THE COMPENSATIONS OF PLUNDER

JAMES A. MILLWARD, SERIES EDITOR

The Silk Roads series is made possible by the generous support of the Henry Luce Foundation's Asia Program. Founded in 1936, the Luce Foundation is a not-for-profit philanthropic organization devoted to promoting innovation in academic, policy, religious, and art communities. The Asia Program aims to foster cultural and intellectual exchange between the United States and the countries of East and Southeast Asia, and to create scholarly and public resources for improved understanding of Asia in the United States.

THE COMPENSATIONS OF PLUNDER

How China Lost Its Treasures

JUSTIN M. JACOBS

THE UNIVERSITY OF CHICAGO PRESS

CHICAGO AND LONDON

The University of Chicago Press, Chicago 60637
The University of Chicago Press, Ltd., London
© 2020 by The University of Chicago
Published 2020
Printed in the United States of America

29 28 27 26 25 24 23 22 21 20   1 2 3 4 5

ISBN-13: 978-0-226-71196-6 (cloth)
ISBN-13: 978-0-226-71201-7 (paper)
ISBN-13: 978-0-226-71215-4 (e-book)
DOI: https://doi.org/10.7208/chicago/9780226712154.001.0001

Library of Congress Cataloging-in-Publication Data

Names: Jacobs, Justin, 1980– author.
Title: The compensations of plunder : how China lost its treasures / Justin M.
Jacobs.
Other titles: Silk roads (Chicago, Ill.)
Description: Chicago : University of Chicago Press, 2020. | Series: Silk roads |
Includes bibliographical references and index.
Identifiers: LCCN 2019049554 | ISBN 9780226711966 (cloth) | ISBN 9780226712017
(paperback) | ISBN 9780226712154 (ebook)
Subjects: LCSH: Excavations (Archaeology)—China, Northwest—History—20th
century. | Excavations (Archaeology)—China—Xinjiang Uygur Zizhiqu—History—
20th century. | Archaeologists—Europe. | Lost works of art—China, Northwest—
History—20th century. | Lost works of art—China—Xinjiang Uygur Zizhiqu—
History—20th century. | Archaeology and state—China—History—20th century. |
China, Northwest—Antiquities. | Xinjiang Uygur Zizhiqu (China)—Antiquities.
Classification: LCC DS793.N6 J33 2020 | DDC 951/.600909—dc23
LC record available at https://lccn.loc.gov/2019049554

♾ This paper meets the requirements of ANSI/NISO z39.48-1992 (Permanence of
Paper).

FOR HAN HAN FROM HAN HAN

CONTENTS

On April 1, 1901, the British archaeologist Marc Aurel Stein paid the fourth of five visits to Han Yaoguang, the district magistrate of Keriya. Over the past three months, this dusty oasis, perched on the southern edge of the Taklamakan Desert in the far northwestern province of Xinjiang along the fringes of the Qing Empire, had served as the launch point for Stein's forays into the nearby sands in search of buried antiquities. Now, however, it was time to go home. After attending to his luggage and men, Stein mounted his horse and set off toward the *yamen*, where he found Magistrate Han awaiting his arrival. In his field diary, Stein noted their "long friendly talk & hope for a future meeting," along with his own sorrow at having "to part from this kind friend." In *Sand-Buried Ruins of Khotan* (1903), the published narrative of his first expedition to Xinjiang, Stein again professed to be "pained by the thought" of "how scanty the hope was of ever seeing his kindly face again." Only when Han rode out to Stein's campsite for a final farewell was Stein able to conclude that the magistrate fully understood "the lasting gratitude I should retain for him and my sincere regret at the parting."[1]

The feeling, apparently, was mutual. Though Han Yaoguang did not bequeath to posterity as rich a textual record as did Stein, an alternative account of Han's time with Stein can be found in the Chinese-language report the magistrate was obliged to lodge with his superiors in the Qing bureaucracy after Stein's departure from his district. These files, typically bland, reveal an administrative obsession with the logistical minutiae of the expeditions of Western archaeologists: where they slept, what they ate, with whom they talked, where they went, how much money they spent, and so on. Much like the sand-covered ruins of Khotan to which Stein had set himself the task of uncovering, however, buried amid the tedium of bureaucratic rubble is the rare archival gem. In this case, the gem is Magistrate Han's decision to include his own glowing opinion of Stein in his file: "He is an outstanding person, of much culture and refinement" (*wei ren wenwen jinya, yi shi jiezhe*).[2]

Clearly, Stein had made an impression. Even the governor of Xinjiang, Rao Yingqi, took note. The very next year, just a few months after Stein published his *Preliminary Report on a Journey of Archaeological and Topographical Exploration in Chinese Turkestan* (1901), Governor Rao obtained a copy and commissioned a translation into Chinese. In a commentary appended to the end of the translation, Wan Rong, the governor's translator, reveals the high esteem in which most Qing officials in Xinjiang of the day held Stein. In an echo of Magistrate Han's assessment the previous year, Wan calls Stein "a highly refined gentleman" (*boya junzi*). At one time, Wan tells his readers, "scholars fond of antiquities competed with each other for copying" the Chinese translation of Stein's report, "eager to enjoy the privilege of reading it first." As for Governor Rao himself, he was said to have "highly praised" Stein's work.[3]

In 1906, when Stein returned to Xinjiang for a second expedition, he found himself bombarded by the effusive tributes of local Qing officials. Zhu Ruichi (figure 1), the prefect of Guma, confessed his admiration for Stein's "stern fortitude and valiant resolve" (*zhi zhi jian, xin zhi rui*). He then continued (figure 2): "Everywhere you set your foot, dear Sir, becomes famous, from the luster you confer on the sands of the Gobi to the distinction you confer on the peaks of the Kunlun." Xie Weixing, the magistrate of Khotan, declared himself to have been "in continual receipt" of Stein's "enlightened teachings." Pan Zhen, the magistrate of Aksu, called Stein "a man of profound and extensive learning" and described his accomplishments as "truly worthy of an admiration that knows no bounds" (*lingren qinyang wuji*). These breathless paeans culminated in 1913, when Stein returned yet again for a third expedition. Dai Chengmo, the magistrate of Keriya, claimed to have never met another foreigner as distinguished as Stein. "In years gone by, I travelled through such countries as Russia, Germany, and Austria, as well as to the Caspian, Black, and Mediterranean Seas, through whose various ports I passed," Dai wrote (see figure 18). "I made the acquaintance of a great many exceptional people, yet the English Minister for Education Aurel Stein . . . would be the most excellent of them all: proper of character, refined of learning, versed in the ancient, familiar with the modern. My admiration for him, having viewed the collection of books he has authored and annotated, is deep indeed." Not to be outdone, Li Shurong (see figure 17), the magistrate of Barikol, called Stein "a man of outstanding character and

Figure 1. A Surprising Bond. Stein (*right*) met longtime Qing official Zhu Ruichi (*center*) on three of his four expeditions to Xinjiang. This photo was taken on May 20, 1915, near the end of Stein's third expedition, when Zhu was the circuit intendant (*daotai*) of Aksu. According to Stein, he was welcomed into Zhu's jurisdiction as an "old friend" (*lao pengyou*). Also pictured on the left is the district magistrate of Aksu. © The British Library Board, Stein Photograph 392/28(794) Recto.

broad mind, unsurpassed in elegance and refinement." For Magistrate Li, seven meetings over six days in the autumn of 1914 were apparently not enough to satisfy his hunger for Stein's presence. "Standing in deep admiration of your formidable mind and wishing to partake of its bounty," he wrote Stein in a farewell letter, "I detest the late hour of our gathering."[4]

And then the Great War broke out. As funding for archaeological expeditions dried up among the European empires, newly flush American institutions began to step into the breach. By 1930, when the now sixty-eight-year-old Stein returned to Xinjiang for a fourth and final expedition, it was Harvard who footed the bill. This time, however, the fawning praise of yore was somewhat harder to find. In Nanjing, Cai Yuanpei, the president of a prestigious government-funded research organization, publicly announced that Stein's first three expeditions to Xinjiang had resulted in the "theft" and "destruction" of China's "national treasures." From the perspective of the Chinese, Cai continued, Stein's "accomplishments" were little more

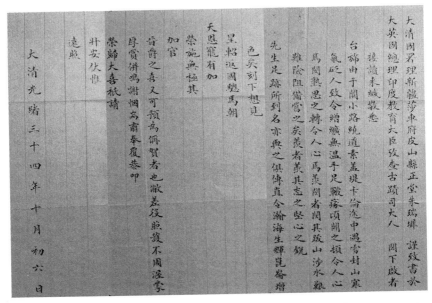

Figure 2. Epistolary Admiration. In 1908, Zhu Ruichi (figure 1), then the magistrate of Guma (Pishan) in southern Xinjiang, wrote a letter to Stein filled with praise for his archaeological work, only one of many such missives Stein would receive from Qing officials in Xinjiang. After expressing his admiration for Stein's "stern fortitude and valiant resolve," Zhu declares that "everywhere you set your foot, dear Sir, becomes famous, from the luster you confer on the sands of the Gobi to the distinction you confer on the peaks of the Kunlun." Stein Papers, Bodleian Library, MS 341–42. Reprinted with the kind permission of the British Academy.

than the "plunder of our cultural artifacts and contempt for our national sovereignty." Wu Jinding, a colleague of Cai in the Department of Archaeology, went on to characterize all of Stein's previous exploits in Xinjiang as the fruits of imperialist deceit and domestic instability. "Come on, Mr. Stein!" Wu wrote in a broadly disseminated polemic. "Are you really going to use an old lie that once worked to deceive the Chinese of twenty years ago to try and deceive the Chinese of today?" Proclaiming that his government had "already killed off" the corrupt officials of the old regime, Wu insisted that the Chinese of his generation would adamantly "resist to the end Stein-style archaeology: walk ten thousand miles, steal ten thousand manuscripts, and write ten thousand boring articles."[5]

Thirty years earlier, Stein had been the toast of nearly every oasis in Xinjiang. Now, however, he was the subject of scathing vitriol throughout China. How can we account for such a dramatic transformation?

FROM EMPIRE TO SPADE

In a short span of just over two decades, from the early 1890s until the outbreak of the First World War, tens of thousands of ancient manuscripts and works of art were taken from the desert sands and mountain caves of northwestern China and deposited in museums and libraries abroad. The agents of this exodus were a diverse group of scholars and politicians whose loyalties lay with the most powerful empires of the day: British, French, German, Russian, and Japanese. Today, the names of these explorers and archaeologists are just as infamous within China as they are famous abroad: Aurel Stein, Paul Pelliot, Albert von Le Coq, Albert Grünwedel, Sven Hedin, S. F. Oldenburg, Gustav Mannerheim, Ellsworth Huntington, Ōtani Kōzui, and Zuicho Tachibana.[6] Though some of these men were more interested in scientific and political surveys than the collection of antiquities, collectively, their expeditions resulted in the first systematic removal of art and antiquities from China to occur outside of a military looting operation. In the modern era, the military looting category includes two scandalous depredations of note: the sacking of the Old Summer Palace by British and French soldiers in the wake of the Second Opium War in 1860, and the despoliation of the Forbidden City by a coalition of eight foreign armies during the Boxer War of 1901.

Compared to other parts of the world, the targeting of China's treasures by Western archaeologists and art collectors—as opposed to soldiers—came rather late in the game. In 1793, more than one hundred years before the Swedish explorer Sven Hedin would prove the feasibility of a taking a caravan into the waterless dunes of the Taklamakan Desert, the Louvre opened its doors to the French public for the first time. As the institutional embodiment of an avowed commitment to the Enlightenment discourse of science, preservation, and education, the Louvre served to legitimize the subsequent appropriation of art and antiquities from throughout Europe and Egypt by a team of savants trailing in the wake of Napoleon's armies. The British Museum, though less eager to embrace the illiterate multitude, played a similar role for resourceful Brits abroad. In 1801, Thomas Bruce, the seventh Earl of Elgin then serving as London's ambassador to Constantinople, seized on Ottoman gratitude for the return of its Egyptian province from the French to obtain permission to remove over a hundred tons of marble from the facade of the Parthenon in Athens.[7]

These early acquisitions for the new museums in Paris and London ushered in more than a century of largely unregulated Western archaeological expeditions and excavations throughout the world. In 1816, the Italian hydrologist and circus performer Giovanni Belzoni, operating under British patronage, managed to dislodge the seven-ton granite head of Ramses II from its millennia-long perch on the western bank of the Nile River at Luxor and float it upstream to Alexandria. From there it proceeded onward to London, where it remains to this day. In 1839, the American scholar and diplomat John Lloyd Stephens, accompanied by British artist Frederick Catherwood, undertook the first systematic survey of Mayan ruins in Mesoamerica, bringing numerous artifacts back to New York, where they later perished in a fire. By 1873, the year in which German American tycoon Heinrich Schliemann uncovered "Priam's Treasure" at the fabled site of Troy, Western scholars and diplomats enjoyed a virtual monopoly on the collection, preservation, and interpretation of the cultural heritage of much of the globe. Even when local elites from the non-Western world began to build their own museums and pass their own antiquities preservation laws, still the Westerners played an outsized role in their development; for nearly one hundred years, both the Bulaq Museum in Cairo and the Egyptian Antiquities Service were managed and led by French scholars, an arrangement replicated in one form or another throughout the Ottoman Empire and its eventual successor states.[8]

From this perch of imperialist privilege the Western scholars promoted their own preferred version of the past. Generally speaking, these narratives favored the inclusion of peoples, places, and events that could somehow be interpreted through the cultural and linguistic prisms of the Hebrew, Greek, and Latin literary canons. This point is evident in the way in which the mysterious identity of the granite head of Ramses II was discussed in European scholarly circles during Belzoni's time. Initially portrayed as the one and only specimen of "fine art" to have been produced during the Pharaonic era, the head of Ramses II was repeatedly identified as that of young "Memnon," a legendary Ethiopian king mentioned in Greek epic poetry as having played a role in the siege of Troy. And since the British imagined themselves to be the most worthy stewards of the Greek legacy, Young Memnon himself was said to be "smiling" at Belzoni "at the thought of being taken to England." A half century later, this ideological slant was explicitly adopted by Heinrich Schliemann, whose excavations in the Troad were motivated almost entirely by his desire to uncover ruins and artifacts associated with events and people mentioned in Homer's *Iliad*.[9]

Although the acceptable parameters of archaeological inquiry could and did expand, they usually did so in a way that continued to reinforce the primacy of the Greco-Roman and Hebraic past. Beginning in 1823, the year the Egyptian hieroglyphs were first unlocked by French polymath

Jean-François Champollion, the exploits of all the pharaohs—not just those of "Memnon"—were gradually incorporated into the rhetorical folds of Western civilization. This process, however, was expedited by the propensity of the hieroglyphs to speak to the concerns of biblical and Greek historiography. For example, the first exhibitions of Egyptian antiquities to be held in the British Museum after Champollion's decipherment of the hieroglyphs were justified on the grounds that the artifacts on display represented "the source from which the arts of Sculpture and of Painting, and perhaps even the Sciences, were handed to the Greeks—[and] from the Greeks to us." In fact, throughout the nineteenth and early twentieth centuries, most Western archaeologists continued to evince the remarkable ability to cast their gaze out over mostly Muslim lands and see nothing but various incarnations of Greeks, Romans, and Jews. This gaze was further adopted by the first generation of Westernized Ottoman collectors and archaeologists to work along their side: the staff of the Imperial Ottoman Museum in Istanbul did not produce a single exhibit on Islamic artifacts until 1889, more than forty years after the founding of the museum. In 1935, a visitor to the national museum in Baghdad expressed his astonishment at "not finding Arab or Islamic antiquities in the museum of a city that was once the Abbasid capital."[10]

These ideological biases followed Western archaeologists well beyond the borders of the Ottoman Empire. In Mesoamerica, the ruins of what would eventually be identified as those of the Mayan civilization were variously interpreted by Spanish, French, and North American travelers as having been built by Greek refugees from Atlantis, a lost tribe of Israelites, or the survivors of a Roman or Egyptian shipwreck. In the 1840s, when John Lloyd Stephens put forth a bold theory of indigenous creation—thereby rejecting transatlantic theories of Mayan genesis—he was motivated to do so in order to support US claims on the lands and peoples of Mexico and Central America. The historian R. Tripp Evans has even gone so far as to characterize Stephens's efforts as a cultural manifestation of the Monroe Doctrine, designed to exclude the Europeans from a newfound American sphere of geopolitical interest. In nineteenth-century India, British archaeologists such as Alexander Cunningham concentrated their efforts almost entirely on the Buddhist ruins of the northern and northwestern frontiers, paying little heed to Hindu and Muslim works. The reason, according to Cunningham, was that these regions afforded the best possibility of identifying "those famous peoples and cities whose names have become familiar to the whole world through the expedition of Alexander the Great."[11]

It was this particular Greek (or, to be more precise, Macedon) figure that would bring Western explorers and archaeologists into the northwestern frontier of the Qing Empire. Much like their predecessors in the Middle East, Mesoamerica, and India, men such as Stein, Le Coq, Grünwedel, and, to a lesser extent Pelliot were most interested in recovering the material remains of peoples whom they could somehow place within their preferred lineage of Western civilization. The fourth century BC conquests of Alexander the Great brought Greek culture, language, and administrative models to the lands and peoples of present-day India, Pakistan, and Afghanistan. The resulting fusion of Greek, Indian, and Buddhist cultures led to the production of what would eventually become known as "Gandharan" art. That these archaeologists were mostly interested in the "Western" side of Gandharan art is suggested by their scholarly backgrounds; most were Indologists by training, inclined to see in monotheistic Buddhism and the earliest Sanskrit canon linguistic and cultural traces of the ancient Indo-European (or "Aryan") race that was widely believed to have conquered the supposedly inferior races of Asia. This intellectual agenda can be most clearly glimpsed in the judgment passed by German archaeologist Albert von Le Coq in 1928 regarding a specimen of Gandharan sculpture in his collection (figure 3). "The drapery falls in noble lines," Le Coq wrote of a Buddhist torso found near Turfan, "not yet degraded by Eastern Asiatic misunderstanding of classic forms."[12]

The degree to which these idealized Greek or Aryan races had "degraded" on contact with the inferior peoples of Asia was measured in precise terms through the once respectable science of anthropometry (figure 4). The personal archives of nearly every single explorer or archaeologist who ventured into northwestern China include at least a few folders or boxes filled with mug shots and data sheets recording anatomical measurements procured from the local population, usually in exchange for various material incentives. In 1906, for instance, Stein bemoaned the resistance of local hillmen in Xinjiang to his "scientific" entreaties, "just as if real live heads were to have been taken instead of mere measurements and photographs with perfectly harmless instruments." The sheer scale and extent of their labors on this front is breathtaking, as suggested by one of Stein's diary entries in 1907. "Finished head measur[ement]s. to No. 400 during morning."[13]

Such data, when combined with ethnographic observations of local customs, sometimes prompted the Western archaeologist to note, with obvious delight, faint traces of various imagined Greek, Roman, or Aryan traits. On his fourth expedition in 1930, Stein took note of his "measuring of many fine specimens of this interesting ethnic relict, the Burush race of Hunza." His degree of interest hinged in large part on determining the precise

Türkisch-manichäisches Buchblatt mit Miniaturen, Chotscho   Hellenistischer Buddhatorso, Chotscho

Figure 3. The Appeal of Gandharan Art. Western archaeologists were initially drawn to Xinjiang by the prospect of finding material traces of Greek and Indian cultural influence in the deserts of Central Asia, be it in the form of early Indo-European languages or works of what became known as Gandharan art. That they were more interested in the "Western" aspects of such traces than in their "Eastern" aspects is evident in the appraisal of German archaeologist Albert von Le Coq, who said of the "Hellenistic Buddha torso" pictured here that its "drapery falls in noble lines, not yet degraded by Eastern Asiatic misunderstanding of classic forms." Albert von Le Coq, *Auf Hellas Spuren in Ostturkistan, Berichte und Abenteuer der II. und III. deutschen Turfan-Expedition von Dr. Albert von Le Coq* (Leipzig: J. C. Hinrichs, 1926), plate 10.

amount of Greek blood that was believed to flow in their veins. Clarmont Skrine, an avid traveler through the mountains of Central Asia who also served two years as the British consul in Kashgar, revealed something of the excitement such determinations were capable of arousing in the minds of these Western archaeologists. While passing through the same Himalayan valleys that Stein would later regard as populated by "interesting ethnic relicts," Skrine concluded that "the Nagaris seem to look more to their remote Greek ancestry than the people of Hunza. In Nagar you see more of the Greek type of features, modified by a liberal infusion of the Pathan nose, than in Hunza." Such observations were not complete without a romantic association with the Greeks of yore. "I tell you," Skrine continued, "when I saw those fellows tearing down on the mark, bow in hand, their hair & shirts fluttering in the wind, I could hardly believe I wasn't back in B.C. and looking at the Parthians or Alexander's Macedonians doing archery practice, for it's exactly what they did in those days."[14]

As Heather Pringle has shown, as late as 1938, a Nazi expedition to Tibet, led by zoologist Ernst Schäfer on behalf of Heinrich Himmler's Ahnenerbe

Figure 4. Searching for Aryans. In order to determine in precise "scientific" terms just when and where the idealized Aryan race had degraded on contact with the supposedly inferior races of Asia, Western archaeologists collected enormous amounts of anthropometrical data from the people whom they encountered during their expeditions. Though the German participants of the Nazi expedition to Tibet in 1938–39 (pictured here) may have gone the furthest in developing a sophisticated racist theory of human evolution in Asia, nearly all of the Western archaeologists and explorers featured in this book were enthusiastic promoters of anthropometry and its ideological underpinnings. Bundesarchiv, Bild 135-KB-15–083 / Krause, Ernst / CC-BY-SA 3.0

outfit, was inspired by the desire to uncover similar traces of ancient Aryan migrations into other remote parts of Asia. Yet the Nazi propensity for drawing on scientific theories regarding race to justify contemporary political agendas was unique only by degree. For most of its existence, the modern Western archaeological enterprise has been deeply implicated in the idea that civilizations are built and governed by superior racial groups. As a result, when faced with the material ruins of such civilizations, Western archaeologists tended to attribute their decline to the influx of an inferior racial stock. This was certainly the case with the ancient monuments and races of Egypt and the Near East. As Elliott Colla and Donald Malcolm Reid have demonstrated, the once noble races of biblical lore were said to have "degenerated" following their subjugation to the Ottoman Turks. Across the Atlantic, the French explorer Désiré Charnay made a name for himself by promoting the thesis that Mayan civilization had been built by the Toltecs, whom he identified as the light-skinned ancestors of an Aryan migration from Asia, a race later brought low by intermixing with the supposedly "inferior" indigenes of the Americas.[15]

The Western archaeologists who undertook expeditions to northwestern China in the first several decades of the twentieth century were fully conversant with these racist scholarly discourses. Such prejudices are on open display in their letters and field diaries, where the peoples of Central, South, and East Asia are often referred to in subhuman terms. In 1908, Stein described the indefatigable labors of a Muslim courier tasked with delivering his letters as the result of "the same canine devotion & calmness whether distance before him 1000 or 100 miles." Three years earlier, the Yale climatologist Ellsworth Huntington said of his Muslim servant Da'ud that "he sticks to me like a dog if I begin to question the route followed by the guide." In 1906, the French sinologist Paul Pelliot expressed concern in his diary about the visible racism of his travel companion, the Finnish intelligence agent Gustav Mannerheim. Not long thereafter, however, Pelliot himself indulged in a racist tirade against his Muslim workers, describing them as "a vile population" and "beasts over the market." Stein once went so far as to place his pet dog Dash, along with his Chinese secretary Jiang Xiaowan, higher up in the social hierarchy than his Indian servants (see figure 9). "He [Jiang] and eager little Dash are always pleasant companions," Stein once wrote to his friend Percy Allen. "With the rest one is again & again reminded that one is dealing with mercenaries." Upon the failure of Harvard art historian Langdon Warner's expedition to Dunhuang in 1925, his wife Lorraine assured her husband's financial backers that the expedition would have succeeded if only the Chinese had acted as "white men" instead of like "swine." When Stein's fourth expedition ended in failure in 1931, his good friend Carl Keller comforted him with the observation that "somehow the Chinese people make me think of masses of objectionable insects, like aphids, or corn borers, or army worms."[16]

Whether such racist attitudes were voiced by the archaeologists and explorers themselves or by their close associates, they were all marshaled in support of an ostensibly scientific expedition that was nonetheless steeped in racist discourses and agendas. Nowhere is this clearer than in the expedition of Ellsworth Huntington. In 1905–6, Huntington traveled through the deserts of northwestern China in search of geological and archaeological evidence of historical fluctuations in the climate and ecology of the region. Ten years later, he would publish the results of this and other fact-finding expeditions throughout the world in *Civilization and Climate* (1915), a hugely influential book that was widely adopted as a textbook in American classrooms during the first half of the twentieth century. In it, Huntington proclaimed that the mental capacities, civilizational aptitude, and social characteristics of the different races of the earth had evolved in response to different environmental factors at various times and places. Huntington's conclusion, formulated in part from the results of his expedition to Xinjiang, pointed to "an ineradicable racial difference in mentality." Just as the "plum differs from the apple," he continued, "so the negro seems to differ from the white man not only in feature and complexion, but in the workings of the mind. No amount of training can eradicate the difference." For his part, Stein was very much a believer in Huntington's theories of climatic determinism. "I entirely agree with you in your opinion about the effect of such a climate on the mentality of races which have suffered from it for untold generations," Stein wrote to his good friend Reginald Schomberg in 1940, while discussing the history of India. "Of course, those who have inherited the result cannot be blamed for it. But it is a pity that they are not plainly told of what their shortcomings are and what these are due to it."[17]

BEHIND THE ARCHAEOLOGICAL CURTAIN

Above all else, it was the revelation of Indic languages and Gandharan art—and the racist assumptions that underlay their evolution—that brought Western archaeological expeditions into Central Asia and China. Though northern and northwestern India preserved a few traces of Gandharan art, most of it had been ravaged by the elements or repurposed at the hands of Hindu and Muslim successors. For British and Russian officials posted to the Raj in India or czarist "protectorates" in Turkestan, the revelation that Indic scripts and Gandharan art could be found within the geopolitical buffer zone separating their two empires was most welcome news indeed. The most coveted destination was Afghanistan, where the archaeological legacy of Alexander the Great was thought to be most bountiful. The emir of Afghanistan, however, repeatedly refused to grant permission for the scientific reconnaissance of his realm. "It appears that three Viceroys, including Lord Curzon and Lord Hardinge, had taken a personal interest in [Stein's] proposed explorations in Afghanistan," wrote Paul Alling, the division chief of Near Eastern Affairs in the US Department of State, soon after Stein's death in 1943, "but had never been able to convince the Afghan Government that no 'political motive' was back of them!"[18]

The emir was right to be suspicious—for it was the rare expedition that set forth without a hidden geopolitical agenda. In fact, Stein found little support among his imperial colleagues in the Raj for his proposed expeditions into Xinjiang until he drew explicit attention to the geopolitical advantages and intelligence such a reconnaissance might be expected to yield. Foremost among such advantages were detailed maps of rival imperial lands. In 1907, Stein told his friend Fred Andrews that "from the time we left this place in June until my arrival at Kanchou, some 24,000 square miles of mountainous ground were mapped in detail." The expedition of French sinologist Paul Pelliot in 1906–8 was sponsored almost entirely by the Russians, who forced Pelliot to take along a less welcome companion—the Finnish intelligence agent Gustav Mannerheim. Not surprisingly, during his time with Pelliot, Mannerheim took copious notes on the obstacles that might confront an armed expedition into Xinjiang one day in the future. "One more valley that crept up to within about 300 paces of the fortress and might some day afford welcome protection to an advancing enemy," he wrote in 1906, "and we crossed an easily destructible bridge over the moat, about 35 feet wide, into the typically Chinese frontier fortress and town of Yangihissar." Upon their return home, men like Stein and Mannerheim invariably handed such data over to their military colleagues. Though much of the intelligence accrued over the course of these expeditions would never be used, those who were involved in its collection knew that anything was possible. "I've got a good deal of stuff which has been duly communicated to Gov't," wrote Clarmont Skrine, the British consul in Kashgar, in 1924, as one of several consuls who had done everything in their power to facilitate the expeditions of Western archaeologists in Xinjiang. "Who knows? Perhaps one day. . . . What a job, Governor of British Turkestan!"[19]

Xinjiang never became British. Nor, despite a few close calls, did it ever fall into the hands of the Russians. It was, and occasionally still is, referred to in Western circles as "Chinese Turkestan" or "Eastern Turkestan." Nevertheless, from 1895 to 1915, a revolving door of Western explorers and archaeologists undertook expeditions into Xinjiang, where the arid climate of the Taklamakan Desert had managed to preserve the ruins of ancient migrants from India, Iran, and Central Asia in conditions unparalleled anywhere else in the world outside of Egypt (figure 5). Nearly all of these expeditions proceeded under the diplomatic cloak of the Russian and British Empires, which maintained the only foreign consulates in the region and whose colonial dependencies offered the quickest, safest, and most strategically fruitful routes into Xinjiang. After a comfortable trip by rail from Saint Petersburg to Russian Turkestan or a somewhat more harrowing trek over the Himalayas from British India, most explorers and archaeologists

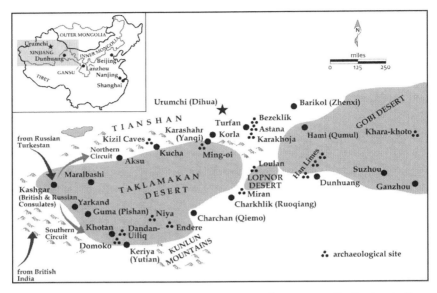

Figure 5. Silk Road Expeditions in Xinjiang, Gansu, and Inner Mongolia. During the first
wave of expeditions (1895–1915), Western archaeologists, depending on their political
loyalties, entered Xinjiang through one of two routes: Russian Turkestan or British India.
All of them, however, eventually ended up in Kashgar, where the British or Russian consuls helped facilitate arrangements with local Qing officials. From Kashgar, they would
then set out on either the northern or southern circuit of the Taklamakan Desert, making
side forays to promising sites along the way. The two circuits would eventually reconnect
at Dunhuang, from which point one could continue on into inner China or return back to
Kashgar along a different circuit. Cartography by Debbie Newell.

found themselves in Kashgar. There, depending on political loyalties, they
liaisoned with either the Russian or the British consul, who would in turn
introduce them to the local Qing officials and help smooth the way into the
field. With his caravan and paperwork all in order, the archaeologist then
began his trek eastward around the northern or southern rim of the Taklamakan Desert, from whence he could strike into the desert in search of
ruins. Though some excavations, like those of the Germans, ended up fo-
cusing on one or two sites in close proximity to a modern oasis, most were
true expeditions, covering hundreds and even thousands of miles en route
to the neighboring provinces of Gansu and Inner Mongolia.

Nearly all of the lands through which these expeditions passed had
experienced major political upheavals and massive loss of life within living memory. Beginning in 1862, a series of Muslim rebellions broke out in
Gansu and quickly spread to Xinjiang. The resulting instability in Xinjiang,
a loosely held colonial dependency of the Qing state since its conquest one

century earlier, opened the door to military incursions from Central Asia. For a little over a decade, the southern half of Xinjiang was ruled by an independent Khoqandi warlord named Yaqub Beg (also known as "Bedaulat"). At a village near Hami in 1907, a village elder told Stein all about the political drama and daily suffering he had witnessed thirty years before:

> Q.[azi] tells me of sufferings of Hami & these roadside vill.[ages] during Muh.[ommaden] rebellion. Hami first taken by Bedaulat's men from Kucha & Aksu. Then Chin.[ese] returned from Anshi, to be driven out & slaughtered by Tungans from Urumchi way. Almost the whole population fled to west & villager town fell into ruin. Hami finally retaken when Chin.[ese] had collected at head of desert route 2000–2500 strong. The vill.[ages] were reoccupied by former owners who returned from West. Greatest losses in life ascribed to Tungans.[20]

In 1884, following the reconquest of the region by Qing armies, Beijing opted to turn Xinjiang into a province. This decision signaled an administrative revolution. The exclusive club of Manchu and Mongol military officials who had once ruled the region before the rebellion were now joined by a substantial cadre of Han civil officials drawn from the inner provinces. Most came from Hunan, prompting one Chinese observer to regard the Qing administration in Xinjiang during these years as a "Little Hunan." With them also came a host of new geographic designations, most of which derived from ancient toponyms first imposed on the region during the Han and Tang dynasties more than a millennium prior.[21] (As a result, many of the places discussed in this book tend to be known by more than one name, variants of which are noted on the map in figure 5.)

It was these newly arrived officials—Manchu, Mongol, but mostly Han— who greeted Western explorers and archaeologists at every oasis in Xinjiang, Gansu, and Inner Mongolia. And, more than anyone else, it was these officials who bore direct responsibility for the logistical success or failure of Western expeditions in northwestern China. No matter how much money, training, or determination the racist imperialist may have had, he would not have been able to organize a single excavation or expedition anywhere in Xinjiang if the local Qing officials did not allow him to do so. Stein, who spent more time in Xinjiang and took away far more antiquities than any other explorer, openly admitted as much. In *Ancient Khotan* (1907), an account of his first expedition in 1900–1901, Stein made it clear that he could not have overcome the many logistical obstacles in his path "without the active co-operation of the Chinese administrators of the districts upon which I depended for whatever was needed during the winter campaign in the desert." Twenty years later, while preparing for his fourth expedition, Stein reiterated in a letter to a colleague that his latest enterprise "will largely if not mainly depend on the good will of the local authorities." Without that good will, Stein continued, "the tracing and surveying of ancient routes and remains, etc., in the now waterless desert areas towards which my operations are primarily to be directed, would in any case be practically impossible."[22]

It is clear that Stein, along with nearly every other foreign archaeologist to pass through northwestern China, possessed such good will in spades. But how did they get it? After all, the Chinese were not fools. They knew all about the maps of their newly recovered and weakly integrated province that men like Stein, Pelliot, Hedin, and Mannerheim routinely compiled behind their backs. "I may mention here that not a soul in Uch Turfan, from the Amban and the O.C. downwards," wrote Clarmont Skrine, the British consul of Kashgar, in 1923, "believes my story of going up into the Tian Shan to shoot ibex; it is taken for granted that I am reconnoitering the Russian frontier." As a result, whenever one of the archaeologists failed to follow Skrine's lead in devising a suitable cover story for the routine gathering of sensitive intelligence, Qing officials were quick to turn him away. On his first expedition, Stein found that his application for "permission to use the ramparts of the Yangi Shahr for theodolite observations was refused by the Military Commandant" of Khotan.[23]

The Qing officials of Xinjiang were not only aware of the sensitive intelligence collected under their watch. They were also aware of just how much of a diplomatic liability Western archaeologists could present to them. After all, Western expeditions in Xinjiang were intimately associated with the British and Russian consulates that aided and abetted them. And the consulates that aided and abetted them were the institutional embodiments of two of the most powerful empires on the planet, both of which were heavily invested in the geopolitical and economic fate of Xinjiang. In 1926, Zhu Ruichi, the circuit intendant of Aksu and author of one of the sugary letters to Stein previously quoted, described the five Russian consulates in Xinjiang as headed by "Russian 'consuls' in name" (qi ming ze wei E lingshi), but who were in fact merely the agents of a forcibly imposed Russian economic "monopoly on the ground" (qishi ji wei longduan zhi suo).[24]

The archaeologists who lodged, dined, and fraternized with these consuls were not merely hollow emblems of their diplomatic hosts. They also carried out substantive political duties entrusted to them by the consul himself. Such duties often took the form of the adjudication of disputes arising from the mostly Turkic-, Hindi-, and Urdu-speaking Russian and British expatriate communities of southern Xinjiang. Though some of these were strictly internal affairs, a fair number involved financial and property disputes between British or Russian expatriates and the Muslim subjects of the Qing. In such cases, the Western traveler temporarily assumed the duties of an honorary consul and was expected to spar with the local Qing official in a makeshift court on behalf of the Russian or British subjects claimed—often in spurious and opportunistic fashion—by his consular host. In 1905, the American climatologist Ellsworth Huntington, having reached the oases of southern Xinjiang by way of India, was entrusted by George Macartney, the British consul in Kashgar, with confronting the Qing magistrate of Keriya on behalf of loosely affiliated British subjects:

> Abdullah Khan, an old Afghan merchant from Kabul and hence a British subject has just come to me with a petition. A large sum of money is due him from various people who won't pay unless compelled to. The Amban won't make them pay because Abdullah is not a Chinese subject. Mr. Macartney wrote to the Amban asking him to see that the money was paid. Now the Afghan, an attractive old man has twice petitioned the Amban in vain. I am going to ask the Amban to do his duty with the threat, well sugared, of telling his chief in Kashgar of his discourtesy to me, and of his failure to perform his work.[25]

Two years later, Stein found that two dozen Hindu moneylenders had assembled to greet him at Yangi-hissar, so as "to offer attention to an officer of the 'Sirkar' which protects them in this land of highly profitable exile." Despite the comfort of their hospitality, even Stein confessed to a sense of alarm at "all the mischief resulting from these hardy Shikarpuris being allowed to fasten themselves on Turkestan soil and leech-like to suck by their usury the substance of its cultivators."[26]

Faced with the powerful threats and influence of a Western archaeologist-cum-diplomat, it is little wonder that some Qing officials were relieved to see their guest depart. The French sinologist Paul Pelliot certainly came to this conclusion. "But, in spite of everything," he proclaimed at a public lecture in Paris in 1909, "a European can always, with the best intentions of the world, be for the Chinese functionary a cause of complications." Should an "incident" occur, the Qing official could be transferred, demoted, or even cashiered, Pelliot rightly observed. To illustrate his point, Pelliot recounted for his audience his own long-delayed departure two years earlier from the oasis of Kucha, where the local Qing prefect was said to have breathed "a

big sigh of relief." Pelliot's assessment echoes the language found on the
Chinese-language passports issued by the Qing Ministry of Foreign Affairs
(Waiwubu) in Beijing for these expeditions. On the passport issued to Stein
in 1905 for his second expedition (figure 6), a short description of his background and proposed activities is followed by a terse order to the Qing officials in Xinjiang and Gansu who were charged with receiving him. "Whenever Stein, with passport in hand, passes through the jurisdiction of local
officials," the document reads, "he is to be immediately inspected, released,
and afforded protection in accordance with the treaties [zhaoyue tuowei
baohu]. If he is detained or obstructed [liunan zuzhi], such actions will be
cause for investigation and prosecution [zhigan chajiu]." Two years later,
Pelliot's passport would contain exactly the same language. On both surviving documents, one anxious official has added multiple red circles beside
these two sentences—the Chinese equivalent to "underlining" a passage of
particular importance.[27]

    This is scary language. It is also language that is difficult to reconcile
with the gushing purple prose addressed to Stein by some of the same officials who once held this very passport in their hands. Indeed, it is entirely
possible that one of those letters was written by the exact same official who
added thirteen red circles next to the bureaucratic admonition on Stein's
passport. After all, the pool of candidates was large. As we have already
seen, professed admiration for Stein was widespread among Qing officials
both during and after his expeditions, from the provincial governor in Urumchi all the way down to the county magistrate of Guma. Were such profes-
sions little more than insincere pleasantries, the rhetorical manifestations
of hollow diplomatic ritual and decorum? This seems unlikely. The reason
is simple: similar assessments of Stein, expressed in a slightly less gushing
tone, also appear in the Chinese letters, telegrams, and gazetteers that Qing
scholars and officials composed solely for the eyes of other Qing scholars
and officials. In his telegram to the governor in Urumchi, Keriya magistrate
Han Yaoguang called Stein "an outstanding person, of much culture and refinement." Wan Rong, the translator of Stein's *Preliminary Report* from his
first expedition, informed his colleagues in the Xinjiang provincial bureaucracy not only that Stein was "a highly refined gentleman," but also that
the governor himself had "highly praised" Stein's work.

    If these proclamations of admiration among Qing officials for Stein
were in large part sincere, we must then explain how they could be uttered against a backdrop of aggressive Western imperialism—an imperialism of which most Qing officials were rightly terrified of falling afoul. The
Chinese historian Wang Jiqing has attempted to solve this very quandary.

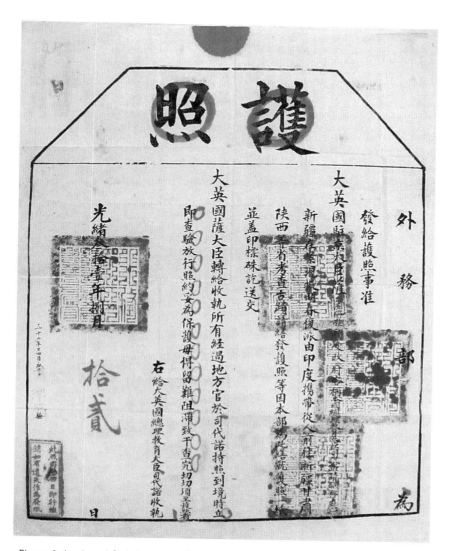

Figure 6. Anxious Administrators. The Chinese-language passport for Stein's second expedition (1906–8) included strict instructions for those Qing officials tasked with hosting him along his route: "Whenever Stein, with passport in hand, passes through the jurisdiction of local officials, he is to be immediately inspected, released, and afforded protection in accordance with the treaties. If he is detained or obstructed, such actions will be cause for investigation and prosecution." Next to these lines one anxious official has added thirteen red circles in order to draw attention to their importance. Stein Papers, Bodleian Library, MS 283. Reprinted with the kind permission of the British Academy.

According to Wang, the flowery praise of Xinjiang magistrates Xie Weixing and Zhu Ruichi, both previously quoted, stemmed from "the foolish minds of foreigner-worshipping local officials." In this vein, Wang is supported by Liu Shiping and Meng Xianshi, who claim that Stein was able to "toy" with Qing officials in Xinjiang because such men were "obviously stupid and dim." With respect to the last will and testament of Jiang Xiaowan, the Chinese secretary who greatly assisted Stein on his second expedition and ordered his son to forever cherish the two watches given to him as tokens of appreciation by Stein, Wang characterizes Jiang's dying wishes as the product of someone "who toadies up to foreigners, worships their ways, and derives all of his self-worth from their opinion of him." In the final analysis, Wang believes that three factors facilitated Stein's success in Xinjiang: "the cultural aggression of the Western powers toward China," "Stein's own cunning nature," and "the corruption and ineptitude of the Qing central government."[28]

In other words, coercion, deceit, and corruption are to blame for the loss of China's treasures. Though it is not difficult to find individual instances of coercion, deceit, or corruption on the expedition trail, the idea that these three factors alone were responsible for the exodus of art and antiquities from Xinjiang—or anywhere else in the non-Western world—begins to buckle under closer scrutiny. With regard to coercion, the suggestion seems to be that the British or Russians were somehow able to use their superior military might to force Qing officials to welcome archaeologists whom they would otherwise prefer to turn away. Not only does the Chinese source base lack empirical evidence for such a view, but so too do the evolving fates of Western archaeological expeditions around the world also undermine this position. As we saw in the case of Afghanistan, any state, no matter how small or weak, was free to refuse permission for foreign expeditions within its territory at any time. Though the emir of Afghanistan had already ceded a large degree of control over his country's foreign affairs to the British, he still felt free to issue what one of Stein's biographers characterized as a "thundering refusal" to the most powerful empire on the planet.[29]

In addition, it is important to note that when Western archaeologists did finally begin to encounter non-Western resistance to their proposed expeditions in the decades after World War I, such resistance nearly always came from states that were weaker and less unified than those which had regularly admitted such expeditions prior to the war. For example, the Ottoman Empire repeatedly allowed European and American archaeologists to undertake excavations and expeditions in all of its territories throughout the nineteenth century. But it was the militarily, economically, and politically weaker successor states of the Ottomans that succeeded in obstructing still powerful and resourceful Western archaeologists for the first time: Turkey and Egypt in 1924, and Iraq in 1935.[30] Similarly, when the Chinese first began to obstruct foreign expeditions to Gansu and Xinjiang in the mid- to late 1920s, the timing of their obstruction coincided with the absolute nadir of political stability and unity across the land. In other words, it was the more resourceful and certainly more unified version of China and other non-Western states that welcomed foreign expeditions, while it was the poorer and often weaker ones that obstructed them. Generally speaking, outside of the relatively rare military looting operation, Western archaeologists did not excavate behind the barrel of a gun—nor were they kicked out in front of one.

We thus cannot single out coercion as a useful explanatory factor. In fact, given what we know about the ubiquitous intelligence gathering activities of Western expeditions, the admission of a foreign archaeologist into one's borders would have made that country even more susceptible to a future military invasion. And yet the Qing officials of Xinjiang, who knew what the archaeologists were doing behind their backs, never once invoked the prospect of national security to reject an application for an expedition, despite their own firsthand experiences of Xinjiang's recent political turmoil. To be sure, rejecting such applications would invite the ridicule and scorn of the Western powers and likely further help to brand the Chinese as "backward" and "unscientific." But these were words, not bullets—and the Chinese knew that the Westerners would continue to denigrate them anyway, regardless of whether or not they acquiesced in an archaeological expedition. Of course, Western armies might also invade Qing or Ottoman territory for any number of unprincipled reasons, but the principled rejection of an application for an archaeological expedition was not among them.

This leaves us with deceit and corruption. Were Western expeditions able to remove so much art and antiquities from China because the Chinese were unaware of the scale of the removals? Or perhaps they knew how much was being taken away, but exchanged their silence for a bribe? As with coercion, both of these hypotheses wither under sustained scrutiny. First and foremost, they must both reckon with the fact that Ottoman and later Qing officials dealt repeatedly with Western archaeologists over a period of many decades. Though it is certainly possible that some officials in some times and places were corrupt, it beggars belief to conclude that all officials in all times and places were corrupt. Similarly, though Western archaeologists could be deceptive on some occasions, they were not deceptive on every occasion. Even had they wanted to be, the practical logistics of removing so many objects, some quite large, over such great distances would have exposed the scale of their operations sooner or later. The reason the removal of the Memnon Head from Luxor was so difficult was because Belzoni had to devise a new way to move seven tons of solid granite over half the length of Egypt. When Lord Elgin shipped his marbles from Athens to London, the combined weight of his precious freight totaled more than 120 tons, all of which passed through multiple Ottoman ports of call. Each time a Western archaeologist left Xinjiang, he took with him at least a hundred heavy crates of antiquities strapped to the backs of braying donkeys and spitting camels.

No Qing official could have failed to notice what Stein and his foreign colleagues were removing from their province. Whenever a foreign archaeologist like Stein or Pelliot arrived in a new jurisdiction, before they did anything else, they were obliged to pay a formal visit to the *yamen* of the local Qing civilian and military officials. Later that same evening or the next day, these same officials would invariably invite him to a formal dinner or tea party, a ritual to be repeated several times during their stay. If there were thorny logistical issues or other troublesome affairs requiring closer attention, another meeting or two would usually be arranged. If the two sides found that they shared some kind of social, cultural, or intellectual bond, yet another one or two daily visits would likely occur. Finally, before he left town, the foreigner would again pay a series of farewell visits to the same group of officials, who might then intercept him on the road for a final cup of tea. All in all, over a three- or four-day stay in town, the foreign archaeologist in Xinjiang could expect to engage in substantive face-to-face interactions with local Qing officials no fewer than three or four times, and perhaps as many as ten or more. And that was only if the foreign explorer was merely passing through. If he used the oasis as a base from which to strike out into the desert sands with the intent of returning in one or two weeks, the entire sequence of official visits would be repeated once more.

All this is to say that the Chinese authorities had ample opportunity to learn what the foreign archaeologist was up to. And the foreigner was usually forthcoming. On January 12, 1901, during his first expedition, Stein noted in his diary the return visit of Han Yaoguang, the district magistrate of Keriya. "Returned visit immediately. Showed him MSS, etc." Three months later in Khotan, when department magistrate Pan Zhen returned his call, Stein "showed him selected specimens of my MS. and tablet finds." On October 9, 1906, during Stein's second expedition, He Jiadong, the district magistrate of Keriya, returned Stein's visit "at 10 AM. & stays two hours for sake of antiques, Hsi-yu-ki, etc." Two months later, his colleague at Charklik, Liu Mo, returned Stein's visit "by 2 P.M. & stays to look at plates, coins, etc." Not only that, but Magistrate Liu even helped identify Stein's latest spoils from the field: "Identifies my Vash-shahri finds except one." Two days later, Liu "asks to see tablets found at Niya Site." When Stein returned to Charklik one month later, he showed Liu the "Chin.[ese] tablets," from which he "recognizes nien-hao [nianhao, 'reign date']." Two days after that, Liu still had not gotten his fill. "Amban calls at 6–8 P.M. to see more tablets."[31]

Two months later at Dunhuang, in the neighboring province of Gansu, district magistrate Wang Jiayan called on Stein, who promptly displayed his "Niya tablets, plates, LA finds." When Stein returned from the nearby desert with wooden tablets dating back to the Han dynasty, he told his friend Percy Allen that "my Mandarin friends at the base" were "duly impressed." Over the remainder of Stein's second expedition, a seemingly endless parade of civil and military officials saw Stein's newly collected antiquities with their own eyes. On July 22, 1907, Chai Hongshan, the garrison commander of Suzhou, returned Stein's visit and was treated to his "Yu-men finds." At Ganzhou, Stein noted the "grand appearance of Titai; showed tablets, etc." On October 3, Li Yougeng, the telegraph commissioner at Anxi, "came to look at Chin.[ese] slips" and helped identify "numerous errors in transcripts made at Ch'ien-fu-tung." Back in Xinjiang, Stein "showed tablets, books, etc.," to four Chinese officials at Hami, while at Aksu, the newly promoted circuit-intendant Pan Zhen, with whom Stein maintained especially friendly relations, procured a long and intimate session with Stein's collection. "I had brought a few specimens of my Tun-huang finds, etc. for Pan-Darin's benefit," Stein wrote to Allen, "& to see him handle & study those relics of Han times was a treat." Pan must have concurred, for he later thanked Stein in a letter for allowing him to "cast my gaze back over several thousand years, as if the ancients were standing right before me." In 1914, Li Shurong, the district magistrate of Barikol, expressed a similar sentiment when he thanked Stein for allowing him "to see the ink traces of the Han and Tang dynasties that you have collected."[32]

After meeting with Stein and learning about his activities, Qing officials were required to submit a detailed report up the chain of command to the governor in Urumchi. These bland bureaucratic documents not only described the exit and entry dates of Stein and other foreign explorers into the magistrate's jurisdiction—along with a host of other mundane logistical minutiae—but also delineated in clear and precise language just what exactly Stein was planning to take out of the country. On May 17, 1901, Pan Zhen, then department magistrate of Khotan, submitted the following report in Chinese to his superiors:

> During our interview, he produced for my inspection clay Buddhist sculptures, wooden tablets, fragments of folded leather strips, and quite a bit of tattered paper with tracings of writing visible, all of which appeared to be ancient Indian characters written in an old Buddhist form. I estimate that the writings on paper are perhaps eleven to twelve hundred years old, while the wooden tablets and leather strips are closer to two thousand years old, from the days before the invention of paper.[33]

But Pan did not stop at a mere description of form. He also revealed the content of these documents, as communicated to him by the polyglot Stein. "The traveler does appear to be able to make sense of the majority of the writings in this script," Pan reported, "and states that they are letters and correspondence between local chiefs and princes from the kingdoms of that time and the Indians who ran errands back and forth." Two weeks later, Han Yaoguang, the district magistrate of Keriya, also recorded an extensive list in Chinese of Stein's newly unearthed antiquities and described a joint examination with Stein of this soon to be exported collection. "Upon examination," the magistrate noted, "I noticed that some of them were inscribed with traces of characters." According to Stein, Han continued, "these are all ancient Indian characters, not of the sort still in use today. They are perhaps twenty-eight hundred years old, a date [Stein] verified by reference to an annotated English version of Xuanzang's account of his trip to the Western Regions to obtain sutras that he kept next to him."[34]

It was meticulous reports such as these that prompted the governor of Xinjiang, Rao Yingqi, to commission a Chinese translation of Stein's *Preliminary Report* (1901) immediately on learning of its publication. The Chinese translation of Stein's report, titled "A Record of Archaeological Exploration in China" (*you Hua fanggu ji*), consists of ninety-eight pages of handwritten text. The translation is loose and imprecise, typical of many hasty translations of foreign works made at this time by Chinese scholars with a shaky grasp of English. Still, it provides a remarkable glimpse into what the educated Chinese elite of northwestern China—those who never had the opportunity to meet Stein or any other foreign explorer—might have learned about the expeditions of Westerners in Xinjiang.[35]

From the outset, Stein's activities are described in Chinese in accurate and unambiguous terms as the "search for ancient relics" (xunfang guji).[36] For any readers still in the dark, the Preliminary Report, both in English and Chinese, made it clear what Stein was after. Time and again, Stein describes in painstaking detail the hundreds on hundreds of documents and antiquities he unearthed from the jurisdictions of Chinese officials in Xinjiang. In an ancient "rubbish heap" at Niya, Stein recounts the recovery of "over 200 documents on wood, of all shapes and sizes." Lest the Chinese lose interest in the accumulation of non-Chinese scripts, Stein made it clear that Chinese material was also included in this haul. "Besides tablets with Kharoṣṭhī writing, which form the great majority," he wrote, "there came to light numerous narrow pieces of wood, bearing Chinese characters, like the two specimens reproduced on Plate VI."[37] His penchant for loose translation notwithstanding, Wan Rong glosses this passage with great accuracy, noting that Stein "obtained over two hundred inscribed wooden documents, among which were narrow pieces with Chinese characters [huawen], which can be seen in Plate Six. The majority of the leather documents were in Kharoshthi."[38] Nor was there any doubt about what Stein intended to do with these objects. Toward the end of his report, in passages faithfully retained in the Chinese version, Stein described the "twelve large boxes" of "archaeological proceeds" (Ch., guwu shi er da xiang) that he "took with him back to England" (Ch., daihui Yingguo), where he was able to "deposit the collection in the British Museum" (Ch., jiang ge jian nazhu bowuyuan).[39]

The original English version of Stein's Preliminary Report included sixteen plates that depicted a representative sample of the documents, statuary, and other objects taken out of Xinjiang by Stein. It is not known whether these plates were also included in the Chinese translation, though this seems unlikely. Regardless, it is clear that Stein made a habit of sending multiple copies of the illustrated English versions of his works to the British consul in Kashgar, who then distributed them to selected Chinese officials throughout the province, including the governor. Even for those who could not read English or procure their own copy of Wan Rong's translation, these richly illustrated reports provided ready visual confirmation of what Stein had removed. On November 11, 1907, Zeng Binghuang, the subprefect of Turfan, revealed to Stein that he "had seen my Prelim.[inary] Report when serving under Pan-Darin." Stein then gave Zeng a copy of his full book, since published, which Paul Pelliot spotted in Zeng's office during a visit to Turfan the following year. "He has Stein's books," Pelliot noted in his diary, with a hint of Gallic disdain, "due to Stein's habit of showing them everywhere." In 1913, Dai Chengmo, the magistrate of Keriya, was even able to

recall the specific title of one of these books, despite the fact that he did not
have his own copy. In his diary, Stein noted that Dai had "seen Anc.[ient]
Khotan at Kashgar & remembers Chin-docs in it."[40]

It is not clear how many copies of Stein's various books, articles, and reports made it into the hands of Chinese officials in Xinjiang. What is clear,
however, is that each copy that did make it into the province was regarded
as a prized possession, to be shared among one's friends and colleagues and
discussed at length. For those who did receive their own copy, expressions
of admiration and gratitude were duly communicated. "I have received the
book you sent as a gracious gift," wrote Aksu circuit intendant Pan Zhen
to Stein in 1908, "and have already browsed through it. Truly, it is a work
that is destined to be cherished and passed around, and it elicits a special
admiration." In a separate letter, Pan described them as "expansive books of
great importance that encompass everything you have experienced, be it the
traces of the ancients or the customs of our contemporaries." In 1913, Dai
Chengmo declared that his "deep admiration" for Stein was based on "the
collection of books he has authored and annotated." In 1925, Shule magistrate Wang Min, the son of a recently deceased magistrate who had once
been close to Stein, expressed his belief that "all the books you have written about your expeditions in Xinjiang are destined to become the subject
of deep respect among learned men, who will compete with one another to
purchase and read them."[41]

In addition to Stein's books, Chinese officials also relied on word of
mouth to keep abreast of his activities in the field. "Whenever I think of my
late father," Wang Min wrote in the same letter, "I recall how every time he
chatted with his friends, he would suddenly change the topic to talk about
your broad learning and thorough understanding of Eurasia, and he would
narrate your travels in Xinjiang." In October 1910, Zhao Weixi, a Qing official passing through Gansu en route to Urumchi, added a colophon to the
end of a *Great Nirvana* sutra from Dunhuang. In it, he recounts how Stein,
here misidentified as a German, "followed the Indus River, crossed over the
Kunlun Mountains, and entered Keriya, from whence he traveled to the old
Jade Gate Pass and thus reached Dunhuang." In Xinjiang, Zhao observed,
Stein "excavated a great number of antiquities," while in Dunhuang he "selected the best of the manuscripts, packing them away in numerous large
cases." As for the source of his knowledge about Stein's activities, Zhao
mentions a conversation with Chai Hongshan, the garrison commander of
Suzhou, who met with Stein on several occasions and appears in Stein's
diary as a witness to his collections.[42]

With the conclusion of Stein's second expedition (1906–8), awareness of his activities began to spread far beyond the administrative circles of Qing officials stationed in the northwest. In 1909, the noted Qing classicist Luo Zhenyu, working from Beijing, obtained copies of speeches published earlier that same year by Stein in London and Pelliot in Paris. Relying on the linguistic expertise of his student Wang Guowei and Japanese scholars in Tokyo, Luo quickly brought *Visiting the Ancients among the Shifting Sands* (*Liusha fanggu ji*) to publication. In it, the educated Confucian elite of the entire East Asian world could now read, in classical Chinese translation, a detailed account of Stein's and Pelliot's expeditions carried out in Xinjiang over the past three years. As with Wan Rong's translation of Stein's *Preliminary Report* seven years earlier, Luo's was as complete and candid an account as the English and French versions were for Western audiences. Even the purchase and removal of nearly twenty thousand ancient manuscripts from the Dunhuang cave library—a transaction neither Stein and Pelliot were eager to publicize before the collection had left the country—was narrated in full, from start to finish.

Last but not least was the publication in 1911, just months before the revolution, of Xinjiang Minister of Finance Wang Shu'nan's *Record of Antiquities in Xinjiang* (*Xinjiang fang gu lu*). Published both in a stand-alone version and as a single chapter in the much larger *Xinjiang Gazetteer* (*Xinjiang tuzhi*), Wang's overview of newly unearthed antiquities in Xinjiang covers the last decade of the Qing dynasty. It also makes clear that foreign scholars had removed enormous numbers of manuscripts and relics from the province. The Japanese expeditions sponsored by Count Ōtani are described as having "excavated a great number of antiquities" (*jue de guwu shen huo*) at Lop Nor, while Stein—again misidentified as a German—was singled out for having "obtained a private contract dated to the first year of the Jianzhong reign [i.e., Tang dynasty] for the purchase of an ox" at Keriya. Albert Grünwedel's removal of a commemorative stele for the construction of a Northern Liang temple in Turfan in 1903 was also deemed worthy of mention, as was Qing diplomat Duanfang's successful attempt to obtain a rubbing of this same stele during a visit to Berlin in 1905. In sum, of the many high quality Buddhist sutras to have emerged from the desert sands of Xinjiang over the past decade, Wang reports that "most of them were taken by Westerners."[43]

As with the covert collection by Western archaeologists of sensitive intelligence, Qing officials almost always knew exactly what—and how much—of his country's buried treasure the foreigner was removing. Moreover, he received no financial compensation for their loss, thus undercutting accusations of corruption. In fact, the Qing magistrates of Xinjiang were far

more likely to spend their own financial resources on the Western archaeologist than they were to accept any money in return. When the Finnish
intelligence agent Gustav Mannerheim left the oasis of Yarkand, he was surprised to find the local magistrate, Peng Xuzhan, ready to open his pocketbook. "His amiability even went so far as to ask," Mannerheim wrote in his
journal, "if I did not require some money for continuing my journey. When
I thanked him and laughingly declined his offer, he begged Liu repeatedly
to tell me that I should by no means feel embarrassed, but should consider
it a perfectly natural thing. These mandarins can really be extraordinarily
kind and they often have very good manners." At other times, Peng's colleagues extended temporary loans to the Westerners, routinely dismissed
lodging and culinary debts, and voluntarily assumed the burden of other
daily expenses.[44]

Why? The explanatory framework of coercion, deceit, and corruption
is inadequate to explain the behavior of Qing officials in Xinjiang, Gansu,
and Inner Mongolia—or the behavior of non-Western officials in any other
part of the world, for that matter. Though instances of coercion, deceit, and
corruption did occur, they did not occur at all times and all places. But the
removal to Western lands of caravan after caravan of art and antiquities
did. The rulers of the Ottoman and Qing Empires, free to reject any and all
applications for an expedition or excavation and well aware that archaeologists habitually collected sensitive strategic data concerning their lands
and peoples, nonetheless chose to admit them nearly every time. The goal
of this book is to develop a new explanatory framework, one capable of accounting for the seemingly counterintuitive behavior of those people whose
proactive and voluntary assistance was indispensable to the successful com-
pletion of an archaeological expedition in the age of Western imperialism.

THE COMPENSATIONS OF PLUNDER

The expeditions of Western explorers and archaeologists in northwestern
China have received very little critical scholarly attention. Thus far, the
field has been defined largely by popular biographers and museum practitioners, who draw heavily on the published accounts left by the archaeologists themselves. When such scholars make use of unpublished letters or
diary entries, they are usually marshaled in further support of a rhetorical
position that can ultimately be traced back to the explorer's own official
version of events. By accepting the archaeologist's own words about his motives and those of the locals at face value, these authors tend to avoid or
marginalize the less savory aspects of these enterprises. In most cases, the

publicly professed agenda of the heroic explorer serves as the implicit, or in some cases explicit, framework for all subsequent analysis.[45]

In recent years, however, a more critical stance has been adopted by a few scholars inclined to focus almost entirely on the unsavory aspects of some of these expeditions. Chief among the targets of this newer group of scholars is the Swedish explorer Sven Hedin, whose persistent Teutonic sympathies eventually placed him on the wrong side of history.[46] The Harvard art historian Langdon Warner, who brazenly cut out cave murals from the actively worshipped Thousand-Buddha Caves near Dunhuang in 1924, is the latest scholar to have joined the ranks of the excoriated.[47] (He will not fare too well in this book, either.) Unfortunately, the moral barometer from which such critiques are derived is decidedly anachronistic: in his exposé of Hedin's handling of antiquities in the first three decades of the twentieth century, Perry Johansson invokes the 2004 "Professional Code of Ethics of the International Council of Museums" as the standard to which Hedin should be posthumously held.[48] Regardless of their moral posture, however, all of these scholars are united in their complete neglect of the Chinese source base. When the rare sinologist actually does dip his or her toes into the expeditionary waters, the result is usually a narrowly focused article or book chapter inspired by the discovery of a single new source, without much attempt to integrate it into larger theoretical concerns.[49]

Scholarship on Western excavations and expeditions in the Ottoman Empire has developed much further. From Napoleon's invasion of Egypt in 1798 to the Iraqi confrontation of James Henry Breasted in 1935, historians have uncovered a rich mélange of nuanced responses to, and interactions with, Western archaeologists. Of particular note is the work of Donald Malcolm Reid, Elliott Colla, and Wendy Shaw, who have managed to recover Ottoman and Arabic perspectives on the Western obsession with the Greco-Roman and Pharaonic antiquities in their midst. In addition, James Goode has documented in detail just when and where the newly independent successor states of the Ottoman Empire managed to put a halt to the unregulated Western appropriation of their many pasts, both material and intellectual.[50] Despite all of their efforts, however, these scholars also continue to adhere to an anachronistic moral barometer of implicit judgment: nationalism. Though most recognize the importance of World War I as a turning point, they still tend to adopt the explanatory framework of coercion, deceit, and corruption as the key to understanding the actions of historical figures on both sides of the dig.

I propose a new theoretical approach to Western archaeological expeditions and excavations in the non-Western world, one that goes beyond the criminalizing and anachronistic discourse of nationalism. Key to this new formulation is an explicit recognition of three factors that defined the course of any archaeological enterprise: class, empire, and profit. Without a proper understanding of how these three variables functioned on the ground during the course of an expedition, we will continue to misinterpret as "criminal" or "shameful" actions that were instead motivated by a host of rational and pragmatic concerns.

With regard to the importance of class and empire, I have taken inspiration from the groundbreaking work of British historian David Cannadine. In *Ornamentalism: How the British Saw Their Empire* (2002), Cannadine highlighted the importance of the class-based transimperial bonds that prompted many British imperial administrators to forge more intimate relationships with their elite indigenous counterparts throughout the empire than either set of elites did with their own lower-class subjects, whom they tended to regard with contempt. Western archaeologists formed a similar transimperial bond with their administrative and social counterparts in China, often interacting with them on a basis of equality and respect that they did not replicate in their dealings with the lower classes. This elite fraternal bond, predicated on a shared recognition of common social, political, and economic markers of status, was further strengthened by racist theories of evolution then in vogue in Western intellectual circles. According to the German scholar Hans Günther, the Chinese and Japanese "aristocracy" of East Asia evinced "a decidedly long skull and an almost white skin, sometimes combined with handsome European features."[51] Such theories both facilitated and justified this transimperial bond. It should not surprise us, therefore, to learn that requests for anthropometrical measurements were invariably directed at the lower-class inhabitants of Central and East Asia—not to the Qing elites with whom Western archaeologists interacted and tended to treat with respect.

With regard to the importance of profit, I have followed the lead of legal historian Stuart Banner. In *How the Indians Lost Their Land: Law and Power on the Frontier* (2005), Banner draws attention to the rational cost-benefit analysis that the indigenous peoples of North America, quickly alerted to the meaning of a "land sale," adopted in their dealings with white settlers. Because the indigenous peoples did not yet regard their plentiful preserves of land as priceless, they were usually willing to trade or sell it in exchange for other commodities deemed far more valuable at the time.[52] As with antiquities, the general backdrop of unequal power relations certainly framed and guided all interactions between the two sides. Against that larger backdrop, however, the specific decision-making calculus of historical actors on the ground was influenced by a rational cost-benefit analysis of the risks and rewards expected to derive from a transactional relationship with resourceful outsiders.

Of course, in the end, the Indians lost nearly all of their land and the Chinese and Ottomans lost a staggering amount of what are now regarded as priceless specimens of art and antiquities. Key to the present reassessment of how these transfers took place, however, is the critical observation that the commodities offered in these transactions—land and antiquities—were not yet regarded as priceless at the time they were exchanged. Only with the institutionalization of state-sponsored nationalism in postrevolutionary China or in the postwar Ottoman successor states would the art and antiquities targeted by Western archaeologists undergo a new, inflated valuation. Before then, as we will see in chapters 1 and 2, these same antiquities may have been viewed as profitable or precious, but they were not regarded as priceless. As such, they could still be traded for anything that was imagined to be of equal or greater value by those who were engaged by the Westerner for their removal. I will refer to this rational and pragmatic barter calculus as "the compensations of plunder."

A few scholars have noted the underlying logic of these so-called compensations with regard to the Ottoman Empire and its successor states. In his classic study of the Elgin Marbles, William St. Clair noted how Lord Elgin failed to make much progress in the negotiations for a *firman* authorizing work on the Parthenon until the British decided to help the Ottoman Empire recover its Egyptian province from Napoleon. Then, "suddenly the Turks began to shower their British allies with favours," one of which was the *firman* for Elgin's work team in Athens. "The granting of the second firman," St. Clair continues, "was just another gift to be compared with the aigrettes, pelisses, horses, snuff boxes, and medals." Wendy Shaw, in her analysis of halting Ottoman efforts during the late nineteenth century to prevent the outflow of cultural artifacts, described the sultan as "willing to dispose of the material remains of ancient cultures in exchange for modern European technologies." Several of the pashas in Egypt were also willing to do the same in exchange for diplomatic aid: from 1826 to 1877, Muhammad Ali, and later his grandson Ismail, willingly gifted three ancient obelisks to France, Britain, and the United States. In a similar vein, Maya Jasanoff has taken note of the ways in which the Egyptian government's gift of the Temple of Dendur to the United States in 1965 in exchange for American aid hearkened back to the earliest days of Western expeditions in Egypt. "It was as if nothing had changed since the days of Muhammad Ali: antiquities could be traded for modern technology and Western development aid."[53]

Unfortunately, none of these tantalizing insights was pursued any further by its author, each being incidental to the narrative at hand. But they are united in their recognition of the fundamental utility of art and antiquities in the era before—and in some respects long after—nationalism: as barter commodities that could be exchanged for anything deemed of value to the giver, without the taint of corruption or immorality. The examples quoted above refer to highly specific transactional exchanges, in which clearly identified artifacts are traded for clearly identified returns. Far out along the expedition trail of northwestern China, however, most antiquity transactions were not so transparently quid pro quo. Rather, they were simply one part of a complex web of relationships in which different parties exchanged various types of goods, services, and capital in hopes of acquiring new resources of a greater perceived value. St. Clair, Shaw, and Jasanoff each illustrated a form of what we might refer to as "diplomatic capital": the receipt of costly diplomatic or economic favors from powerful Western states in exchange for freely available objects deemed of far less value to the relatively impoverished giver. As Jasanoff's critique of the Egyptian government's gift of the Temple of Dendur to the United States in 1965 shows, diplomatic capital is the most enduring and precious form of capital, the only one capable of transcending the inflated valuations of nationalism.

Most of this book is concerned with tracing the exchange of three forms of capital whose value was greatest not in the imperial corridors of power, but rather in the local vicinity of the excavation itself: economic, political, and social. As we will see in chapters 1 to 3, economic capital was of greatest appeal to the destitute lower classes of northwestern China, while political and social capital was highly coveted by the Qing ruling elite. Because most of the Muslim and Chinese people who sought out these three forms of capital did not become acculturated to nationalist ideologies within their lifetime, the allure of each form of compensation continued well beyond the rhetorical enshrinement of nationalism in the decades following the Chinese revolution of 1911.

In the era before nationalism, most of the people with whom the Western archaeologist interacted on the expedition trail tended to privilege the claims of tangible and personal social and political networks over those of abstract and impersonal collective ones. With respect to art and antiquities, this mode of interaction can claim a long and distinguished pedigree in China. In fact, most of the Confucian elites who welcomed Western archaeologists into their jurisdictions could rightly portray themselves as heirs to an unbroken tradition of antiquarianism and cultural connoisseurship that far exceeded, in both time and space, that of any comparable tradition in the West. As Shana Brown and Patricia Ebrey have shown, the collection, preservation, and study of antiquities in China goes back at least as far as the Song dynasty (960–1279). For nearly a thousand years before Western archaeologists and explorers first arrived on their doorstep, Confucian elites had been inscribing political and cosmological significance into the material remains of the earliest Chinese dynasties and empires. Moreover, they approached the past through the lens of a perception of cultural continuity, not discontinuity. Thus, unlike with Western scholars, who took some time to warm to the idea that the material remains of places such as ancient Egypt were within the purview of their civilizational genealogy, in China, everything inscribed in Chinese characters over a three-thousand-year period was considered fair game for serious scholarly attention and preservation.[54]

In the century or so immediately preceding the arrival of men like Stein and Pelliot in China, however, Western perceptions of the political utility of art and antiquities underwent a dramatic shift. Once viewed as the embodiment of the individual virtue of monarchs and social elites, art and antiquities began to be associated with the rise and fall of distinct "nations," whose members were posthumously believed to have been collectively responsible for their creation. According to Wu Hung, this shift in perception was reflected in the peculiar obsession with the depiction of "ruins" in Western art during the eighteenth and nineteenth centuries. This momentous transition, given powerful voice by Romantic poets and essayists, helped transform antiquities into the politicized emblems of nations that had risen and fallen over the course of history.[55] As Western empires expanded beyond the European continent and exerted dominion over diverse peoples around the world, the recovery, preservation, and display of art and antiquities served to justify their rule over alien peoples, who were now regarded as distinct "nations" subsisting under an imperial umbrella that contained many other nations.

By linking the art and antiquities of nations to the legitimacy of their empires, Western scholars infused a political valuation into these objects, one that made them virtually priceless—for to neglect the forgotten cultural heritage of the nations over which one ruled was to forfeit the right to serve as the resurrector of the "forgotten" glory of those nations, a glory now symbolized by their picturesque ruins. The Confucian elites of China experienced no such shift in their perceptions of the political value of similar cultural remains. Though they had been venerating Chinese art and antiquities for over a thousand years, far longer than the Westerners, they did not associate these objects with the collective virtue or glory of the nations over which the political legitimacy of Chinese emperors might be derived. As Wu Hung as shown, there was no Chinese counterpart to the visual depiction of ruins in contemporary Western art. When tropes of material ruin and destruction were invoked in the literary production of Confucian elites, they were applied to the rise and fall of individual dynasties that had presided over Chinese civilization—not to the rise and fall of Chinese civilization itself, nor to the "nations" that might be imagined to compose it.[56] In other words, political virtue was still a private affair in China. Though art and antiquities were pregnant with political value, such value redounded only to the person or family who owned the object. The emperor's treasures were nothing more and nothing less than the emperor's treasures; to the extent that they reflected political virtue and the right to rule over the empire, they reflected the exclusive virtue and legitimacy of the ruling house then in power and the dynasty over which the members of its lineage had presided.

Long before the arrival of Western archaeologists in the late nineteenth century, Chinese collectors had already placed an extremely high value on their art and antiquities. But they did not value them in the way that Western scholars had (only recently) begun to value them: as political emblems of the many nations whose collective cultural identities now imparted legitimacy to the rulers of a multiethnic state. The presence of Tibetan urns, paintings, and other cultural treasures in the Forbidden City was not viewed as representative of the Qing emperor's right to rule over the "Tibetan nation" writ large; rather, it represented his right to claim an exclusive patronage relationship with the influential religious leaders of the Yellow Hat sect of Tibetan Buddhism, who in turn exercised their own individual authority over the Tibetan masses. Such cultural artifacts did not belong, either literally or figuratively, to the Tibetan people, nor were they viewed as somehow representative of the creative genius or national character of the Tibetan people. The same could be said of pretty much any work of art or antiquity, produced by the craftsmen and artists of any ethnic or religious community, in any of the private collections owned by Qing elites. The Qing emperor, instead of placing such precious objects into a public museum, where they might broadcast his political legitimacy to all the people belonging to the many nations under his rule, instead stored them out of sight in the bowels of the Forbidden City, managed by officials in the aptly named Inner Household Department (Neiwufu).[57]

It is this crucial shift in perceptions regarding the value of art and antiquities that I have relied on in formulating several important definitions that will appear throughout this book. In short, I propose the following hierarchy of valuation among the various peoples who interacted with the material remains of the past in China: worthless, profitable, precious, and priceless. The first two valuations—worthless and profitable—will generally apply to the modes of interaction adopted by lower-class Muslim and Chinese peasants. I reserve the valuation of "precious" to refer to the high—but nonetheless negotiable—value ascribed to Chinese art and antiquities by various Confucian elites. As we shall see in chapter 2, though the educated elites of China certainly valued such things, and had done so for millennia, they were still willing to trade or sell them to other elites for a form of compensation—economic, political, or social—deemed of equal or higher value. Finally, I apply the valuation of "priceless" to refer to a mode of interaction adopted by Western archaeologists and collectors, who regarded these objects as collective emblems of those nations over which they saw themselves—or their imperial sponsors—as current or future political stewards. The reason I describe such valuations as priceless is because nothing, in theory, could induce the Western archaeologist to sell or otherwise exchange the art and antiquities he had obtained during the course of his expedition, for the simple reason that nothing, in theory, surpassed the political value of objects from which the right to rule over the collective nations of the world was now increasingly thought to derive.

The implications of all this are enormous. Because the educated elites of China did not yet infuse objects with the collective identities of nations—that is, nationalism—there were still a great many forms of compensation whose value exceeded that of the art and antiquities in their midst. As I will show in chapter 2, this was just as true of their dealings with other resourceful Chinese as it was of their dealings with the resourceful foreign archaeologist. As a result, it was one's relationship with the archaeologist himself that was deemed of greater value than possession of the artifacts he targeted. Not only that, but this relationship and its associated benefits were also deemed to counterbalance most of the imperialist depredations and strategic liabilities that the Western archaeologist brought with him into China. As we shall see in chapter 1, to the mostly Muslim lower classes, an artifact could be sold no more than once, but a long-term relationship with a Western archaeologist could yield repeated economic returns over many years. Similarly, as I will demonstrate in chapters 2 and 3, with regard to the Chinese elites, an artifact might be precious and the Westerner might be arrogant and haughty—but still the value of what the archaeologist could provide in other forms of compensatory capital could manage to outweigh the cabinet of unpleasantries occasioned by their loss.

With the postwar and postrevolutionary institutionalization of nationalist ideals in non-Western museums, however, the domestic value of the artifacts sought by the Western archaeologist began to skyrocket. Once a new generation of fully Westernized Chinese elites began to do as their Western counterparts did—that is, conflate the material culture of the past with the political legitimacy of newly conceived nations—the art and antiquities of China attained a valuation just as priceless within China as they had already attained outside of China. Not surprisingly, this new valuation soon gave rise to conflicts and tensions that were wholly absent from earlier archaeological expeditions, when only one party to the transaction regarded the objects targeted for removal as priceless. Henceforth, the moral barometer of our own day and age quickly took shape: anyone who participated in the removal of newly nationalized artifacts from their "rightful" national boundaries was now complicit in a criminal act of betrayal against that very nation. Reformulated in terms of the evolution of the "compensations of plunder," we might say that as the rhetorical value of the artifact increased, the material value of the resources yielded by the Western archaeologist in exchange for that artifact began to decrease. This is a process that will be treated more fully in chapter 4. And yet, as will become clear in chapters 5 and 6, the value of each form of capital offered by the archaeologist far out along the expedition trail still proved surprisingly resilient even in the face of nationalist deflation.

In the major cities of the eastern seaboard, however, one small but powerful group steadfastly adhered to the new nationalist valuation: Westernized Chinese scholars working outside of high political office. The reason for the latter caveat is simple: much like the Egyptian politicians who gifted the Temple of Dendur to the United States in 1965, even the most principled nationalist Chinese elites, so long as they occupied high office in a politically unbalanced world, could not ignore the allure of free diplomatic and political capital, even long after they had inoculated themselves against the temptations of social and economic capital.

THE SOURCE BASE

This study is based on a rich array of published and unpublished sources in English, French, and Chinese. The value of the English and French records is obvious. Stein, Hungarian by birth and educated in Germany during his adolescence, took his PhD at Oxford and spent the rest of his life in service to the Raj. Because the British government in India was the primary diplomatic and financial sponsor of Stein's first three expeditions to Xinjiang (1900–1901, 1906–8, 1913–15), with Harvard assuming financial obligations for the fourth (1930–31), nearly all of the records associated with his expeditions—applications, letters, field diaries, account books—are in English. The same combination of British and American patronage also facilitated the lone expedition (1905–6) of Yale climatologist Ellsworth Huntington, whose letters from Xinjiang back to his family in New Haven provide rare insights into aspects of these expeditions that his European colleagues tended not to comment on. In addition, the ill-fated expeditions of American art historian Langdon Warner and paleontologist Roy Chapman Andrews in the 1920s are also documented in English. All of these sources derive from the relevant archival holdings in Oxford, Harvard, Yale, and the American Museum of Natural History in New York.

The study of other expeditions has been made possible through recently published scholarly editions of diaries and letters previously inaccessible or else available only in heavily censored form. Included in this category is the Russian-sponsored expedition (1906–8) of Finnish intelligence agent Gustav Mannerheim, who kept his diary in Swedish but later oversaw its publication into English. In 2008, the Finno-Ugrian Society published a fully revised version of the 1940 edition, restoring all of the passages that Mannerheim previously omitted. With regard to French, documentation of the expedition (1906–8) of famed sinologist Paul Pelliot, who set out together with Mannerheim through Russian Turkestan but later parted ways in Xinjiang, has long been unavailable to researchers. That changed in 2008, when the Museé Guimet in Paris published a complete edition of Pelliot's field diary, along with a selection of letters he sent from Xinjiang and Gansu.[58] Unfortunately, there are several explorers and archaeologists whose expeditions can only be incorporated into the present analysis through their own published works in English or through the insights of other academic scholars. This is due to a variety of limiting factors: the range of my own linguistic expertise, a lack of archival access, or the physical loss of the records in question. Expeditions affected by one or more of these conditions include those of Swedish explorer Sven Hedin, the Russian explorers Sergey Oldenburg and Pyotr Kozlov, the German archaeologists Albert von Le Coq and Albert Grünwedel, and the Japanese scholars Ōtani Kōzui and Zuicho Tachibana.

As a result, this study derives a significant portion of its empirical source base from published and unpublished archival material produced in English and French by Stein, Pelliot, Mannerheim, Huntington, Warner, and Andrews while they were on the expedition trail. Though each expedition will yield unique insights at different points in the narrative, those of Stein—and, to a lesser extent, Pelliot—clearly predominate. There are good reasons for this. Even if the records of every explorer could be consulted in their original language and condition, Stein would still be the most suitable historical figure through which to tackle the present research agenda. First, he spent more time on the expedition trail than did any other archaeologist. Second, his many expeditions took place against vastly different geopolitical and chronological backdrops: two in the late Qing, one in the immediate aftermath of the 1911 revolution, and one amid the rise of Chiang Kai-shek's Nationalist government nearly two decades later. This allows us to see how certain phenomena and themes endured or evolved over the course of three separate decades and many different political contexts. Third, Stein was by far the most "successful" of all the foreign archaeologists; his caravans were responsible for removing many tens of thousands of artifacts from China. (Here the distinction between "explorer" and "archaeologist" is important: Hedin probably spent just as much time—and across just as many decades—in the field as did Stein. Unlike Stein, however, Hedin rarely excavated, thus sparing him the enmity of later Chinese nationalists.)

After Stein, Pelliot (figure 7) is the second most important archaeologist on the list. Although he undertook only one expedition to Xinjiang and Gansu, Pelliot was the rare scholar who was able to converse and interact with the Chinese entirely on their own cultural and linguistic terms. Whereas nearly all of his Western rivals approached northwestern China from the perspective of Indology or Turkic studies, Pelliot alone was fluent in Mandarin Chinese—in addition to Turkic and Persian—and fully proficient in the Chinese literary canon. His unique scholarly background helps to account for the divergent fates of one of the most spectacular discoveries of all time: the hidden "cave library" at the Thousand-Buddha Caves near Dunhuang. First uncovered by the itinerant and illiterate Daoist priest Wang Yuanlu in 1900, Cave 17, as it later came to be called, would ultimately yield more than forty thousand objects of historical, literary, religious, and artistic value, all of which had remained untouched and forgotten for nearly nine hundred years. In 1907, Stein gained access to the cave and negotiated with Wang for the sale of approximately one-quarter of its contents. Hot on Stein's trail, Pelliot arrived the very next year and acquired another one-quarter of the original collection. Pelliot's acquisitions, however, are generally considered superior to Stein's. Because Pelliot could read Chinese and had a better sense of the historical and literary value of what he was removing, he managed to avoid procuring endless copies of the same Buddhist sutras. Instead, Pelliot amassed one of the greatest collections of inadvertently preserved secular documents, literary texts, and monastic records from antiquity anywhere in the world.

Figure 7. French Sinologist Paul Pelliot. In 1907, the precocious French sinologist Paul
Pelliot, operating under Russian patronage and with the Finnish intelligence agent
Gustav Mannerheim in tow, entered Xinjiang and followed the northern circuit to the
provincial capital of Urumchi and thence on to Dunhuang in Gansu. In 1908, one year
after Stein first gained access to the hidden "cave library" at the Thousand-Buddha Caves
and removed nearly ten thousand manuscripts, Pelliot—pictured here inside the cramped
confines of what is now known as Cave 17—managed to acquire an additional ten
thousand manuscripts. Unlike Stein, however, Pelliot was fluent in Chinese, proficient
in the Confucian literary canon, and eager to share his finds with Chinese scholars on the
eastern seaboard. Paul Pelliot, "Trois ans dans la haute Asie," *L'Illustration* 135 (January–
June 1910): 265.

For all of these reasons, Stein and Pelliot stand head and shoulders above the rest, both in terms of what they did and in terms of how they are remembered. In reconstructing their interactions with local Chinese and Muslims on the expedition trail, the following chapters will make liberal use of the unpublished diaries and letters they composed while in the field. Some readers may be skeptical of such sources. After all, they did originate from the pens of men who were accustomed to being treated in accordance with the deference and respect that an agent of a powerful Western empire typically received during that era. And yet it is important to remember that these are records of people, places, and events that Stein and Pelliot did not intend for the eyes of their contemporaries. Unlike published articles and books, which invariably portray their authors as cultural heroes engaged in the altruistic pursuit of politically disinterested science, private letters and field diaries often reveal events and commentary that are unflattering to those involved.

In dealing with this source base, I have taken much inspiration from the work of Qing legal historians Matthew Sommer and Robert Hegel. One of the great virtues of Sommer's and Hegel's scholarship is to show how historians can recover the "voice of the voiceless" from records that were created and edited by elites. In documents from Qing court proceedings, the testimony of largely illiterate peasants, rebels, shopkeepers, and drifters, among many other members of the less privileged sectors of Chinese society, are recorded at great length and in surprising detail. Though such testimony provides an invaluable window into the lives of people who otherwise would never have left such detailed accounts of their daily activities and thoughts, Sommer and Hegel rightly note that even the ostensibly verbatim oral testimonies of such people were ultimately edited by Qing elites. By accounting for the known prejudices and censorial habits of the creators of such documents, however, they manage to recover otherwise unrecoverable evidence of the daily interactions, motivations, and desires of people who rarely appear in historical narratives produced by privileged elites.[59]

As with the court documents bequeathed to historians by Qing magistrates, the unpublished letters and field diaries of Western archaeologists in China contain a wealth of information about people who otherwise would not appear in the historical record. By accounting for the known biases and editing proclivities of men who were undeniably both racist and imperialist, I have attempted to recover the voices of these voiceless figures to the greatest extent possible. Much as Sommer and Hegel have approached the edited records of Qing court cases, I recognize that men like Stein and Pelliot were forced to balance a competing set of priorities. On the one hand, they could not help but reveal their deep prejudices regarding class, race, and culture when dealing with peoples they regarded as vastly inferior in nearly every imaginable way to themselves. Just like a Qing magistrate, however, Stein and Pelliot also needed to obtain as complete and accurate an understanding as possible of the actions, motivations, and habits of the people over whom they exercised authority. Otherwise, it would be difficult to do their job. That Stein and Pelliot often regarded the men in their caravan with varying degrees of suspicion, scorn, and bemusement does not necessarily mean that they were incapable of understanding why such people acted in the ways that they did. In other words, the undeniable bias of the observer does not automatically discount the empirical value of his observations.

A few examples may help to illustrate the utility of this source base. Let us begin with the case of Ram Singh, the cartographer sent to accompany Stein by the Survey of India. In the winter of 1906/7, Singh repeatedly complained about his lack of comfort on the expedition trail. He then began to drag his feet on his assigned tasks. "Had to hurry on R.[am]S.[ingh] who was taking his meal at 8 A.M. declaring he could not get up earlier," Stein wrote in his field diary. Singh then did the unthinkable. "Insolent attitude & outburst on acc.[ount] of my remonstrating. Attempts to leave by asking camelmen to unload. Stopped this barefaced insubordin[atio]n." Even after Stein quelled Singh's attempt at "insubordination," Singh continued to give his employer an earful. "Presumes to state his opinion about me personally," Stein noted in the same entry. Four months later, tensions between the two men flared up once again:

Had to administer "specific" to R.[am]S.[ingh] about his interference with transport & claims of "Survey [of India]" camels. Followed it up by friendly enquiry into [illegible] complaints. Probed his bitter feelings about work supposed to have been done for others' credit. Residua: too long marches . . . cooking shared with Naik—& latter's snoring; bad quarters at [illegible]; no superior pony, and—too little ease & comfort. Has no wish to get "credit", only pay & a safe return. Asked him to let me know thereafter of any discomfort at the time, & to believe in my wish to help in return for good work. When desired to save objections, etc., claims to be doing all that can be expected "in Dep[artmen]t" & special merit for saying good morning, etc. Sad hominis speculo.[60]

In these unpublished excerpts from Stein's field diaries, the actions and motivations of Ram Singh are consistently denigrated and mocked by his employer, who concludes his entry with a suitably elitist insult in Latin. And

yet if we as historians cannot bring ourselves to look beyond Stein's unsavory prejudices, contenting ourselves with little more than a righteous condemnation of his haughty imperialist ways, we will then fail to recover the
otherwise irretrievable voice of the "voiceless" Ram Singh—however medi-
ated his voice may be. Once we manage to penetrate Stein's formidable rhetorical gloss, we can see that these passages contain revelations that would
have proven deeply embarrassing for Stein had they been made public. The
issue was not with Singh's allegedly lethargic behavior and desire for creature comforts; elsewhere, Stein was perfectly happy to publish pejorative
comments about "lazy" servants and "indolent" natives whenever and
wherever they bothered him. The problem was that Singh had openly defied
Stein's authority as leader of the expedition and questioned his presumed
infallibility as a heroic man of science. Perhaps of even greater interest is
Singh's alleged comment about his "bitter feelings" toward "work supposed
to have been done for others' credit." The oft-denigrated natives, it seems,
were fully aware that, despite all the hardships that every member of the
expedition must endure, in the end only the Western archaeologist would
reap the benefits of fame and fortune.

This is merely one example of the ways in which the unpublished records of these expeditions can help restore the voices of the voiceless, even
if we can only recover those voices indirectly. Needless to say, Stein never
published a single word about his unpleasant interactions with Ram Singh.
Readers of Stein's books and articles know only that Singh was a competent
if nondescript Gurkha cartographer who was later awarded a prize by the
Royal Geographical Society for his services on the second expedition. The
diaries and letters of other Western archaeologists evince a similar utility.
As we will see in chapter 1, despite his openly racist scholarly agenda, Ellsworth Huntington has left us with the single most complete and revealing
account of the various forms of economic compensation made available to
Muslim peasants on the expedition trail. In a similar vein, we will also see
how Pelliot, in the midst of weaving a salacious and somewhat misogynist
anecdote about the sexual behavior of a young Muslim girl, inadvertently
reveals how local Muslims could put Buddhist antiquities to uses wholly
unanticipated by educated elites, Western or otherwise.

These same sources can also be used to contest, verify, or otherwise supplement the letters and diaries left by other Western scholars. For example,
when Stein and Pelliot first witnessed the excavation methods of German
archaeologists Le Coq and Grünwedel in Kucha, Turfan, and Kara-shahr,
they could scarcely believe their eyes. Pelliot was the first to see the indelicate handiwork of the Germans, who "made 'holes' and conducted them-

selves more in 'Sarte,' seeking objects for their museums more than working for science." The following year, Pelliot concluded that the Germans "have completely ruined the Ming-oi" at Kara-shahr by hacking at the frescos and putting "strong glue in the hollow inscriptions; why great gods?"[61] Stein, a far more guarded commentator than Pelliot, also found it difficult to reserve judgment on the Germans. Like Pelliot, however, he would only criticize the Germans in private. "You will understand the awkward dilemma I had to face," he wrote to his good friend Percy Allen from Ming-oi in December 1907, "when I found ruin after ruin of big temples, monasteries etc., dug into with the method of a scholarly treasure seeker, yet barely explored with any approach to archaeological thoroughness." After repeatedly encountering seemingly deliberate gashes to murals the Germans left behind, along with a general "indifference to the fate of all that was left in situ," Stein described Le Coq's excavation methods as a "system for which the German language supplies the express term of 'Rabbau.'" The passage of time did not lessen Stein's distaste for German depredations. "It has needed practice to examine calmly the way in which Lecoq's & Grunwedel's assistant," Stein observed on his third expedition in 1915, "had ruthlessly hacked the frescoes to the right & left of the pieces they wanted." The Russian explorer Sergey Oldenburg was far more blunt. "It is sheer robbery, clever, ingenious, but robbery all the same—not scholarly research."[62]

Other revealing passages can often be found whenever one explorer interacted with the same Muslim or Chinese person who had previously interacted with another explorer. Though few archaeologists would ever publish a contrary word against their Western colleagues in public—Le Coq's gentle mocking of Grünwedel in the published account of their joint expeditions being the lone exception—they eagerly recorded unflattering impressions of one another in their private diaries and letters. These impressions sometimes offer tantalizing glimpses into the thoughts of people whose voices are otherwise irretrievable, even if they were not illiterate peasants. On February 9, 1908, Pelliot paid a visit to Enguang, the Manchu prefect of Anxi, just outside of Dunhuang. During the course of their conversation, Pelliot learned that Stein, "speaking to the amban of T'ang seng [i.e., Xuanzang]," the celebrated Buddhist monk who traveled to India in the seventh century and brought back Sanskrit sutras to translate into Chinese, had "naturally portrayed himself as a Buddhist." But Enguang, whom Pelliot otherwise regarded as "quite an imbecile," was nonetheless skeptical of Stein's claims: "Mandarin asks me if this faith is sincere."[63]

Both Chinese and Western scholars have long followed Stein's lead in attributing much of his success on the expedition trail to his skillful invocation of Xuanzang, which is often said to have ingratiated Stein with his Chinese hosts. The implication is that such a deceitful tactic succeeded in paving the way among dim-witted and corrupt Qing officials to the unlawful theft of Chinese art and antiquities. Of course, this facile explanation requires us to ignore the obvious fact that numerous other archaeologists also managed to remove thousands on thousands of artifacts from northwestern China without once uttering the name of Xuanzang or professing any affinity for Buddhism. The above quoted passage from Pelliot's diary, however, makes it abundantly clear that even the most "imbecilic" Qing official was skeptical of Stein's invocation of Xuanzang. Not only that, but Enguang's skepticism can be deduced in spite of the absence of any surviving Chinese documentation left by Enguang himself.

The private correspondence of other explorers also helps to chisel away at the aura of infallibility that has accrued to Stein over the years. On October 30, 1905, Huntington wrote to his family about "old Abdulla," Stein's guide from his first expedition four years earlier. At some point, Abdulla admitted to Huntington that he had withheld knowledge of routes and sites from Stein while employed in his service. When Huntington asked him why, Abdulla replied:

> "Oh the camelman and the cook, and the hostler frightened me. They did not want to go further into the sand, or to stop at any more places than necessary. They said, 'Don't tell him. He knows of the "millstere" (as they call an old Buddhist chortan) but not of the other places.' So when the Sahib said 'Abdullah do you know of any other houses?' I said 'Mr. Sahib, if you kill me I should still say there were no more ruins. I never saw any or heard of any!'"[64]

Even if Huntington has partially misquoted or mistranslated what Abdulla may have told him, the basic historical value of this remarkable confession remains. Though neither Stein nor Huntington would admit in public that Stein's illiterate peasant guides had managed to deceive him, such things would be lamented in private. On July 14, 1907, even Stein revealed as much. "Mo-Daloi & guides now owned up to full knowledge of route leading in 4 more marches to Kia-yu-kuan," Stein noted in his field diary. "Barefaced acknowledgment that previous lies told in order to escape a troublesome track!"[65]

Throughout this book, we will find that the private documentation of Western archaeologists often stands in sharp contrast to the official narratives put forth in the public eye. For instance, in *Buried Treasures of Chi-*

nese Turkestan (1928), Le Coq took great delight in recounting a practical joke he and his assistant, Bartus, played on the Muslim elders of Turfan. When the elders expressed an apparently earnest desire to be able to greet the Germans in their own language on their return for a future expedition, Bartus decided to teach his unsuspecting hosts the following two phrases: "Good morning, old fat head" and "Good morning, old tippler." When Grünwedel returned to Turfan six years later, Le Coq assures his readers, he was indeed greeted by the Muslim elders of Turfan with the same inappropriate phrases Bartus had taught them. But the letters of Ellsworth Huntington present a very different picture of local Muslim reactions to these unseemly German shenanigans (albeit not the exact same shenanigan). On March 14, 1906, Huntington wrote to his family from Turfan, where he had just participated in several audiences with the young Muslim prince of Lukchun. The prince, Huntington says, "asked me why the German archaeologists who have been exploring Turfan carried away all sorts of useless things, even samples of earth." Huntington, unaware of Le Coq and Bartus's boorish behavior, attempted to explain "as well as I could." The response of the boy prince? "Ah, I knew those Germans were liars. Their leader, Lecoq, told me the earth was to be put in water and drunk as medicine."[66]

If the unpublished documentation of Western archaeologists in northwestern China can yield such refreshing examples of non-Western agency in English and French, what can the Chinese source base reveal? The answer is quite a lot. Just as with the Western-language documents, however, the utility of the Chinese side is dependent on a proper understanding of the ideological biases involved in the production of any given source. These sources include official telegrams, privately circulated gazetteers, personal letters addressed to the foreign archaeologists, translations of Western archaeological reports and the prefaces or postfaces appended to them, and, perhaps most revealing of all, the modern Chinese colophons added to ancient manuscripts found in Turfan and Dunhuang. Prior to World War I, nearly all of these sources are reflective of the concerns and priorities of the Confucian-educated officials whose careers unfolded against the backdrop of the last several decades of Qing rule. These men, most of whom lived and worked in a bureaucratic and social bubble largely divorced from any meaningful contact with the Muslim and Chinese peasants of the northwestern frontier, rarely commented on the lower-class subjects who interacted with the Western archaeologists. As a result, the earliest Chinese materials are most valuable for what they can tell us about the nature of the relationship that developed between educated Chinese and Western elites, a topic to be treated in depth in chapters 2 and 3.

In the decades after World War I, the types of sources produced by those Western archaeologists who continued to try their luck in China changed very little. But the Chinese source base witnessed the rise of an important new perspective: that of Westernized Chinese scholars in Beijing who began to accompany Western archaeologists on their expeditions into the northwest, with varying degrees of authority over their international colleagues. Several of these scholars, such as Chen Wanli, Xu Xusheng, and Huang Wenbi, kept detailed diaries of their travels. Unlike their Confucian-educated forebears, however, these men paid acute attention to the actions and attitudes of the lower-class peasants with whom they were obliged to interact. The end result is an embarrassment of empirical riches for these latter expeditions, where it is often possible to trace divergent or convergent Western and Chinese responses to the exact same person or event. Another salient feature of the expeditions to occur after World War I is the more proactive role of various government bodies within China regarding the activities of the Western archaeologist. During the late Qing, the central government in Beijing did little more than issue a passport, delegating most administrative affairs to the local officials in Xinjiang. By 1930, however, Stein had to navigate through a complex web of various official and unofficial Chinese organizations, each of which was deeply invested in his every word and movement: the Xinjiang provincial government in Urumchi, local officials posted to the oases of the Taklamakan Desert, the Nationalist government and Academia Sinica in Nanjing, and the Commission for the Preservation of Antiquities and various universities in Beijing.

Regardless of the type of Chinese source, it is important to note that the vast majority of those used for this study were never intended to be read by anyone outside of a very small circle of like-minded colleagues within China. By and large, the Chinese source base is characterized by highly educated Chinese elites talking in private to other highly educated Chinese elites about Western archaeologists and the art and antiquities targeted by them for removal. In fact, the only types of documents that their authors ever imagined would be seen by Western archaeologists were the personal letters sent to Stein and Pelliot. These letters, it bears mentioning, were posted after Stein and Pelliot had already left the jurisdiction of their author, and in some cases after Stein and Pelliot had already left China entirely. In other words, whatever benefits a given official may have thought he could accrue through the composition of a flowery letter to a resourceful person like Stein would have largely disappeared by the time Stein actually read the letter. Rather than view such missives as an insincere attempt to curry favor with a resourceful imperialist susceptible to flattery—though some may also have been that—this study will treat these documents as tangible emblems of an unexpected social bond made possible by the gradual revelation of shared political, social, and cultural interests.

There are also a handful of sources, found among Stein's papers, that were written by the local educated elites of the Turkic-speaking Muslim oases of the Tarim Basin in southern Xinjiang (figure 8). Their descendants are known today as "Uyghurs." Prior to the 1930s, however, they were referred to by Westerners as "Turki" (or "Eastern Turki") and by the Chinese as "Turban Heads" (*chantou*). Anyone who is hoping for such documents to reveal evidence of an anti-imperialist subaltern voice, however, will be sorely disappointed. On the contrary, all of the Uyghur-language sources in Stein's papers—eight single-spaced documents and a handful of paper slips and other fragments—are composed of various petitions and administrative orders regarding local disputes in the villages through which he passed during his expedition. One of them, for instance, is a complaint from a Tatar named Mahmud Bay who is trying to reclaim some loans. Another outlines the grievances of a group of villagers from Qarakash, who accuse another group of villagers of stealing their allotment of canal water and bullying the local irrigation supervisor, or *mirab*.[67]

Why were these documents in Stein's possession? Though we can only

Figure 8. Harnessing the Agents of Empire. These two Uyghur-language documents, preserved in the personal papers of Aurel Stein, record the grievances of local merchants and villagers in the villages through which Stein passed during his expedition. The fact that they were found among Stein's papers suggests that the local Muslims of Xinjiang regarded him as a resourceful agent of a powerful empire who could help them negotiate or resolve various disputes in between his archaeological labors. Stein Papers, Bodleian Library, MS 341–42. Reprinted with the kind permission of the British Academy.

speculate, the most likely answer is that he was called on to help negotiate or resolve the disputes outlined in these documents. As we have already seen and will continue to see in the chapters that follow, the Western archaeologist was viewed by the local residents of the lands through which he passed as much more than simply an archaeologist. To them, he was also a resourceful representative of a powerful Western empire, with whom one might interact in any number of self-interested ways unanticipated by the rigid nationalist narratives that would later accrue around these expeditions. It is important to remember that the art and antiquities of the non-Western world were not taken abroad by agentless abstractions such as "empires," "imperialism," or "racism." Rather, they were removed by flesh-and-blood individuals who leveraged tangible resources to initiate mutually productive relationships with the people who lived in the vicinity of these antiquities. And, more than anything else, it is these sorts of relationships that determined the course of every Western expedition to northwestern China—and, I would argue, throughout the rest of the world. Though everyone involved in these expeditions had principles that they were prepared to defend and lines that they dared not cross, the nature of these principles has been lost to time. Instead, we continue to adhere to an anachronistic moral barometer of nationalism that would have been utterly unfamiliar to nearly everyone who aided and abetted the Western archaeologist in the era before World War I.

The goal of this book is to recover the pragmatic barter calculus that guided the actions of rational historical actors on the expedition trail. Only then will we be able to replace our ahistorical standard of judgment with a contemporary standard of judgment—and thus truly understand how China lost its treasures.

✧

This book is composed of six chapters. Chapter 1 analyzes the perceived value of the material remains of the past among the mostly illiterate, lower-class Muslim peasants of Xinjiang before, during, and after the arrival of the Western archaeologist. It then highlights the forms of economic capital that these same Muslims were generally willing to accept in exchange for their physical assistance with the removal of these objects to a foreign land. Chapter 2 applies a similar analytical framework to the Confucian-educated Han, Manchu, and Mongol officials and scholars of the late Qing era who interacted with the foreign archaeologist or the objects he coveted, and establishes the perceived value of these objects among the literate elites of the late imperial era. Chapter 3 then outlines the nature of the transimperial relationship that formed between educated Western and Chinese elites on the expedition trail, a relationship based on the exchange of a diverse array of political and social capital. Chapter 4 takes the narrative beyond the 1911 revolution and World War I to understand where, when, and how a new nationalist valuation of China's art and antiquities took hold among the domestic ruling elite. It also traces the political and economic tribulations that prevented a wholehearted adherence to the new valuation within China, thereby encouraging additional foreign expeditions to Xinjiang and Gansu from the eastern seaboard. Chapter 5 narrates the experiences of the first generation of Westernized Chinese scholars to accompany Western expeditions to the northwestern borderlands, along with the oftentimes surprising ideological convergences and divergences they encountered with their newfound Western colleagues. Chapter 6 then reconstructs the various developments and competing interests that led to the first successful obstruction of Western expeditions in China, thus marking the end of an era.

CHAPTER ONE

Sahibs in the Desert

On December 1, 1906, amid the dusty dunes of an excavation near Maralbashi, the French sinologist Paul Pelliot learned that three of his heads were missing. Over the course of the next five days, Pelliot launched an investigation into who among his workers had managed to abscond with the terracotta fragments. At last, on December 6, after threatening to withhold the wages of his men and submit a report to the local Chinese magistrate, Pelliot learned the full story. "The daughter of a local chief has many lovers," Pelliot wrote in his diary, "and one of them, one of our laborers, has reconciled himself to her good graces by giving her a gift of three heads, one of which was restored to us a few days ago." In a letter to his mentor Émile Senart, a well-known Indologist, Pelliot added some more color to the story. "The notable had a daughter, and this girl behaved rather badly," Pelliot wrote. "To conciliate her favors, one of my men had given her a gift of the three heads, and the other jealous suitors of the beauty had denounced their happy rival." Unfortunately for the girl, Pelliot continued, after securing the return of all three heads, "the poor child found herself pregnant . . . with her short, very short shame."[1]

This story of a fleeting romance on the fringes of the Taklamakan Desert helps to illustrate an important point: The objects uncovered from the desert sands of Xinjiang could be used for many different purposes wholly unrelated to the political and scholarly agenda of the Western archaeologist. To Pelliot, who intended to place the material proceeds of his excavations into a French museum, the three terracotta heads represented not only an opportunity to contribute to the oft-invoked Enlightenment goals of science, preservation, and education. They also represented an opportunity for France to advertise itself as the foremost Western patron of those goals. In that sense, the heads were literally priceless, since no amount of mone-

50

tary compensation could recoup their political and scholarly value, either to Pelliot personally or to the French empire more generally. To the people of China, however, in an era before museums and nationalism, these same objects might serve an entirely different purpose altogether. It is not clear from Pelliot's letter and diary whether the heads in question were given to the Muslim laborer's paramour for their resale value or for their aesthetic value (Pelliot did describe them as particularly beautiful). What is clear, however, is that they did not change hands in service to a political, cultural, or scholarly agenda.

In the absence of such agendas, the heads could still be regarded as profitable or precious, but they were unlikely to be regarded as priceless. As such, in order to procure the consent of the local populace for the removal of such objects, the foreign scholar needed only to offer something in exchange that met or exceeded their perceived value among the Muslim peasants of Xinjiang. As this chapter will show, the reason why Western archaeologists so often succeeded in achieving their goals was because they consistently managed to provide a form of capital that exceeded local valuations of the objects targeted for removal. Contracted by what must have seemed to be an endlessly resourceful and wealthy outsider, the Muslims of Xinjiang began to regard the foreign archaeologist as a great "sahib." Even when some of these foreigners resisted the application of such a grandiose label, they still found it impossible to shirk the financial and social obligations that it cast on them. Willingly or not, so long as the sahib met these obligations during his march through the desert, most of the impoverished Muslims of Xinjiang would prove willing to endure all manner of physical hardships and rhetorical denigrations for a chance to procure his fair share of economic compensation.

THE PROFITABLE PAST

The oasis tillers of the Tarim Basin had been digging for, or stumbling on, the ruins of ancient civilizations for many centuries before the first Europeans arrived. In the sixteenth century, Mirza Haidar, a scholar of the ruling Dughlat tribe, recounted the story of a local ruler, Aba-Bakr-Mirza, who set prisoners to work digging up "old cities," with "the earth dug from them to be washed." By such means, Haidar concluded, "innumerable treasures in precious stones, gold and silver were discovered." In search of precious stones and metals, a ready form of economic capital in all times and places, most of these treasure seekers preferred to let nature do the work. "Even today," wrote Russian explorer Nikolai Przhevalsky in 1888, "the residents of Khotan, Keriya, Niya and other still surviving oases venture into the sands annually, during autumn and winter, in search of the ruins of old settlements uncovered by storms. They say that gold and silver objects can be found there on occasion." Most of these "storms" swept in from the desert without warning, bringing a violent gale of thick, swirling dust that coated everything in its path. These *buran*, as the locals called them, uncovered what had long been buried. In 1908, Stein learned that the peasants of Bugur treated dust storms as an economic opportunity. "Ground close-by appar.[ently] eroded as people go there after Burans in search of 'gold.'" The rare downpour of rain was equally conducive to such operations. In 1917, just outside Karashahr, the Chinese envoy Xie Bin observed that "every time there is a great wind or rain, the locals go out to search for pieces of gold."[2]

Just below gold on the hierarchy of treasure were ancient coins. On his second and third expeditions, Stein learned how the Astana graves near Turfan had been exploited by the local Muslim population as early as the 1860s, when the Khoqandi general Yaqub Beg temporarily wrested the southern oases away from Qing dominion and oversaw a period of economic deprivation. "Acc.[ording] to Latif these graves first attracted attention after plundering of graves started near Kara-khoja," Stein wrote in 1914. "There first said to have been burrowed by Tungans during Bedaulat's [i.e., Yaqub Beg's] time." Though Stein's informant claimed that only the "Tungans"—that is, Chinese Muslims, or "Hui"—plundered these tombs, another foreman "avows that their 'Chantu' [*Chantou*, 'Turban Head,' or Uyghur] forefathers shared in the plundering." Why did the people of Turfan open these graves? "The villagers declare," Stein wrote, that during the hardship of the "last great rising" they "systematically searched all graves for valuables, such as silver ornaments, etc." In addition to silver ornaments, Stein also learned that the tombs were searched "for sake of coins placed between lips of dead." Fortunately for the Western archaeologists who later targeted these same sites, the locals were interested only in precious metals. "Statues, MSS. and the like were fortunately of no saleable value in those happy days," Stein later noted with relief. During his third expedition, Stein discovered how quickly a local tomb raider would abandon a site if no gold, silver, or coins emerged. "Honest ghorchi Mashik expresses his decision never to search graves again since the first intact tomb he had now seen ix. 2 had proved to contain so little of what to him seemed of value!"[3]

If the object in question could not be immediately spent or exchanged in the bazaar, it usually met with one of three fates: passive disposal, aggressive destruction, or pragmatic transformation. In 1906, Stein heard from a local Muslim headman "that about 40 years ago, in Bedaulat's time, 20 Domoko people dug at this mound for saltpetre. They found none but discovered a packet of papers which was thrown away as useless." If such things were not simply thrown back into the pit from whence they came, they tended to make suitable toys for children, whose rough handling was tantamount to disposal. On his first expedition in 1901, Stein met Abdullah Khan, who revealed the fate of inscribed tablets he had stumbled on while digging for precious metals outside of Keriya. "He found them with four others in a sand-buried house and took them away as curios," Stein wrote. "The two brought to me he threw away on his way home, and the rest he gave to his children to play with who in due course burned them!" Pelliot, too, heard of the indelicate hands of local children. When twenty-three bundles of Indian manuscripts were found in a stupa near Kucha, "the treasure hunters, not knowing what to do with this booty, offered it to Temur Beg's uncle, Ghanizet Khodjam, who was chief of this part of the city." Ghanizet Khodjam, however, "did not pay much attention to it, and little by little the books, torn by the children . . . were all lost. No one suspected that these old papers could be of any interest."[4]

Handing manuscripts and tablets over to one's children or tossing them back into the sand can be regarded as an expression of passive indifference, even if the end result was equivalent to disposal. Perhaps just as common, however, was the aggressive destruction of anything viewed as incompatible with local religious beliefs. The German archaeologist Albert von Le Coq reported on the actions of a Muslim peasant in Turfan, who five years before his arrival had "found great cartloads (araba) of those manuscripts 'with the little writing' (i.e., Manichaean) for which we were making such diligent search. Many had been ornamented with pictures in gold and colours." But afraid in part "of the unholy nature of the writings," he "straightway threw the whole library into the river!" In 1907 at Turfan, Stein interpreted "evidence of wilful burning" in the interior of a Buddhist shrine as suggestive of "Muhammadan iconoclasm." At another nearby Buddhist site, Stein found "everywhere abundant proof of wanton destruction. Painted surfaces purposely scraped off, faces picked out, etc." Such religious vandalism continued over the years. In 1914, Stein found in a frescoed Buddhist shrine in Turfan that "Buddha paintings [are] all disfigured." During the Sino-Swedish expedition in 1928, Xu Xusheng observed how earthen pagodas at Bezeklik were all surrounded by Buddhist altars. "But there are no Buddhas, and all that remains is peeling paint. From the looks of the peel marks, I would conclude that someone purposely came to destroy these." The occasional propensity of the Muslim inhabitants of Xinjiang to seek out and destroy Buddhist iconography was well known to their Chinese rulers. In a colophon attached to the end of a *Great Nirvana* sutra obtained from Dunhuang, dated to between 1911 and 1914, one anonymous Chinese official stationed in the northwest rejoiced in the realization that the present manuscript had "managed to avoid being burned for ritual sacrifices or being consigned into the river."[5]

If the ruins and antiquities of the Taklamakan Desert did not succumb to the whims of passive disposal or hostile destruction, they were most likely to be subjected to the process of pragmatic transformation. In other words, they would gain a second life as manure for the fields or materials for construction. While traveling through Xinjiang in 1893–95, the Russian explorer V. I. Roborovsky observed near Turfan that "the ruins are quickly falling out of existence because the natives . . . break down the eroded walls, crush them and use its clay for fertilizer on their fields." In 1900, a group of Russian scholars led by Sergey Oldenburg concluded that Xinjiang was suffering from "a merciless destruction of old monuments, with their stucco used for fertilizer and the masonry knocked down to be used in building dwellings." In Berlin in 1924, Le Coq told Edward Forbes, director of the Fogg Museum at Harvard, that "when a Mohammedan found one of these frescoes he knocked it down and carried off the pieces for his gauliang [*gaoliang*, 'sorghum'] pit, and that the others were only too pleased to have him [i.e., Le Coq] take them." On his third expedition in 1915 near Karashahr, Stein encountered "half destroyed walls which are being carted off for manure." Later Chinese observers witnessed the same thing. At the Bezeklik caves in 1928, Xu Xusheng took note of "some new residents, who are cultivating fields all around. I saw some of them knocking down the wall for manure!" Two years later at Turfan, Huang Wenbi echoed Xu's lament. "The locals quarry the site for use as fertilizer in their fields, which means that all the antiquities have been dispersed far and wide."[6]

Much of the destruction of ruins and antiquities in Xinjiang, be it through passive or aggressive means, can be easily explained. In short, the Muslim populations of northwestern China viewed the material remains of the ancient Buddhist—and occasionally Manichaean—past through a lens of cultural discontinuity. Unlike the Western archaeologists, who saw in Gandharan art the Hellenistic influences of ancient Greece—and thus a connection with the evolution of Western civilization itself—the Muslims of Xinjiang found only pagan disbelievers. Much like their co-religionists in Egypt and much of the Ottoman Empire, they saw little of redemptive value in the monuments and writings of a heathen people. As historian Rian Thum has noted, the "sacred histories of local gods, Buddhist sutras, rules for Manichaean priests, and Christian scripture, written in Khotanese,

Sanskrit, Sogdian, Tocharian, and Chinese were of little interest to the later Muslims of Altishahr," or southern Xinjiang.[7] In 1928, the Chinese archaeologist Huang Wenbi witnessed such indifference firsthand. "Whenever I collect these sorts of artifacts," he wrote in his diary, "the Uyghurs all just laugh at me." Those who did identify with the pre-Islamic cultures of Central Asia—and not merely as an extension of the Greeks—responded in a very different way. In Yarkand, Le Coq recounted the story of how his expatriate Hindu host, Rai Sahib Bhuta Ram, on learning "that old Indian manuscripts were packed in my cases . . . begged me to allow him to make a reverential offering to them." With Le Coq's consent, the man "brought flowers and began to scatter them and drops of water on the cases, round which he and some friends walked in solemn procession. When I noticed that my presence disturbed him, I went away after the first glance. But this pious veneration for the intellectual labour of their forefathers expended on these documents had something touching about it."[8]

And yet there are limits to this explanatory framework, for it is clear that the Muslims of Xinjiang were more than happy to sift through the tombs of known Muslim graveyards as well. Pelliot, while overseeing a dig in an old cemetery near Tumshuk, halfway between Kashgar and Aksu, claimed to be "happily surprised, in the attitude of the inhabitants . . . that they did not scruple to overthrow the tombs that abounded in Toqqouz Sarai." All this despite the prominent presence of two *mazar*, or Muslim shrines. Though Pelliot gave his workers the benefit of the doubt in suggesting that they simply may not have known about the Muslim character of the graveyard, it appears that some sort of deliberate self-deception was involved. "If the workers, while giving the first days' *ketman* blows on skulls, had some hesitations," he wrote, "the growing attraction won them over quickly, and they said to themselves that being only workers, the sin, if there was sin, fell back on those who paid them." Clearly, it was poverty rather than ideology that inspired such labors. Later, a Muslim man approached Pelliot and attempted to sell him a skull. Pelliot again assumed the best of the situation. "They are trading them, provided they believe they are skulls of pagans!" For his part, Stein was relieved to learn that the Muslims of Turfan attached few scruples to tomb raiding, regardless of the religious affiliations of the corpse. "The damage done by such 'irresponsible digging' is not yet extensive," he told Allen, "and the lead given by it is anyhow useful as proving that religious objections could not be justly raised."[9]

With the arrival of Western scholars in the last decade of the nineteenth century, the passive disposal of portable antiquities and aggressive destruction of immovable ruins quickly became a thing of the past. Once the people

of the southern oases learned that ancient manuscripts and terra-cotta figures could yield an immediate economic profit, their former indifference
or hostility gave way to pragmatism. This transformation began with the
establishment of Russian and British consulates in Kashgar. First to arrive
on the scene was Nikolai Petrovsky for the Russians in 1882, followed by
George Macartney for the British in 1890. In 1891, Petrovsky began to purchase manuscripts, statues, coins, and other ancient curios from local treasure seekers as far east as Khotan. These he sent back to Saint Petersburg,
thus stimulating European interest in the Gandharan art and Indo-European
languages of Central Asia. Before long, Macartney did the same. Though the
purchasing activities of Petrovsky and Macartney gave rise to a new valuation for antiquities among the local Muslims, they did so only in the limited
environs of Kashgar and Khotan. It was the explorers and archaeologists
inspired by their acquisitions who introduced this new market into every
corner of the province.

   In 1895, while traveling under the Russian flag, the Swedish explorer
Sven Hedin first proved the feasibility of venturing out in the desert sands of
the Taklamakan for weeks at time, a necessary benchmark for the excavation of most ancient sites in Xinjiang. Hedin, however, did not come to dig.
That task was left to Stein (figure 9). In 1900, Stein ventured into Xinjiang
for the first time. German, French, American, Japanese, and Russian expeditions followed close on his heels. Everywhere they went, they encouraged
the locals to think of the antiquities in their midst in economic terms. In
1906, Pelliot acknowledged the role he and his colleagues had played in
transforming the marketplace for antiquities in Xinjiang. While excavating
the aforementioned site at Tumshuk, Pelliot observed how its prior neglect
by other archaeologists redounded to his benefit. "The population was only
interested in our excavations for the money it earned," he noted, making a
careful distinction between the sale of labor and the sale of artifacts. "Perhaps, as it must have already arrived at Khotan, at Tourfan, and no doubt at
Koutcha, the natives, seeing the price which the Europeans attach to 'heads'
and 'letters,' will seek to earn money by selling some antiquities to the foreign residents of Kachgar, but it is a branch of commerce which has hitherto
been unknown at Toumchouq." In other words, because Tumshuk was vir-
gin soil, so to speak, Pelliot did not have to contend with the sort of market
incentives that had raised the value of portable antiquities in other oases.[10]

   Not surprisingly, the exploitation of an undervalued site could only
work once. After all, it did not take long for the local Muslim peasants to
grasp the prospect of even greater profits, beyond the mere sale of their labor,
if they could succeed in cutting out the Western middleman altogether and

Figure 9. All the Sahib's Men. A rare group photo of Stein alongside his Chinese, Indian, and Uyghur assistants toward the end of his second expedition in 1908. The pecking order in Stein's party was clear: Stein (center, seated), his classically educated Chinese secretary Jiang Xiaowan (second from left, seated), and his dog Dash. After the dog came the uneducated or merely technically educated Uyghur and Indian assistants: Ibrahim Beg (far left, standing), Jasvant Singh (center, standing), Lal Singh (second from right, seated), and Naik Ram Singh (far right, standing). "The petty ways of my Indian Assistants & their indifference to any higher aims put my Chinese helpmate's value into double relief," Stein confessed in a letter to his friend Percy Allen in 1907. "He and eager little Dash are always pleasant companions. With the rest one is again & again reminded that one is dealing with mercenaries." M. Aurel Stein, Ruins of Desert Cathay: Personal Narrative of Explorations in Central Asia and Westernmost China, vol. 2 (London: Macmillan, 1912), plate 296.

take possession of the coveted artifacts themselves. This led to direct competition between the archaeologist and the impoverished locals. "Thanks to Stein," wrote British consul Clarmont Skrine in 1922, "the people here realize that objects other than gold ornaments . . . have a value for mad Europeans and so there are two or three people here who have got small collections from Yotkan, Domoko & other sites." Most of these rival collections were the result of bold freelance sallies into the desert by enterprising peasants who were willing to risk life and limb in order to turn a maximum profit off of their labor (figure 10). But some were the result of subterfuge and deception. In 1901, toward the end of his first expedition, Stein exposed the forgery operations of Islam Akhun, who had been selling fake

Figure 10. Antiquities For Sale. Western archaeologists were not the only ones willing to brave the hostile conditions of the Taklamakan Desert in search of antiquities. In 1922, Clarmont P. Skrine, the British consul in Kashgar, photographed this collection of antiquities for sale in Khotan. The mostly Buddhist paintings and sculptures on display here were likely sold to a local middleman by poor Muslim peasants and shepherds hoping to supplement their income by searching for salable antiquities during their spare time. Collection of the Royal Geographical Society, image no. S0005897. Copyright © Royal Geographical Society. All rights reserved. Reproduced with permission.

manuscripts in mysterious unknown scripts to Europeans in Khotan and Kashgar for six years. "When asked how he first got the idea of manufacturing 'books,'" Stein recorded after a day of interrogation in the presence of the local Chinese magistrate, "he said that he was in the habit of collecting coins, etc., among the villagers. When about 1894 Badruddin began to press him for MSS. from 'the old towns' (which he did *not* explore & where he did not expect to get them) he tried to produce them in another way."[11]

The forgeries of Islam Akhun represented the extent to which the Muslim peasantry of the Taklamakan oases was willing to go in order to turn the tables on the foreign archaeologists. Most did not need to resort to trickery, however. So long as they were willing to venture out into the desert themselves, anything was possible. In a world bereft of the abstract claims of nationalist ownership, newly excavated objects belonged either to he (or she) who found them or to he who paid the wages of those who found them. Sometimes the two sides stood in near comical proximity to one another. "Whilst we were occupied there two old women went to work opposite us, on the other side of the stream, amongst several shapeless mounds," Le Coq recounted in his book. "Some of these were only chance heaps of loess, but one was opened to good purpose, for it was a ruined *stupa*, and gave these treasure-diggers, before our very eyes, some strange demon-heads and a great quantity of Tocharian and Indian manuscripts in various Indian scripts." Le Coq was certain that these women, who could neither read what they had found nor appreciate its historical significance, had stumbled on this magnificent hoard purely by chance. But it mattered not. "We were obliged to buy their booty from these extremely disagreeable women at a fairly large price, paying nine shillings for about one hundred fine sheets of manuscript."[12]

In order to prevent the acquisition of buried artifacts by rival Muslim peasants, Stein and other Western archaeologists adopted several tactics. The first was simple and straightforward: get there first and excavate as thoroughly as possible. "I could not help clearing the site completely," Stein wrote to Allen from Keriya in 1906, "for being so near the oasis it would have been swarming with seekers for 'Khats' [documents] as soon as I had turned my back. It was better not to leave anything for their 'explorations.'" If the archaeologist could not get there first, a second tactic was then deployed: the offer of attractive wages for labor, with additional monetary incentives for anyone who found the most coveted artifacts, such as manuscripts. Near Turfan in 1914, Stein "heard that in expectation of my 'demand' Kara-khoja people had started digging up more graves." Faced with the prospect of having to pay inflated market rates for antiquities excavated by another party, Stein tried to convince the local Muslim headman that such activities ultimately detracted not from his own purse, but rather from the remuneration of the local workforce Stein intended to hire. "Urged Nazir Dogha to stop this exploitation in interest of village labourers."[13]

If Nazir Dogha chose to stop these villagers from digging into tombs, it is likely that he did so in expectation of securing his own cut of the wages promised by Stein for the village laborers. From the perspective of the local Muslim begs, or village headmen, there were two ways to profit off of an excavation in one's district. The easiest way was to take charge of rounding up hired labor, then as middleman demand that the wages for these men pass first through his own hands, with predictable results. "The Loblyq also recalls Sven Hedin, a generous Sahib," Pelliot learned in 1907, "but who was accompanied by this 'scoundrel and thief of Imam Bai,' who always pocketed more than half of what the Sahib told him to hand over to the inhabitants." On one occasion, Pelliot's men even offered to reveal the location of a concealed artifact in exchange for daily wages that did not pass through the hands of their beg first. Pelliot refused, claiming that such demands were "too much for my principles." Most likely Pelliot simply did not want to set a precedent of negotiating with his workers. But he also knew that to deny the begs a generous share of the profits was to encourage them to draw on corvée or minimally compensated labor, then direct the dig themselves without the participation of the foreign archaeologist. Though this was considerably more work and hassle for the begs, it would ensure them the maximum margin of profit. The begs sometimes pursued this option anyway, eschewing a partnership with the foreign archaeologist altogether. In 1907, Stein made meticulous plans to subvert the operations of one such conglomerate. "Arrang[emen]ts for Korla base. Taher Beg's trepidation about wrath of local Begs, etc., when Kok-Darwaza is to be attacked! Decide to get 30 men ready without disclosing objective."[14]

As a result, whether they labored under foreigners or begs, workers in the field had every incentive to try and maximize their income. For neither beg nor archaeologist was there the guarantee of a monopoly over the archaeological proceeds of any given site. Knowing that they could likely obtain a higher price in the urban marketplace than any reward offered by their employer for an artifact successfully concealed, the hired hands often engaged in a tense game of cat and mouse with their overseers. In 1901, Stein paid a man named Ibrahim to guide him to the site where he claimed to have found Kharoṣṭhī tablets the previous year. Afraid that Ibrahim, now alerted to the market value of objects he had previously entrusted to the indelicate care of his children, would attempt to replenish his lost stock, Stein took suitable precautions. "Proceeded myself with all available men to the 'house' where Ibrahim had found a year ago the inscribed tablets," Stein noted in his diary. "He had been kept under observation since yesterday to prevent eventual interference with the remainder of finds." Pelliot also found the use of surveillance necessary. "I left the ruins a guard of four men, to prevent untimely visits like that of these two Sartes who last night have scratched and irretrievably lost the mud heads (also rather mediocre) that we had left under the stupa." In a letter to Senart, Pelliot confessed his frustration at the limits of such oversight. "Despite all the surveillance," he wrote, "it is difficult to prevent a worker from sliding a small piece, just revealed by his ketman, into a fold of his clothes." Even when such pieces did not make it into the folds of their clothes, still the workers tried to outsmart the foreigner. In one case, they attempted to trick Pelliot into doling out additional reward money for an artifact culled from the main site. "Shortly afterwards, a child brought me a little terracotta head, grimacing, and which was evidently removed during the excavations by one of our workers. He ordered a child to bring it to me, in the hopes that I would not recognize the origin and provide money."[15]

Aware that clumsy attempts at subterfuge could lead to discharge from the caravan and an attendant loss of wages, some laborers decided to wait until the Western archaeologist had left the excavation site altogether before making their move. After all, no matter how industrious or resourceful the foreigner may be, there were limits as to how many antiquities his camels could carry away. In 1901, during his first expedition, Stein made the decision to rebury some statues that he had uncovered in the vicinity of the Rawak Stupa north of Khotan. Unable to take the statues back with him to New Delhi or London, he hoped by such means to preserve them for a future expedition. By the time he revisited the site on his second expedition just five years later, however, the statues were gone. "I found the court of the latter even more deeply buried under the dunes than when I carried on here excavations in 1901," he later wrote, "and, alas! the fine stucco relievos then brought to light completely destroyed by treasure-seekers in spite of careful reburial." Though Stein here deploys the pejorative label of "treasure-seekers" to describe his local competitors in the field, we might instead refer to them as "subsistence diggers," so as to highlight the pragmatic economic calculus of their actions. In other words, the impoverished Muslim peasants of Xinjiang might collect a modest initial profit from the provision of their labor on any given dig. Once the Western archaeologist had led his laborers to a different site, however, the same laborers could later supplement their wages by returning to the original site and removing anything of saleable value that their former employer had failed to take away.[16]

Regardless of how and by whom these profits were reaped, it is clear that they never moved beyond the realm of tangible economic capital, even after the transformations wrought by the purses of foreign archaeologists. This is why the new market for antiquities ended the local Muslim practices of passive disposal and aggressive destruction, but did not affect the practice of pragmatic reuse. For the first time, the begs and peasants of Xinjiang strove to secure possession of their own artifacts for sale on the marketplace. But this was still a form of acquiring tangible monetary profit rather than a demonstration of service to abstract political or scholarly ideals. As a result, the new modes of interaction did not conflict with the long-standing practice of quarrying immobile ruins for fertilizer or bricks, for such actions merely served as a substitute for an otherwise necessary investment of financial resources in agriculture or construction. The only practices these new interactions conflicted with were the now economically wasteful habit of destroying or disposing of such things.

To most of the sedentary Muslim populace of Xinjiang, then, the antiquities beneath their feet were still merely profitable and little more. As a result, the only possibility of conflict with the Western archaeologist over the removal of these objects lay in negotiations over the amount of economic capital allotted to the begs, treasure seekers, and laborers involved in their recovery. So long as the financial compensation on tap equaled or exceeded both the perceived value of the object in question and the cumulative effects of the hardships incurred in the process of its removal, there was no possibility of irreconcilable conflict between the two sides. Instead, there were only negotiations over how much economic capital should trade hands in exchange for helping the Western scholar implement an archaeological monopoly over his preferred site. It is to those economic compensations that we now turn.

THE COMPENSATIONS OF COOPERATION

In 1905, the Yale climatologist Ellsworth Huntington undertook an expedition to Xinjiang in order to gather evidence for his theory about environmental determinism and its effects on the evolution of different human races. Huntington was unique among Western archaeologists during the initial wave of expeditions, for he was the rare American among their ranks. In his letters back home, Huntington constantly drew attention to the rigid expectations of class and decorum that his European counterparts often took for granted. "This boat is very English," he wrote to his sister Beth en route to India. "I told you about wearing dress-suits at dinner. It further appears that if a man fails to at least put on black for dinner, the captain sends him a note!"[17]

Upon his arrival in Xinjiang, Huntington found that he was immediately treated by everyone other than a Chinese official as a "sahib," a label that clashed with his professed egalitarian ethos. This distinction was made very clear during one of his first visits to the house of a local beg. "For Muhammedans the Beg says that he provides only the rug and felts," Huntington wrote in one of his letters home, "but for 'great' guests and Chinese he furnishes the cushion and table after the Chinese style." While crossing a river near Khotan, Huntington chafed at the realization that "the Sahib had to have a horse led out for him. I just longed to jump in all over and get cool, but dignity would not allow it." After several months of such treatment, Huntington began to deplore his special status. "This role of great man that every foreigner must play in the Orient has some decided disadvantages," he wrote to his sister. "In the first place one gets tired of being always treated as different from others. . . . In the next place it makes one selfish. One gets into the habit of always sitting in the best place, eating the best food, riding the best horse, sleeping while others get ready to start, and in general being pampered." It also meant isolation and loneliness. On one occasion, Huntington noted how his men verbally abused a local village headman when he inadvertently placed two felts on the ground side by side:

> Was it proper, they said, that a great guest should sit and eat with little men close to him? So felt number two was moved off a hundred feet to another tree, and I ate my bread, sour milk, and mulberries alone. Isn't it ridiculous? I eat with people of all sorts more or less, but our own men do not like it. They want to make out that their Sahibs are very great men indeed. It lowers one greatly in the eyes of the people, too, if you are at all familiar. On the other hand one wants to see everybody and be friendly with them. It is ever so hard to steer a safe middle course.[18]

Here we see Huntington, against his wishes, being groomed by his servants to embrace a prestigious and exclusive social identity with which he himself was apparently uncomfortable. Stein, too, often found himself pressured to conform to the expectations of a sahib, whether he liked it or not (though he usually did). "Overtook baggage at ford unsafe for donkeys & found two dirty Kirghas at spot 'where Sahibs always camp,'" he wrote on his fourth expedition, highlighting the words of his men, "and accordingly undesirable." Huntington, too, could be just as resistant to such pressures. "This time I refused to have my horse led," he wrote in July 1905. "The Chinese interpreter was sorry, because if my horse was not led it was not proper for his to be. He was still more sorry when his horse began to fight with Ibrahim's, and he fell off into a foot of water." When Huntington arrived in Keriya, he found that the Chinese magistrate "was not dressed officially as he ought to have been and he put himself instead of me in the chief place." Though Huntington claimed that he could not have cared less, his men were apparently outraged. "Isn't it petty?" he continued. "These things mean nothing to me except as they affect others, the men etc." Stein once noted how a Chinese official roused the wrath of his secretary, Jiang Xiaowan, "by not bowing to ground & offering 2nd seat." Jiang then exited the room in a "stormy departure." Huntington was exhausted by such theatrics and once admitted to being "tired of being somebody and long to play nobody." But his men would have none of it, for only a great man was worth serving. When Huntington received a much grander reception at Khotan, his men openly rejoiced. "If only I could make you see it all! Our men were greatly impressed. They say that for years no European has been received with so much ceremony." Stein also noticed the buoyant reactions of his men toward the grand receptions afforded him. "Impression of official welcome awaiting me eastwards reflected in followers' conduct. Even H.[assan] A.[khun] all eagerness."[19]

Although Huntington occasionally fought against his transformation into a sahib, he nearly always relented "for the sake" of his men. But Daniel Barrett, his traveling companion and fellow American, did not. Barrett's repeated refusal to conform to the expectations of a "great man" produced a near mutiny among his men. On one occasion, Barrett told Huntington how much he dreaded a formal meeting with a Chinese magistrate and his soldiers. "Barrett simply hates such formalities, and began to debate how to get out of it. I jokingly said, 'There is no way, but for you to be sick.' He took it seriously." After Barrett later embarked on a five-mile detour to avoid meeting up with a beg who had come out to greet them, his men approached Huntington and vented their frustrations. Their "chief grievance," Huntington later told his father, "is that the men want a Sahib who is a Sahib. They are ashamed of a man who shuns his fellows especially the great; dresses like a tramp; saddles his own horse; eats on the floor; takes his exercise naked where all can see him; sleeps alone in the mountains; never can tell beforehand where he is going; in short as Rasul says 'a wild man, an animal.' If only I could laugh and say 'It is not so,' I should not mind. But it is all true, and has been troubling me for months."[20]

Barrett's eccentric behavior negated one of the chief appeals of a foreign sahib for the impoverished lower classes: proximity to wealth and power. As Skrine later observed, the prestige of a foreigner in Xinjiang "depends very much upon the size of one's caravan. Nobody gives one any credit for being a hardy traveller and a lover of the simple life; it is merely supposed that one is not a real 'sahib' and cannot afford to travel better." Huntington also embodied this perception, however reluctantly. "It is considered essential, you know, that a man of any importance should never go anywhere without a retinue." The very presence of an entourage confirmed the exalted status of its leader. "I suppose I am a 'darin' [Ch. *daren*, 'great man']," Huntington once mused, "because I call on governors, have a big red card, and am accompanied by an escort." Such an abundance of superfluous hangers-on could strain the finances of the foreign explorer. To make up for the low cost of goods and services in Xinjiang, Huntington observed, "one has to support an army. Nominally I have five men, but four others are attached to us in one way or another, and have to receive baksheesh [i.e., tips] and sustenance. And a still larger number turn up at meal-times. You can't send them off for in the first place you are a Sahib, in the second you never know how many may be your host or your guide, and in the third place it is the custom for a rich man to feed an army." During the Sino-Swedish expedition in 1928, Sven Hedin also drew attention to the economic responsibilities of a sahib after he was obliged to throw a feast in the governor's honor. "When one gives a dinner for such a potentate, who comes with an escort of fifty men," he wrote afterward, "one must also provide food for the whole of his company. We had therefore laid tables for them in the courtyard with food ordered from the bazaar."[21]

These comments reveal the chief reasons why the lower classes of Xinjiang eagerly associated with the foreign archaeologist: his economic resources and political clout. First and foremost, the sahib was supposed to be generous with his money. In his summary of the servants' complaints toward Barrett, Huntington noted how "his eccentricity and his extreme care about every penny gall them. They like a Sahib for whom they do not have to apologize." For what sort of sahib did one not have to apologize? Huntington's men told him that they had "travelled with Sahibs who were extravagantly liberal." Unlike these model sahibs, however, "they are ashamed of the parsimonious way in which this has been run." Huntington also heard of two other anonymous British travelers, whose hired men "were bitter in their complaints of the meanness with which they had been treated and paid."[22]

Most Western archaeologists, regardless of their personal inclinations, duly conformed to the expectation that they be liberal in their outlays of cash, regarding it as a shrewd investment in the overall success of the expedition. Ten years after Hedin completed his third expedition, Pelliot learned that he still had a reputation as "a generous Sahib." Pelliot himself fully understood the importance of cultivating such a reputation. "The Mandarin military man announces an escort of two soldiers as far as Bongour," he wrote in 1907. "We would have done well [without them], since they will do nothing, and they will have to be paid by a gratuity which tenfolds their pay; but noblesse oblige." On one occasion, the local Chinese official himself drew explicit attention to the importance of the "gratuity" his men had received from the foreign sahib, however reluctantly such gratuity may have been dispensed. "My servants were remiss in attending to your needs, and they are deeply appreciative for their bountiful rewards," wrote Zhu Ruichi, the prefect of Guma, to Stein in 1908. "Each one of them expresses the most sincere gratitude."[23]

In addition to being generous with his economic resources, the magnanimous sahib was also expected to bring his servants with him into the halls of power, where they might improve their career prospects by catching the attention of another "great man." In 1906, Huntington passed through Urumchi and obtained an audience with the Manchu governor Liankui. Because his Muslim servant Da'ud had "been very faithful in spite of his shortcomings," Huntington asked Liankui to give Da'ud the post of beg. The governor

> promised to do so and when he called on me asked to see the man. Poor Da'ud, most horribly frightened, was brought in, and after falling on his knees at the door and bowing his close-shaven head to the ground half a dozen times advanced nearer to be looked at. I suppose it was the great experience of his life, one that he will boast of till his death, for as Ibrahim said, a man like that could not procure a personal interview with the Futai [*futai,* governor] if he paid 5000 dollars.[24]

Here we see Ibrahim, another one of Huntington's hired servants, appraising the value of the sahib's political connections in precise economic terms. For Ibrahim and Da'ud, their relationship with Huntington was literally priceless: no amount of money—not even five thousand dollars—could buy what he had given them. This was the sort of coveted career advancement opportunity that Barrett, "who shuns his fellows especially the great," denied his own men, much to their disappointment. Most archaeologists followed Huntington's lead. On his second expedition in 1906, Stein was able to report that "Islam Beg, my faithful old retainer, has just been promoted to a fat Begship, and as news of this sort spreads like wildfire, I may expect willing services further ahead too." Later, Stein visited Islam Beg's "fine country house at Altunche . . . a creation of Pan-Darin's favour &—my recommendation." With another favored servant, Ibrahim Beg, Stein assured him "of continued employment by a Minute or Patent addressed to succeeding Keriya Hsien-Kuans." During a meeting with Financial Commissioner Pan Zhen in Urumchi in 1914, Stein "put in recommendation for plucky Tungan officer and Roze Beg." The following year, Stein "put in good word for Aksakal's son & Mahsud" with the magistrate of Kucha. On his fourth expedition, Stein bumped into a former servant in Tashkurgan who had since become a beg. "Attributes his rise to service on my journey."[25]

Not every hired hand received such glowing recommendations, however. Only those who pleased the sahib would be able to transform his political connections into economic capital. With regard to Hassan Akhun, his unruly camel factotum, Stein once wrote a letter declaring "that he is neither rogue nor fool nor coward, but a 'handful.' Wonder how many poss.[ible] employers will care to handle it." But for those who obtained the sahib's favor and thus managed to further their career, the gratitude was long lasting. "Whenever I think of the unique distinction that has been conferred upon me I cannot help thinking that I am indebted to you more than any body else for it," wrote Sir Kander Khan from Lahore in 1914. "Kind and sympathetic as you have always been to me I owe you almost every thing good that I enjoy in this life. I owe my position and honour to you." On his first expedition in 1901, Stein noted the attentions of an educated Chinese man "who wants to follow me as Munshi [i.e., secretary]." Mannerheim observed that idle men would sit "in a vestibule all day on the chance of being able to render a service," while Huntington noted that "these people want to do everything for a Sahib or anyone whom they think important, but they won't do a thing for one another." Indeed, the political-cum-economic clout of foreign archaeologists in Xinjiang was so high that one elderly Muslim man insisted on having Pelliot "write the names of all the surrounding qazi and his own" as "so many candidates for future positions" in the event that the Europeans should one day conquer Xinjiang, drive out the Chinese, and need a new crop of local officials.[26]

The majority of those who hired out their labor to the foreign archaeologist did not leave such lasting impressions on him. Nevertheless, they too usually managed to improve their economic fortunes by engaging with his expedition. Let us begin by trying to make sense of the daily wages on offer for the unskilled labor force that most archaeologists sought to secure. It is nearly impossible to determine a fixed scale of the absolute value of wages across different times and places. Wages were paid out in various currencies, and the value of these currencies changed from oasis to oasis, with different explorers using different reference points for their exchange rates. Mention of thirty taels of silver paid out as wages to a servant in Kashgar could mean something very different from the same thirty taels of silver paid out in Hami. As a result, the detailed lists of wages and salaries found in Stein's account books are of little use unless we know the value of these numbers relative to local wages in different places and times. This means that the most useful estimates of the value of economic compensation are those that were formulated in explicit relation to local and international reference points.

Once again, Huntington's letters help to shed light on an issue that the European explorers rarely commented on in explicit detail. In 1905, using American currency as a reference point, Huntington observed that the annual income of an ordinary unskilled laborer in the southern oases of Xinjiang was about $15.00, or $1.25 per month. He then listed the monthly

wages of his four most important men. Ibrahim, his chief factotum, translator, and guide (and likely the same man for whom Stein later secured a
lucrative promotion as beg), earned 40 rupees per month, or $13.00—nearly
ten and a half times the going rate for unskilled labor. Da'ud, the man Huntington introduced to the Qing governor in Urumchi, received six *sers* per
month, or about $4.80, more than four times the going rate. Two other men,
Handum Bai and Tokhta Akhun, received $3.20 and $2.40 per month, respectively, or two to three times above market rate. "All get good pay,"
Huntington wrote to his family in New Haven, "and two get what is considered very high, like five or six dollars a day with us."[27]

Of course, the four men named in Huntington's letter should not be
grouped into the category of unskilled labor, for each brought special skills
to the table. Still, it is clear that these were very generous wages. There is
other anecdotal evidence as well. In 1906, Pelliot complained about the ab-
surdly high wages that Le Coq and the Germans had paid out for unskilled
labor in Kucha. "They have powerful financial means," Pelliot noted. "Instead of the 16 kopecks cost of a worker at Koutcha, the Germans gave
five times more, and this naturally led the workers to ask for even more."
Three months later, Pelliot provided rare context for the wages he paid to
his own unskilled laborers at a nearby site, noting that "the natives work
willingly with us, for 25 kopeks per day." In other words, Pelliot's men on
this occasion were paid 9 kopecks, or one-third more, than the going market
rate. On another occasion in 1907, Pelliot recorded daily wages of one and
a half *misqals* for his laborers. We can put this into context when Pelliot,
just one month later, referred to "an exceptional balance of 2 1/2 misqal
per day" for exemplary workers he selected to follow him to a remote site.
In other words, if two and half *misqals* per day represented "an exceptional
balance," then one and half *misqals* seems likely to be at or slightly above
market rate. We can further bolster this point by noting that Stein, too, just
a few months later, also paid out wages at Pelliot's "exceptional" rate, with
the result that his men all clamored to continue their employment with
him. "Paid off labourers by 9 A.M., all volunteering to follow me to fresh
sites. Wages + reward average 2 1/2 M.[isqals]."[28]

In sum, it appears that Western archaeologists did not pay below the
going market rate either for skilled or unskilled labor, and often paid considerably more. Regardless, it was clear that the locals, not the foreigner,
determined the scale of wages to be paid. "I wish," Stein wrote to Allen in
1907, "it may be easier . . . to catch & keep coolies" once he left Gansu.
"In these parts humanity is scarce & exacts high wages for a minimum of
labour." These findings echo the situation in contemporary Egypt. Flinders

Petrie, a British archaeologist active in Egypt for nearly four decades beginning in the 1880s, noted how the village sheikhs, similar to the begs of Xinjiang, "tried to stop the people from working, because they did not get the money through their hands." But the Egyptian peasants, Petrie continued, "are so glad to get regular pay without any deduction that they say they intend to work, shekhs or no shekhs, as long as there is pay to be had." As a result, so long as they are "paid regularly," Petrie concluded, the peasants "defy anything short of open violence to stop them." On average, those who volunteered to do manual labor for Petrie tended to make about twice as much as they would in their usual occupations. In fact, there was such an abundance of eager hands that Petrie once admitted to "discharging for laziness freely," as "there are so many applicants for work."[29]

What made these wages especially attractive, both in Xinjiang and Egypt, was the fact that nearly all excavations took place in the winter, during the agricultural off season. This meant that they constituted a form of supplementary rather than substitute income. Furthermore, the scale of the economic impact on local communities was often immense. The foreign explorer purchased tens of donkeys, ponies, camels, and carts for transportation in each oasis, in addition to many other supplies and services: food, fodder, crates, fuel, guides, repairs, and clothing, to name just a few. In the tiny and impoverished oasis of Charklik, Stein noted one of his routine purchasing sprees. "Supplies gathered: 200 Characks grain, 50 Ch. Kunjara; men's food for 2 months; labourers (50) with one month's food. Prices far higher than at Charchan. Rice at 6M. per ___; flour 2 1/2 M." Regardless of what the locals charged for their services and goods, the foreigner was obliged to pay it, for he had few alternatives. But once he proved able and willing to foot the bill, the locals signed up for his expedition in droves. "Started at 8 A.M. for Abdal after paying off 120 labourers," Stein noted in 1906, giving a sense of the scale of his operations. Two months later, Stein "sent to Abdal for every available man in addition to the 18 men engaged; also for photo.[graphic] materials & supplies." Even when they were called up for service by the local authorities on the foreigner's behalf—as involuntary labor—the locals still regarded the promise of a reliable wage as a boon. Accustomed to providing unpaid corvée labor for their sheikhs and begs, the peasants of southern Xinjiang were pleasantly surprised to be offered a decent wage for a day's labor. In the oasis of Shahyar near Aksu, Stein noted how he allayed "fear of a new 'corvee'" among his laborers with "promise of pay & timely repatriation."[30]

We might say that the arrival of a Western archaeologist in the poor and remote oases of Xinjiang was akin to an economic stimulus package of sorts. He bought copious amounts of supplies, commissioned numerous skilled and unskilled services, and paid fair and often generous wages to a large number of men during the agricultural slack season, when much of the male workforce was idle. He also paid for the roof over his head. Most often this came in the form of local residences, whose occupants vacated their rooms either of their own volition or on the orders of the local authorities. "A wonderfully hospitable country!" exclaimed Mannerheim in 1907. "You come and install yourself in almost any home you choose, and the owners put the best face on it they can." The reactions of these occupants ran the gamut, from the "tenacious dowager who refused to stir" her quarters for Stein and required official "intervention before room could be secured," to the two military officers who "seemed to think it quite natural" that Mannerheim "had taken possession of their house in their absence." In 1914, Stein recorded how Ibrahim Akhun "at once offered his house for our accommodation" in Karghalik. For some, the arrival of a foreign archaeologist into their home was an eagerly anticipated novelty. On one occasion near Dunhuang, Stein noted "children's delight at 'kvartelyozas' [Hung. *kvárté-lyozás*, 'billeting']."[31]

Regardless of individual sentiments, it is clear that the lodging of a foreign guest, willingly or unwillingly, represented a financial windfall for the owners of the house. Mannerheim recounted how the mother-in-law of one such residence "proudly refused the money I offered for our lodging with one hand, but not only accepted it with the other, but turned away and checked it" as he left. At the abode of delighted children, Stein recorded how the "ladies of house send a little mite to receive our rent. Civility on all sides." With somewhat less civility, Mannerheim took note of an "unbearably cross hostess" near Barikol, whom he "placated to some extent by a pair of scissors, a needle and thread, mirrors, brooches and some postcards with pictures of nude women (the cards were especially appreciated)." When all that proved insufficient, Mannerheim added an additional three *liang*, "more than she usually could get monthly for her hovel, but the old woman was not satisfied and I had to spend still more on the witch." In his account ledgers, Stein regularly recorded the outlay of three or four *misqals*—about two or three times the market rate for daily unskilled labor—for the "rental of house." Stein found that one of his landlords "would accept no payment but appreciated 'Chit.'" In the mountains outside of town, the nomads also expected a handsome reimbursement for any hospitality provided to the foreign archaeologist. "I ask the price of the sheep," Pelliot wrote near the start of his expedition in Xinjiang. "The Kirghiz declares that there is no price and that he is too happy to have us as his guests; I know what that means, that I will have to pay more than the price."[32]

Wages, supplies, services, and lodging were reliable sources of economic capital, ones readily available to the less privileged classes of Xinjiang. Not only that, but these financial outlays were supplementary to the economic fringe benefits described above, such as an audience with the governor or a letter of recommendation. But even these provisions did not exhaust the store of economic capital on tap. In addition to the conventional forms, there were also two other less obvious incarnations: medicine and navigation. Both depended on a widespread belief among the people of Central Asia in the near magical effects of Western science. In 1906, Pelliot learned from his Muslim host in Ferghana that an oral legend had been circulating in the region regarding the origins of Western wealth and power. "It is said, however, that all the books of Aplatoun [Pers., 'Plato'] and the others, with all the secrets of modern science, were preserved in the house of Aplatoun, in the middle of a desert," Pelliot recorded. "It is said that the Faranghi [i.e., Franks] have obtained these books, and from it comes their present superiority." For those who still needed a bit more convincing, the Westerner relied on his own servants to sing his praises. "A Chinese man asked Ting one day, 'This Mr. Pelliot must be a little bonkers to spend so much money to look for heads, they have no value.' Ting, who in the end thinks maybe a little like him, replied, 'Europeans know things that neither you nor I know or understand.'"[33]

What the Europeans understood better than anyone else was how to cure an illness. And to judge by the contents of their field diaries and letters, everyone else in Xinjiang knew it, too. "In the little places through which I now passed between Bugur and Kucha many people knew me—they were former patients," the German archaeologist Albert von Le Coq recounted in his book. "And when the report of my coming reached their ears—which, indeed, it very soon did—they waited for me at the *sarai* with offerings of milk and, alas! of fruit also." Le Coq's medical treatments were in such high demand during his stay in Turfan that his landlord, Saut, began to charge the locals for access to his tenant. When Le Coq learned of this unauthorized extortion, he threatened to report him to the local Muslim prince for corporal punishment. For many of the local Muslims, Western medicine was not only viewed as effective, but trustworthy as well. In 1917, Xie Bin reported that the governor of Xinjiang recently "sent three officials with medical training here to the south to administer medication to the locals. But the Turban people are superstitious and religious, and very closed-minded. They do not trust Han medicine nor its alleged effects, and it is difficult to get them to see its benefits." Not just any Westerner would do, however. Only those hailing from distant empires could be trusted to truly care about the health of their patients. "As soon as he knows that there is a physician among us, he needs a consultation," Pelliot noted of one patient in Russian Turkestan, "for, like all the Sartes we have seen, he has no confidence in Russian physicians. Scheduled for tomorrow."[34]

As long as they were not Chinese or Russian, Western archaeologists found themselves besieged by requests for medicine. Louis Vaillant, a member of Pelliot's party and a trained doctor, gave numerous consultations to the begs of Kashgar, "because it goes without saying that they have a few afflictions for which they want European medicine." The Chinese scholar-official Pei Jingfu also thanked Vaillant for medical treatment when the French expedition passed through Urumchi. On his second expedition, Stein was approached by a family of Mongols who "asked for medicine to help two children, bitten by . . . dog some 10 days ago." On his return to Khotan, Stein took up duties as an improvised nurse to Jiang Xiaowan, his Chinese secretary. "He suffered awful pains for days & kept me busy as improvised doctor & superintendent of nursing," Stein wrote in a letter to Allen's wife. "But at last he got over the attacks & is now slowly regaining strength & spirits. Faith in my medicines was the main cure." On his third expedition, Stein was "interrupted by call of one of yesterday's convives who hoped for treatment of eyes." One week later, Stein recorded his offer to Chai Hong-shan, the garrison commander of Suzhou, "of Boric treatment for eye which rhuma caused by Tun-huang winds has affected." In the mountains of Inner Mongolia, Stein's healing powers were once again put to the test. "Malum in his usual irritable temper causes fracas by striking young Mongol who retaliates with tent pole. M.[alum] gets his left humerus fractured & first-aid work keeps me busy till 12–20 A.M."[35]

No matter the political climate, the medicines of Western explorers were always in high demand and could be used to smooth out otherwise rocky relationships. In 1921, during the height of the warlord era in China, American paleontologist Roy Chapman Andrews found himself surrounded by hostile bandits in the mountains of Shaanxi. "Fortunately for us," he later informed his patron J. P. Morgan, "their captain had a bad wound in the hand, and as I have some medical experience I was able to fix him up fairly well and spent the next day dressing heads, legs, arms and bodies that had been more or less shot to places. The result was that the brigands treated us very courteously and when we were ready to go, gave us a guard of honor until we were out of their territory." On his fourth expedition, Stein gave Tabloids to the magistrate of Charchan and wrote to the British agent at Amritsar to send further medicine for his host. Near Kucha, the local commandant, "a poor sickly figure, returns call. Tells also of his digestive trouble for which medicine is sought. Could help only with Soda mint Tabloids." When one patient left, others took his place. "Patient at Yamen with stricture, etc., expects quick treatment by a 'yao' [medicine]," Stein wrote the following day. On the third day, "more patients from Yamen apply for medicine." In 1928, during the Sino-Swedish expedition, David Hummel, one of Sven Hedin's Swedish colleagues, treated the brother-in-law of Governor Yang Zengxin. "The mandarins especially were very impressed by this successful cure," Hedin later wrote, "and the doctor's reputation spread and redounded favourably upon the whole expedition."[36]

Not all requests for Western medicine were as advertised. In 1906, Pelliot recorded his conversation with the seventy-seven-year-old Qoutloug Beg, "a great womanizer despite his age," who did "not tire of the excellence of the French/European women of thin size that he saw in the Suez and Misr." Claiming to have dreamed of these women for a long time, Qoutloug declared that he "would have willingly added them to the 65 women he had already successively married since his tender adolescence." He then inquired of Pelliot "whether he can still expect a summer of Saint-Martin from our pharmacy"; that is, a medicine that facilitates unseasonably warm "weather" late in life. "Despite the precedent for the Duke of Richelieu," Pelliot wrote, referring to a lecherous eighteenth-century French nobleman of advanced years, "I do not dare to promise this to him." Stein also received such requests. In 1901, Han Yaoguang, the elderly magistrate of Keriya, began his farewell visit with Stein by asking for medicine "for two members of Zenana ['women's quarters'], though origin.[ally] as if for Amban's own person!" Later, Stein realized that the magistrate harbored a much greater ambition for his wives. "During afternoon calls from Begs & Chinese official all eager for 'dora' ['medicine']," Stein noted. "Amban desires through Abdulla Beg a nostrum for obtaining a son."[37]

Unless they asked for an aphrodisiac or a son, the people of Xinjiang generally came away from these medicinal interactions healthier than when they arrived. And because the foreign archaeologist knew that this constituted a form of strategic goodwill, he tended not to charge for his services. In that sense, Western medicine was a form of highly coveted economic capital, freely dispensed to people from all classes and all walks of life. Related to this belief in the efficacy of Western medicine was a similar conviction in the lucrative benefits of Western navigational skills. Unlike with medicine, the Muslims of Xinjiang were initially skeptical of the foreigner's

reliance on a compass and map and had to be convinced of the wisdom of
their use. In 1914, while marching to Barikol, Stein witnessed such skepticism firsthand. "Our hapless guide had all along felt convinced that the
village we made for was a fata morgana," he wrote. "His face showed pity
for beguiled barbarians who would make for a place without safe guidance
of a ta-lo [Ch. *dalu*, 'main road']." Gradually, however, the navigational accuracy of the compass and map made true believers of everyone. "It is great
fun to see the wonder of the, to them, almost miraculous way in which I
seem to know the road where there is no road and where I have never been
before," Huntington wrote in 1905. "Da'ud is so convinced of its accuracy
that he sticks to me like a dog if I begin to question the route followed
by the guide." The following year, Stein described his men as "cheered by
the accuracy with which the ruins were struck across this most forbidding
desert." Not long afterward, Stein brought another reticent party safely
through a fifteen-thousand-foot glacier. "The look of our Chinamen's faces
when through the mist they caught sight of the broad open valley beyond &
felt assured of escape," he told Allen, "was a thing to remember."[38]

The demonstrated ability of the Western archaeologist to emerge from
the wasteland unscathed opened up an intriguing opportunity. In 1906, Pelliot overheard the following conversation between a Chinese merchant
from Aqsu and a gold and jade sifter from Khotan. "'How can these Europeans know,' said the great merchant, 'that there are objects in the earth?'
'It is,' replied the gold washer, 'that they have a large telescope, with which
they discover everything from far away. If they had not been able to see from
their homes to the land here, why would they have made such a long trip
to us from home?'" The "objects" in question were nearly always assumed
to contain gold inside, no matter what the archaeologist said. "Vaillant's research intrigued Hassan Beg, who believes we are looking for gold," Pelliot
observed in 1906. His Muslim host then asked if Pelliot, "in the face of any
land whatsoever," could perform "a process of divination to know exactly
what it contains." The assumption, of course, was that any such divination would reveal the presence or absence of gold. Early in his career, Stein
learned just how tenacious such assumptions could be when a Pathan officer refused to believe he was searching for antiquities in Swat. "Nonsense,
he only pretends that. If people dig in old ruins, it is to find treasure and
nothing else. Every one knows that." In 1913, during a meeting with a Russian consular official in Kashgar, Stein learned that his reputation as a gold
digger had preceded him. "Had heard of my Taklamakan finds—of gold."[39]

The combination of Western navigational skills and a widespread belief in buried treasure presented a golden opportunity for the impoverished

Muslim masses. Stein witnessed this opportunistic initiative firsthand, much to his frustration. In 1908, Stein spent eight long days in futile pursuit of a collection of ruins that local informants claimed to have visited in years past. "Having convinced myself that there was nowhere room for a ruined site of 'more than a thousand houses,' I puzzled over explanation of all these atrocious lies," he wrote in his diary. Stein then recalled the words of one of his guides, who claimed that "the Sahib not fearing Jins [jinn, 'demon'] may be credited with finding 'old towns' which to other mortals never show themselves twice." When another guide "stoutly stuck to his story of having actually seen the 'old houses'" seven years earlier yet was "by no means worried about an answer to query as to why he could not find them now," Stein finally realized what had happened. "All that my guides hoped to do was to put me on the track of those mysterious ruins for the gold of which they were lusting since long years." In other words, the locals weren't telling lies, for they were convinced the ruins did indeed exist. They just needed the foreign sahib, with his "powerful Wilayeti [Urdu, vilayeti, 'foreigner'] arts," to discover "those forts & houses they had seen in their dreams & where they might then dig at ease for all kinds of riches." Despite this wild goose chase, Stein was again taken for a ride on his third expedition. "It became clear that the alleged ruins were like Musa Haji's of the type which once seen cannot be found again," he wrote with considerable irritation in 1914. "Repeated expeditions before had been fruitless and my informants' eagerness prompted only by hope that by chance I might overcome magic spell."[40]

In this case as in others, Stein failed to overcome the wizardry of the desert. But the steadfast perception among the oasis dwellers of Xinjiang that he alone was fit to do battle with the hostile jinns of the dunes and lead them to a hidden cache of gold suggests that the navigational skills of foreign sahibs, when properly manipulated, were also regarded as a legitimate form of economic capital. That this compensation consistently failed to materialize does not seem to have lessened the value of its appeal.

THE DEPREDATIONS OF COOPERATION

Not everyone came away pleased with the results of his interactions with the foreign explorer. We have already taken note of several aggrieved parties who emerged during the course of these expeditions: the laborers whose wages were pocketed by local begs, the "tenacious dowager" who refused to vacate her home for Stein's party until forced to do so by the Chinese authorities, the guides who lied to Stein about their knowledge of sites in

order to shorten their terms of service, and Ram Singh, Stein's Indian cartographer, who submitted a laundry list of complaints to Stein about various inconveniences in camp. Other than the garnishing of worker wages
by local begs, however, most of these complaints tended to emphasize the
physical discomfort and daily hardships that were associated with the demands of the archaeologist. It bears repeating that none of these expressions
of dissatisfaction stemmed from an attempt to enforce anything resembling
the moral barometer of our own day and age with regard to questions of cultural sovereignty. Rather, the overwhelming majority of complaints were
of a far more mundane—if no less consequential at the time—nature: the
snoring of one's tent mate, the real or imagined dangers of the desert or
mountains, separation from one's family, and a general reluctance to perform the type of labor demanded by the exacting sahib.

Within this list, fear of injury or death far from home was the most common source of resistance. Though Stein often belittled such fears, both in
print and in his diaries and letters, it is clear that the occasional risk to life
and limb was very real indeed. During one of the many excavations undertaken by Albert von Le Coq at the caves of Kizil, a local worker was seriously injured when part of the cave collapsed on him. The Chinese authorities investigated the matter and Le Coq was forced to pay reparations to the
family. In 1895, the Swedish explorer Sven Hedin mismanaged his party's
water supply, with the result that two of his four Muslim servants died in
the desert. Another man was saved only when Hedin found a pool of sweet
water and administered a rejuvenating mouthful in his boot. The trauma of
such experiences was widely retold in Xinjiang. In 1913, when Stein passed
by "Hedin's pool" and "thought of what Hedin must have felt when he
emerged from jungle belt hereabout & found bed dry," he was able to re-
live the experience with one of the men who had narrowly escaped death.
"Kasim retains every detail of H.[edin]'s story incl.[uding] boots & all."[41]

Although Kasim remained undaunted by his brush with death and continued to work with Western sahibs—including Stein—for many decades
thereafter, others were less enthusiastic. On his second expedition in 1908,
Stein learned of a group of laborers contracted on his behalf in Khotan who,
"with evid.[ent] relief," had aborted their trek into the desert "when Ghazi
Sheikh had met them & told them 'that they were going to death.'" Another
group of men was likewise "full of apprehensions," Stein noted the same
year, "but treat them as a matter of Kismet [fate]." In northwestern Gansu,
Stein confessed to "misgivings about transport, the Suchou pony men protesting against a march into mountains." There was a widespread belief,
both among the pony men and sometimes even among the local Chinese

authorities, that "wild Tibetans" and possibly even dragons would ambush them in the mountains. On his third expedition, Stein again encountered troubles with Gansu pony men, who forced him to renegotiate his intended route. "At last some contractors produced & softened by assurance that I shall not travel by Hsao-yao-kou Pass."[42]

A decade and a half later, some men still believed that the prospect of injury and hardship outweighed the allure of economic capital. "Paid off temporary Kashgar followers who had proved unwilling to face winter in desert," Stein wrote on his fourth expedition. The passage of another half century did not dull the memory of the suffering such men had once endured. In 1979, a Sino-Japanese expedition to Niya interviewed a ninety-two-year-old man who claimed to have guided Stein into the nearby ruins in 1906. He did not wax poetic over the experience. "I remember we found an old pot with a lot of red papers inside," he told the film crew. "I know it was very cold at the time we found them. I didn't like it too much." But it wasn't just the men who suffered. At times, it was the women whom these men left behind who registered their opposition most vociferously. "I just signed the contract with the djigit Yakoub," Pelliot noted in his diary in 1906. "The other, yielding to his wife's tears, renounced his departure." The next year, Stein similarly found himself "obliged to let Tokhta Akhun remain, at request of his old mother."[43]

Once contracted for service, the members of the sahib's caravan sometimes undertook acts of passive resistance. "Up by 6 AM., but busy till 10 AM. in tearing off caravan from its fleshpots," Stein wrote in 1906 near Charklik. Stein's penchant for early wake-up calls and a consistent aversion to urban environments—London and Charklik alike repulsed him—did not sit well with his men. "Up by 3.45 A.M.," he noted on September 10, 1907, the day of his departure from Jinta, a town in northwestern Gansu. "But absence of cartmen, Sieh's lateness & accounts extortionate delay start till 7.15 A.M.! A trying wait, due to allurements of cheng [city] & Ya-men." On other occasions, the tactics adopted by his laborers could be just as amusing as they were frustrating. "Tried to get what rest I could before the rise fixed for 3 A.M. and—found to my chagrin when I awoke at 5–30 A.M. that no one was stirring," he wrote in 1913 near Maralbashi. "Afrazgul had my alarm watch, heard it strike &—went to sleep again when his efforts to awake the others were met by comforting assurance—that as four camels were missing and the ponies, too, had decamped we should not be able to move!"[44]

To Stein, the most frustrating source of passive resistance was that exhibited by Li Yuansun (figure 11), the Chinese secretary hired for his third

Figure 11. Secretary Li. Not everyone who joined a Western archaeological expedition found that the compensations outweighed the depredations. Foremost among these malcontents was Li Yuansun, the Chinese secretary (*shiye*) who accompanied Stein on his third expedition. Pictured here at the frigid site of Miran in January 1914, Li insisted on the letter of his employment—writing Chinese letters—and refused to undertake any other task desired by Stein. "Li never opens his mouth if he can possibly help it," Stein wrote in a letter to Allen, "and has to be driven to give help." He later concluded that "evidently the poor little fellow very sorry for his job." As a result, Stein skewered him both in his private correspondence and in *Innermost Asia*, the published narrative of his third expedition. Copyright © The British Library Board, Stein Photograph 392/28(331).

expedition.[45] Much like Ram Singh before him, Li repeatedly insisted on the contractual nature of his employment and refused to do anything he was not explicitly hired to do—such as teach Stein Chinese. "Ssu-yeh [*shiye*, 'secretary'], after condescending to some conversation in morning, promptly marched ahead," Stein noted in December 1913. Three months later, Stein again bewailed "Li's helpless indolence: he was heard to declare that writing letters was his only function. Feel sadly the badness of bargain." Stein, like most Western archaeologists, regarded his expedition as a great enterprise. As such, he was pleasantly surprised when Jiang Xiaowan, the secretary from his second expedition, took an acute interest in Stein's scholarly agenda and went above and beyond the call of duty to help facilitate its success. But for Jiang's successor, it was just another job, and a distasteful one at that. Li, Stein wrote in a letter to Allen in 1914, "is a hopelessly lethargic person, just a machine for inditing Chinese letters." Stein most deplored Li's lack of engagement during their many audiences with Chinese officials. "Li keeps his usual silence and is with difficulty prodded into saying a dozen words," Stein wrote in his diary on November 19, 1914. "Busy at cracking nuts." On another occasion, Stein confessed how he "missed Chiang's alert diplomatic help. Li sits by like a piece of wood and expectorates all the time. Invincible vis inertiae." When it came time to settle accounts, Stein once again bemoaned Li's lack of enthusiasm for his job. "Attitude of indolent torpor preserved to end. Sorry for T[ae]ls. 824 paid out to this living mummy."[46]

In addition to passive resistance, some men actively tried to arrange their own discharge from the caravan. On his second expedition, Stein faced increasingly combative behavior not only from Ram Singh, his Gurkha cartographer alluded to previously, but also from Naik Ram Singh, a Sikh sapper. "Worry with Naik who neglects two summons & then turns up 'illuminated,'" Stein wrote in his diary on June 20, 1907, just weeks after he had succeeded in securing nearly one-fourth of the contents of Cave 17 at Dunhuang. "Excuse that he was asked to pack tobacco!! Asks for dismissal which anywhere would be readily granted." The very next day Ram Singh also made a scene. "R.[am] S.[ingh] vindictive with interpreter & tries to make a scene, but fails to suggest a substitute," Stein noted. "Evid.[ently] bent on getting off to Shanghai on plea of illness. Talks of previous thoughts of suicide, with a sneer at example set by 'officers'! Advisable to treat as patient."[47]

Some of Stein's Chinese assistants also made attempts to cut their employment short. In April 1907, while tracing the ruins of Han watchtowers in the buggy and desolate marshes west of Dunhuang, Stein received what

he regarded as a suspicious request from the Chinese secretary he had contracted in town. "Tsao-Daloi asks leave for family accident (a la Punjab)."
On January 1, 1914, during his third expedition, Stein woke up to news
that Li Yuansun, his disgruntled Chinese secretary, was missing. "An hour
later crest-fallen Ssu-yeh, more crumpled up than ever, appeared," Stein
recorded in his diary. "They had wandered back to river but lost the track
again & bivouacked without food. A good lesson to Li who is ever bent on
deserting." Rather than brave the desert dunes on their own, some workers thought it better to try and force Stein to camp in proximity to reliable sources of water. On February 2, 1908, Stein encountered the "semi-
mutinous conduct of Shahyar men who in their alarm clamoured for return
to well of C. 325." Ultimately, Stein allayed their fears "by argument about
advantages which their departure would cause us as to ice supply!"[48]

As is clear in many of these examples, most manifestations of discontent were defused through little more than a frank exchange of words. On
his third expedition, Stein noted how a "bickering conflict between A.[fraz]
G.[ul] & Shams Din had revived this morning & threatened to breakout
into affray. Lost hours over bringing my myrmidon's childlike temper to
reason." On the rare occasion when words failed, however, the sahib was
permitted to respond in punitive fashion. Once, after Ram Singh had "come
to better sense" and apologized for his earlier behavior, Stein nonetheless
insisted on a "written reply to my Memo calling for explanations." This
was military discipline, and Singh was lucky to get off so lightly. Hasan
Akhun, the "unruly" camel factotum, was once sentenced by Stein to a
public whipping for his part in a brawl. The resulting welts, Stein informed
his readers in *Sand-Buried Ruins of Khotan* (1903), "had a very salutary effect upon the young offender." Iliazov, a Muslim servant hired by Pelliot in
Russian Turkestan, was "shaken" (*secoué*) by Mannerheim after Mannerheim found him sleeping in Pelliot's bed. Before the expedition was over,
Pelliot, too, would end up striking the Chinese cook he had brought with
him from France. "Ting was still so drunk today that I slapped [*flanqué*] his
hands for the first time."[49]

In lieu of corporal punishment, the archaeologist could also choose to
hand his men over to the local authorities. In October 1906, Pelliot did precisely that after "one of the excavators, an older man, wished to conduct
himself with a younger worker according to the rules of oriental morality,
and gained a knife in the shoulder." When Pelliot suspected another worker
of having stolen one of the three terra-cotta heads lost at Maralbashi, he had
"the thief brought back to the house." When the man showed "no sign of
repentance," Pelliot "finally deliver[ed] him to the Chinese Mandarin" for

punishment. (In a subsequent letter to Senart, Pelliot defended his actions by claiming that "this little Chinese official does not have the right to beat anybody.") In October 1913, Yusuf, one of the assistants Stein had hired in Kashgar, "saw fit to rebel against taking charge of big camera. Announces a la Ramzan his intention to leave." Stein made it clear what would happen to Yusuf if he were to follow through on his threat. "Reply that alternative to service detention at Yamen."[50]

The ability to invoke the specter of official intervention by the Chinese authorities proved useful on more than one occasion. On his second expedition, Stein faced "insolent behaviour" from the Taghliks ("Mountain People") south of Khotan, who refused to welcome him into their closely guarded domain. "But their taming is proceeding," Stein later told Allen in a letter, "thanks to the fear of the 'Khitai' [Chinese] and a little humorous handling." Similarly, while exploring the ancient Han watchtowers in the intolerable marshes west of Dunhuang, Stein informed Allen that he was "always counting my men knowing that they would all like to decamp at the first chance. Luckily some herdsmen on the route near Tun-huang are respecting authority & have brought back the first who tried to desert!"[51]

THE GOLDEN GOOSE

In his pursuit of priceless artifacts, the Western archaeologist could be haughty, overbearing, and vindictive. But he could also be quite generous with his resources. And when he contracted the services of people who did not regard these artifacts as priceless, it did not take many of these resources to obtain the consent of the locals for the removal of the objects in their midst. In fact, he needed only to offer a form of compensation equivalent to the combined local market value of the artifact and the real or perceived hardships of the expedition trail. As we have just seen, the archaeologist did not always match this subjective valuation. This was particularly the case with regard to educated assistants such as Li Yuansun and Ram Singh, who were not permitted to collect their own artifacts for sale on the open market. For them, the chief form of compensation was their fixed salary, which, when measured against the hazards of a two-year expedition in the desert, often proved insufficient to justify their hardship. With the mostly unskilled and illiterate Muslim laborers in Xinjiang, something as simple as the Muslim holiday of Ramadan or bazaar day could provide enough of a disincentive to work with the sahib. "I had also wanted workers today, Monday, but this is the main day of bazaar," Pelliot wrote in May 1907. "There are scarcely five or six; I have postponed the resumption of the excavations until tomorrow."[52] When the compensations of cooperation proved insufficient to motivate those who had signed up for work, passive resistance and active obstruction were the result.

More often than not, however, the Western sahib not only matched local valuations of the artifacts he sought and the work he demanded, but he also far exceeded them. And even with some of the salaried assistants, the nature of the work Stein demanded of them could evince a compensatory appeal similar to that which the Western scholar himself derived. Jiang Xiaowan, the Chinese secretary for Stein's second expedition, was apparently one of those who derived a great deal of satisfaction from the mostly clerical and linguistic work Stein assigned him. "The petty ways of my Indian Assistants & their indifference to any higher aims put my Chinese helpmate's value into double relief," Stein once noted in a letter to Allen, referring to Jiang. "He—and eager little Dash are always pleasant companions. With the rest one is again & again reminded that one is dealing with mercenaries." Because Jiang got along so well with Stein, he was able to draw on a host of compensations denied to Li Yuansun and Ram Singh, among others. Chief among these compensations was lifelong employment as the Chinese secretary in the British consulate in Kashgar on the conclusion of the expedition. In his last will and testament, Jiang instructed his son to cherish the two watches Stein had given him in recognition of his seventeen years of service to England, and referred to them as evidence that he had done something worthy in his life. In his final words, Jiang asked for Stein, his "most honoured patron," to help settle his debts, employ his son in the consulate, purchase a coffin, and pay for the transport of his body back to Hunan. In response, Stein sent a check for 300 rupees to cover the cost of transporting Jiang's body to Hunan, while the British consul hired his son to do clerical work in the evenings. Similarly, Lal Singh, the Sikh surveyor who was dispatched from India to replace the discontented Ram Singh in the midst of the second expedition and later served as cartographer on the third expedition as well, also appears to have cultivated something akin to friendship with Stein. In 1930, as Stein set off from Srinagar en route to Xinjiang for his ill-fated fourth expedition, his diary records a "farewell to dear old Lal Singh whose visits had been daily."[53]

"Mercenaries" or not, those who participated in an archaeological expedition tended to do so voluntarily, in reasonable expectation that the services they rendered would be compensated fairly and sometimes generously. Compared to the modest value of artifacts for sale on the local antiquities market and the general unlikelihood that any given expedition would result in serious injury or death—widespread retelling of Hedin's

fatal blunder notwithstanding—most people tended to favor engagement
over disengagement. And for those lucky few who were able to leverage
the sahib's political prestige into audiences with the Qing governor or a
"fat" promotion to a begship, the potential compensation could be limitless. Though the Westerner had the writ of the Chinese authorities behind
him, this writ was seldom invoked. When it was, it was usually invoked
over disciplinary matters that had arisen on the expedition trail after the
voluntary contraction of services. In other words, most conflicts concerned
what we might characterize today as workplace disputes. Only rarely, as in
the case of Stein and the Taghliks and a couple of Stein's grueling marches
north and west of Dunhuang, was the specter of official intervention ever
invoked as a means of overcoming otherwise intractable resistance. Even
then, the available evidence strongly suggests that such resistance was born
entirely out of fears of physical privation, "wild Tibetans," and a widespread
belief in the presence of dangerous dragons or *jinns*. If the historian looks
for principled resistance echoing our own discourse of cultural sovereignty,
he will not find it.

Had the Western archaeologist not offered an attractive economic proposition to the people of Xinjiang and Gansu, they would have shunned his
expeditions. After all, as this chapter has shown, the enterprising peasants
of northwestern China were not only free to refuse his entreaties for employment, but they were also more than capable of venturing out in the
desert alone to grab hold of the exact same antiquities themselves. Some
would continue to do both. A far greater number, however, made the con-
scious and rational decision to work with the foreign archaeologist on what
were regarded at the time as acceptable terms. Generally speaking, they
did so not because they were sympathetic to, or impressed with, the Westerner's professed adherence to the abstract Enlightenment ideals of science,
preservation, and education. Rather, they did so because he was the most
resourceful sahib in the desert, one who dispensed a reliable form of compensation that was perceived to be of greater value than the cumulative sum
of what he asked in return.

CHAPTER TWO

Accumulating Culture

On September 7, 1908, Aisin Gioro Zailan, a disgraced Manchu prince living in exile in Xinjiang, wrote a long letter to the French sinologist Paul Pelliot. Zailan had met Pelliot the previous winter in Urumchi as Pelliot made his way through Xinjiang en route to Gansu. "Last year we met in the northern court, where we rejoiced in wine and food," Zailan wrote. "Holding hands as we engaged in pleasant conversation about antiquity and our present age, we took no notice of how quickly time passed by. But then you mounted your steed and ventured eastward, and I have not stopped mourning your absence." Pelliot was an unlikely recipient of such syrupy sentiments. Just eight years earlier, the two men had faced off against each other in Beijing on opposite sides of the Boxer War. "We had fought in 1900," Pelliot later recalled, "but time soothes many things." Time can certainly do that. But so, too, can a shared love of Chinese antiquity. "In the spring you took your rest at Dunhuang," Zailan continued in his letter, "touring the ancient grottoes with joy, gazing upon the Buddhist relics with reverence, and tracing the remnants of steles with your hand." News that Pelliot, "an erudite scholar and lover of antiquity" (*boxue haogu*), had managed to "take hold of texts to verify the histories" (*yuanjing zhengshi*) greatly pleased the exiled prince. "Your study of these forgotten manuscripts will contribute to the progress of humanity and shine a glorious light on our frontier landscape."[1]

In addition to this letter, Prince Zailan gave Pelliot something else: a 1,300-year-old manuscript from the hidden "cave library" at the Thousand-Buddha Caves (*Qianfodong*) near Dunhuang. And that was not the only such manuscript in Pelliot's possession. Soon after he arrived at Dunhuang, the local prefect gave Pelliot another "two manuscripts from the Ts'ien-fo-tong of Touen-huang," both Tang dynasty sutras, to which "he does not attach a price."[2] Though no money changed hands, it would be a mistake to conclude that the Qing officials of northwestern China did not receive anything in exchange for such gifts. In the previous chapter, we saw how the uneducated Muslim peasants—or merely technically educated Indian and Chinese assistants—tended to regard the Western archaeologist as a "sahib in the desert," from whom they expected to extract various forms of tangible economic capital. This chapter will lay the groundwork for an understanding of how the educated Confucian elites of the late Qing empire could regard the Western archaeologist not as a thief but rather as someone who treated art and antiquities in the same way that the Chinese themselves had long done: as intangible forms of political and social capital.

The exchange of political and social capital took place at precisely the same time that Western explorers were removing tens of thousands of antiquities from the jurisdictions of Qing officials. As a result, if we are to reconstruct the full perspective of the educated Confucian bureaucrat on the Qing frontier, we must recover more than just his interactions with the foreign scholar. We must also recover his interactions with the same sort of material culture that the foreign scholar himself targeted for removal. Only then will we be able to make sense of the perceived contemporary value of the "goods" he was willing to exchange with the Western scholar. As we shall see, unlike the mostly illiterate Muslim peasants, the Confucian elite was not culturally disconnected from the artifacts that lay hidden in the desert sands and caves of the northwest. Though they showed little interest in newly unearthed Indian, Iranian, Turkic, and Tibetan antiquities, anything inscribed with Chinese characters evinced an enormous appeal to the educated Confucian gentleman, be he Mongol, Manchu, or Han. The lower classes may have regarded such things as little more than profitable. To the Chinese elites, however, these same objects were very precious indeed.

Patricia Ebrey, in her study of Chinese collecting practices in Emperor Huizong's court (1100–1125), and throughout the Song dynasty (960–1279) more broadly, has described Confucian interactions with art and antiquities as a form of "accumulating culture." As Ebrey and other scholars such as Shana Brown and Thomas Lawton have demonstrated, this accumulation of culture was one of the chief means by which educated Chinese elites gained and maintained their coveted status as refined gentlemen. As Scarlett Jang repeatedly reminds us in her study of imperial collecting practices, however, such collections were private, not public. That is, the trade in gentlemanly status was negotiated through private social and political networks, not collective ones. In other words, the Confucian gentleman accumulated culture on behalf of himself. Should he choose to transfer his accumulations of culture to someone else, such transfers would take place in exchange for a new privately held asset: social or political capital. In the event any of these accumulations of culture were lost or destroyed, such loss was interpreted as a commentary on the moral failings of their previous owner—and the previous owner alone. This was precisely the case with the collections of Emperor Huizong, who neither regarded them as the tangible property nor figurative embodiment of his subjects. The emperor's treasures belonged to no one but the emperor, and they represented the virtue of no one but the emperor. Therefore, when the Song capital of Kaifeng was sacked by invading Jurchen forces in 1127, Confucian commentators viewed the subsequent dispersal of Huizong's collection as a moral commentary on the failings of Huizong himself.[3]

As we shall see in this chapter, the educated elites of the late Qing dynasty continued to engage with art and antiquities in a way that would have been familiar to Emperor Huizong and his fellow Song collectors. After all, Prince Zailan and other Qing officials were still willing to give men like Pelliot the precious Dunhuang manuscripts that they held in their possession. For his part, however, Pelliot would only give that same manuscript to an institution that claimed to represent all the nations of the French empire, both ancient and modern. He would not give it to another private individual, no matter how much social or political capital that individual might offer in return. This is the crucial distinction between what I have termed "precious" and "priceless." The goal of this chapter is to illustrate that distinction through a close analysis of how late Qing scholars and officials engaged with the thousands of ancient artifacts and manuscripts that came into their hands in Gansu and Xinjiang during the early decades of the twentieth century.

After canvassing the range of interactions between Confucian elites and the sort of objects they associated with a culturally continuous past, we will take a look at what they thought about the activities of the Western archaeologists who removed these same objects. The evidence will show that while the Chinese *regretted* the loss of so many precious treasures, they did not *criminalize* that loss. The reason is simple. As far as the educated Qing elites were concerned, the Western archaeologists were doing little more than what they themselves had long done: accumulating culture. As such, there was nothing in the acquisitive actions of the foreign gentleman to preclude the solicitation of a mutually productive relationship by a fraternal colleague of empire.

EXCAVATING THE CULTURALLY CONTINUOUS PAST

Generally speaking, the Qing officials posted to northwestern China were educated and wealthy men. Their lack of poverty meant that they had little incentive, except in extreme circumstances, to treat art and antiquities as an unvarnished form of economic capital. And their cultural identification with much of what emerged from the desert sands, an identification bred through years of Confucian education, meant that they would not knowingly destroy or dispose of anything that came into their possession. With that in mind, we can now ask the following three questions. First, what did the Qing officials of Xinjiang and Gansu have in their possession? Second, how did they get it? And finally, what did they do with it? The answers to these questions will help us to understand why the Confucian elite of late imperial and early Republican China not only condoned the collecting activities of Western scholars but also actively assisted in the removal of antiquities.

The collecting preferences of Confucian elites tended to focus on manuscripts and steles written in Chinese. Their classical training was rooted in philology, with a near sacred veneration for the written word. Such was this regard for the Chinese script that many religious depictions of Chinese hell courts include at least one image of a sinner being tortured or disemboweled for having burned or discarded inscribed paper. In addition to written texts, be they on stone, wood, paper, or silk, the Chinese scholars and officials also targeted objects that had once been created, preserved, and handled by privileged elites like themselves. Though sympathetic toward Buddhism and perhaps even a true believer himself, the Confucian gentleman showed little interest in acquiring for his own collection the same sort of religious statuary and public artwork that the illiterate commoners tended to worship. In 1924, Edward Forbes, the director of the Fogg Museum, visited the German archaeologist Albert von Le Coq at his museum in Berlin and "asked him whether the Chinese Government didn't object to his taking" such things. In response, Le Coq told Forbes that "the Chinese Government was made up of educated Confucian gentlemen, who simply couldn't understand how he, a Christian scholar and gentleman, could take any interest in such 'Dröck' [Dreck, 'rubbish'] that was fit only for the most low-brow of the Chinese common-people." Four years later, the Chinese archaeologist Huang Wenbi echoed Le Coq's assessment. "People in our country are accustomed to emphasizing research on the upper classes and ignoring the lower classes," he noted in his diary during the Sino-Swedish expedition.[4]

But so long as the object in question was a Chinese manuscript or stele, the Qing officials of Xinjiang and Gansu did not need the prodding of any Western archaeologist to teach them the value of its preservation. They simply needed to know where to look. Long before Hedin, Stein, and Pelliot ventured out into the Taklamakan Desert at the turn of the century, the Chinese had already independently identified the location of several steles from the Han and Tang dynasties. In 1879, in the mountains northeast of Aksu, one of the soldiers involved in the Qing reconquest of the region stumbled on the rock inscription of Liu Pingguo, an Eastern Han general who in AD 158 commissioned a pavilion at the site. In 1906, when Pelliot met with Zhang Zaoguang, the prefect of Maralbashi, "he apologized for the poverty of the country and offered each of us a copy of the rubbings of the only two Han steles found in Turkestan so far. His stupefaction is profound when he finds that both of them, that of P'ei Ts'en and that of Lieu P'ing-Kouo, have long been familiar to me." Several months later, after a visit to Circuit Intendant Pan Zhen in Aksu, Pelliot received a letter from Pan "containing the decipherment of the inscription of Lieou P'ing-kouo."[5]

Although these steles and their rubbings were treasured possessions, they were very few in number and acquired only by chance. Before the arrival of Western archaeologists, this was the chief way in which a Chinese official stationed in Xinjiang might come across the odd stele or manuscript. As Stein was fond of observing, the educated Confucian gentleman had not been reared on the virtues of outdoor exertions. Once while on the march in Gansu, Stein bemoaned the complaints of his "timorous" men, whom he regarded as "queer products of an ancient civilization which has never encouraged pluck or 'roughing.'" When Chinese officials near Dunhuang expressed their astonishment at Stein's discovery of ancient Han watchtowers and inscribed wooden tablets just a few days' march from town, he thought it a natural result of their cloistered upbringing. "The Chinese can scarcely be blamed for having no knowledge or tradition of their existence," Stein wrote to Allen, "so decayed are the ruins & so far away from their beloved *Ta-lo*, 'the big road.'" At times, Stein could not resist taking a lighthearted jab at his "overly civilized" hosts. "Dr. Chiao Mou-lin, a slender delicately featured man, wisely kept to his chair under the shelter of a country umbrella," Stein noted during a rainy excursion to some ruins outside of Nanjing in 1930. "His thin Chinese slippers might well have stuck on the way."[6]

As a result, Stein was convinced that the Chinese scholars of his day exhibited a marked "inability to comprehend scholarly work in the field." There is some truth to this statement, at least with respect to the late Qing

era. It is certainly true that no Qing scholar ever embarked on anything
resembling an archaeological expedition before Stein's first expedition
in 1900, nor at any point during his second (1906–8) or third expeditions
(1913–15). But he should have known better than to suggest that the Chinese were not willing to match him spade for spade at sites that did not
require the rigors of an expedition. The Chinese suffered from a handicap in
the field, but it was only a handicap, not a debilitant. After all, the vast majority of the Chinese who lived in Xinjiang during this time were attached
to the official Qing bureaucracy. There were few Chinese gentry or peasants. Many of the officials, steeped as they were in the Confucian classics
and annals of history, carried out earnest scholarly labors. Yet their identity
as scholars was forced to take a back seat to their primary identity as administrators. In other words, they were officials first and scholars second.
During a visit with Yarkand magistrate Peng Xuzhan in 1906, Mannerheim
listened patiently as Peng "complained of the amount of work he had to do,
as in Kashgaria the mandarin had to attend to everything. Irrigation in particular claimed a great deal of attention."[7]

Expeditions into the dunes the Chinese could not—and frankly would
not—do. In the 1902 postface to the Chinese translation of Stein's *Preliminary Report* for his first expedition, translator Wan Rong observed that
when his colleagues in the Qing bureaucracy see "Mr. Stein crossing mountains and rivers, or travelling through the desert, they laugh at his folly."[8]
They did not laugh at suburban excavations, however, so long as they could
be managed from the confines of their government office. As was the case
with the Liu Pingguo stele in 1879, Chinese officials, consumed with bureaucratic obligations, needed only someone to point them in the right direction. In the 1890s, the British and Russian consuls in Kashgar began to
oversee some of the first organized digs in the nearby desert. But the results
of these digs, publicized only within European scholarly networks, were
composed entirely of manuscripts in non-Chinese languages and popular
Buddhist works of art, things in which the Chinese showed little interest. It
was only with Stein's first expedition in 1900 that Qing officials truly began
to grasp the sinological potential of the Taklamakan. Once they realized
that Chinese manuscripts and steles could also be found in the desert sands,
they immediately jumped into the fray.

The evidence for Chinese excavations during the first decade of Western
expeditions to Xinjiang (i.e., 1900–1910) is sparse but suggestive. In 1917,
the central government envoy Xie Bin learned from officials in Urumchi
that the first organized digs had begun in 1901, the same year as Wan Rong's
translation of Stein's *Preliminary Report*. "In the twenty-seventh year of

Guangxu [i.e., 1901]," he wrote, "Turfan Prefect Wen Lishan excavated a copy of the *Lotus Sutra* from the middle of the ruins, which dated from the tenth year of the Kaiyuan reign of the Tang." Also that same year, at a site near Keriya, Stein reported on the excavations of a local beg and his Muslim laborers. "The men deny any finds of value having been made yet it is difficult to believe that mound after mound should have been opened with much labour if no results rewarded the work," Stein observed. "The Beg seems afraid of the Amban [Qing official] forming too great an opinion of his 'finds,' and the labourers may have been instructed to tell accordingly."[9]

The beg's concern about the jealous attentions of nearby Chinese officials seems to have been well founded. In 1900, the circuit intendant of Kashgar told Stein of coins and seals that had come into his possession from a site some 70 *li* outside the city, all believed to date to the Han dynasty. In 1915 outside Khotan, Stein noted some "extensive burrowings . . . where an Amban some 12 years ago [i.e., 1903] is said to have set a large number of men to work." In 1906, Peng Xuzhan, the magistrate of Yarkand, gave Stein "a batch of coins dug out 'not far from Yarkand ya-men.' Seem to be Sung pieces." In 1907, the Chinese telegraph operator at Ganzhou, Li Yougeng, showed Stein "old bronze mirrors & vases said to come from He-shuei-kwe, the old site n[ea]r Kanchou." In 1928, the Chinese archaeologist Huang Wenbi came across an inscription that suggested Chinese excavations near Kucha in 1910. "Within one of the caves there was an inscription . . . dated to the second year of Xuantong [1910]. It read: 'At this spot I excavated two pages from a Buddhist sutra.' This must mean that a Han person once dug here." The following year, Huang also stumbled across two "tourist" placards erected by previous Chinese magistrates. At a site near Aksu, Huang was taken aback by a "a wooden board inscribed with the words: 'The Tang city of Qieshi.' It was erected in 1925 by Magistrate Yang Yingkuan." One week later, Huang found "a wooden sign, erected by the magistrate of Bachu county, Duan Quan. On it appeared the words, 'Ancient ruins of the Tang state of Weitou,' followed by several lines of description: 'According to historical records the ancient remains of the state of Weitou lie here.'"[10]

Despite these tantalizing clues regarding excavations throughout Xinjiang and Gansu, it is clear that the overwhelming majority of organized Chinese digs took place at Turfan. As Stein once put it, "the natural conditions [at Turfan] were singularly favourable. The Turfan basin (sinking to circ. 400 ft. below sea level!) is remarkably dry & quite exempt from drift sand & erosion. On the slopes of the low hills ruins were quite safe, too, from moisture." Because a system of underground canals had spared Turfan from dependence on melted alpine water, the oasis had never been abandoned to the desert sands. This meant that the current town was in close proximity to its decaying predecessors. The end result, Stein observed, was that anyone so inclined "could carry on their operations almost everywhere from comfortable shelter of modern houses." Among Western archaeologists, the Germans exploited these advantages most fully, using Turfan (and, to a lesser extent, Kucha) as an extended base for each of their expeditions. As far as Stein was concerned, work at Turfan or Kucha, "'tame' sites which could be worked as it were, from a drawing room window," hardly constituted an "expedition." How much easier his work would have been, Stein confessed to Allen, "if local conditions were as comfortable in the desert as they are at the sites of Turfan & Kucha."[11]

Of course, to the Chinese officials as well as the Germans, these conditions were a boon. Turfan, with its ready abundance of Chinese and Central Asian treasures, had something for everyone. In his *Record of Antiquities in Xinjiang* (*Xinjiang fang gu lu*, 1911), Wang Shu'nan, the Xinjiang Minister of Finance, underscored the ease with which anyone could dig in Turfan. "Most manuscript fragments have been excavated by Easterners and Westerners in the village of Sanpu, which is east of Turfan, and Tuyou Gorge, which is in Shanshan," Wang wrote. "Sometimes they are excavated, sometimes they simply appear [*shi jue shi xian*]." Wang also drew attention to the activities of Turfan subprefect Zeng Binghuang, whom Stein and Pelliot both met in 1907–8. According to Wang, Zeng "is a learned lover of antiquities [*haogu duowen*]. In his excavations he has acquired the remnants of numerous manuscripts." Zeng's prized possession was a Chinese stele from the Northern Wei era, which he acquired in 1908. Another celebrated stele from the Tang dynasty followed in 1910. "In the tenth month of the second year of Xuantong [November 1910], Sub-District Deputy Magistrate Zhang Qing came to Sanpu to excavate antiquities," central government envoy Xie Bin learned in 1917, "and he found a stele inscription from the tomb of Zhang Huaiji of the Tang era. . . . They also found Zhang Huaiji's body, still in excellent condition."[12]

To the Chinese officials, much of Turfan's appeal came from its geographic proximity to Urumchi, the provincial capital, where all of the most powerful and wealthy Chinese resided. From about 1906 or 1907 onward, the road from Urumchi to Turfan began to witness a heavy traffic in Chinese antiquities. Already by 1907, Mannerheim found that "it is more difficult, however, to secure ancient objects here [Turfan] than at Khotan and the prices are considerably higher." Every time an official in Turfan unearthed something spectacular, his colleagues in Urumchi were quick to hear about it. In 1912, Duan Yongen, the prefect of Fuyuan, added a colophon to the end of a Dunhuang manuscript. In it, he informs us that the incoming magistrate of Turfan recently "packed his luggage and went to take up office in Turfan. Occasionally he would find manuscripts from the Six Dynasties and Tang era in containers, and would invite me to mount them and write a colophon to mark the occasion." The following year, Dan Qi, an envoy from the central government, met with the minister of education in Urumchi and learned all about the thriving trade in Turfan. "Turfan has the most ancient temples," Dan observed. "These temples have all collapsed and are now buried under the sand. But the foundations remain. . . . Often stored within them are precious objects [zhengui zhi pin]."[13]

In Urumchi, the largest and most exquisite collections belonged to the most powerful officials. Wang Shu'nan had so many manuscripts from Turfan that he disposed of them freely as gifts. "I gave this fragment of a *Commentary on the Great Perfection of Wisdom [Da zhidu lun]* manuscript to Zifeng as a gift," Wang wrote in a colophon in 1914. "It was unearthed from the ground in Sanpu near Turfan in the second year of Xuantong [1910] amid tattered pieces of papers and other miscellaneous items." That same year, Orlando Hobbes, a member of one of the Japanese expeditions led by Zuicho Tachibana, met Wang in Urumchi. "At Urumutch the Provincial Treasurer had some very valuable documents in the dead language," he wrote to his family back home, "similar to those excavated by Mr. Tachibana." Wang's exquisite collection became so well known throughout China that some distant observers eventually came to confuse Wang with his Western competitors in the field. In 1944, the writer of an anonymous colophon appended to a Dunhuang manuscript mistook Wang as the discoverer of the Dunhuang cave library—itself imagined to be in Xinjiang rather than Gansu—and blamed the dispersal of Wang's collection on the Westerners. "From the Dunhuang stone cavern in Xinjiang came many remnants of Tang-era manuscripts," he wrote. "They were preserved for many years without being dug up. During the Qing dynasty, they were discovered by Wang Jinqing [Shunan] of Xincheng, who accumulated a great many through excavations. But they have long since passed into the hands of Westerners, who packed them up and transported them beyond the ocean to foreign countries."[14]

Another major collection was amassed by Liang Suwen, who worked with Wang in the provincial treasury. We can obtain a sense of the scale of Liang's acquisitions through the eyewitness account of Song Xiaolian, a former governor of Heilongjiang then serving in Beijing. "I heard that Mr. Liang Suwen, formerly an official in the Xinjiang treasury, obtained a large number of Northern Dynasties and Tang-era manuscripts, contracts, and government documents from Gaochang," he wrote in 1913 in a colophon appended to a copy of a *Lotus Sutra* from Turfan. "This fall in the capital, Suwen invited some people to view his collection, so I rushed over to take a look. The collection filled the entire room, to the point where I was only able to glance through half of it despite exerting a day's efforts there." On his third expedition, Stein got a firsthand glimpse of the excavations undertaken in Turfan by officials such as Wang and Liang. At Toyuk in 1914, Stein took note of "a number of ruined structures," among which "Niaz Darogha working for an Amban said to have found a good deal of MSS." A few months later at the Astana graves, Stein learned of one Muhammad Jiza, who "had worked them for supplying Chinese at Turfan and Urumchi and others on own speculation." Another part of the tomb complex had been searched "by Ahmed Dogha who had been asked to supply antiques by the late Turfan 'Loye' [*laoye*, 'district magistrate']." Before long, Stein concluded that any site targeted by the Chinese in Turfan was not worth spending much time on, because the Chinese had likely already cleared it. "As this cemetery with its Chin.[ese] character offered little hope of interesting finds," he wrote in 1915, "I moved by 1 P.M. 1/2 m. to N. to the group of tombs where Mashik declared to have found stucco images in the one he opened."[15]

By this time, Chinese officials in Khotan and Keriya also began to oversee their own excavations. These appear to have been far more organized and systematic than the tentative efforts of the previous decade. In 1913, near Khotan, Stein met a man named Kasim, who "brought a packet of Tibetan, Chinese Brahmi documents on wood & paper. Other finds said to have gone to Amban & Badr[uddi]n." As this passage suggests, the Chinese officials of the southern oases had even begun to find some use for non-Chinese manuscripts. Three months later, at a site outside Keriya, Stein found a "low shapeless mound" in a state of "complete destruction due to digging which Daud Beg effected last summer with 17 men in endeavor to secure more for Amban." The magistrate in question was Dai Chengmo, with whom Stein maintained close and friendly relations, and the find consisted of "a packet of 15 large leaves, evid.[ently] Pothi shaped," along with "plenty of parcha khats [pieces of paper]." Though all appeared to evince various Indian scripts, "half [were] taken by Beg for Amban." During a subsequent meeting with the magistrate, Stein learned the fate of these acquisitions, expressing his surprise that Dai, a Chinese official from Hunan, would take such an interest in Central Asian manuscripts. "Amban mentions a big Pothi bundle which he obtained from Domoko—& has sent away to Hunan!"[16]

In addition to voluminous manuscripts and a handful of steles from Xinjiang—most but not all of which came from Turfan—Qing officials

posted to the northwestern frontier also came into possession of a great
many manuscripts from Dunhuang. The flights of fancy from our anonymous author of a 1944 colophon notwithstanding, none of these manuscripts were "excavated" by Chinese officials (nor was Dunhuang located
in Xinjiang!). In fact, every last one of them was discovered by the illiterate
Daoist monk Wang Yuanlu (figure 12), who alone is responsible for their
further dispersal from Cave 17. To Stein, Pelliot, and other foreign archaeologists, Wang "sold" these manuscripts under the pretext of a donation to
his temple. To the Chinese officials, however, Wang did not sell them. He
gifted them. This realization brings us to our next question: How did the
Chinese interact with the antiquities in their midst?

UNPACKING MODERN CHINESE COLOPHONS

To the Confucian elites, art and antiquities were invested with abstract
moral and cultural significance. When a Confucian gentleman acquired, preserved, or analyzed an artifact, such acts were regarded as the cultivation of
his own personal virtue. Patricia Ebrey has described this process as one in
which educated Chinese attempted to "accumulate culture" as a means of
bolstering their cultural, social, and political standing.[17] As a result, unlike
the illiterate peasants, the self-professed Confucian gentleman almost never
destroyed or disposed of manuscripts or works of art, for they were intertwined with his identity as a civilized person. First and foremost, then, art
and antiquities were a form of social capital. They provided a material conduit through which one gentleman could demonstrate to another gentleman
his adherence to the abstract cultural ideals of their common social class.
From this foundation sprung a secondary form of capital: political. In other
words, one of the best ways for an educated official to curry goodwill with
another educated official was to acknowledge his ability to appreciate these
same cultural ideals.

The social and political functions of art and antiquities in China are
perfectly illustrated by the fate of most of the ancient manuscripts from
Cave 17 (figure 13) at Dunhuang that were not taken away by foreigners.
Beginning with Aurel Stein's first visit to the caves in 1907 and ending
with the outbreak of World War I in 1914, numerous scholars from every
major Western empire acquired several hundreds and occasionally even
thousands of such manuscripts. Almost without exception, these manuscripts were then transferred to a museum, library, or university, institutions that claimed to embody a commitment to the abstract ideals of the
Enlightenment: science, preservation, and public education. In the West,

Figure 12. The Guardian of Dunhuang. At some point during the last decade of the nineteenth century, the itinerant Daoist priest Wang Yuanlu made his way to Dunhuang and took up residence in a derelict temple just opposite the Thousand-Buddha Caves. In 1900, while undertaking restorations of the neglected caves with donations procured in town, Wang noticed a crack in the ceiling of the corridor entranceway in what is now Cave 16. He broke through the plaster and discovered the hidden "cave library." Over the next two decades, the illiterate Wang, unable to read or assess the historical value of the more than forty thousand manuscripts, paintings, and banners that had come into his possession, proceeded to transform his newfound discovery into lucrative economic capital for the further restoration of the caves and accumulation of spiritual merit. In managing his closely guarded inventory, Wang proved adept at misrepresenting the true extent of his hoard to inquisitive outsiders, leading each to believe that he had acquired the last of his cache, all at a suitably inflated price. M. Aurel Stein, *Ruins of Desert Cathay: Personal Narrative of Explorations in Central Asia and Westernmost China*, vol. 2 (London: Macmillan, 1912), plate 187.

Figure 13. The Dunhuang Manuscripts. Nearly all of the ancient manuscripts that passed
through the hands of Chinese officials and scholars in Xinjiang and Gansu could be traced
back to excavations in Turfan or the hidden cave library in the Thousand-Buddha Caves
near Dunhuang. In this composite photograph developed by Stein, the entrance to the
cave library (now Cave 17) is visible to the right, while the Buddhist statues of Cave 16
seem to fix their gaze on some of the scrolls purchased—and later superimposed on the
original negative—by Stein in 1907. These were the sort of scrolls on which Confucian
elites felt compelled to add their own modern colophons. M. Aurel Stein, *Ruins of Desert
Cathay: Personal Narrative of Explorations in Central Asia and Westernmost China*,
vol. 2 (London: Macmillan, 1912), plate 188.

the treatment of antiquities was beholden, at least in theory, to the ideals
of collective ownership by the people or nation. These ideals were given
substance by preserving art and antiquities in public institutions that were
designed to cater to that nation. By contrast, the Dunhuang manuscripts in
China, where such institutions did not yet exist, would meet with a very
different fate.

Instead of donating their acquisitions to public institutions, Confucian
elites gave them to other like-minded elites, convinced that only a cultured
gentleman like himself could be trusted to cherish, preserve, and study the
gift. This conviction stemmed from the realization that the antiquity itself reflected the individual virtue of its new owner; thus to destroy, dispose, or otherwise neglect the antiquity in one's possession was to tarnish
one's own claim to civility. Wang Yuanlu, the illiterate Daoist caretaker of

Cave 17, was carefully attuned to the logic of the Confucian mind. In 1900, seven years before he met Stein, Wang discovered the hidden cave library and came into possession of tens of thousands of ancient manuscripts, all of which dated to between the fifth and eleventh centuries. His first "customer," however, was not Stein. It was the Chinese officials of northwestern Gansu, from whom Wang hoped to induce a donation to his temple in exchange for receipt of such exquisite cultural treasures.

In this hope Wang was sorely disappointed. From 1900 to 1906, Wang chose the most complete and aesthetically pleasing specimens from his newfound hoard and sent them as gifts to various officials in neighboring jurisdictions. Wang never got a penny in return. Luckily for him, however, the Chinese officials who received his gifts did not inquire further into their source, nor did they visit the caves themselves. What they did do was distribute these manuscripts among their friends and colleagues as gifts intended to cultivate social and political goodwill. By the time Stein and Pelliot visited the caves in 1907 and 1908, it is clear that the Dunhuang manuscripts had already spread far and wide, from Urumchi in the northwest to Lanzhou in the southeast. Seeing how the Chinese valued these scrolls so highly, Pelliot found it odd that no one in China had yet attempted to track them to their source. "It is curious that there are important historical documents," Pelliot wrote from the caves in March 1908, "and that no Chinese scholar has come to get involved."[18]

We now know why. In what can only be described as a shrewd business move, Wang Yuanlu seems to have concealed the true extent of his supply, leading the Chinese officials to believe that there were only a few hundred manuscripts in all, and those already dispersed. As early as 1903, Ye Changchi, a prominent scholar and Qing official active throughout Gansu, revealed his conviction in this belief. "I have heard that these sutras come from a rock cell in the Thousand Buddha Caves," he wrote in his diary, "and that the door of the cave had been sealed with molten iron and not opened since ancient times." Inside this cave, he learned, "were stone ledges on which hundreds of scrolls were heaped up, and the manuscripts I have received are from among these. At the time none of the monks and laymen realized their value and so divided these among themselves." Ye was not only misled about the true extent of the manuscript hoard. He was also wrong about the monks not knowing their true value. In fact, we might say that it was precisely because Wang appreciated their value so much that he sought to control access to his "goods," carefully manage his "stock," and "sell" them on his own terms.[19]

With Wang, the goal was to exchange manuscripts for cash, no matter how hard he tried to portray such transactions as "donations." With the Chinese officials and scholars, however, cash was the last thing on their minds. In order to interrogate these minds, we turn now to an analysis of the colophons they regularly added to the ends of the Dunhuang and Turfan scrolls.[20] The very existence of the colophons themselves underscores the highly personal nature of the social and political capital these manuscripts were imagined to yield. To men like Stein and Pelliot, conditioned to think of their acquisitions as reflective of the commitment of their respective empires to the lofty and abstract ideals of the Enlightenment, the scholar was not supposed to insert himself into the fabric of the artifact itself. The artifact was no longer a living thing, subject to the evolving uses and adaptations of different owners in different times and places. Once acquired by the man of science, it was supposed to be transformed into a sterile exhibition piece, fixed in both time and space and forever divorced from daily contact with the evolving agendas of those mired in the real world—at least in theory.

The Chinese of the late Qing era were still a decade or more away from subscribing to these ideals. To them, antiquities were regarded as dynamic objects whose social and cultural identities were inseparable from the individual gentlemen who owned them. As such, it was perfectly acceptable to merge one's own identity with that of the antiquity itself, for owner and object were imagined to be mirror images of each other. This helps to explain why none of the Dunhuang manuscripts removed by Westerners from China contain anything other than catalog notations written on the manuscript itself, while those that remained within China are filled with contemporary literary annotations added by nearly every Chinese official and scholar through whose hands they passed. These annotations, or colophons, provide us with startling insights into how educated Chinese interacted with antiquities in the days before the Western discourse of scientific preservation delegitimized such practices.[21]

In October 1910, Chai Hongshan, the garrison commander of Suzhou, decided to give away his copy of a *Great Nirvana* (*Da ban niepan jing*) sutra from Dunhuang as a gift. The lucky recipient was Zhao Weixi, a Qing official traveling through Gansu en route to Urumchi. The reason we know about this gift is because Zhao made a note of it on the sutra itself (figure 14). In a colophon containing more than four hundred Chinese characters, Zhao narrates the discovery of the Dunhuang cave library, including the pivotal role of Stein. His narration is filled with errors, among which are his beliefs that the cave was opened in 1896 and that Stein was

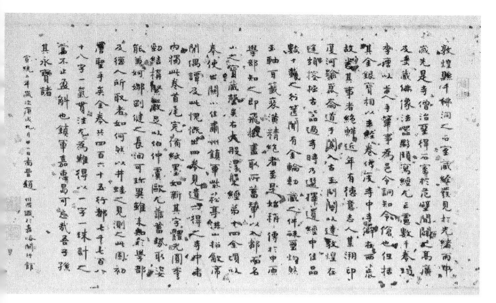

Figure 14. The Living Manuscript. Educated Chinese elites of the late Qing and early
Republican eras regarded art and antiquities as privately owned representations of the
moral character and cultural credentials of the individual Confucian gentleman who had
acquired them. As such, they felt free to inscribe their own personal identities onto the
ancient manuscripts that came into their possession, most often in the form of colophons. In this lengthy colophon appended to a *Great Nirvana* sutra from Dunhuang in
October 1910, the traveling Qing official Zhao Weixi indulges in nearly all of the literary
conventions typical of such inscriptions: an error-filled narration of Stein's and Pelliot's
visits to Dunhuang in 1907–8, speculation on the identity of the manuscript's ancient
scribe, a gracious account of the moment when a newly respected colleague gifted the
manuscript to its present owner, a gushing appraisal of the aesthetics of the calligraphy,
and a warning—apparently rarely observed—to one's descendants to never sell the manuscript. Beijing daxue tushuguan and Shanghai guji chubanshe, eds., *Beijing daxue tushuguan cang Dunhuang wenxian* [Dunhuang manuscripts stored in the Peking University
Library], vol. 1 (Shanghai: Shanghai guji chubanshe, 1995), 124.

German. Pelliot is not mentioned. In the second half of the colophon, Zhao
tells us how he came into possession of this manuscript. During a banquet
convened by Garrison Commander Chai, the two men took out four scrolls
to examine. "We found that this is the only one from the temple collection
to be complete from start to finish, with ink that looks new," Zhao wrote.

The paper and ink appeared to be brand new, while the characters were
vibrant and smooth, tender yet muscular. In composition the structure

was tight and orderly, comparable to that of [Tang calligraphers] Ouyang Xun and Yu Shinan. Bursting with latent vitality, in form and appearance the characters succeeded in harmonizing elegance and grace with a firm, robust bearing. Such a thing is truly rare and precious.

Concluding that his sutra could only have been written by "the hand of a Tang genius," Zhao went on to count every single line (465) and character (7,788), "all of which look as though they were written in one breath. Truly, an amazing feat!" It is in his final lines, however, that Zhao highlights the chief value of the sutra. "How can I ever forget the generous favor bestowed upon me by the Garrison Commander? My children shall cherish this for eternity."[22]

They did not. As subsequent colophons make clear, this *Great Nirvana* sutra passed through the hands of at least two more owners before eventually ending up for sale on the shelves of the Haiwangcun bookshop in Beijing. Presumably, it was purchased from there by Chinese scholars of a later generation, who demonstrated their belated adherence to Western scholarly ideals by placing it not in another private collection but rather in the Peking University library. The impermanence of possession is a recurrent theme in these colophons. In 1935, Cen Dongshi noted how his sutra had been a gift from Wu Jingshan, a retired military official once stationed in Suzhou, who "had stored these manuscripts in a trunk for many years" before giving them out as presents. Cen's manuscript changed hands at least once more, eventually ending up in the Tianjin Municipal Museum of Art. In 1942, a man by the name of Jia Lu marveled at the journey that one of the Dunhuang sutras had undergone. "In order to survive [for over a thousand years], I believe that this scroll must have had its own god watching over and protecting it," Jia wrote. "Today, however, it has fallen into possession of Haiwangcun." In 1943, Chen Jikan, a former governor of Gansu, expressed his fear that the *Great Nirvana* sutra in his possession might not survive the tender vagaries of fate much longer. "I know that I cannot keep this manuscript forever," he wrote. "My only wish is to find someone to look after it, care for it, and not let this invaluable ancient ink be destroyed at the hands of anyone from my generation." If they lived long enough to learn the fates of their manuscripts, both Jia and Chen would have had cause to rejoice: Jia's ended up in the Peking University library, while Chen's found its way to a museum in Shanghai.[23]

They were the lucky ones. For every Dunhuang or Turfan manuscript that eventually ended up in a Chinese museum or library, just as many were lost in the endless shuffle of private social and political networks throughout the country. In 1944, Xu Chengyao, a former circuit intendant in north-western Gansu who obtained more than two hundred manuscripts from Dunhuang during his tenure, added a colophon to a *Sutra Spoken by the Buddha on the Names of the Buddhas (Foshuo foming jing)* manuscript owned by his friend. In it, he reflected on the tragic fate of the scrolls that once filled his collection. "They have been scattered about and are now mostly lost," he wrote, "while those that have survived by chance are not many." On another colophon the previous year, Chen Jikan lamented the scarcity of those manuscripts he had once handled so frequently. "Those manuscripts that my friends and I competed for so intensely back in our days in Gansu are now dispersed all over the world."[24] Among the manuscripts that survived within China, it is notable that none appear to contain a colophon from any date prior to 1910. Though not every manuscript was graced with a modern colophon, it was a fairly common practice, especially on the most complete and aesthetically pleasing scrolls—precisely the sort given away by Wang Yuanlu to Chinese officials in the years before he learned how much Westerners were willing to pay for them. All this suggests that the apparent lack of any such colophons from the first decade of dispersal within China reflects a fairly high rate of attrition for the early batches gifted away by Wang.

Clues to possible sources of this attrition can be found directly within those colophons that did survive. Recall that Zhao Weixi made mention of receiving his Dunhuang manuscript "during a banquet convened by Garrison Commander Chai Hongshan." Like his colleague Wu Jingshan, Chai did not place his manuscripts in a museum or library as did Stein and Pelliot. Rather, they were stored in a "trunk," and constantly packed and unpacked, rolled and unrolled, as circumstance and occasion dictated. Most of these occasions were social. "In the second month of the *xinhai* year of the Xuantong emperor [March 1911]," wrote one anonymous author of a colophon appended to a *Great Nirvana* sutra, "Huizhai took out all the Dunhuang stone cavern manuscript rolls that he has collected from the second year of the Jiande reign period of the Northern Zhou. The paper used for this scroll is 1,340 years old." The venerable age of the manuscript did not deter further additions, however, for this notation is followed by a list of the names of twelve people who looked at this scroll while it was on display. Over the next seventeen years, this sutra would amass six additional colophons, the last in 1928 by Ma Xulun, a prominent politician and scholar who expressed his "unlimited joy" at perusing the scroll.[25]

Many other manuscripts collected within China from Turfan and Dunhuang evince a similar life history. No matter how delicately they were handled, it is clear that they were constantly furled and unfurled over a period of many decades. Cheng Zongyi, a former magistrate of Jiuquan, recalled in his colophon how "Mr. Bingran took out this manuscript for our perusal." Xu Yili expressed his gratitude to Yuan Wenbai, who "once served in Yumen County, only 100 *li* from Dunhuang. Often he would take out his collection of manuscripts for our perusal." Chen Zhigao, a former magistrate of Anxi, drew explicit attention in his colophon to the very act of unrolling these ancient scrolls. "To unfurl this scroll is to give it new life," he observed. Though that may well be true in a metaphorical sense, in a practical sense each new unfurling added yet another imperceptible layer of wear and tear to manuscripts that were already more than a thousand years old. At times, this wear and tear was quite perceptible indeed. The most obvious example comes in the form of the colophons themselves, which could tally up to several hundred characters each. "Mr. Peixin has asked me to record some of my memories and review the fading threads of my old dreams," wrote Xu Chengyao on the *Sutra Spoken by the Buddha on the Names of the Buddhas* manuscript owned by his friend, "and so I have unconsciously jabbered on for too long." Xu, however, did not jabber on for so long that future admirers could not find space to record their own names. The last colophon, dated to 1947–48, includes the signatures of thirteen more men who were invited to view the sutra.[26]

What did they all talk about? The history of the dispersal of the Dunhuang cave library, to be sure, along with the endless gratitude each person felt toward whoever had displayed or given the manuscript away as a gift. By far the lion's share of such colophons, however, was devoted to the ultimate litmus test of the Confucian gentleman: the appraisal of calligraphy. Few activities allowed Chinese elites to show off their literary prowess and cultural credentials more than the assessment of the calligrapher's craft, long considered the hallmark of any cultivated gentleman. As the American philosopher John Dewey discovered in 1919 during an extended stay in China, educated Chinese talked about their script "with all the art jargon: 'Notice the strength of this down stroke, and the spirituality of the cross stroke and elegant rhythm of the composition.'" The writers of Dunhuang and Turfan colophons did the same. In descriptions so hyperbolic and ethereal that any effort at translation is approximate at best, the Chinese officials and scholars of the northwest competed with one another to leave the most distinct and ostentatious appraisal they could possibly muster. In the third colophon to his *Great Nirvana* sutra, Zhao Weixi declared that "the ancients believed that the critical evaluation of calligraphy was a sacred task. . . . Thus I, too, will critique this manuscript." As we already saw, Zhao's appraisal included references to the Chinese characters as "vibrant and smooth, tender yet muscular." He also believed that the anonymous ancient scribe, whose characters were "bursting with latent vitality," succeeded in "harmonizing elegance and grace with a firm, robust bearing."[27]

Nearly all of the surviving colophons are filled with such purple prose. In 1912, Duan Yongen, a longtime northwestern official, described the writing on a Turfan manuscript as if he was watching a theatrical performance. "Like a graceful dance, it is elegant and flows effortlessly." Two years later, the Xinjiang official and scholar Wang Shu'nan said of a *Sutra on the Heroic-March Concentration (Shoulengyan sanmei jing)* from Turfan that it revealed "a pure representation of the clerical script for seal characters. It is written in an elegant flow that is interspersed with rich splashes of recklessly bold ink dashes." Declaring each character to be worth a thousand pieces of gold, "enough to cure your hunger," Wang concluded that the ancient scribe achieved "intensity through elegance and grace. The entire page is overcome with mesmerizing beauty. No one has seen such a thing for over a thousand years." In 1921, Cheng Zongyi, the magistrate of Jiuquan, described the calligraphy on his friend's *Lotus Sutra* as "tight and firm in structure, harmonious in spirit." In 1941, a *Diamond Sutra* found at Haiwangcun yielded two colophons that described its script in transcendent terms. "The calligraphy is refined and tight," wrote a man who signed his name as Qinyu. "It is just like the pure blue essence of the flame in the furnace." This was followed by the notation of one Qigong, who portrayed the characters as "springing across the page like the rays of a rainbow. Who can write anything more beautiful than this?" Song Xiaolian, who was invited to view the massive collection of former Xinjiang treasury official Liang Suwen in Beijing, surely could have provided an answer. "It was like entering a treasure cave, with all five senses mesmerized," he gushed in 1913. "Or like traveling through the Buddhist heaven, with all thoughts obliterated. So beautiful! So extravagant! I could only sigh while viewing them all. What have I done to deserve such ocular pleasures?"[28]

As these excerpts make abundantly clear, most comments were directed toward tasks of a scholarly nature, such as calligraphy, in an effort to shore up the learned credentials of the writer. This obsession with calligraphic form tended to obscure any interest in the actual content of these sutras: Buddhism. Because Pelliot, and to a lesser extent Stein, took away those manuscripts of greatest historical interest—secular, philosophical, and literary documents—most of what remained in China were endless copies of the same handful of familiar Buddhist sutras. As a result, the style of writing used to copy these sutras tended to provide the greatest element of interest for their Chinese owners. "The collectors of Dunhuang manuscripts have been interested in the miscellaneous secular documents [*zashu*] and have not lavished much attention on the Buddhist sutras," wrote one colophon author in 1944. That said, some sutras were cherished for their perceived religious powers. In 1910, Zhao Weixi, the author of the earliest surviving colophons, described the genuine spiritual attraction of his *Great Nirvana* sutra. "Suffering from extreme loneliness interrupted only by sleep," he wrote in his second colophon, "I discovered that this manuscript alone was capable of driving my fears and anxieties away. After reading this sutra all of my evil defilements have been flushed out and eliminated. [Within this manuscript] lies not only the power of the Buddha but also a noble task for learned scholars." The next day, Zhao rode out to do some hunting and succeeded in shooting "one yellow goat and two wild turkeys." Later that evening, he "took out this manuscript and began to read. Immediately my body and mind were purified. Not only is this sutra pleasing to the eye; it can also help me atone and repent for this afternoon's activities."[29]

Be it for aesthetic or spiritual reasons, Chinese elites regarded these manuscripts as extremely precious. Perhaps the most memorable description was provided by former Gansu governor Chen Jikan, who referred to them as "among the foremost treasures of all that is between Heaven and Earth." A somewhat less poetic assessment was put forth by Harvard art historian Langdon Warner, who also grasped the aesthetic and spiritual allure of these manuscripts. "These rolls avert fire and flood and bring good luck," he wrote in 1924. "They make splendid gifts to higher officials and sell for hundreds of taels each." Either way, it is important to note that they were regarded as the private possessions of individual owners and their tangible social and political networks. The writers of the colophons were very clear about this. The colophon that Wang Shu'nan appended to the *Sutra on the Heroic-March Concentration* from Turfan, for instance, ends with an explicit recognition of ownership. "Mr. Gongdu should cherish this forever," he wrote in 1914. Because these sutras belonged to no one but their current owners, they were at the mercy of the social and political networks through which these owners circulated them in pursuit of social and political capital. The lucky ones survived wholly intact as gifts or as goods for sale in a bookstore or antiquities shop, where they might eventually be acquired by a museum or university.[30]

The unlucky ones, however, were lost entirely during the course of a lengthy peripatetic career or were cut up into as many gifts as its owner saw fit in the pursuit of social and political capital. The indelicate fate of one ever-shrinking *Great Nirvana* sutra was documented over the course of

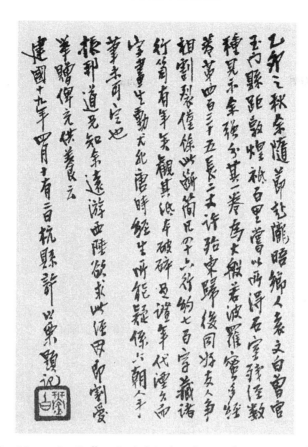

Figure 15. One Manuscript, Endless Capital. In their desire to leverage as much social and political capital as possible out of privately owned Dunhuang manuscripts, some Chinese elites even went so far as to cut a single scroll into multiple fragments, each of which could then be given to whomever the original owner wished to curry favor with. In this colophon appended to a *Great Nirvana* sutra from Dunhuang in 1930, Xu Yili observes (in the fourth and fifth lines from the right) that on his return to the interior from Gansu, his friends "competed with one another to cut off their own piece" (*zhengxiang gelie*) of this manuscript, to the point where "all that remains is this small fragment" (*jin yu ci duanjian*). Gansu cang Dunhuang wenxian bianweihui, Gansu renmin chubanshe, and Gansu sheng wenwu ju, eds., *Gansu cang Dunhuang wenxian* [Dunhuang manuscripts stored in Gansu], vol. 5 (Lanzhou: Gansu renmin chubanshe, 1999), 308.

multiple colophons, some undated. According to Xu Yili, the author of the first colophon in 1930 (figure 15), his *Great Nirvana* sutra began to shrink the moment he left his government post at Yumen in Gansu and returned to the eastern seaboard. It was at that point that all his friends "competed with one another to cut off their own piece [*zhengxiang gelie*]." Later, a subsequent colophon describes how the author "managed to obtain a portion" from the original scroll. In the end, Xu Yili wrote, "all that remains is this small fragment [*jin yu ci duanjian*]," consisting of about seven hundred characters. The sutra's turbulent journey, however, was still not complete: this final fragment was later given to one Feng Sizhi, who in turn gave it to one Zhang Ziying.[31]

None of the men through whose hands these manuscripts passed thought that they belonged to anyone other than he who had acquired it by discovery, gift, or purchase. There was certainly no sense that they belonged to an abstract collective entity such as "the Chinese nation." This was made abundantly clear in 1910, when the famous Qing official and scholar Luo Zhenyu convinced the Ministry of Education to arrange for the transport of all remaining Dunhuang manuscripts to Beijing for deposit in the Imperial Library. Though the Imperial Library was precisely the sort of receptacle where historical treasures might be preserved on behalf of the abstract nation, the Ministry of Education refused to pay for the transport, forcing Luo to draw on his own personal savings. "Talk with Mr. Hu-Shih of Ch. MSS. brought to Peking," Stein wrote during a meeting with the famous Chinese philosopher during a visit to Nanjing in 1930. "6000 T[ae]ls. from private donor." In the end, the fate of the entire enterprise was determined by private individuals rather than collective bodies. Not only was the money allotted for Wang Yuanlu—Luo Zhenyu's personal funds—siphoned off by local officials, but also the manuscripts themselves were brazenly seized by these same officials all along the route to Beijing. An anonymous colophon on Zhao Weixi's *Great Nirvana* sutra, dated to between 1911 and 1914, bore witness to this event. "Officials from the Ministry of Education then hurried to round up a few camels of their own," the writer noted, after describing the acquisitions of Stein and Pelliot, "but the very last remnants were either used to line their own pockets or are hardly fit to cover sauce jars." In the very next colophon, the poet Chang Tingjiang claims that the hemorrhage of manuscripts continued after their arrival in the capital. "During the former Qing, those [manuscripts] that the Ministry of Education managed to bring to Beijing saw the best of the collection seized and taken away by people the moment the carts arrived in the capital."[32]

With the passage of time, such actions would come under severe criticism and ridicule. Yet it is clear that these opportunistic Chinese elites, few of whom believed in the political legitimacy of the nation, were simply acting in accordance with the widely accepted norms of their day. And these norms privileged the claims of tangible and personal social and political networks over those of abstract and impersonal national ones. The emperor himself would have agreed. In the aftermath of the 1911 revolution and overthrow of the Qing dynasty, the boy emperor Puyi and his thousands of attendants found themselves in dire financial straits. Regarding everything in the Forbidden City as the private property of the Aisin Gioro clan, which had ruled the Qing Empire for more than two and a half centuries, the eunuchs who served this clan began to sell the art and antiquities of the palace to private dealers in Beijing. Later Puyi himself, along with his brother Pujie, did the same.[33]

Other fallen Qing officials acted similarly. As Thomas Lawton and Lara Jaishree Netting have documented in detail, when the Manchu connoisseur Duanfang lost his head in 1911, his family promptly placed his substantial collection up for sale. John Ferguson, a Canadian missionary turned foreign advisor to the new Republican government, was well positioned to exploit the sudden glut of art and antiquities. In 1914, Duanfang's family contacted Ferguson to discuss a sale. "The family," Ferguson wrote, "has been left with not much else than the art specimens which the father collected during his life." That same year, Ferguson declared that "the market here has never been so favorable as at present." The reason, he concluded, was "due to the necessity of selling collections on the part of those who are no longer in office. . . . It has nearly driven me to bankruptcy to try to buy as much as I have." Though Ferguson was purchasing on behalf of American museums, the unemployed Qing officials and their families who entered into negotiations with him do not appear to have been motivated by this association. Rather, they sold to Ferguson simply because he was deemed worthy of appreciating their value—and because he was the highest bidder.[34]

The fact that so many of the Dunhuang and Turfan manuscripts ended up in Beijing and Shanghai bookshops suggests that the heirs of Qing officials in the northwest treated their antiquities in the very same way. The preferred mode of interaction was to leverage one's collection into social and political capital, even if this meant the permanent loss or mutilation of the object. Of course, if one's circumstances became dire enough, these same objects could also be transformed into bald economic capital. Regardless, the tangible and intangible benefits derived from all three forms of capital redounded to private individuals alone. As Jing Liao has shown, throughout Chinese history, imperial and private libraries "rendered no service to the public."[35] It did not occur to Prince Zailan or any of his Qing colleagues that the proper place for their collections was in a distant museum or library, boxed off in a glass cabinet for the edification of the vulgar masses. The proper place was wherever their owners deemed it possible to squeeze the maximum amount of profit from their perceived social and political value. For Prince Zailan, this calculation took the form of a complimentary gift to Pelliot of a rare and precious Dunhuang manuscript. For Pelliot, this took the form of a symbolic gift to the people of the French empire—as embodied by its publicly accessible institutions—and the many nations which that empire claimed to represent.

THE VICARIOUS ACCUMULATION OF CULTURE

So long as the Chinese elites considered art and antiquities to be merely precious and their Muslim subjects viewed them as merely profitable, there was no possibility of intractable conflict with the foreign archaeologist. There was only mutual competition, cooperation, and negotiation, none of which transgressed any moral or legal boundaries of the day. For the educated Confucian elite, it was enough that the Western archaeologist presented himself as a mirror image of himself: a scholarly gentleman who intended to preserve, study, and cherish whatever antiquities he acquired in China. "A deep and abiding love for antiquity [*haogu shenxin*]," longtime Xinjiang official Pan Zhen wrote to Stein in one his letters, "is something particularly worthy of respect and admiration [*you lingren qinyang*]."[36]

In their letters to Stein and Pelliot, the Chinese officials of Xinjiang often praised the foreign archaeologist as a virtuous gentleman whose scholarly books were destined to change the world. "Be it the traces of the ancients or the customs of our contemporaries," Pan added in another letter, "there is not one that you have failed thoroughly to uncover and investigate, presenting them in expansive books of great importance that encompass everything you have experienced. This is truly worthy of an admiration that knows no bounds." Stein's books, they were convinced, embodied the lofty commitment to the preservation, study, and dissemination of knowledge about China's glorious past. "The history of Xinjiang in China since Han and Tang times has also benefitted from your investigations," wrote Shule magistrate Wang Min. "These are significant accomplishments." Surely sales of the resulting book, he added, in a well-worn allusion to immortal literary creations in Chinese history, "are not unlike when paper became expensive in Luoyang?" In his letter to Pelliot, the exiled Manchu prince Zailan concluded that the Frenchman's "study of the forgotten [Dunhuang] manuscripts," in the form of a "great record of your travels, one destined to become a brilliant work of literature that stuns the world," would "contribute to the progress of humanity and shine a glorious light on our frontier landscape."[37]

Acting in the belief that they were assisting a like-minded scholarly gentleman in the investigation of China's past, local officials went above and beyond the call of duty to help Stein and Pelliot exploit promising new archaeological sites. In March 1901, the magistrate of Keriya paid a visit to Stein and "informs me that he too has heard now of two 'old towns' N. of *Gulakhma*." In November 1906, Pelliot learned that the sub-prefect of Faizabad had prepared for his visit by asking "in advance which were the old sites of his district," and then personally "came to us on the main road to announce that he had charged one of his subordinates to guide us in our visit." In 1907, in the dusty town of Jinta in Gansu, Stein noted that Sub-Prefect Zeng Liangsheng was "eager to arrange for my visit to ruins," while the magistrate of Dunhuang "refers to large ruined site 60 li from Kan-chou." The subprefect of Turfan, Zeng Binghuang, gave Pelliot a detailed map of his district and pointed out where Pelliot was most likely to uncover the best relics. The prefect of Luntai spoke to Pelliot of "the former Louen-t'ai whose ruins are according to him about 70 *li* to the south-east of Bongour," while the magistrate of Aksu "tells me about ruins on the side of Aqsou, towards a place called Tsiang-kia, about 60 *li* from the highway." On his third expedition, Stein obtained from Li Shurong, the magistrate of Barikol, "most useful information about sites at Guchen, my next goal." Stein also rejoiced at the willingness of Keriya magistrate Dai Chengmo to share everything he knew about nearby sites. "He possesses a good deal of geographical and antiquarian knowledge, and our talks have been long," Stein noted. "His help is most useful."[38]

Of course, Qing officials were obliged to facilitate the bare logistics of an expedition and ensure that no physical harm befell the foreign explorer while in their jurisdiction. Beyond that, however, they were under no compulsion to share detailed knowledge about possible sites. And yet that is exactly what they did, over and over again. Sometimes they even gave Western scholars precious items from their own collections as gifts. On June 30, 1906, the prefect of Yarkand, Peng Xuzhan, gave Stein "a batch of coins dug out 'not far' from Yarkand ya-men. Seem to be Sung pieces." In addition to the Dunhuang manuscripts gifted to Pelliot by Prince Zailan and Enguang noted at the outset of this chapter, there was also the prefect of Maralbashi, who, "having learned that antiquities lovers were here, apologized for the poverty of the country and offered each of us a copy of the rubbings of the only two Han stones found in Turkestan so far."[39]

In fact, during the entirety of the roughly two decades when foreign explorers embarked on the first wave of expeditions to Xinjiang, one searches in vain for even a single instance of a Chinese official or scholar deploying the lexicon of criminality to describe their activities. Instead, the removal of antiquities abroad was consistently expressed in Chinese through the application of morally neutral verbs such as "obtain" (de), "collect" (huo), "take" (qu), "transport" (yun), "send" (ji), "carry" (xie, dai), "excavate" (jue), and "dig" (wa). Even when they described the most invasive and destructive acts, such as cutting a cave mural out of the wall with a chisel and saw, still they did not call it "theft" or "vandalism." In 1917, when central government envoy Xie Bin learned from the local Muslims of Charklik that wall murals filled with "natural scenery and people" had been cut out and removed by Stein, he described the act as "chiseled out [chanbao] by the British Stein, packed in felt, and taken away." At the Kizil Caves near Kucha, Xie merely noted that most of the wall murals "have been cut out [bao] and carried away [xiequ] by foreign explorers."[40]

Why didn't the Chinese regard such acts as "theft"? The answer is simple: because they did not recognize any prior claims on objects not already held in someone's private collection. Art and antiquities were not yet imagined to belong to an abstract "Chinese nation," from which they might plausibly be "stolen." Instead, they were imagined to reflect the personal virtue of their individual owners, who could, if they so chose, transfer that virtue to another individual. Absent an identifiable owner, however, cultural relics of the late Qing period simply could not be "stolen." In his Record of Antiquities in Xinjiang (1911), Xinjiang Minister of Finance and noted scholar Wang Shu'nan observed that "most" of the Six Dynasty–era sutras to emerge from Turfan "were taken by Westerners." Wang did not condemn the foreigners, however, for having obtained the lion's share. He merely urged his colleagues to join the fray. "The earth does not love its treasures [di bu ai bao]," Wang continued. "Henceforth, who knows how many more will emerge from the ground?" This was not the first time a Confucian scholar had defended the free market of Chinese antiquities. In 1903, a preface to one of the first studies of the Shang dynasty oracle bones unearthed near Anyang described the bones as "long buried, yet suddenly exposed by the opening of a new footpath. The earth does not love its treasures. Once struck by the light of day, they supply lovers of antiquity and connoisseurs of the marvelous."[41]

This is not to say that the Chinese were thrilled with the loss of so many precious treasures. In most of those instances where Chinese officials and scholars describe foreign removals without condemning the remover, the original passage often begins with an expression of "regret" or "misfortune" (xi). This was the case with Luo Zhenyu's first descriptions of

Pelliot's acquisitions of the Dunhuang manuscripts in 1909 and 1910, and it was the case with Xie Bin's comments on Xinjiang antiquities in 1917 as well. "To see them all lost to foreign countries," Xie wrote, "is a cause for regret [kexi]." The vast majority of these early expressions of regret, however, were aired with specific reference to Stein's and Pelliot's removal of the Dunhuang manuscripts in 1907–8. In fact, the only known expression of regret in Xinjiang contemporary to the first wave of foreign expeditions (i.e., 1895–1915) was that of Financial Commissioner Wang Shu'nan. In 1911, Wang wrote that the loss of so many Six Dynasties and Buddhist manuscripts in Turfan was "regrettable" (xi).[42]

With regard to those Dunhuang manuscripts sold by Wang Yuanlu to Stein and Pelliot, however, Chinese emotions could run quite high indeed. Zhao Weixi, in a colophon appended to his *Great Nirvana* sutra in October 1910, referred to the "immense shame" (kuikai) he felt when discussing their loss with Suzhou garrison commander Chai Hongshan. Three months later, while penning his fifth colophon to the same sutra, he recounted how Pelliot "took away the cream of the crop" (jue qi jingying) to Paris, an event he regarded as "a deep humiliation for our people" (wuren zhi dachi). "How could I have known," he continued, "that the teachings of the sages would be taken to the West?" Three colophons later, an anonymous commentator added a similar lament. "The monk in the hills sold them all to foreigners," he wrote. "When will they return?" Clear across the empire in Beijing, the scholar Yun Yuding recorded his heartache in his diary. "The chariot has returned to Paris," he noted. "How can this be anything other than a hateful and painful event?"[43]

The heartache was greatest, however, for the great Qing scholar Luo Zhenyu. On August 19, 1909, in a letter that has since become famous in China, Luo told his friend and fellow scholar Wang Kangnian of "a piece of news I have to pass along that is at once extremely joyous, hateful, and sad." The news concerned "the ancient manuscripts and woodblock prints from the Tang and Five Dynasties era stored in the stone cavern at Dunhuang, which were acquired [de] by the Frenchman Pelliot." The fact that "most of them have already been shipped to France" was the "hateful" part (ke hen). The fact that Pelliot had allowed Luo to copy and photograph a small portion of his collection while he passed through Beijing, and that he had assured Luo the cave still retained a considerable number of manuscripts for the taking, was the "joyous" part (ke xi). But the realization that Stein and Pelliot had already taken the choicest pickings and that the Chinese would be reduced to sifting through scraps were the "sad" parts (ke bei). "I don't know for certain that any more remain there," he told Wang, "but if so, speed is of the essence. The first carriage has already departed, and no one knows what will happen to the next one."[44]

Unlike Stein, Pelliot witnessed all this sorrow in person.[45] In the widely publicized account of his expedition, "Three Years in High Asia" (1910), Pelliot recounted a poignant moment with the Manchu antiquarian and influential Qing official Duanfang. "The viceroy Touan-fang borrowed one of our most precious documents," he wrote, "and, as collectors in all countries leave with regret what they hold in their fingers, it took me six weeks to get it back." Fortunately for the Chinese, Pelliot was willing to furnish copies of his acquisitions on request. When Luo asked Pelliot to send facsimiles of the most important manuscripts from Paris, Pelliot readily agreed, noting that "it is the least we owe them" (*c'est bien le moins que nous leur devions*). Still, for the educated elites of China, Dunhuang was a wound that would never fully heal. In publishing a Chinese translation of Pelliot's account, Luo (or his translator) added a curious passage, one that does not appear in the original French. In the paragraph where Pelliot describes the magnanimous reception afforded him by Chinese scholars in Beijing, their treatment of the Frenchman is glossed in the Chinese version as a means of "repaying injury with kindness" (*yide baoyuan*). As the decades wore on and the permanency of the loss began to sink in, sorrow turned to bitterness, even among the old Confucian elite. In 1943, Chen Jikan, a former governor of Gansu, wondered how things might have turned out differently. "If the stone caverns had remained sealed then their contents could have been preserved in pristine condition for another thousand years," Chen wrote in a colophon appended to a *Great Nirvana* sutra from Dunhuang. "Yet within only a few decades after their discovery, they have all been scattered and lost [*lunyi yi jin*]. Now they are scarce and precious, like a phoenix or a blue moon [*xi ru xing feng*]."[46]

These are melancholy words. And yet, much like the intimidating instructions given to local officials on Stein's passport analyzed in the introduction, such words should not be taken out of the larger context. Without a doubt, the loss of the Dunhuang manuscripts was regarded by some Chinese elites as a "hateful" event almost immediately after they learned of its occurrence. But still their ire was not directed at the foreign gentlemen who had taken them—it was directed at the illiterate Daoist caretaker who had sold them. In other words, their dissatisfaction was expressed in terms of class, not nation. For example, in 1910, when Zhao Weixi described the loss of so many Dunhuang manuscripts abroad, his lament was articulated as a "great humiliation for our people" (*wuren zhi dachi*). But who were Zhao's "people"? As William Rowe has shown, the term *wubei*, often used inter-changeably with *wuren*, was frequently invoked by late imperial Chinese elites as a way of referring to "people like us"; that is, educated officials or the Confucian literati as a whole. It did not refer to what we might now conceive of as a supposedly homogenous "Chinese nation," one undifferentiated by class. As we saw previously, in 1943, former Gansu governor Chen Jikan, in ruminating over the fate of the Dunhuang manuscript in his possession, also invoked the term *wubei* in a similar sense. "My only wish is to find someone to look after it, care for it, and not let this invaluable ancient ink be destroyed at the hands of anyone from my generation."[47]

It is clear that in most times and in most places, educated Confucian elites went out of their way to aid and abet the activities of Western archae-ologists in their jurisdictions, far beyond the bureaucratic injunction to en-sure his safety and not throw obstacles in his way. Whenever Qing scholars and officials reflected on the removal of art and antiquities to a foreign land, the most common response was one of "regret," followed by a renewed resolve to emulate the foreigner and get into the field themselves. Prior to World War I, Chinese scholars and officials never once drew on the lexicon of criminality to describe what had transpired along the expedition trail. On the contrary, many of them, including Luo Zhenyu, continued to maintain friendly and substantive relationships with Western scholars long after they knew what they had taken and how they had taken it.

We now know why. Art and antiquities were precious to the Chinese elites—very precious—but they were not priceless. Breathless paeans about them constituting "the foremost treasures of all that is between Heaven and Earth" to the contrary, every artifact did indeed have its price, even if that price was only rarely articulated in monetary terms. As such, they could be exchanged for various forms of capital that were perceived to be of equal or greater value to the giver. To do so was not to betray the Chinese nation, because the Chinese nation had yet to be enshrined as the basis of political legitimacy in China. To trade art and antiquities with the Western gentleman in exchange for social and political capital was to treat him as the Confucian elites had long treated one other. The many modern Chinese colophons appended to the Dunhuang and Turfan manuscripts make this abundantly clear.

The fact that each and every artifact, no matter how precious, could be exchanged for some other form of social, political, or economic capital with-out moral opprobrium does much to explain why the educated elites of the late Qing and early Republican eras interacted with Western archaeologists and collectors the way they did. Because the accumulation of culture in

China was designed to showcase the personal virtue of the collector rather than that of the "nation," the accumulation of such culture by a foreigner was not yet viewed as "theft." On the contrary, as we will see in the next chapter, it was regarded as yet another opportunity to exchange social and political capital with a newfound gentleman of a newly respected empire.

CHAPTER THREE

Gentlemen of Empire

In July 1902, Rao Yingqi, the governor of Xinjiang province, commissioned a Chinese translation of Stein's *Preliminary Report* (1901). In a postface appended by the translator, Wan Rong, Stein's expedition is presented as a useful learning experience for Qing officials in Xinjiang. Stein, Wan tells his readers, "has used 9,000 rupees and spent eighteen months, incessantly climbing mountains, traversing rivers, and seeking out antiquities and ancient sites. He tracked every matter to its source and investigated its nature." Unfortunately, Wan continued, his Chinese colleagues in the Xinjiang bureaucracy had yet to fully appreciate the significance of Stein's activities. "The ignorant ones may ridicule his roundabout wanderings and take no notice of them," Wan wrote. "But there is a reason behind every matter and an underlying principle behind everything that exists." This is why, he concluded, Westerners such as Stein undertake such arduous expeditions. By "exploring the ancient, they understand the modern; they observe the physical objects and recognize the principles behind these." He then concluded with a call to arms:

> The natural sciences of the West are all developed on the basis of observation; their weapons and technology are advanced through learning. Aspirations of studying natural phenomena lead to wealth and power, but the principle of going from studying to political might seems coincidental to people. They all marvel at the natural sciences and are in awe of Western weapons and technology, yet when it comes to seeing Mr. Stein crossing mountains and rivers, or travelling through the desert, they laugh at his folly. This is just being ignorant![1]

During the first two decades in which Western archaeologists undertook expeditions to Xinjiang, Qing officials posted to the region were engaged in a lively debate about how best to integrate Xinjiang with the rest of the empire, in hopes of harnessing its natural and human resources for the rejuvenation of imperial wealth and power. At the forefront of every official's mind was the existential crisis brought about by successive political setbacks. In Xinjiang and Gansu, successive Muslim revolts during the latter half of the nineteenth century revealed the tenuous hold of Qing administrators in the vast lands of the northwest. Along the eastern seaboard, the Qing central government suffered disastrous military defeats in the Sino-Japanese (1894–95) and Boxer wars (1900–1901), both of which resulted in hefty indemnities to foreign powers that seriously impaired Beijing's ability to fund the organs of government in Xinjiang. In response, Qing officials formulated various policies designed to reverse local and imperial fortunes. These included the adoption of an ill-fated Confucian civilizing project in Xinjiang, followed by a comprehensive reform agenda, known as the "New Policies" (xinzheng), slated for implementation throughout the realm.[2]

Faced with the repeated humiliation of their empire by Western and Japanese forces, Qing rulers did not turn away from the outside world. On the contrary, they actively sought out the best minds that Europe, America, and Japan could offer, hoping to discover the secrets of Western and Japanese wealth and power for themselves. Thus began an unprecedented era of receptivity to anything and anyone that promised to rejuvenate the Qing state and help it regain parity with the other imperialist powers of the day. This was the context in which Governor Rao both commissioned and "highly praised" the Chinese translation of Stein's report, followed by Wan Rong's glowing acclaim for Stein and sharp rebuke of any official who dared mock his forays into the desert sands. Qing officials gravitated toward Stein because he represented a model of science and development that they could emulate in attempting to develop Xinjiang along Western scientific lines. In this sense, Stein was a form of political capital for any bureaucrat who wished to promote such ideals among his subordinates.

ACCUMULATING POLITICAL CAPITAL

It wasn't just Stein who provided such capital, however. The French sinologist Paul Pelliot also found himself the subject of Chinese paeans to Western scientific expertise. On January 4, 1908, while excavating in Turfan, Pelliot sent his servant to ask the local subprefect, Zeng Binghuang, for a map of the region. The servant brought back not only the map, "reproduced with great care," but also "a large placard where Tseng Ping-houang celebrates my scientific merits." Because Pelliot was viewed by his Chinese hosts as the very embodiment of what they themselves one day hoped to become, his opinions were solicited with high regard. Five months later, the magistrate of Anxi spoke to Pelliot "as always about the reform, and asks me, once in Pekin to tell him of my impression of the present state of China." In 1906, the Finnish explorer Gustav Mannerheim also found Qing officials eager to pick his brain. "During our visits to the Chinese authorities," Mannerheim wrote from Kashgar, "they were interested in informing themselves about the political situation in Russia." One month later, the magistrate of Yarkand, Peng Xuzhan, admitted to Mannerheim that "old Chinese laws were not suitable to present conditions" and "required revision." Though Chinese culture should not be forgotten, Peng continued, "all that was useful among other nations should be learnt." Two years later in Khotan, Stein found the local magistrate "full of curiosity about things western in spite of his age."[3]

Chinese curiosity about the secrets of Western science was consistently noted by the foreign archaeologists. At a dinner party en route to Khotan, Stein noted the topics of conversation with his Chinese hosts, which included "accounts of railway wonders & all the timesaving of Western inventions." At Kucha, Pelliot talked with Magistrate Yuan Yanxun "about balloons, which he just knew the name, and balloons which he had no idea." The balloons that Yuan knew nothing about but was eager to inform himself were emblems of advanced atmospheric science. "Go and tell a Hunanese who abominably jabs in his patois," Pelliot observed with frustration, "that the earth is surrounded only by a mattress of relatively thin atmosphere, beyond which it is the void. At last he seems to have understood." More than twenty years later, the Chinese officials of Xinjiang were still eager to learn about the latest scientific advances in the West. "Interrupted during morning by call of old Tung-ling," Stein noted on his fourth expedition. "Interested like the rest in tent, bamboo poles." Western science—and the archaeologists who embodied it—were so highly regarded that some officials refused to believe that Western ingenuity had its limits. When the Swedish explorer Sven Hedin inquired about an appropriate gift for the Muslim prince of Hami, a Chinese general told him that the prince "had heard that in Europe there was a kind of lens that enabled its user to see through one side of the mountain while standing beside it." Hedin insisted that "such a thing currently does not exist in the world," but the general "simply did not believe us. We had to explain it to him for half a day before he finally gave up." The next day, Xu Xusheng, the Chinese co-leader of the expedition,

paid a visit to the prince himself. "He continued to persist about the telescope that can see through mountains," Xu wrote in his diary. "No matter
how I tried to explain it to him, he would not believe me."[4]

The unusually high regard that Western science elicited among Chinese
officials in Xinjiang meant that any appropriation of Western ways was regarded as a form of progress, however superficial. In 1906, Ellsworth Huntington met the Muslim prince of Lukchun, who proudly displayed a field
glass for his American guest. Because it was manufactured in Germany,
the prince had "so high an idea of its value [that] he paid $65 for a little
repairing worth $1 done at Urumchi by some lying Russian Sarts whose
work was so poor that the glass was still out of order." Two years later at
Kashgar, Pelliot responded to a question about the health of his emperor by
informing his host that France had no emperor. "When I say that we have no
Emperor," Pelliot wrote in his diary, "his Excellency Wang brings his stool
closer, very keenly interested, but a little secretary who accompanies him
is very proud to be able to explain to him that France is a Min-tchou-kouo
[*minzhu guo*, 'democratic country'] with a Chang-yi-yuan [*shangyi yuan*,
'upper house'] and a Hia-yi-yuan [*xiayi yuan*, 'lower house']." Knowledge
of foreign ways would not have been a source of pride for Qing officials of
the previous generation. But now such knowledge was eagerly flaunted and
deemed indispensable for career advancement. In the dusty town of Jinta
in Gansu, Mannerheim received a call from the son of the local magistrate.
"He had lived in Germany and had learnt a little German which he murdered unmercifully," Mannerheim noted. "His studies in a military school
in Peking had been interrupted by bad health and in 2 or 3 years he was to
take a civil examination in which his knowledge of European languages was
to be a trump card."[5]

The sudden prestige associated with Western learning also spilled over
into the material realm. Though most explorers preferred to see the Chinese
adhere to "traditional" ways, the Chinese themselves were eager to West-
ernize. In 1906, Mannerheim expressed his dismay on discovering that the
magistrate of Khotan preferred "a horrible modern clock" over "a beautiful
Chinese vase" he had chosen as a gift. Stein found that the Muslim prince
of Hami made use of "furniture arranged in Chinese fashion yet with chairs
& tables evid.[ently] worked in imitation of European articles." In a beg's
mansion in Turfan, Stein took note of "Europe luxuries in form of Chintz-
covered ceiling" and "Russian trunks, cups, etc.," while a magistrate in
Aksu "seems to indulge in many Europe fashion[s]." In a yamen in Yarkand,
Stein found that "Europe things prevail, from cane camp chairs to cups,
etc." Russian and French liquors were required accessories for any respect-

able feast. At a banquet thrown by his good friend Pan Zhen, Stein noted with approval Pan's "quiet unostentatious concessions to Western style: knife & fork (which we did not need); light Russian wine &—small bowls changed at every course." He made a careful distinction between Pan, who symbolized "sensible conservative progress," and the "barbarous mixture of Western luxuries with time honoured fashion at other hosts' tables." Fortunately, "of things foreign such as other Mandarins indulge with pride now, he had none."[6]

It was clear that Pan was the exception. Despite Stein's reservations, Western fever was in full bloom among the Chinese officials of Xinjiang. In 1910, a British member of the Otani expedition found that the rooms of Prince Zailan, the exiled Manchu prince in Urumchi, were decorated "exactly like European, with nice chairs, beautiful ornaments on the table, English cigarettes, and Russian tea glasses, with the holders of silver." Three years later, Stein caught his first glimpse of "glass in windows" along with "other signs of Western comfort" in an office in Keriya. Not only that, but the magistrate's thirteen-year-old son "attends in Europe clothes." As a result, by the time of his third expedition, Stein had a pretty good idea of the sorts of gifts most likely to impress his Chinese hosts. "Now that the Chinese are taking to aping Europe ways," he wrote to his friend Fred Andrews in 1914, "silver cigarette cases and Chinar left trays might find appreciation." Such things were viewed as ideal souvenirs "for Europe-aping Mandarins & the like delighting in showy rubbish." In fact, Stein came to regard the Chinese as so besotted with Western material culture that he considered giving them "silver buckles or silver pins with stones such as a demi-European might like to wear."[7]

During the height of Western expeditions to Xinjiang, foreign archaeologists were the very embodiment of all that the West had to offer a developing country like China. But they didn't merely represent Western wealth and power. They were also skilled practitioners of the same sort of scientific expertise widely believed to have facilitated such wealth and power in the first place. And when prompted, they were more than happy to share that expertise with local elites intent on modernizing their districts. In July 1907, on the outskirts of Kucha, a local Muslim headman told Pelliot about a debate regarding the feasibility of building a tunnel to supplement the shortfall of the Kucha River. "Some have concluded that it is possible; others that it is not," Pelliot noted. "He hoped that I could clarify the question, which is of paramount importance. One would not hesitate to spend 70,000, 80,000 taels for such an enterprise." The following year in Gansu, Li Yingshou, the subprefect of Gaotai County, complained to Pelliot that "almost all the land immediately irrigable has been cleared here; the rest is invaded by *chor* that should be washed to make it flow." Li then asked Pelliot "if we have no plant to absorb this salt." In formulating his response, Pelliot drew on his experience in the French colonies of Indochina. "I tell him that to my knowledge, the best way is to make canals on these lands and flood from time to time, and I ask him why they do not try a *noria* at the base, supplementing the elevation with buckets, as one irrigates with man's arms all the fields a little higher from the Tonkinese delta."[8]

Stein, too, was willing to lend his assistance for local development schemes. In his case, however, it was the resources of British India rather than French Indochina that proved most useful. "Exchanged visits with lively old Hsien-kuan, Fu-tai-tsin, who had come into charge some 8 months ago from Ili," Stein recorded in his diary on March 25, 1908, near Lop Nor. "Seems anxious to develop the district & followed eagerly explanations about Punjab irrigation." Just three days later, Stein "was taken out of my way by a big posse of Yuzbashis & Begs to inspect the new canal of Sampula which is to reconquer quite a goodly slice of desert." The local headmen asked Stein if he could help them "effect an accurate levelling of line to spare needless excavations" and to "get help for a correct alignment of the canal." Stein responded by sending his Indian surveyor Lal Singh out to "do the needful levelling by the 'durbin' (i.e., clinometer)," asking only for "an annual present of walnuts to be duly despatched to Kashmir when the trees of the new colony *in spe* will have begun to bear fruit!" Two months later, the Muslim headman of Uch-Turfan openly lamented to Stein that in Xinjiang "there were no rulers like Firangs who would bring water through the mountain from the Tushkan R." Stein wondered, not without justification, if this lament was due to "an echo of stories about the Swat canal spread by Hajis who have recently passed through Peshawar?"[9]

Regardless of the source of this high regard for Stein's expertise, the locals were united in their belief of its efficacy. On his third expedition, Stein accompanied a "whole posse of Sheiks & labourers" about to commence work on a new dike near Charchan. Stein warned the sheikhs that "the river after lake has been formed" was likely to "seek a fresh outlet elsewhere," a hypothesis he later verified by on-site analysis. "My interposition thought particularly timely because the *Kara-su* flow below Mazar has begun," Stein noted in his diary, "& was expected to reach site of *tugh* in 4–5 days when the work would become much more difficult." As thanks for Stein's intercession, "Tokhta Akhun in presence of Sheiks agreed to send me five dry apricots year by year as a tribute on oasis saved." Two decades later, on his fourth expedition, Stein's technical expertise was still a

Figure 16. Gentlemen of Empire. From 1926 to 1943, Stein maintained an intimate correspondence with Pan Zuhuan, the younger son of his longtime friend and career northwest official Pan Zhen (figure 19). As he had done with the elder Pan, Stein bonded with his former patron's son over common political and social interests, not least of which was their shared conviction in the civilizing power of their respective empires. In 1930, Pan Zuhuan would play a decisive role in helping Stein overcome early opposition to his fourth expedition in Xinjiang (see chapter 6). Stein Papers, Bodleian Library, MS 21. Reprinted with the kind permission of the British Academy.

highly valued commodity in Xinjiang. The fact that Chinese intellectuals in Beijing now regarded him as a "thief" meant little to Pan Zuhuan (figure 16), the magistrate of Shule, who proposed accompanying Stein up into the mountains south of Kashgar to investigate Pan's "plan of creating a reservoir for irrigation by damming outflow of Karakul or Bulun-kul." In one of his last acts on Chinese soil, Stein spent an evening "passed over writing full report on Karakul L. dam scheme" for Pan and expressed his wish that

Pan "may see his cherished scheme started before he gives up charge of the district in the near future."[10]

During the late Qing and early Republican eras, foreign archaeologists in Xinjiang were both emblems and purveyors of a Western modernity that was highly coveted by the local ruling classes. This fact alone would have assured them a warm welcome. But there was more. Men like Stein and Pelliot also provided their hosts with an invaluable opportunity to display their imperial authority over their own subjects. In other words, when Western archaeologists were welcomed by Chinese officials into their jurisdiction, they were greeted not only as virtuous scholars and scientists but also as fellow imperial administrators steeped in the ideologies and institutions of colonial rule. In stark contrast to the realms of science and modernity, the Chinese officials in Xinjiang did not suffer from an inferiority complex with regard to their status as imperial officials. Rather, they regarded themselves and their Western guests as fraternal agents of enlightened colonial regimes, ones in which the benevolent representatives of superior civilizations exerted transformative rule over the denizens of inferior civilizations. We might think of this phenomenon as a form of "transimperial bonding" similar to that which David Cannadine has identified in the colonies of the British Empire. It took root through a shared conservative ethos and occupational solidarity before bearing its fullest fruit in the form of military displays and the staging of elaborate banquets.

As William Rowe has shown, most educated Chinese of the late imperial era did not conceive of their society in terms of a finely graded hierarchy defined by multiple economic classes and status groups. Instead, they tended to think of it in far simpler binary terms: rulers vs. ruled. If this was true of the Han heartland, it was even more so of the non-Han frontier. The "rulers" of the inner provinces habitually referred to their subjects (i.e., the "ruled") as "ignorant," "stupid," and in constant need of reform (or, in Confucian parlance, "transformation"). Out in Xinjiang, the Muslim masses were also grouped into such pejorative categories but were further maligned for their complete lack of historical contact with Confucian culture. In 1909, Provincial Commissioner Wang Shu'nan observed that, compared to the interior provinces, "the mixture of Xinjiang's races" and "the vulgarity of their character" meant that "the borderland is hard to transform." The Turkic-speaking Muslims of the southern oases were described as "stubborn" and "ignorant," while the nomadic Kazak and Kyrgyz tribes were regarded as "lawless and wild in the extreme." As a result, any talk of "self-government" for such peoples would have to be delayed until such a time as they could become gradually acculturated to Chinese civilization.

After all, in the estimation of Wang, "the ability to self-govern depends primarily on the degree of civilization."[11]

Without exception, every foreign explorer to pass through Xinjiang would have seconded Wang's opinions, both toward the lower classes of their own countries and toward the subject populations of their own colonies. In 1915, one year after the outbreak of World War I, Stein commended the way in which "the educated classes" of England had "responded splendidly" to the war effort. But he thought it "bitter to read of big crowds idling around football matches and none of those sturdy loafers answering appeals to enlist." If only their womenfolk would shame them "into doing their duty," Stein continued, "those who return from the war will be men of far greater value to the nation and humanity in general." In other words, the lazy and profligate masses of England would be "transformed" by the experience of being led into war by their social betters. Stein gave voice to this deep-seated aversion to the lower classes of Europe in other ways as well. Upon seeing repeated evidence of destructive German excavation methods in the vicinities of Turfan and Kucha, Stein refused to believe that Grünwedel or Le Coq might have been responsible. "One must assume that neither of the two learned men supervised these operations," Stein wrote in 1915. Instead, he unfairly ascribed all blame to their assistant, Bartus, who was disparaged by Stein, on the basis of hearsay alone, as "an old sailor" and "an old N.C.O. of the German Navy." These were meant to be insults. On another occasion, Stein drew attention to the unflattering appearance of Li Yuansun (see figure 11), his much-maligned Chinese secretary from his third expedition, by describing his clothing in class-based terms. "The enclosed photo shows you on left the Amban of Maralbashi with regulation felt hat," Stein wrote to Allen. "Next my hapless Ssu-yeh dressed in black like a coal-heaver."[12]

Such prejudices followed Stein wherever he traveled. In 1907, he made a careful distinction between the refined upper classes of China and their unrefined subjects, regardless of race or religion. "The Chinese are pleasant enough people whenever one can make use of their education," Stein explained. "But with the common & garden folk one needs a good deal of patience." Once, while despairing over the reluctance of his "dirty & unkempt" pony men to do his bidding in the mountains of Gansu, Stein imagined an "amusing parallel" in which "some worthy slum-dwellers from the East End" of London would be transported for "service on the Afghan border." In searching his lexicon for an appropriate word with which to praise his Turki postal courier, Stein decided to credit his "canine devotion & calmness whether distance before him 1000 or 100 miles." Pelliot also thought little of the lower-class Muslims of Xinjiang. After foiling an attempt by one Turki man to sell him an artifact at fifty times its estimated value, Pelliot revealed his utter contempt for the entire race. "All the same, these Turks," he wrote. "Treat them with care, and immediately they abuse it; if you show the teeth a little, they go to bed. Unable to behave by themselves, they need masters; they are born serfs." On another occasion, Pelliot was dismayed to find that his generous offer of a higher daily wage for his laborers was met not with gratitude, but with increased demands for even higher wages. "I have increased the wages by a third for all my men today," he noted in his diary, "and the result was that, expecting nothing, they said nothing; but, receiving something, they thought they deserved more, and so claimed; what a vile population! And beasts over the market!"[13]

Faced with such contemptible subjects, Muslim or otherwise, both Chinese officials and Western archaeologists believed that efforts to "transform" them must proceed at a snail's pace, thereby ensuring the continued dominion of rulers over ruled. In 1929, Pan Zuhuan, the magistrate of Shule County and son of Stein's longtime mandarin friend Pan Zhen, wrote to Stein about the stubborn intractability of his Muslim subjects. "The mohammedism in this country, as you know very well," Pan explained in halting English, "prevents the local people having any progress; their lives are nearly as the primitives. It is a hard task of working among them." Pan ended his letter with a rhetorical question, to which he provided his own answer. "How do you think, if it is possible to make the people of 9th or 10th century following the civilization of the 20th century at once? On account of the great differences of custom, language, and religion between Chinese and Mussulmans the latter certainly do not like us, but their weakness of mind makes them still to be governed by the former."[14]

Stein was in complete agreement. "All you say about the differences between the actual conditions of the Turki population and the modern civilization which apparently it is intended to make them benefit by," he replied, "is perfectly true. I feel sure that all Chinese administrators who have inherited the historical sense of their own great civilization must appreciate the time which the desired changes will take." Stein, of course, was speaking from his own experiences as a British colonial administrator in the Raj. Like his fellow Western archaeologists, Stein identified—and was identified—as a member of the ruling class, whether in India or elsewhere. In 1907, Stein was invited by the magistrate of Jiayuguan in Gansu to join him in watching a street theatrical performance from a privileged vantage point. "Ambulant audience on road, elite on terrace of temple," he noted in his diary. The following year, Stein reacted to news about "Bengal sedition" in India with the conclusion that "there is evidently plenty of trouble in store for ruled & rulers alike." Once during a visit with Yang Jinbang, the garrison commander of Hami, Stein listened closely as his host told him "official version of attack" by rebels on a nearby fortification. Apparently seeing in Stein the mirror image of a fellow ruler, Yang "describes his narrow escape from bullet which grazed his hat. . . . Hat produced in evidence." Such troubles between ruler and ruled, he was convinced, stemmed from ill-informed attempts by liberal statesmen to transform the poor benighted masses too quickly. Often referring to the "poisonous by-products of 'modern education'" among non-Western peoples, Stein, much like his Chinese counterparts, was convinced that the natives were not ready to rule themselves. In 1930, in a letter to his good friend Carl Keller in Boston, Stein concluded that "the problem of saving poor old India from the defects of its own inherited mentality is difficult enough." Unfortunately, he continued, in a striking echo of Pan Zuhuan's comments to Stein in a letter the previous year about the futility of attempting to transform "primitive" Muslims in Xinjiang, "it has been complicated by the well-meant but intrinsically futile attempt to foist western democratic institutions upon a society still as far as the masses go in a prehistoric stage of evolution."[15]

Stein's emphasis was on the masses of India, not its educated native elites, among whom he counted many close friends and colleagues. But between these two classes of rulers and ruled, most of the rulers agreed: an unbridgeable gulf stood betwixt them. During his time in Xinjiang, the German archaeologist Albert von Le Coq was much dismayed to see the native servants of Western travelers adopting Western dress, for it blurred the boundaries between master and subject. "It is greatly to be desired, in the interests of all Europeans travelling in these districts," Le Coq later wrote, "that Indian or other Asiatic servants should wear clothing that plainly distinguishes them from the European travellers, so that these awkward misunderstandings may not occur." Though the natives may one day earn the right to be considered civilized and wear such clothing, that day was far, far in the future. Several decades later, Stein responded to the rise of Gandhi in India by suggesting to Keller an experiment designed to demonstrate "India's incapacity of ruling itself at this stage—or any other." In short, the Raj should "let every European official go on six months' leave at the same time," Stein wrote. "Before that time were up the mass of Indian people would clamour for their quick return to India." As for Gandhi himself, Keller regarded him "as a complete ass" and assured Stein that Gandhi did not make "much of a hit in this country. I believe he is regarded as sort of feeble-minded." Stein was much gratified. "What you write about

Gandhi & the movement for which he is used as the tool, is only too true,"
he replied. In another letter, Stein concluded that "the economic assets of
England in India are too great to be sacrificed to Hindu incapacity for self-
government."[16]

This was the shared conservative ethos of empire on which Western
archaeologists found common ideological and occupational ground with
their Chinese hosts. As transimperial members of an exclusive club of "rulers," both in a colonial and noncolonial context, the educated Chinese and
Western elites believed that they—and they alone—could bring enlightened
and rational rule to the uncivilized masses of the world. It should not surprise us then to find the comparison of different colonial regimes to be a
frequent topic of discussion. "The New Dominions," Stein wrote to Allen
in March 1907, employing the English translation of Xinjiang, "are a sort
of India for Chinese officials, where everybody knows everybody else—or
his friends & antecedents at least." Two weeks later, Stein expressed the
same sentiment to the magistrate of Dunhuang. "Explain to Wang resem-
blance of Indian and Hsin-ch'ang administration," Stein wrote in his diary.
Six months later, Stein noted "talk of Tun-huang & India" at an official
banquet in Ganzhou. The next year at Guma, Stein recorded "talk of distant
homes [that] united us exiles from far east & west & the thought of the past
when the men of the Hans had met here Indian monks & Persian traders."
For Stein and other Western explorers, the imperial Chinese elites were just
as civilized as they were, and their common dominion over inferior peoples
was evidence of that superiority. After a banquet at Aksu in 1908, Stein confessed that he now began to "suspect faintly the assimilating power of Chinese culture!" The Yale climatologist Ellsworth Huntington went even further, declaring the Chinese "the cleverest and most highly civilized people
in Asia and the most like us."[17]

A conservative ideology of empire provided fertile ground for the development of a transimperial bond between Chinese host and Western
guest. This bond was further strengthened through the repeated display
and discussion of the administrative insignia and duties of their respective ranks. In fact, many of the foreign archaeologists were issued grossly
inflated titles by their home governments so as to ensure favorable treatment on their expeditions. This fact has led one Chinese scholar to suggest that men like Stein were able to "intimidate" and "cow" local officials
into bending to their every whim. This, however, was standard practice in
any context where formal audiences with officials of another state could
be expected. In 1865, when the Qing court decided to send its first official delegation to Europe, both the leader of the delegation and its admin-

istrative functionaries were given elevated titles and ranks, so as to "make them more impressive." The inflated titles of these Qing emissaries did not, however, grant them any advantages in subsequent diplomatic negotiations. They merely allowed them to be treated as equal members of a fraternal ruling class of officials.[18]

In Xinjiang, there is little doubt that the inflated diplomatic titles of Western archaeologists made a big impression on the local officials. In 1905, Huntington, a Yale professor, noted that the inclusion of "a small commission from the Department of Agriculture" on his passport made it "seem to these people" that he and his colleague Daniel Barrett were "high American officials." Two years later, Stein, who by then had begun to travel under the grandiose title of "Great Superintendent for Education in India in the Great British Empire" (Da Yingguo zongli Yindu jiaoyu dachen)—he was actually Registrar of Punjab University and Principal of the Oriental College in Lahore—was warned by his Chinese secretary "that having no fine uniform, etc., I shall not look sufficiently the big personage I am officially assumed to be! Well, we should have to invent some polite excuse for having left all that finery (which does not exist & which I could not even usurp) 'at my Indian Yamen.'" As usual, Pelliot took jealous note of the grand reception Stein's titles brought him. "Stein has been received here with great honors," Pelliot wrote in Gansu. "By order of the governor of Lan-tcheou, the civil and military authorities (including the tao t'ai) went to meet him in full costume, and at his departure, the tcheou kouan escorted him for two days in the mountains." Regardless of their diplomatic rank, all Western archaeologists were treated by the Chinese officials as fraternal colleagues of empire. In 1906, during a visit to the magistrate's yamen in Yarkand, Gustav Mannerheim, a Finnish member of Pelliot's party, observed that "the ordinary entrance is from the side behind this platform, but for persons of rank and foreigners the back wall is opened."[19]

Inflated or not, these titles, along with the administrative careers they represented, resonated in meaningful ways with those Chinese officials tasked with hosting foreigner explorers. At the most basic level, they were emblems of a shared professional identity, one the Chinese were just as eager to flaunt as were the foreigners. In Khotan, Mannerheim noted how the local military officer allowed himself to be photographed "sitting in a tent with the insignia of his rank on a table by his side." During an audience with Chen Wengan, the subprefect of Dunhuang, Pelliot took note of his host's "crystal button and no peacock feather," but then further learned that Chen had been "awarded thirty-two inscriptions for merit." For most Chinese officials, however, the preferred method of revealing their exalted official status was to talk about the number of times they had been received by the emperor in Beijing. During an audience with Yao Wenlin, a magistrate near Aksu, Pelliot learned that his host had been "received twice in imperial audience, and on this subject has made quite lengthy stays in Pekin." The Muslim prince of Hami, Shah Maqsut, never failed to regale his foreign guests with stories of his audiences in Beijing. "He went to Pekin four times," Pelliot learned in 1908, "and a *shou* ['long life'] inscription from the empress' hand adorns his palace." Stein, too, heard all about these prestigious trips by the prince, who "chatt[ed] freely of his visit to Peking, his Haji subjects." That the Western archaeologists paid careful attention to such fine distinctions of rank is evident in the reaction of Alan Priest, a member of Langdon Warner's second expedition to Duhuang in 1925, on learning that one of his hosts was not as exalted as previously thought. "We are disgusted to learn that the personage we called upon yesterday morning is not the Dalai Llama at all but only the Panshan . . . Llama who is second in importance and comes from Western Thibet," Priest wrote. "He was just as much fun but one doesn't like to call on the pope and find he has been taken in by a mere cardinal."[20]

In sum, both sides thought it was important to ascertain whether or not they were interacting with social and political equals by discussing and displaying the emblems of their rank. Once the elite status of both parties was confirmed, neither wished to see the other diminished in any way. In fact, they wished for the opposite. Stein's many interactions with Chinese officials are notable for how often each party expressed a wish for the imminent promotion of the other, while sympathizing with any news of a demotion. In 1908, during an audience with Pan Zhen in Aksu, Stein "told P.[an] of my wish to see him installed at Urumchi." That same year, Xie Weixing, the magistrate of Khotan, signed off on a letter to Stein "with respect and wishes for your promotion." Zhu Ruichi, the prefect of Guma, expressed the same wish in somewhat more flowery language (see figure 2). "At the moment, I can imagine that you are returning to your home country in a carriage pulled by piebald horses to have an audience with your king, who will grant you untold awards and infinite honors," Zhu wrote. "I would like to congratulate you in advance on your imminent promotion." When Stein saw Pan Zhen again in Urumchi in 1914, he reminded Pan "of my wish at Aksu to see him as Fu-tai [*futai*, governor] and hope to see it yet realized."[21]

When any member of this exclusive group of rulers suffered a professional setback, his colleagues immediately circled the wagons. In 1907, when the magistrate of Dunhuang was demoted on account of a local uprising, Stein found that "official feelings here are not regret at lives lost, but sympathy with Wang for the check in his career." Stein, too, made a point of consoling the cashiered magistrate. "Delayed further by call of sympathy on Wang-Daloi," Stein wrote three months later, "who has been summoned to give account of Tun-huang rising." In his diary, Stein seemed to identify with Wang's travails. "Struck by his worn look. Rioters had destroyed his Yamen & all his belongings." In Aksu the following year, Stein called on the disgraced garrison commander Tang Yongshan, who "seems to appreciate doubly attention paid to one in disfavour." Tang, sensing the presence of a fellow imperial colleague, then made "allusions to cabal which led to his suspension," before asking Stein "whether gov[ernmen]t. with us, too, relies on secret informers for watching of its officers." In Urumchi, Pelliot commiserated with the exiled official Pei Jingfu, who "tells me that he received a telegram a few days ago announcing that examination of his case will resume at Kouang tong [Guangdong], in a spirit that will probably allow him to return in good grace in a few months."[22]

The Chinese officials and Western archaeologists in Xinjiang and Gansu shared a conservative imperialist ethos, an obsession with diplomatic rank, and an acute sense of occupational solidarity. It should not surprise us, then, to find that these same Chinese officials viewed their recently "promoted" Western counterparts as uniquely positioned to help facilitate their own rise within the Chinese bureaucracy. At a remote town in the vicinity of Kashgar, Pelliot found that Wang Yingqi, the local garrison commander, "obviously wants me to recommend him to tao-t'ai of Kashgar," a none-too-subtle hint that Wang personally delivered to Pelliot's Chinese servant. After another official learned that Pelliot "got along very well with Yin-hi," his superior, he "had a snack prepared for the time of our coming and invited his colleague." At a tiny oasis near Aksu, an aspiring Chinese clerk brought "a poem to my address, to which he appends a verbal request to recommend him to the governor of Ouroumtsi. I can easily imagine that he must not be overly pleased in this hole, where there are in all 15 to 20 houses." When Pelliot finally reached Urumchi, he met with all the top officials and literati. "Finally I take leave of Mr. P'ei and Kouei Yu," Pelliot wrote on December 24, 1907. "Kouei Yu is an excellent man who offers us a small snack; he would like another post and asked me to say a word for him, which I already did yesterday through Kouo P'ong the intermediary."[23]

The greater the Western personage, the greater his influence. For each career Pelliot promoted, Stein promoted two or three more. In 1906, the district magistrate of Charklik, Liu Mo, convinced Stein to allow his Chinese secretary "to add to my letter to Pan-Darin some eulogies of his colonization work at Vash-shahr." It seems that Pan Zhen, by then the circuit

intendant of Aksu, had made it known far and wide among Xinjiang officialdom that Stein occupied a special place in his heart. Toward the end of
his second expedition, Stein rejoiced at the acquaintance of Khotan district
magistrate Xie Weixing. In him Stein saw "with pleasure" the mirror image
of a model official of the Raj, imagining Xie as an "energetic D.[istrict]
C.[ollector] eager for chance enlightenment." Stein then told Xie "how glad
I should be to let Pan know of so efficient a successor." On his third expedition, Stein used the return visit of the military commandant of Charklik as
an opportunity to "tell Tsai of Vash-shahri Beg's energetic action." In one
instance, Stein noted that a local magistrate in Gansu, after learning of Garrison Commander Chai Hongshan's deep regard for Stein, "feels evid.[ently]
advantage of showing himself ready to help." A Muslim military officer
near Korla paid a visit to Stein in order "to make friends—& secure recommendation." Meanwhile, the Muslim magistrate of Kara-kum complained
to Stein about the Chinese administration and expressed his "wish to work
where European control is at hand. He recalled his help about Abdur Rahim
& evid.[ently] wished to be recommended to Mac.[artney], a well-earned
service." On one occasion, Stein went so far as to dangle the prospect of his
own recommendation to an official in exchange for assistance in the pursuit of his recalcitrant pony men and deserting servant. "Found out soon
that the commandant was out of favour with Ti-tai, having failed to present
himself when Bai took office," Stein noted in his diary. "Emphasized Tsui's
[Chai Hongshan's] friendship & dropped hint as to my event.[ual] recommendation which would help to make my host again persona grata."[24]

If we had any evidence of Chinese indifference and hostility toward, or
obstruction of, foreign explorers during this time period, then we could take
more seriously the claim that Stein was abusing his power and twisting the
arms of his Chinese hosts into doing his bidding against their will. In the
near total absence of such evidence, however, we must accept these interactions for what they appear to have been at the time: the voluntary exchange
of political favors designed to promote and further the careers of fraternal
colleagues of empire. Far from being intimidated or cowed by Stein's exalted
rank, it appears that the local officials of northwestern China actually embraced the opportunities it afforded them to buttress their own status and
position. Nowhere is this realization more clear than in the various wel-
coming rituals faithfully carried out by Chinese officials immediately on
the arrival of the foreign explorer: military displays and banquets.

Whether the foreigner wanted it or not—and he usually did not—
Chinese officials frequently prepared an elaborate military reception and
farewell for their guest. Upon his arrival at Khotan in 1906, Stein was

greeted "with whole military drawn up on road. Fanfares." The following year at a small outpost near Ganzhou in Gansu, Stein noted that he was "received with popguns & bagpipes & drums played outside Yamen." The next month at Jinta, "30–40 quaint soldiers, in black uniforms with red matchlocks, make pretence at presenting arms." Upon his return to Xinjiang, Stein "had a solemn send-off by 'garrison' (some 30 'men,' incl. little boys, etc., under Ma-Ta-jen)." Once, he failed to anticipate a farewell parade and was mortified to find his wardrobe inadequate for the occasion. "Had to face a full-parade send-off, outside N suburb, in plain clothes!" Mannerheim also experienced the formal grandeur of such occasions. In Khotan, magistrate Peng Xuzhan "escorted us to our carriage with great courtesy and a salute of three guns was fired as we stepped on to the platform of boards." In Jinta, Mannerheim "called on the highest military mandarin of the place" and was received with "a salute of 3 shots" while "some musicians in a pavilion played some extraordinary Chinese music." Huntington, too, recounted for his family the novel experience of a military reception: "As I came through the mock entrance guns were fired." Even unrelated requests by the foreigners were seized on as a pretext to bring out the soldiers. When Huntington's travel companion Daniel Barrett "said that he would like to see a soldier to examine his equipment," it was "interpreted as meaning a lot of soldiers and a procession in our honor." Similarly, Mannerheim's request to photograph a military officer in Khotan led to the mobilization of "a drill in my honour for which he dressed up in full array." Not only that, but "the entire garrison, 3 officers and 104 men, stood in the square in front of the old man's tent with rifles (muzzle-loaders) and fixed bayonets. It was a sight fit for the gods."[25]

On his third expedition in 1913, Stein found (much to his relief) that the troubles of the revolution and other crises of the past two years had diminished the enthusiasm of local officials for such ostentatious military displays. In Aksu, toward the end of his expedition in 1915, Stein described a "grand reception by Mo Tajen at N. end of suburb; conducted in state to quarters; military guard, etc." as "a novel experience on this journey." That was fine by him. The year before, outside Ganzhou, Stein reflected on the "pompous reception of 1907 & was glad to escape it." Huntington, too, regarded such military receptions as "fearfully formal." On one occasion, Stein even referred to the "preposterous preparations for my reception." By the time he reached Aksu in 1915, however, Circuit Intendant Zhu Ruichi ensured that Stein would not escape his oasis without a revival of the old ways. Before he could leave, Stein was "escorted by Begs, four Muham[maden] pings [bing, 'soldiers'] in Europe uniforms & an Afghan

posse comitati." The exasperated Stein was then paraded in a "solemn progress through city with popguns, etc. to proclaim et urbi." By the time it
was over, Stein was exhausted: "Ceremonious leave brought relief."[26]

There are several important lessons to take away from these descriptions of military receptions. First, they were totally unnecessary. No treaty
obliged the Chinese officials to make a grand display of weaponry and soldiers on the reception of a foreign scholar. Officially, Stein was a "Great
Superintendent for Education" and Huntington was a representative of the
US Department of Agriculture. They were not generals. That such displays
were superfluous can be seen in the repeated surprise of Huntington and
Mannerheim—and increasing exasperation of Stein—at being treated so
grandly. Second, the foreigners usually were not impressed with what they
saw. If the goal had been to frighten or intimidate the foreigner, then the
Chinese consistently failed to do so. Third, these displays were often incon-
venient and taxing for the foreigner, who tended to be embarrassed by such
attentions. It is clear that Stein did not enjoy them, nor did he relish the
role he was expected to play in them. Finally, they were a spectacle in and
of themselves. Shrieking music, loud popguns, armed escorts, colorful uniforms, formal salutes, staged training exercises, and solemn parades through
the streets—all of these ostentatious manifestations of Chinese authority
were meant to be heard or seen by everyone within earshot or eyesight. In
other words, military displays were undertaken for the benefit of the Chinese host, not the foreign guest. As men like Stein quickly discovered, the
foreign explorer was little more than a shiny prop in an elaborate ritual performed by opportunistic officials intent on displaying their power not over
the foreign archaeologist, but over their own subjects. And the greater the
guest, the greater the pretext for a grand display.

If this was the case with shows of military force, it was even more so
with shows of culinary force. In fact, the reactions of foreign archaeologists
to the endless round of official banquets that they were obliged to attend
make for some of the most entertaining of all source material for this chapter. Clarmont Skrine, the British consul in Kashgar from 1922 to 1924, has
left us with one of the more blunt assessments of these oft-maligned feasts.
"The Chinese in their entertaining consider the convenience of their guests
less than any other consideration," Skrine wrote in a letter to his family in
1923, "and they have a perfect genius for giving parties at the wrong time."
On one occasion Skrine complained about having "wasted 4 of the middle
hours of Saturday having an enormous meal at the Dao Tai's Yamen, (I had
seen the old man 3 times during the preceding week & there was no need
whatever for this infliction)." Just one year after assuming his post, Skrine

was fed up. "Again, with the Chinese hospitality is not real—it is all forced & formal. It is their 'face' that counts, not your convenience, their chah-jings, farewell feasts etc. are all calculated to give a maximum of inconvenience to the incoming or outgoing guest, but they whiten the face of the Chink which is all they care about."[27]

Although Skrine's choice of words is not to our liking today, his basic assessment of the political and social functions of official Chinese banquets finds considerable resonance in the accounts of foreign explorers. In 1900, during his first expedition, Stein reported to Allen that "I have had so far every attention shown to me by the Chinese officials who are very pleasant people to meet—except when they ask one to dinner." In 1905, Huntington observed that "dinner was something of an ordeal, but I waded through the thirty courses quite successfully." The next year, Stein informed his friend Fred Andrews that the local magistrate "helps & honours your humble servant in every way, e.g. by a grand feast for which all Begs of Khotan came & which was a long—and trying affair." By this time, however, Stein had begun to take pride in his ability to weather a Chinese feast. "I was treated to a great luncheon party by the side of the Tao-tai's lotus ponds," he wrote from Kashgar in 1906, "and may take it as a proof of renewed strength that I could look back upon the treat without the slightest regret." In the next oasis over, Yarkand magistrate Peng Xuzhan treated Stein to a "prolonged but digestible feast." Though time may have improved Stein's palate, it did not free him of the obligation to clean his plate—over and over again. "Return oppressed by food after two weeks' careful dieting," he complained from Keriya on his fourth expedition in 1931.[28]

Why was Chinese fare so roundly dreaded by foreign explorers? In short, the guests were many, the hours were long, the occasions were endless, and the food was composed of indigestible delicacies. Indeed, the expensive Chinese delicacies with which the foreigners were mercilessly regaled—sea snails, shark's fins, fish entrails, sheep's stomach, pigeon's eggs, fried sheep fat, and, as Skrine once put it, "an extraordinary water-weed sort of plant which looked like what one sees in sewage channels"—were each calculated to impress the host's guests with his culinary art and deep pockets, not with the pleasure of consumption. When Mannerheim partook of a meal at the Russian consulate in Kashgar, he judged the vastly inferior fare acceptable in exchange for the gain in time. "At present we certainly eat worse, but it costs us less time." Mannerheim, after noting that Chinese "dishes are served up with good taste and are more remarkable for their artistic appearance than for their flavour," went on to observe that "many of the dishes seem repulsive," with the "same flavour of steam and fat."

In the deserts of Xinjiang, seafood from the distant coast was particularly pricey—and thus particularly prestigious. After a small repast in Dunhuang in 1907, Stein learned that "the few far-fetched dishes cost 10 Sers!" One month later at Suzhou, Stein "sat feasting for nearly four hours on delicacies which I should vainly attempt to analyze or remember." In 1913, Stein was shocked to find the same rare treats at the poor and remote outpost of Charchan. "Return for their dinner at 3 P.M. Long feast with luxuries unlooked for in Charchan." Two decades later, nothing had changed. "Then wait for Huo Hsienkuan's dinner," he wrote from Guma in 1930. "Reach Yamen by 10 A.M. but no notice had been taken of my request for an early & modest meal."[29]

The reason Stein's request was ignored was because, as Skrine observed, these dinners were more about the needs of the Chinese officials than they were about the needs of the foreign explorer. According to the British intelligence agent Reginald Schomberg, "the visitor, or victim, is the last person considered." At Barikol in 1914, Stein, suffering from intense pains in his face, "remained in bed till 11 A.M. and hoped to escape Chen-tai's dinner." Unfortunately, the garrison commander's "distressed appeal forced me to go out to feast by 3 P.M. bandaged and with swollen face." Bandaged or not, Stein's coveted presence lent an essential air of transimperial authority to such occasions. Without the exalted gentleman of another great empire, a Chinese official posted to the impoverished desert frontier would lose a rare opportunity to display his wealth, taste, and patronage over his own subordinates—both Muslim and Chinese. In his description of the 1906 banquet at Khotan quoted previously, Stein noted the presence "of all Begs of Khotan." On his first trip to Urumchi in 1914, Stein found "among guests both P'an (in big medieval fur cap) and Pen (of Yarkand and Uch-Turfan). . . . Also Chiang, the Wai-chuan-chu and Li, a learned Private Secry. of Tou-tou." Feted at Aksu the next year, Stein was joined by "two Hsiens, the Tung-lung, Yue-yuan and one other official besides Li & myself."[30]

If it sometimes seemed like the whole of local officialdom turned out to partake of such feasts, it is because they often did. "By 6 P.M. to grand dinner at Tao-tai's," Stein noted on his fourth expedition. "Military honours with pop guns & fanfares. Whole of local officialdom gathered at long table in hall formed by combining Pan Ta-jen's old office with an adjoining room. International display of flags." Five months later at Kashgar, Stein attended the "Tao-tai's dinner party, a huge feast on quite western lines. Whole official world present incl.[uding] Chang. Endless succession of dishes keeps us till 11 P.M." The list of invitations appears to have been determined solely by whomsoever the magistrate wanted to impress. On one occasion, Stein noted that "convives include his children's mentor, the Customs Amban & a couple of Ssuyehs." On another, "other convives follow (Postmaster, Customs man, Wireless super[intendan]t, Tao & Tao-tai's secretaries; Pan Tsi-lu & . . . Chang." The magistrate so often crowded the dining table beyond capacity with carefully chosen guests that Stein could scarcely believe his luck when he once found himself alone with his favorite host. "Welcomed in cool large Yamen," Stein wrote in 1908 from Aksu, where Pan Zhen then held the post of circuit intendant. "Delighted to find that we two were the only guests. Happy hours by the side of my old scholar friend."[31]

This touching exception simply proves the rule: except in cases of extraordinary friendship, a Chinese official would not waste on a single individual such a valuable opportunity to display his wealth and power, regardless of the comfort of his foreign guest. When it came time to dine, the foreign guest was but a prop on the yamen stage, with the Chinese official cast in the starring role. In this as in so many other ways, foreign archaeological expeditions in northwestern China were not just about archaeology. For the local Chinese officials posted to the distant and isolated frontier, they were a rare and unexpected source of valuable political capital.

ACCUMULATING SOCIAL CAPITAL

In addition to political capital, Chinese officials also extracted precious social capital from their foreign guests. As the Chinese translator of Stein's *Preliminary Report* observed in 1901, Western archaeologists were scientific celebrities on camelback, doing things that no other man had ever done before. To know one was to brag about knowing one. In 1925, Wang Min, the son of the recently deceased magistrate Wang Xujun, revealed the ways in which his father's acquaintance with Stein provided him with an endless source of conversational fodder. "Whenever I think of my late father," Wang wrote in a letter to Stein, "I recall how every time he chatted with his friends, he would suddenly change the topic to talk about your broad learning and thorough understanding of Eurasia, and he would narrate your travels in Xinjiang." Pan Zuhuan, the son of Pan Zhen, also noted the extent to which his father regularly talked about Stein. "In 1907 at my age of 14 I was with my father, who had been the Tao-tai of Aksu then," Pan wrote in 1930, in English. "It keeps in my mind still that you were passing there some time in that year, and interviewing my father in a corner-house near the garden of the Taotai Yamen had a very friendly talk. I looked [at] you through the window glass and thought that it would be a great pleasure if I could talk with you in English directly, as my father told me so often about you."[32]

Figure 17. An Overnight Friendship. When Stein reached the quiet town of Barikol on
October 3, 1914, he could not have anticipated how quickly a friendship would develop
between himself and the local magistrate, Li Shurong. Li, "a lively & truly scholarly
man," called on Stein seven times over the course of six days and gave Stein this portrait
of himself before his departure. "Across multiple meetings over several days," Li later
wrote in his letter to Stein, "I was able to see that you are a man of outstanding character
and broad mind, unsurpassed in elegance and refinement. . . . You, Mr. Stein, do not shirk
from any danger or obstacle in scouring grottoes or collecting wooden slips. In pursuit of
these things, you practice archaeology with a stunning perseverance and thoroughness
that is unheard of." Stein Papers, Bodleian Library, MS 341–42. Reprinted with the kind
permission of the British Academy.

The reason why Stein was such a hot topic of conversation was because
he was believed to have done things no mere mortal could have done. Wang
Min recounted how his father "singled out for particular praise your steadfast determination to succeed despite untold sufferings unimaginable to
others. Truly, these were things that no one else could measure up to."
Barikol magistrate Li Shurong (figure 17) also thought Stein was without
peer. "You, Mr. Stein, do not shirk from any danger or obstacle in scouring
grottoes or collecting wooden slips," Li wrote in 1914. "In pursuit of these
things, you practice archaeology with a stunning perseverance and thoroughness that is unheard of." In 1908, Zhu Ruichi, the prefect of Guma,
confessed to a feeling of "grief" and "deep sorrow" (see figures 1 and 2) on
hearing that Stein had "encountered snowcapped mountain peaks and a bit-

ter cold air that pierced through to the bone and rendered all clothing immaterial." Upon further reflection, however, "my thoughts turned to admiration. What I mourn is the thought of the hardships you must endure while
scaling mountains and fording bodies of water, and of the difficult straits
in which you continually place yourself. What I admire, however, is your
stern fortitude and valiant resolve." The Qing officials of Xinjiang described
Stein's exploits by deploying the same literary conventions that Confucian
elites had long used to describe the travels of famous poets, scholars, and
officials in Chinese history. "Everywhere you set your foot, dear Sir," Zhu
wrote, "becomes famous, from the luster you confer on the sands of the
Gobi to the distinction you confer on the peaks of the Kunlun."[33]

But it wasn't merely the educated elites of Xinjiang who regaled their
colleagues with stories of Stein's feats. The Turkic-speaking Muslim inhabitants of Xinjiang also regarded him as someone worth talking about. During
his three-year stint as British consul at Kashgar in the early 1920s, Skrine
learned that "the name of Stein is well remembered in these parts." During
his travels through the southern oases, Skrine "heard many stories about
the great explorer; how in the dreaded Qaranghu Tagh or 'Dark Mountains'
south of Khotan he bridged an abyss with wire and thus pulled himself and
his party across; how in the same mountains he was laid up with frost-bite
and would have perished if help had not been obtained from the Leh road,
and so on." In 1923, Skrine hired Ibrahim Beg, one of Stein's former guides,
to lead him on the caravan trail. When Stein learned of Ibrahim's exemplary
service to Skrine, he wrote to Ibrahim to express his thanks and included a
picture of himself. Unbeknownst to Stein, both his letter and portrait served
as a valuable form of social capital for his old guide. "Sir A. Stein sent a
letter to me," Ibrahim informed Skrine the following year, "which I read out
to all my friends here." When the Chinese archaeologist Huang Wenbi re-
traced parts of Stein's route a few years later, he found that the locals could
still recall with stunning precision sites and people associated with him:
where he ate, where he slept, where he excavated, which paths he took,
whom he hired as guides, etc. Nor was Stein the only Western explorer to
make such an impression. Though the British traveler Henry Deasy passed
through Xinjiang as early as 1897, three years before Stein's first expedition, the "stable in which his ponies were kept" was still "pointed out with
pride" to Skrine. Another man, in an attempt to claim the aura of foreign celebrity for himself, "told me with pride that it was his father, Rahim Khalfa,
who really helped Deasy to cross the mountains."[34]

These examples of social capital all derived from direct participation in
or knowledge of the activities of a Western archaeological expedition. Other

forms of social capital were far more superficial, dependent on little more than the mere fact of the foreigner's celebrity rather than the achievements that had facilitated such celebrity in the first place. Nevertheless, this too was a lucrative form of social capital. In 1907, the garrison commander of Barikol departed from strict rules of etiquette and insisted that Mannerheim inspect the face of his wife, who, along with her sister, "came pattering in on their tiny feet" for inspection, "just like a couple of horses that their owner was proud of." It was only after Mannerheim offered a few words of praise that the garrison commander revealed the true purpose of this disconcerting display, and "enquired whether I thought that he or the Chent'ai T'ang at Aqsu had the lovelier wife." Apparently, the favorable appraisal of a Western archaeologist was a highly valued commodity. When Stein passed through Hami the same year, the Muslim prince (*wang*) showed him a previous traveler's book "with account of visit to Wang who expected more glowing records."[35]

In the event that the foreign explorer could read and write Chinese, the substantive form of such "glowing records" expanded accordingly. In 1906, a Chinese secretary in the yamen at Maralbashi shared with Pelliot a book that "he composed on the relations between the universe and man" and for which "he would like to have a note written by me; he would add my portrait, and this book would secure his fortune, etc." Pelliot, after learning that the man had been waiting patiently for days to see him, "dispatched him by promising to examine his work when I had more leisure time and to send it back with my annotation in a few days." One month later, another man insisted on taking Pelliot back to his house, "where he showed me a poem he had composed" and hoped that the Frenchman would second the opinion of the local magistrate, who "negligently wrote at the end of the piece [hao-che], 'good poetry.'" Pelliot reluctantly obliged. Sometimes even the foreign explorer himself was the subject of the poem. "As I was writing these lines, I was interrupted by another call from the same young man," Mannerheim wrote from Jinta in 1907. "He brought me a poem he had written in my honour—a curious form of politeness to a stranger." When he reached the provincial capital of Urumchi, Pelliot made a similarly positive impression on the Manchu governor Liankui. "He is an intelligent and sophisticated man [*jingming lianda*]," Liankui wrote to the French ambassador in Beijing. "Truly, he is a profound scholar with a passion for antiquity."[36]

For some, neither the passage of time nor shifts in politics could dull the luster of the archaeologist's appraisal. In 1930, Zhang Xinhai, a councillor in the Ministry of Foreign Affairs, invited Stein into his home. "Mrs. Chang presents her nice little daughter of 2 1/2 years and chubby Chang Ping-chung, the 5 months old boy," Stein noted. "Asked to write first entry in his scarlet biographical volume." A decade later, some people in China still valued the social capital represented by an association with Stein enough to disregard his newfound reputation as a "thief." As late as 1939, Aitchen Wu (Wu Aichen), a former Nationalist official in the same ministry, sent Stein a copy of his forthcoming book, *Turkistan Tumult*, and told him that he "would be most grateful if you would be so kind as to write a preface thereto. Nothing would please me more than to obtain just a few words from the one and only authority on the subject—your good self."[37]

In lieu of words, a photograph could serve just as well. On his second expedition, Stein learned that the garrison commander at Hami "keeps an album of his European visitors," while the Muslim prince, Shah Maqsut, asked Pelliot "for my photograph 'because all traveling travelers gave him theirs.'" In Khotan, Stein noted that he was "photoed by Amban's son." Procuring a photograph of a Western archaeologist was regarded as a rare privilege. Pan Zhen told Stein that his portrait helped to bridge the thousands of miles that later separated them. Wang Min referred to Stein's "precious portrait" and how it elicited "feelings of intense adoration and reverence in me." In return, Chinese officials sometimes gave Stein a portrait of themselves. In 1908, Xie Weixing, the magistrate of Khotan, who professed to be "greatly distressed" at Stein's imminent departure and "unable to control my emotions," offered "an everyday photograph of my debased appearance. May you take it back to your country and not feel a sense of loathing and revulsion when you look at it, and may it remind you that of all your admirers in this country, the greatest still holds office in Khotan." In 1914, Li Shurong, the magistrate of Barikol, presented to Stein "my portrait as a token of remembrance and repeat my expressions of deep admiration."[38]

Most Chinese officials, however, did not have a picture of themselves to give. In the first decade of the twentieth century, cameras were large and cumbersome pieces of technology, and it required the expertise of a trained handler to process the plates on site. As a result, most Chinese officials eagerly sought out a photo opportunity with the foreign archaeologist, who brought such rare and expensive technology to their distant desert doorstep. Near Aksu in 1906, Pelliot found that the local magistrate "expressed his desire that we make his photograph in the morning," a request to which Pelliot eagerly acceded as a "means of acquitting ourselves towards him." When the magistrate's servants "boldly approached and asked me to take them in groups also," Pelliot again acquiesced. The next year in Kara-shahr, a Torgut Mongol nobleman asked Pelliot "to take and send him a photograph." The Mongol further demanded that he "paint him a proof, so that one sees his red button, his black tunic, his white dress, and especially that

I erase the case which he has on the right eye." Pelliot did as requested, and the photograph assumed a place of honor in the Mongol's yurt, alongside "some pictures of sanctity." The following year another Mongol prince put on two different costumes for two different portraits. As Pelliot readied to leave, he was "soon overtaken by a Mongol official that the *wang* sent to send us back; I suspect, at once, that the *wang* desires the proofs; in effect, it is demanded, and for this very evening; I can not naturally give any, but promise to send it from Lan-tcheou."[39]

Stein, too, found his photographic skills in high demand. At Dunhuang in 1907, Stein was asked to take a formal portrait of the magistrate's entire family. "His grey-haired mother, a dignified matron, sat for family group." In Barikol in 1914, Stein was "called back" by the garrison commander "to take his portrait, much against my attention, for inguinal muscle shows again signs of strain." In Urumchi, Stein's meeting with the Russian consul was cut short by a "queer irruption of Mongols who want to be photoed!" A decade later, Skrine, too, was imposed on in such fashion by Ma Fuxing, the chief military officer in Kashgar. "Very soon after he arrived he asked me through Harding whether I would take his photo, & then we realized why he had come in uniform alone of the guests; he wanted to be photoed in his joy-rags! I had to take him out on to the terrace and take 3 different photos of him." These portraits were much valued by their recipients. In Khotan in 1906, Stein noted that "photos received with great relish" by the magistrate, Che Yuheng. On his third expedition, the European postmaster at Urumchi reported to Stein that Pan Zhen "seems pleased that you were able to take his photograph before you left and he has been delighted with your visit. Whenever I see him he talks of you and is always greatly interested in your work and movements."[40]

It is clear that these photographs, whether they depicted the foreign archaeologist or his Chinese hosts, were in great demand. It should not surprise us, then, to learn that the reproduction of either in a foreign publication enhanced its value still further. To be merely photographed by the foreign archaeologist was one thing. It was quite another to see that photograph later published in his book. Stein's literary and photographic portraits of Pan Zhen, for instance, became so familiar that Mannerheim recognized him immediately on his arrival in Aksu. "From Macartney and from Stein's book," he wrote in 1907, "I had learnt a good deal about him and would have recognised him by an illustration in the book." These widely disseminated photographs conferred a minor degree of celebrity on the depicted Chinese officials, who eagerly collected the books in which their portraits appeared. In 1926, Pan Zuhuan, the son of the recently deceased Pan Zhen, learned that Stein intended "to edit another set of books in which you will print our photo which was taken by you." He told Stein that he "should appreciate it very much if you would kindly let me know where they may be ordered and what is their cost. I anxiously desire to have them all for remembrance." In response, Stein gave Pan copies of several of his books and pointed out in "the index the references I have made repeatedly to your beloved and honoured father."[41]

As emblems of a special relationship with a celebrity scientist and a tangible reflection of the advanced technology he brought with him, the photograph provided its recipients with a measure of both social and political capital. The same could also be said of guns. One of the more striking features of the diaries of Western archaeologists is just how often they reveal evidence of the discussion, exchange, and discharge of firearms with local military authorities. In July 1907, Pelliot recorded how the khan-wang of the Torgut Mongols "sent for me to show him a Mauser rifle, a Mauser revolver of the box-shaped model, and a Winchester rifle." Fortunately, Pelliot went "with some precautions, because once he opens the Mauser, I see it is loaded." One month later, Pelliot talked shop with Li Chenglin, the military commandant of Kucha, "who knows the names of quite a lot of European rifles, but this is probably the limit of his military science." Stein, too, found time to bond with his military hosts over firearms. "Long visit of Chen-tai who examines arms and takes some shot cartridges," he reported from Barikol in 1914. Stein then returned the call. "Call also on Chen-tai who displays his armoury of repeaters of all sorts sporting guns, etc." Little had changed by the time Stein returned for his fourth expedition. "Return call of Tunglung at former Russian fort, now much dilapidated," he wrote from Tashkurgan. "Queer collection of rifles in his room as mixed as his soldiers among whom Tungans, Chinese from Kansu, Turkis, etc."[42]

On occasion, this form of martial bonding went well beyond the mere inspection of arms. At Aksu in 1907, Garrison Commander Tang Yongshan proposed to Mannerheim "that we should do some target shooting." Much to Mannerheim's dismay, "the general forced me to shoot first, standing in the pavilion, where a crowd of servants had brought tea and various kinds of cakes. My first shot was a hit, my second a miss, the three others hits. The general scored 5 hits." Two days later, Mannerheim returned to photograph Tang and his wives, and the ritual was renewed. After tea, the two men spent "another hour on the shooting range in order to test my rifles, this time with a miss for the Chent'ai and nothing but hits for me." But that was not all. To Mannerheim's surprise, Tang then called out his wives and daughters to the shooting range, so that his foreign guest could "admire the proficiency" of his womenfolk. Their expensive dresses and bound feet proved no hindrance at all. "The couple of dozen shots they fired at a distance of about 180 metres were all hits," Mannerheim wrote, "to the great delight of the Chent'ai."[43]

Western firearms also made for great gifts. In 1928, the Chinese and Swedish members of Sven Hedin's expedition were approached by Tsetsen Puntsag Gegeen, the Incarnate Lama of Karashahr and the regent for the khan-wang of the Torgut Mongols. According to Xu Xusheng, the Chinese co-leader of the expedition, Gegeen "mentioned to Mr. Hedin that he had heard that foreigners have guns with a telescope attached. He wanted to know whether or not we had one." When Hedin took one out of storage for the regent, "he was ecstatic, saying that he wanted one." The next day, two Chinese military officials paid a visit and "presented Mr. Hedin and me with a bearskin." They then announced that Gegeen, after having laid eyes on the vaunted rifle, "was so excited thereafter that he was unable to get a good night's sleep, and that he implored us, no matter what, to either sell it to him or give it to him as a present." Not surprisingly, Hedin, realizing how highly regarded such a gift would be, duly followed suit and parted with the telescoped rifle.[44]

The prestige associated with Western photographs and firearms is wonderfully illustrated by the purchasing habits of Duke Zailan, an exiled Manchu prince in Urumchi. "The Prince is said to have a passion for rifles, cameras and gramophones," Mannerheim reported in July 1907, "of which he has no less than three enormous ones in his house. The main point seemed to be that they should be expensive." To the duke, these three material possessions, all of which were intimately associated with foreigners, represented the pinnacle of good taste. We have already illustrated the allure of cameras and rifles. As for the gramophone, we can more readily reveal the presence of the form of social capital embodied by its possession rather than the gramophone itself: that is to say, entertainment. "The life of a Chinese official is curious," Mannerheim once observed after a visit to the yamen:

> He sees little beyond the clay walls of his yamen. He never ventures outside the door without a crowd of brightly clad servants, mounted and on foot, in a carriage (higher officials in a litter), through the windows and door of which, opening in front, the view is limited. He does not speak the languages of the people and, indeed, does not come in contact with anyone but his thoroughly depraved circle of Begs, interpreters, servants and helpers. The only society he has is that of his wife or wives and occasionally a mandarin on a tour of inspection or passing through, as closely

confined and guarded as himself, pays a visit. And so it goes on, year after year. Never any leave or a pleasure trip or a visit to his native place.[45]

Far out along the impoverished and isolated desert frontier, surrounded by people deemed far inferior to himself, the Chinese official was indeed a lonely soul. And the well-traveled, highly educated, and technologically adorned foreign archaeologist was a most welcome diversion. In 1905, Huntington noted that one magistrate's "invitation to visit Guma was repeated no less than five times, the attractions of the place being set forth at great length." Mannerheim received the exact same invitation. "He begged me to spend some time in Guma on my way back, which I shall certainly avoid doing." After Mannerheim stayed true to his word, he learned from another magistrate of the disappointment of his would-be host. "He expressed his regret that I had chosen another road. He had ordered a room to be heated and prepared for me in his yamen." What sort of entertainment might have been on tap? Elevated conversation on a diverse array of topics, to be sure. But sometimes it was simply a chance to let down one's guard with a rare social equal. "I never saw such a funny sight in my life," wrote the British consul Skrine, attempting to describe a game he played with Chinese officials in Kashgar one night after dinner, "as the fat old Taoyin with his cheeks bursting, puffing away at a feather six inches from his nose, and the Commander-in-Chief of the local forces making frantic efforts to grab it over his shoulder!"[46]

Most of the time, however, the alleviation of boredom was a far less boisterous affair. In one desolate outpost along the southern Taklamakan, Stein felt a twinge of sympathy for the "poor Sieh who looks after Dak service in this dreary place." When Stein attempted to leave the next day along the "cheerless" road, the "poor Siye insist[ed] on keeping me company for a mile. Regret to have no present for him." At Turfan, Stein found that the local magistrate "vainly urges my stay for another day." During a stay in Khotan, Stein "felt rather feverish when Amban's son arrived for long talk—about nothing." On another occasion, Stein "returned in twilight to be caught again by anonymous Chinese visitors, incl.[uding] English-knowing clerk out of employment." Stein attributed such unexpected attentions of well-wishers to the tedium of official life in a remote outpost. "Tashkurghan is a trying place to spend two years in," he wrote in 1906, "and this may account for the warm welcome given to a stray visitor." But one did not have to be an official posted to the desert frontier in order to experience the thrill of novelty associated with the visit of a foreign archaeologist. In 1925, Alan Priest, a member of Langdon Warner's second expedition to Dunhuang, described the scene as he took leave of the Panchen Lama in Taiyuan. "When we crossed the court," he wrote, "we turned around in time to catch the Living Buddha getting a surreptitious peek at us through the window curtains of the throne room. He must have scrambled down off his dais and skipped to the window before we were well out the door."[47]

On one occasion, it seems as if the prospect of a legitimate diversion was coveted more than the alleviation of boredom. As he attended to logistical arrangements in the Gansu oasis of Suzhou in 1907, Stein found the local prefect, Jin Chengyin, to be unusually helpful, having seen personally to the implementation of orders for labor, supplies, and transport. Later, Stein learned from Jiang Xiaowan, his Chinese secretary, that the prefect's "empressement to arrange personally for my start was due largely to the convenient excuse it offers for getting away from telegraph." Why did Prefect Jin want to avoid the telegraph? As it turns out, news of the recent uprising at Dunhuang had finally made it to the provincial capital, and the prefect of Suzhou was terrified of being sent into the fray. According to Stein's secretary, Jin "apprehends orders from Lanchou to proceed to Tun-huang & hopes to escape this responsible task of enquiring into emeute ['riot']."[48]

Last but not least, we must also acknowledge the fact that a genuine friendship could sometimes develop between the foreign archaeologist and his Chinese host. In 1925, the son of Wang Xujun, whom Stein had met on two separate occasions, lamented how his father "never got a chance to read your letter in person. This is cause for enormous regret. If only he could have seen it with his own eyes before he passed away, who knows how high his exuberance would have enabled him to leap?" These were not empty words. Three years earlier, Skrine told Stein about a recent meeting with Wang, then in good health. "I have remembered you to several old Chinese friends of yours," Skrine wrote, "including dear old Wang, who is now Hsien-kuan of the New City. The latter says he has always regretted missing a last chance of meeting you; he arrived at Hami or some such place, from one direction the same night as you arrived from the other, and didn't know you were there till afterwards." A similar sentiment appears to have marked Stein's relationship with Zhu Ruichi (see figure 1), whom Stein first met on his second expedition. "Found him as cheerful & lively as on my Guma visit in June 1908," Stein wrote in 1915. "Welcome as a lao pang-yu [lao pengyou, 'old friend']."[49]

By far the most substantive and long-lasting of Stein's friendships with Chinese officials, however, was that shared with Pan Zhen (figure 19). Stein met Pan on each of his first three expeditions and maintained substantive correspondence with Pan (and later his son) for more than forty years. In

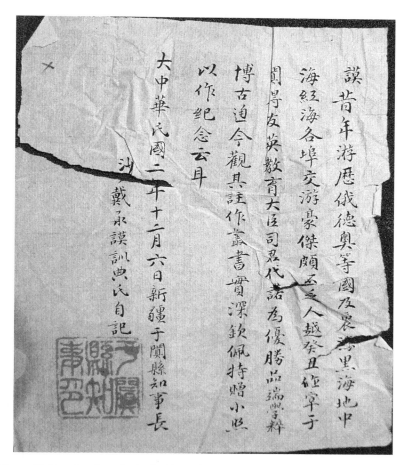

Figure 18. Bragging about Stein. On December 6, 1913, Keriya magistrate Dai Chengmo wrote the following note about Stein: "In years gone by, I traveled through such countries as Russia, Germany, and Austria, as well as to the Caspian, Black, and Mediterranean Seas, through whose various ports I passed. I made the acquaintance of a great many exceptional people, yet the English Minister for Education Aurel Stein, whom I did not befriend until the *guichou* year [1913] when in the role of magistrate of Keriya, would be the most excellent of them all: proper of character, refined of learning, versed in the ancient, and familiar with the modern. My admiration for him, having viewed the collection of books he has authored and annotated, is deep indeed. I present a little photograph, as what one may term a simple memento." Stein Papers, Bodleian Library, MS 341–42. Reprinted with the kind permission of the British Academy and translated with the generous assistance of Ely Finch.

Figure 19. "Dear Old Pan." Stein first met Pan Zhen (*center*) in 1900 when Pan was serving as the magistrate of Khotan. Eagerly anticipated reunions followed in Aksu in 1908 and Urumchi in 1914, where the sixty-five-year-old Pan, pictured here with both his sons, told Stein that he "trusts to our meeting fourth time!" Though Pan's death in 1925 prevented such a meeting, Stein continued to correspond in English with his younger son Pan Zuhuan (*left*; see also figure 16), who later recalled his first glimpse of Stein two decades earlier in Aksu: "It keeps in my mind still that you were passing there some time in that year, and interviewing my father in a corner-house near the garden of the Taotai Yamen had a very friendly talk. I looked you through the window glass and thought that it would be a great pleasure if I could talk with you in English directly, as my father told me so often about you." Sir Aurel Stein, *Innermost Asia: Detailed Report of Explorations in Central Asia, Kan-su, and Eastern Iran*, vol. 2 (Oxford: Clarendon Press, 1928), plate 298.

1908, afraid that his route may force him to bypass Pan's jurisdiction in Aksu, Stein told Allen that "it seems hard to have to forego the pleasure of meeting my old friend once more in this life." When Stein ended up in Aksu after all, he confessed to a "sad feeling at what may be a real farewell." Such fears turned out to be premature. When Stein returned for a third expedition in 1913, Pan was installed in the post of financial commissioner in the provincial capital of Urumchi. But when Pan learned that Stein's route once again threatened to prevent another meeting, he urged Stein to revise his itinerary. "I saw Pan Ta-jen yesterday and gave him your message," wrote one Mr. Tudhope, the foreign postmaster in Urumchi, to Stein in 1914. "He seems a little disappointed that you should be so near and yet not think of coming to Tihwafu so that he might again see you." Stung, Stein added a quick detour to Urumchi, where "Mr. Tudhope's assistance [with translation] brings dear old Pan nearer." When the conclusion of this third reunion drew near, Stein was unable to hide his grief. "Heart heavy at thought that I am not likely to see my old friend again," he wrote in his diary. Pan, however, then nearing seventy years old, "trusts to our meeting fourth time!"[50]

That never happened. But the bond between these two men was apparently so strong that Stein continued to correspond regularly with Pan's son, Zuhuan, long after the death of his father. In 1926, Pan Zuhuan assured Stein "of our deep gratitude for your continual remembrance and unceasing friendship for my father, whom you will be sorry to hear passed away not long ago. It is a great sorrow to us that he did not read with his own eyes, and feel with his own heart, the amiable words of his old friend." In response, Stein informed Pan that "there can be no one outside your dear Father's own family and most intimate circle of friends who feels deeper sorrow on account of his passing away or cherishes his memory with deeper respect and attachment than I do." Much as Pan Zhen had once instructed his sons to emulate Stein, Stein now revealed that he had spoken similarly of Pan. "How often have my friends in Europe and India heard me talk in genuine admiration of your Father's old world integrity, of his noble character which made the people wherever he held office look up to him as the ideal Magistrate!" As we shall see in chapter 6, during Stein's fourth expedition in 1930, the younger Pan lobbied tirelessly on Stein's behalf and even put himself forward as a candidate to accompany Stein into the desert. For his part, Stein looked into employment and study opportunities for Pan outside of China. When those failed to materialize, the two men continued to correspond about a possible reunion in Kashmir for years to come, with Pan expressing a desire to leave the wartime government in Chongqing and work for the British consul in Kashgar. Pan's last letter to Stein reached him in September 1943, just one month before his death.[51]

Only a small handful of Chinese officials ever developed anything close to the sort of intimate relationship that Pan and his son seem to have enjoyed with Stein. But as we have seen, the procurement of social capital from a foreign archaeologist did not depend on the cultivation of a genuine friendship. On the contrary, such capital derived its value from little more than the reputation of the archaeologist as a scholarly celebrity, one who was willing to share his name, likeness, and gadgets with anyone who stood to benefit through association with them.

THE PRICELESS GENTLEMAN

In this chapter, we have shifted our focus from the lower-class Muslim and Chinese peasants who provided physical labor for the Western archaeologist to the educated Confucian elites who staffed the Qing bureaucracy and often took up scholarly pursuits on the side. Such men did not view the Western archaeologist as a potential economic patron. Instead, as we have seen, they tended to see him as they saw themselves: as a "gentleman of empire." The Western explorer, however, was not just any gentleman from any empire. To the Confucian elite of the late Qing and early Republican eras, he was an exceptional gentleman from an exceptional empire. As such, he was the living embodiment of the scientific progress that was imagined to be responsible for the advent of unprecedented Western wealth and power in the modern world. In accordance with this perceived identity, the Qing officials of Xinjiang and Gansu proceeded to extract two forms of capital from their esteemed guests: political and social. Compared to the tangible economic capital coveted by the lower classes, these new forms of capital were largely intangible; that is, their value to the Confucian elite lay largely in the rhetorical uses to which they could be put. Though material goods often did change hands within such encounters, these goods were valued not for their intrinsic monetary worth, but rather for their symbolic political and social value.

The Chinese response to Western archaeologists cannot be reduced to a binary "either/or" proposition. As was the case with the response of the lower-class Muslims examined in chapter 1, the Confucian elites of China saw in the foreign explorer both things to admire and things to fear. But as the past three chapters have attempted to show, Western archaeologists could not have procured the degree of assistance and cooperation necessary to undertake a successful expedition or excavation if the drawbacks of cooperation outweighed the advantages. Just like their mostly illiterate subjects, Chinese officials and scholars harbored regrets and anxieties about their relationship with the foreign archaeologist. But these regrets and anxieties were not enough to dissuade them from going out of their way time and again to lend their enthusiastic and voluntary aid to what they regarded as a great enterprise worthy of admiration. Chinese art and antiquities were precious, to be sure, but they were not so precious—priceless—that their loss could not be tolerated, provided that some form of even more precious compensation was tendered in exchange.

To the Confucian elites of late imperial China, this compensation took the form of political and social capital. As with the Muslim lower classes, the only thing that was priceless to Qing officials and scholars was their personal relationship with a resourceful and cultured agent of a foreign power. To the illiterate laborers, he was a sahib in the desert; to the Qing officials and scholars, he was a gentleman of empire, one just as intent on "accumulating culture" as they were. So long as the art and antiquities coveted by the Westerner were worth less than the compensations he could offer— knowingly or unknowingly—in return for their removal, Chinese and Muslim perceptions of the limitless value of his dual identities would remain stable. Should the value of the art and antiquities in China become inflated, however, the value of the compensations made available by cultivating a relationship with someone like Stein or Pelliot would decrease accordingly.

After 1911, that is exactly what happened.

CHAPTER FOUR

The Priceless Nation

In the realm of art and antiquities, the recipe for conflict is simple. When two parties regard the same object as priceless, neither negotiation nor compensation is possible. So long as the parties in question are both competing for objects in the lands of a third party—such as the Anglo-French dispute over the Rosetta Stone in Egypt from 1799 to 1802—the struggle may be fierce and bitter, but neither side will criminalize the triumph of the other. (The French have never called for the return of "their" Rosetta Stone from the British.) When one of these parties hails from the source country itself, however, resort to the discourse of criminalization is assured. This begs the obvious question. Namely, how and when did the Chinese, stewards of the host country, begin to view their art and antiquities as priceless? In other words, when did the Chinese begin to view their cultural treasures as the Western archaeologists did, as inclusive emblems of the Chinese nation rather than as exclusive emblems of individual Confucian virtue? Phrased in this way, the answer is obvious: the Chinese adopted the Western view of the value of antiquities when the Chinese themselves became Westernized.

In the realms of science and technology, this transition was already well underway by the 1870s. In the aftermath of the Second Opium War (1856–60), prominent Confucian intellectuals began to advocate for the adoption of "useful" Western innovations (yong), which were to be grafted on top of an unchanging Chinese "substance" (ti). Though this signaled the encroaching Westernization of the material world in China, it stopped well short of transforming the intellectual world. For that, another three decades would need to pass. It was only in 1895, following a shocking military defeat to Japan, that the indisputable primacy of the Chinese world order would come under attack for the first time. Just five years later, the traumatic effects of the Boxer War would sweep away any remaining doubts regarding the wisdom of full-scale Westernization in every realm of Chinese life. This was the decade in which influential Confucian statesmen first began to embrace the transformation of the Chinese mind along Western lines, often through a Japanese intermediary.

In the realm of art and antiquities, this embrace took the form of support for the idea of a national museum open to the general public. In the summer of 1898, the Confucian reformer Kang Youwei proposed the establishment of museums as a means to "develop the people's learning." As Kang's proposal makes clear, museums were discussed in the context of educational reform, since they were regarded as a means of educating the people. But so long as the Qing court remained committed to the traditional civil service examination system, which was accessible only to the wealthiest and most privileged of men, any such reform would be piecemeal at best. That changed in 1905, with the abolition of the civil service exam. As Lisa Claypool and Qin Shao have shown, that same year, the Confucian reformer Zhang Jian, having just returned from an extended trip to Japan, submitted a formal proposal to the Ministry of Education for the creation of an "imperial museum-library" in Beijing. To Zhang, the education of the Chinese people could not be entrusted to schools alone. Rather, there must be "libraries and museums to supplement and support the school system." When the Qing court declined to implement his proposal, Zhang returned to his hometown of Nantong in Jiangsu and sponsored the construction of his own museum, paid for entirely out of his own funds. In 1912, after seven years of planning and construction, the Nantong Museum finally opened its doors.[1]

The Nantong Museum was the first museum in China to be controlled by a Chinese person. But it was not open to the general public, nor was it national in scope. Much like the private collections and libraries of the traditional Confucian elite, the Nantong Museum was accessible by invitation only. For instance, in 1908, when Pelliot learned of the magnificent library and antiquities collection of Duanfang, he had to ask Duanfang for a formal invitation to visit through the French embassy. "You indicate that your countryman Dr. Pelliot would like to examine the antiquities in my collection," Duanfang wrote back to Edmond Bapst, the French ambassador in Beijing. "He is most welcome. Upon his illustrious arrival, I will put aside all my work and receive him in person. Everything in storage will be brought out for his scrutiny, as reciprocation for the diligent concern you have shown in making this introduction." Though Zhang Jian did not need to bring his collection "out of storage" for the guests in his museum, his museum was similar to the private collections of yore in requiring a personal introduction before anyone would be admitted through its doors.[2]

Here we see the class tensions that would continue to plague the over-haul of the antiquities trade in China for many decades to come. In theory, by the first decade of the twentieth century, a few prominent Chinese intel-lectuals were ready to pay lip service to the idea of a public institution that safeguarded the empire's cultural treasures on explicit behalf of the Chinese nation. Luo Zhenyu also submitted proposals for an imperial museum about this time. In practice, however, each of these reformers was still tethered to the idea that the art and antiquities in his possession reflected both his per-sonal virtue and his own unique ability to commune with the sages of an-tiquity. As such, they continued to believe that they could do with their ar-tifacts as they pleased and were unwilling to cede actual control over these precious objects to any institution that professed to serve the vulgar masses. In other words, these men became walking contradictions. Luo Zhenyu, for instance, was instrumental in advocating for new antiquities preserva-tion laws and the establishment of museums, and he was the driving force behind the transport of some eight thousand manuscripts from Dunhuang to Beijing. And yet he himself dealt in the sale of antiquities for many de-cades, earning his livelihood by selling off ancient paintings from his own collection to private buyers at home and abroad. In 1913, Song Xiaolian, the former governor of Heilongjiang, observed that "ever since the Frenchman found and excavated the stone cavern at Dunhuang, our countrymen have been moved to develop a preservationist mindset. This constitutes intel-lectual progress." And yet he wrote these words as part of a modern colo-phon newly inked on an ancient Dunhuang manuscript that belonged to his friend, and as we saw in chapter 2, others of his generation had absolutely no qualms about cutting up similar manuscripts as gifts for their friends. For Song and other like-minded elites reared within the old imperial order, "preservation" still meant preservation in the collections of respected Con-fucian gentleman, not national institutions.[3]

   With most Chinese either deeply conflicted or quietly ambivalent toward these new ideas about public ownership of art and antiquities, some Westerners decided to take matters into their own hands. In 1908, Freder-ick McCormick, a journalist for *Harper's Weekly* and the Associated Press, founded the China Monuments Society in Beijing and continued to serve thereafter as its secretary. Alarmed by the rapid deterioration and loss of China's cultural heritage, McCormick drew on an extensive network of American expatriates throughout the country in order to publicize the in-creasingly dire situation. In 1914, the society headlined a memorial to the new Republican government in Beijing urging it to "support and encour-age the Chinese officials and people in taking effective means to conserve their antiquities for China's benefit and the benefit of other nations." At the same time, McCormick helped bring about the remittance of $100,000 from the US Boxer Indemnity Fund to finance the construction of a new museum in Beijing. Many years later, McCormick took full credit for having supposedly awoken the Chinese to the priceless value of their heritage. "The Chinese whom I interested in cultural objects and their protection took just that one word for their activities in succession to my enterprise," he wrote to Roy Chapman Andrews in 1932, "and, according to press reports, have made life miserable for the explorers and students, educational institutions and museums abroad."[4]

Regardless of who is to take credit for this awakening, it is clear that the awakening only took place in fits and starts over a period of several decades. And the most important parts of the process—the formulation of antiquities preservation laws on paper and the opening of a national museum in the capital—were indeed undertaken by the Chinese themselves. After the 1911 revolution led to the abdication of the last Qing emperor, various proposals for such laws and institutions were submitted to Yuan Shikai, the newly inaugurated president of the Republic of China. On June 14, 1914, Yuan finally issued an order prohibiting the export of antiquities from China. That same year, the first limited exhibition of art and antiquities from the Forbidden City was opened to the general public (or at least those who could afford the astronomical price of admission, which was equivalent to about forty-four pounds of wheat flour). Yet the objects provided for this exhibition by members of the deposed Qing court—who continued to live within the Forbidden City—were regarded as a temporary "loan" to the Republican government. In other words, they still formally belonged to their private aristocratic owners—not to the Chinese nation. On paper, of course, President Yuan had made a careful—and, in China, quite novel—distinction between "articles of clothing and daily use," now deemed property of the Aisin Gioro clan, and "treasures and historical relics," now deemed the property of the state. In addition, a committee was formed to prepare for the eventual transformation of the Forbidden City into the National Palace Museum—just as soon as sufficient funds could be gathered. In the meantime, however, Puyi and his household continued to treat everything in the Forbidden City as their private property for another decade, until the populist warlord Feng Yuxiang finally evicted them from the premises in 1924.[5]

Part of the reason that it took so long to nationalize the Forbidden City in fact as well as in theory was because of the turbulent political situation that gripped the country. In 1916, President Yuan died after an ill-fated attempt to restore the monarchy. For the next three decades, China would be plagued by a succession of warlords, civil wars, and foreign invasions. Amid such a precarious political climate, few Chinese politicians evinced much appetite for devoting scarce financial and political resources to the implementation of antiquities export laws and museum blueprints formulated by Yuan's administration. To do so would require an enormous expenditure of financial and political capital to which they simply did not have access. Not only that, but they also had far more pressing matters to attend to, such as the looming extinction of the Chinese state. Furthermore, it is clear that not everyone in China was a true believer in these initiatives. This meant that there was no guarantee that foreign archaeologists and collectors would encounter a united front against their activities. Everywhere they went, they were bound to encounter plenty of influential Chinese elites—as well as legions of impoverished and illiterate commoners, Muslim or otherwise— who still placed a far higher value on the "compensations of plunder" than on the objects targeted by such "plunder."

Despite all this, a significant change had taken root. For the first time, art and antiquities were imagined—at least on paper—to embody the collective cultural heritage of "the Chinese people" writ large rather than that of an exclusive Confucian elite. In addition, this new concept of collective ownership was substantiated, however precariously, in the creation of publicly visible institutions and laws. Officially, China's cultural heritage was now the property of its people: the "Chinese nation." No matter what someone did with his collection behind the curtains, in public he was obliged to acknowledge the collective theoretical claims of the abstract nation on that same collection. In 1911, when the Ministry of Education instructed the magistrate of Dunhuang to keep an eye on the Daoist priest Wang Yuanlu and "take responsibility for ensuring that no more manuscripts are lost to private buyers," it was giving voice to the idea that the only legitimate collections were those purchased by the government on behalf of the people. In 1917, Xie Bin proposed the imposition of a government monopoly on the purchase of all antiquities in Xinjiang, so as "to collect and store these artifacts for archaeological use." He also suggested that objects deemed unworthy of being designated as part of the Chinese cultural heritage, such as mummies, could be shipped and sold abroad to raise funds for the government. "The income generated by these mummies would be sufficient to supplement to some degree the financial situation in Xinjiang," he wrote. Regardless of how such things were treated, their fate was supposed to be determined by collective bodies that purported to speak on behalf of the Chinese nation, which now served as the basis of political legitimacy for the new Republic. In 1919, when the provincial Ministry of Education in Gansu learned that Wang had once again managed to sell manuscripts that he had somehow concealed from previous government inspectors, it reminded the magistrate in Dunhuang that "the protection of antiquities is the same both among foreigners and Chinese." As such, for Wang to regard the contents of Cave 17 "as items that he can give away as presents or sell for profit does not conform with the proper way of preserving antiquities."[6]

On paper at least, the Dunhuang manuscripts and every other artifact in China were now priceless. The reason they were priceless was because they were imagined to represent the collective artistic genius and labor of every single person in the nation, an idea newly inscribed into concrete laws and institutions. As a result, nothing could ever compensate for the perceived scale of such a loss. With the legitimacy of the state now intertwined with notions of popular sovereignty, any politician who publicly acquiesced in the loss of priceless "national treasures" was risking political suicide. Behind the scenes, however, almost no one on the ground was willing to defend this new valuation, no matter what they said or did in public. To treat the art and antiquities of China as priceless in both fact and theory was to forsake the tangible and reliable compensations of plunder in exchange for the intangible and unreliable compensations of an abstract discourse. As a result, if we want to identify the first attempt to obstruct a foreign archaeological enterprise in China on the basis of the new principles of the collective ownership of the nation, we must seek out those Chinese statesmen who were least indebted to the foreigners—and thus had the least to lose from turning their backs on the compensations of plunder.

THE ENIGMA OF GOVERNOR YANG

In December 1911, revolutionary conspirators inspired by the October uprising in Wuchang attempted to seize power in Urumchi. The Qing governor, Yuan Dahua, having learned of the intended coup beforehand, made quick work of the rebels. The same script was not observed in Ili, where the entire New Army garrison rose up the following month and executed their commander, then set out on a march toward Urumchi. At the same time, the Muslim peasants of Hami, long oppressed by the local hereditary prince, Shah Maqsut, laid siege to his citadel and managed to defeat Qing reinforcements sent from the capital. In the midst of these crises, Governor Yuan learned of the abdication of the last Qing emperor in Beijing, an event that prompted him to resign his post and exit the province. For his successor, he designated Yuan Hongyou, the circuit intendant of Kashgar. As soon as Yuan set out from Kashgar to make the long journey to Urumchi, assassins from the underground fraternal order of the Elder Brotherhood, taking advantage of the political chaos, ambushed Yuan's caravan and cut him and his wife to pieces. Next in line for the governorship was Yang Zengxin (figure 20), a former circuit intendant of Aksu then serving as judicial commissioner in Urumchi. If the Ili revolutionaries, Hami rebels, and Elder Brotherhood assassins were not daunting enough for Yang, he was soon confronted with a fourth threat: in May 1912, the Outer Mongols, acting under Russian encouragement, invaded the neighboring outpost of Khobdo. As governor, one of Yang's first instructions from Beijing was to send reinforcements to lift the siege at Khobdo.[7]

This was the immediate backdrop for Stein's third expedition in Xinjiang. As he descended on Kashgar in the fall of 1913, Stein saw the embers of war and revolution everywhere he set foot. "Morning from 10 A.M. used for official Yamen visits," he wrote on September 24. "New Tao-tai no improvement on old Yuan who was murdered last year while with his wife." Noting a "strange want of fine clothes & attendant pomp" among Chinese officialdom, Stein sensed a general malaise and anxiety regarding the present state of affairs. "Difficulty about non-existing Yayes. Chinese establishment reduced to absolute minimum," he observed in Tashkurgan. "Talk of Chinese helplessness & loss of prestige." In Kashgar, Kichik Beg told Stein that he "deplores uncertain condition since there is no Emperor. Though all harvests since 1908, with exception of one were excellent & water abundant, no new lands opened. . . . High prices since a year or two attributed to uncertain political outlook." At his last official audience before leaving Kashgar, Stein recorded the "pathetic appearance tow.[ard] close of entertainment of great seals of office of Tao-tai, brought carefully locked in red-lacquered cases. In them the dignity & pomp of better days seemed to linger."[8]

Once he left Kashgar, Stein came face to face with the horrors of ongoing political crises. As he approached Charklik, suspicious movements in the nearby trees prompted Stein to arm himself for the first time ever in China. "The total absence of wayfarers from Charklik since we got to high road had struck me as strange and this reception to border seemed suspicious," he wrote in his diary. "So we halted and loaded carbine & revolvers." When he finally reached Charklik, Stein learned that there had indeed been cause for worry. A band of Elder Brothers had just overthrown the local garrison and executed the Chinese officials. Stein's arrival coincided with the restoration of provincial authority by Hui soldiers sent from Urumchi. "Send my presents and enquire about call," Stein noted, "[but] am asked to put off visit as Tun-ling busy with having the Kamarbaz prisoners executed. All 8 were

Figure 20. Xinjiang Governor Yang Zengxin. Rising to power amid the chaos and violence of the 1911 revolution, Yang Zengxin would prove to be both a shrewd and ruthless diplomat and an ardent collector of Chinese antiquities. In 1915, Yang took advantage of newly passed legislation in Beijing concerning the protection of antiquities to drive Stein out of Turfan, where he and other Chinese officials had long sponsored their own excavations and were eager to impose a monopoly on the antiquities trade. More than a decade later, Yang was still in power when Sven Hedin returned to Xinjiang. Yang was assassinated in 1928. Courtesy of the Sven Hedin Foundation, Museum of Ethnography, Stockholm.

duly despatched outside W gate of Bazar during forenoon." Later, when Stein left town for a dig in the desert, he was forced to pass by a "heap of bodies of executed Kamarbaz. Gruesome sight of heads severed from bodies. All appar.[ently] killed together. Miserable get up of bodies."[9]

Even before he became an eyewitness to the turbulence of the revolution, Stein had already anticipated the possibility of a change in attitude among the Chinese toward his expedition. In June 1913, as he waited impatiently to set off from his Kashmir camp for Xinjiang, Stein wondered "what this delay might mean, anticipation by competitors from Berlin, America, etc.,—or a complete change in the Chinese attitude?" Any such change would not come from the local officials, who treated Stein more or less as they had before. It was Yang Zengxin, the new governor in Urumchi, who would determine the fate of Stein's expedition. And Yang, as we have just seen, was engaged in a trial by fire. "Back in the early Republic," Yang once mused, "I was a vicious bully. It was only later that I became Amitabha [Buddha]." He had little choice in the matter. Beset by foreign and domestic threats on all sides, Yang resorted to ruthless violence and shrewd diplomacy to eliminate or neutralize each and every one of his rivals. In dealing with domestic threats such as the Elder Brotherhood, Hami rebels, or Ili revolutionaries, bloodshed was an inevitable part of the solution. But in dealing with the foreign imperialists, Yang knew that he could not rely on brute force of any kind. "Today China is weak and poor," he wrote in 1915. "Xinjiang has been abandoned and isolated, cut off from all assistance. In the face of powerful neighbors, we have only one means of keeping the peace: scrupulously adhere to the letter of the treaties."[10]

The treaties (or, as later historians would call them, the "unequal treaties") were a series of diplomatic agreements signed by the Qing government in the aftermath of various military defeats at the hands of Western—and later Japanese—powers. Though they gave foreigners a whole host of economic and political privileges in China, they also reminded them of what they were not allowed to do. Governor Yang could not kick the Russians and British out of his province, but he could try to curtail the scope of their activities, which had rarely conformed to the letter of the law. More than any other governor of his day, Yang was determined to rely on the resources of his own province alone. This meant that he rarely accepted loans or any other form of aid from outsiders, be they foreign or domestic, knowing that to do so would be to put him in their debt and offer a pretext to meddle in the internal affairs of his province. Yang's demonstrated ability to keep hostile foreigners and domestic rivals at bay would later win him rare accolades from the few foreigners who met him. "I was fortunate to meet probably the greatest living Chinaman," wrote the British intelligence agent Reginald Schomberg as he passed through Urumchi in 1928. "This is no exaggeration, for with slender resources beyond his own genius, this old man . . . had given the province peace and prosperity, when every neighbouring country was wracked by war or distracted by faction. How he did it, I never understood, and the more I saw of Sin Kiang, the more bewildered I became, and the more I admired his achievement."[11]

Yang's agenda as governor is important to making sense of how he treated Stein on this expedition. For the first time, Stein would be asked to conform to the letter of the law rather than the spirit of accommodation. On September 30, 1913, during a long talk with George Macartney, the British consul in Kashgar, Stein heard for the first time about "recent orders against surveying & arch.[aeological] investigation." The prohibitions against surveying could not have come as a surprise, for such activities had always been illegal, at least in theory. In practice, however, so long as the archaeologists did their clandestine work out of sight or behind the cover of a suitably benign pretext, these same officials were often happy to turn the other cheek and take refuge in the compensations of social and political capital. In 1913, however, with Xinjiang verging on a state of anarchy, that would no longer be the case. Almost immediately upon Stein's departure from Kashgar, local officials had already begun to submit reports to Governor Yang in Urumchi about Lal Singh, the Indian surveyor whom Stein had sent ahead to map uncharted lands. When Singh reached Charklik (not yet under a state of rebel siege), Yang instructed the local prefect, Hu Dianhua, to search his luggage for evidence of surveying. In his report back to the governor, Hu tells us what happened next. "I went personally to Lal Singh's quarters to look into the matter and found that his luggage contained cartographic equipment," Hu wrote. "When I asked him what it was, he told me that it was photographic equipment. Luckily, I knew exactly what it was, and thus was not deceived."[12]

By the time Stein reached Charklik one month later, Hu was dead. But his report on Lal Singh's surveying set off the first major diplomatic row with a Western archaeologist. Stein learned of the obstruction in the form of a circular telegram sent to Macartney by Chang Yongqing, the inspector of Kashgar. "Foreign travelers are not allowed to survey important strategical points in China," Chang informed Stein through Macartney's English translation. "On this matter, the Chinese Government have repeatedly made communications to Foreign Envoys who have agreed (to the proposition)." Inspector Chang ordered Macartney to tell Stein "that Lal Sing must travel in a manner conformable to treaties, and must not survey." The letter of these treaties had not changed since Stein's earlier expeditions. But war and revolution had finally given the Chinese a pretext to enforce them. On December 26, when Stein learned about the "bad news" from Macartney, he immediately identified the prefect's actions as having originated in "insolent obstruction from Urumchi." He was right. In acting thus, Governor Yang was simply invoking the same treaties that had governed the foreign presence in China for half a century. "It will serve no purpose to argue matters with the Taotai," Macartney told Stein from Kashgar. "He will say—in fact he said it to me this morning—that orders not his and at any rate, are conformable to instructions from Peking."[13]

By invoking the letter of the treaties, however, Yang ensured that the matter would eventually be adjudicated in Beijing, not Urumchi. This was "bad news" for the governor. Though Yang himself may have had little to lose by antagonizing the British in Xinjiang, significant diplomatic capital was at stake for President Yuan Shikai's administration in Beijing. As a result, it took only a few days for John Jordan, the British ambassador in Beijing, to resolve the situation in Stein's favor. "I have to inform you that I brought the matter to the notice of the Chinese Government and requested them in the interests of science to accord such special facilities as would enable the objects of the expedition to be successfully carried out," Jordan wrote to Macartney on January 22. "I have now received a communication from the Wai Chiao Pu [Ministry of Foreign Affairs], copy and translation of which I enclose, informing me that the Tutu of Hsinchiang [i.e., Yang Zengxin] has been instructed by telegram to accord favourable treatment and protection to Sir Aurel Stein." After a bit more back and forth, it was further determined that such "favourable treatment" was to include surveying in any district "where archaeological remains were in existence." Stein had prevailed. And yet it was clear that the new governor of Xinjiang was willing to apply pressure wherever the letter of the law permitted him to do so. In June 1914, Macartney informed Stein that the circuit intendant of Kashgar told him "that he had already a file of some hundreds of pages about you: the Urumtchi lot had blamed the last Taotai for having allowed you to travel without a proper *Chinese Govt.* passport; and at one time there was a talk of stopping you. But you need have no apprehension *now*: your position has been regularized by subsequent orders from Peking."[14]

Indeed it had. As we noted earlier, Chinese politicians and intellectuals of the early Republican era were a study in contradictions. On the one hand, they wanted desperately to measure up to Western political and cultural ideals on paper. On the other hand, unless it was a matter of life and death, they rarely had either the financial resources or the ideological inclination to inject concrete substance into these ideals. For Governor Yang in Xinjiang, the postrevolutionary political environment in Xinjiang was quite literally a matter of life and death; hence, the obstruction of Stein's surveying activities, which had long been tolerated. With the governor's bold attempt to align words with actions undermined by politicians far more indebted to foreign interests than he was, both Stein and Yang made a show of reconciliation. In December 1914, Stein was lured to Urumchi by the prospect of seeing his old friend Pan Zhen once more. Once in the capital, Pan organized several audiences and banquets for Stein with Governor Yang. Stein found Yang "a fine burly figure with bluff but hearty manners," and was pleased to learn of his interest in antiquities, as evidenced by their "talk of Loulan, Tun-huang, etc." Yang then promised "effective help" for the rest of Stein's expedition, which Stein found "strange after last year's attempt." Stein left Urumchi in high spirits, ascribing to "Pan's influence" the way in which "the Provincial Governor has shown himself all attention for me, the queer attempt at obstruction made just a year ago being clean forgotten."[15]

Stein was right to credit Pan alone for his reception in Urumchi. For unbeknownst to either man, Governor Yang had already begun to prepare for a second assault on Stein. This time, he would attempt to enforce the letter of the new antiquities export law passed by President Yuan just six months earlier—a law no other governor, not to mention the president himself, had yet bothered (or would bother) to enforce. Upon his departure from Urumchi, Stein returned to Turfan, where his men had been digging continuously since late October. On February 1, 1915, after three months of excavations at nearby sites, Stein received a letter from Zhang Shaobo, the governor's secretary of foreign affairs. "Present of Kara-shahr fish accompanied by letter informing me that Chiang, Secr.[etary] of For.[eign] affairs, had expressed himself interested in my welfare and—asked for news of me," Stein wrote in his diary. "Reminiscences of a year ago put me on guard." Ten days later, Stein's suspicions were fully vindicated. Hu Wenbing, the magistrate of Turfan, broke the news. "I have received detailed reports regarding your Excellency's arrival into this district after departing from the provincial capital," Hu informed Stein. "Now I have received a communication from the Office of the Civil Governor [i.e., Yang Zengxin] that reads as follows:

In recent years travelers from various countries have, after arriving at their destinations, indiscriminately excavated [suiyi wajue] ancient graves and temples, where they have discovered steles and other ancient artifacts. These they pack up and take away. This is certainly not something that any country will permit [wei shijie ge guo suo bu xu]. Now I have received a communication from the Ministry [in Beijing] to protect and preserve local ancient artifacts [baocun difang guwu]. The aforementioned traveler has entered into the jurisdiction of Wood Gorge within said district to investigate antiquities, and for the time being he still has not left. The local magistrate should therefore proceed to inform him that he is only permitted to make visual observations [guanlan kaocha], and cannot wantonly excavate and take away ancient artifacts.

After noting that Stein had spent far longer in Turfan than originally planned, Hu concluded his letter with a question intended to dispel any and all ambiguity as to its intent. "Do you or do you not intend to excavate antiquities?"[16]

Fortunately for Stein, his work in Turfan was nearly complete anyway. Over the next couple of weeks, he learned that the orders for obstruction were entirely the work of Governor Yang and his foreign affairs secretary, Zhang Shaobo. "You are right in thinking that the obstruction originated in Urumtchi," Macartney informed Stein. "In fact, the Gov.[ernor] and Chang . . . For.[eign] Deputy, have both a hand in it. What this letter means is that you have no right to excavate—though you may examine sites; also that you have no right to take out of China what you have excavated." Hu Wenbing, the local magistrate who was tasked with delivering this most unwelcome news to Stein, took pains to assure Stein that he did not share their sentiment. "The Amban was most apologetic when I saw him," Stein wrote to Allen in Oxford, "and without raising awkward questions (all the work at Murtuk, etc., had been done with his full knowledge!) was only anxious to be able to report to Urumchi that my 'surveys' of the ruins were finished there & my departure impending." Regardless of Hu's personal views toward Stein, however, he was still obliged to make a show of compliance. "While baggage was being packed with no regret on my part at departure from dark noisy quarters," Stein wrote as he prepared to leave Turfan, "Zayid Akhun Shangye turned [up] with instructions 'to attend upon me.' It was clear that surveillance was intended."[17]

Despite such measures, no further attempt was made to curtail Stein's activities. Once he left Turfan, it was like nothing had ever happened. In fact, when Stein arrived in Korla, the local magistrate even went so far as to apologize for his role in relaying the obstruction orders of the previous year regarding Lal Singh's surveys. "He referred to trouble of last year over Lal S.'s surveying & how matters were put right from Peking," Stein noted in his diary. "Secured apologetic about his own share in sending me the obstructive order." One week later, Stein found the next magistrate down the road to be "v.[ery] attentive & appar.[ently] anxious to please P'an [Zhen]," Stein's influential friend in Urumchi. At Aksu, Stein found Zhu Ruichi, whom he first met on his second expedition seven years earlier, "as cheerful & lively as on my Guma visit in June 1908. Welcome as a lao pang-yu [lao pengyou, 'old friend']." At Zhu's dinner the next evening, Stein "noticed discreet avoidance of queries about the hao-tung-hsi [hao dongxi, 'good things'] supposed to be brought away by me." In June 1915, Stein finally returned to Kashgar and paid a final round of calls on the Chinese officials. "Return call of Tao-tai & tutti quanti at 11 A.M.," he wrote on June 5. "Books produced & plates shown without awkward questions." Nevertheless, one month later, as Stein packed his crates for transport over the Himalayas, he did endure a brief scare over "an enquiry about the contents of my cases which preceded this call." But nothing came of it. "No reference made however, to prohibited export of antiques such as I had feared."[18]

Everything Stein had excavated in Xinjiang and Gansu over the past two years accompanied him safely out of the country without incident. So what are we to make of Governor Yang's unprecedented efforts to sabotage his expedition? The prohibition against surveying is easily explained by the geopolitical crisis then gripping the province in the aftermath of the revolution. But the prohibition against the excavation and export of antiquities, the first of its kind in China, is harder to make sense of. In his politics, Governor Yang was neither reformer nor radical. In 1913, at the start of Stein's third expedition, he was forty-nine years old and a longtime graduate of the old civil service examination system. He actively suppressed the agents of revolution in Xinjiang, railed against Han nationalism, and even went so far as to support President Yuan Shikai's attempt to restore the monarchy in 1915. In every aspect of his upbringing, education, and politics, Yang Zengxin was firmly a creature of the old Confucian imperial order. He was not in the least bit Westernized. During his lifetime, Yang repeatedly attacked the importation of Western ideas into China. Instead of promoting ideas such as democracy and the sovereignty of the people, Yang authored numerous philosophical treatises on the virtues of Confucianism and Daoism.

He also collected antiquities. Like many of his colleagues in the northwestern bureaucracy, Yang was known to have obtained his own Dunhuang manuscripts. But he also seems to have had quite an impressive collection of steles from Turfan. In 1928, just months before his assassination, Yang hosted the members of Sven Hedin's Sino-Swedish expedition in Urumchi. Huang Wenbi, one of the Chinese archaeologists, has left us an eyewitness account of what he saw in the governor's private collection. "After the meal," Huang wrote on March 11, "we went inside to look at three different steles. One was an inscription of a Tang-era manuscript. Another was a commemorative inscription for the construction of the Qubin Temple, and the last was from the Northern Zhou period. As the characters were all quite clear, I asked General Yang if I could take a rubbing, and he agreed. We set a date, and we retired afterwards." Much in the way that Pelliot had to apply for permission to visit Duanfang's private collection in Jiangsu, Huang also had to secure Yang's consent to see and study his private collection in Urumchi. One week later, Xu Xusheng, the Chinese co-leader of the expedition, was also invited to view Yang's antiquities. "After dinner we made our way to the governor's office to take a look at two ancient artifacts. One was a sutra, no date recorded, and the other was a king's stele from Gaochang, also without a date. Both were antiquities from the Sui and Tang eras." In addition to Yang's collection, other officials in Urumchi also showed off their ancient wares. When Huang met the head of the division of internal affairs, he found that he "had in his possession an ancient seal that had been found somewhere near Shaya," along with a "stele unearthed in April 1921 from Tuyoq." The stele was "now in the office of the provincial government." Another prized possession was the "Zhang Huaiji stele," which Huang found installed at the guildhall for Chinese from Jiangsu and Zhejiang.[19]

All of these artifacts came from Turfan. As we saw earlier, Turfan constituted by far the richest and most easily accessible storehouse of antiquities for Chinese officials in Urumchi, who had been digging there since at least 1901. Stein was well aware of this, at one point suggesting that the most effective rhetorical defense of his activities would be to highlight the "unchecked destruction in which the local people and the kwans [guan, 'officials'] employing them have been allowed to indulge." As such, Stein suspected that the true motive behind the obstruction orders was nothing more than jealously. "Evid.[ently] prolonged stay here has roused jealous apprehensions," he wrote after receiving the governor's letter in Turfan. And well it should. At one point in his diary, Stein recorded the total weight of all the antiquities he had packed into crates in Turfan: 16,000 pounds! Though this number represents the entirety of what he accumulated throughout the expedition, still the scale is immense.[20]

And yet it was not much different from what he had taken away on his second expedition just seven years earlier. Back then, everyone from the Qing governor in Urumchi clear on down to the prefect of Guma was absolutely enamored of Stein, and none of them begrudged any of his acquisitions. Not only that, such sentiments continued throughout the entirety of his third expedition—with the sole exception of Turfan. Even there, the local magistrate felt embarrassed by the role Governor Yang forced him to play in putting an end to Stein's excavations, even going so far as to apologize for his actions. From Korla to Kashgar, other apologies followed by those Chinese officials still more interested in leveraging social and political capital out of Stein than in kicking him out of their jurisdictions for the sake of an unfamiliar abstract discourse. In fact, one of the reasons that Stein later agreed to return to Xinjiang for a fourth expedition in 1930 was because he saw through Governor Yang's gambit. That is, it wasn't an earnest attempt to implement a newly embraced antiquities export law by a true believer in the popular sovereignty of the Chinese nation. Rather, it was a shrewd attempt by a conservative scion of the old Confucian order to invoke a new rhetorical pretext to preserve his exclusive access to the most fruitful archaeological site within reach of Urumchi. Stein, well aware that none of the other officials in Xinjiang shared the governor's agenda, likely concluded that most of his old Chinese friends would welcome him back into Xinjiang with open arms—and he was right.

By 1915, antiquities in China were priceless, but only when the Chinese wanted them to be. Over the past twenty years, new Western ideas about the value of art and antiquities had gradually led to the formulation of new Chinese laws and the construction of new Chinese institutions. But these laws and institutions were only as effective as the people tasked with their enforcement. If the compensations of foreign "plunder" outweighed the compensations of a principled defense of national sovereignty, then the former would continue to triumph over the latter. What changed in Turfan in 1915 was the convergence of a newly available political tool—the nationalist discourse of cultural sovereignty—with the rise of a Chinese governor who loved to collect antiquities and lacked any incentive to engage the various forms of capital offered by the foreign archaeologist. As a result, in driving Stein out of Turfan and threatening him with the confiscation of his collection, Yang had little to lose and everything to gain. Yet this cost-benefit calculus of the governor applied only to Turfan, the source of most of Yang's own antiquities. That Governor Yang was not a true believer in the new antiquities law can be plainly seen by the near total absence of any follow-up inquiries regarding Stein's collection after he left Turfan. Once Stein exited the governor's personal stomping grounds, he was out of sight and out of mind.

The reluctance of most Xinjiang officials to enforce the new antiquities laws continued throughout the next two decades—and Stein knew it. In 1928, the British consul in Kashgar highlighted the distinction between "official" and "unofficial" knowledge of Western collections in Xinjiang. "Although the Chinese know un-officially that I have things of this kind they do not know it officially," the consul wrote to Stein, "and an awkward situation both for me and for them might arise if they knew that I was sending you things of this kind when they are confiscating similar things" from other foreign travelers.[21] On paper, Chinese officials were now required to enforce the law when they learned of its transgression. But since most of these officials were raised and educated during the late imperial era, few were inclined to enforce the nationalist logic that animated such laws. As a result, they simply preferred not to know about such transgressions in the first place, thus allowing them to continue to draw on the diplomatic, social, and political capital offered by the foreign explorer. In order for the new antiquities laws to be respected and enforced consistently throughout the land, a new crop of fully Westernized political actors would have to exert their influence on the national stage of China. Such men, guaranteed by virtue of their education to be true believers in the Western ideals enshrined in their constitution, must have everything to gain and nothing to lose from the obstruction of foreign archaeological enterprise.

WAR AND REVOLUTION

"So the great conflagration has come which has threatened for years." Thus wrote Aurel Stein to his good friend Percy Allen on August 14, 1914. Just ten days earlier, Britain declared war on Germany, marking the entrance of the last major European power onto the battlefield. Though Stein was holed up in the mountains of Gansu, convalescing from a serious leg injury he suffered when his horse reared back and fell on him, news from Europe was never more than a post office away. "Relieved by receipts from P.O. Lanchou telegram reports," Stein noted on August 22, while passing through a small town in northwestern Gansu. "Alsace held by French; Liege still in Belgian hands. England's declaration of war against Austria-H[ungary]! Cattaro bombarded by Montenegro. Trade routes supposed to be safe." Hungarian by birth, Stein had long transferred his loyalties to Britain and committed himself to the welfare of its empire. Ever since, he wrote to John Scott Keltie, secretary of the Royal Geographic Society, "I have eaten the salt of British India and have felt proud of taking my humble share in the work of the Empire to which I was attracted by every sentiment even long before I came out first to India." In Stein's mind, Britain was fighting not only for itself but also for the good of the entire world. "May the command of the sea forever protect England," he wrote to Allen from Turfan in January

1915, "and may the Empire which has been beneficent for mankind so long, emerge safe from this struggle in which so much is at stake and for which the big talking demagogues have done so little to prepare the nation!"[22]

As Stein had hoped, the Empire did indeed survive the war. But it was no longer the confident purveyor of Western civilization that its most ardent supporters had long imagined it to be. In fact, the outbreak of World War I signaled a dramatic turning point in the history of Western archaeological expeditions in the non-Western world. From this point forward, American museums and universities would flex their newfound wealth under the flag of a growing diplomatic power, while cash-strapped European institutions would find themselves forced to take comfort in the overflowing collections of yesteryear. Win or lose, countries such as Britain, France, Germany, and Russia no longer evinced enthusiasm for financing, outfitting, and protecting their archaeologists in the field. This was particularly the case in the Middle East, where many Westernized Muslim elites had long been willing to cooperate with their European colleagues in the field of archaeology. With the postwar dismemberment of the Ottoman Empire, however, many of these same elites began to speak in the name of exclusive nations rather than of cosmopolitan empires. In search of a new national identity distinct from their imperial predecessors, Middle Eastern nations such as Egypt, Turkey, Iraq, and Iran gradually turned to art and antiquities to fill the ideological void.[23]

In China, a similar transition was underway. Though it managed to avoid the doomsday fate of the Ottoman Empire, China during this time was still afflicted by an acute identity crisis. The 1911 revolution and its tumultuous aftermath brought about not only the end of imperial rule but also a halt to the cautious optimism that had begun to prevail among Chinese reformers in their ability to modernize the empire along Western lines. In 1916, the death of President Yuan Shikai severely diminished the authority of the central government in Beijing, which was no longer able to control the actions of local military officials in the provinces. Much like Governor Yang in Xinjiang, these warlords paid lip service to the republican ideals of the new state but little more. In practice, they adopted only those policies and discourses most suited to carrying out their own personal agendas. As a result, new ideas about the priceless potential of art and antiquities to fill the void of a postimperial Chinese identity were quick to appear on paper, but slow to emerge on the ground. As we saw above, Governor Yang was ready to enforce the new antiquities laws, but only when it suited his own interests. Again, antiquities in China were now priceless—but only when the Chinese wanted them to be.

Although Yang's attempt at obstruction was half-hearted and driven almost solely by his desire to acquire the antiquities of Turfan for his own private collection, the fact that he made any attempt at all is remarkable. The reason is simple. Unlike President Yuan's administration in Beijing, which consistently failed to observe its own new laws prohibiting the export of antiquities abroad, Yang Zengxin was not indebted to any foreign power. Determined to curb Russian and British influence in Xinjiang, Yang likely viewed the outbreak of World War I as a golden opportunity to test the new geopolitical waters. Because he was not interested in taking out foreign loans or undertaking a wholesale program of Westernization in his province, Yang had little to lose and everything to gain. By contrast, the central government in Beijing, along with the governors of most other provinces, were much more dependent on the diplomatic and financial goodwill of foreign empires. In his capricious enforcement of the new antiquities legislation, Governor Yang proved willing to dispense with this goodwill in exchange for what he was now cynically characterizing as the "priceless" antiquities of a single oasis. But for every other politician in China, to enforce the new antiquities laws would be to pay an unacceptable diplomatic and financial price. To them, the antiquities of China still bore a price tag that they were willing to honor in exchange for something deemed even more valuable.

It is important to note, however, that even when someone like Governor Yang chose to enforce the new rules, he could still only enforce them to the extent that Beijing would allow. After all, Yang was merely the governor of a single province, obliged to follow the lead of his central government when push came to shove. And for the time being and for many decades to come, Beijing was still vulnerable to the pushing and shoving of the foreign powers. This means that even the occasional appearance of a temporarily "principled" stance by someone like Yang was doomed to fail in the end, for Yang and every other governor was irrevocably tethered to Beijing. Unlike in the newly independent countries of the Middle East, where relatively unified central governments and their officials took the lead in obstructing Western archaeologists, no politician in Republican China proved capable of playing a similar role. In searching for the origins of a consistently principled stance toward antiquities in China, one based on the new priceless potential of a national identity, we must look to those who had everything to gain and nothing to lose. Due to the severely compromised political arena in Republican China, this criterion excluded nearly everyone who served in high political office.

It did not, however, exclude newly Westernized Chinese scholars who worked in national institutions of higher learning. As we are about to see, it was men like these, with nothing to lose and everything to gain, who proved most willing to turn the Western valuation of art and antiquities back against its original appraisers.

THE RISE OF WESTERNIZED CHINESE SCHOLARS

Chinese scholars immune to the lure of the compensations of plunder did not appear overnight. It took nearly a decade before the first generation of fully Westernized students was ready to confront its mentors. In the meantime, they were eager to obtain professional experience as an apprentice. The first such relationships developed not in the field of archaeology, but rather paleoanthropology and paleontology. In 1914, the Ministry of Agriculture and Commerce invited Johan Gunnar Andersson, a Swedish geologist and paleontologist, to take up an official position in Beijing as mining adviser to the Chinese government. Upon his arrival, Andersson worked closely with Ding Wenjiang, the director of the National Geological Survey. Ding, one of the first Chinese with a complete Western scientific education, obtained all of his degrees from British universities, acquiring a level of fluency in English, French, and Latin said to rival that of any British scholar. In 1915, Ding met Andersson for the first time. Over the next ten years, the two men helped identified deposits of fossil fuels for the government, unearthed ancient hominid fossils such as Peking Man, and uncovered the first material evidence of Neolithic cultures predating the earliest Chinese historical narratives.[24]

Most importantly, however, Andersson and Ding played a central role in training the first generation of professional Chinese scientists within China who were willing to engage in actual fieldwork. Andersson himself highlighted this distinction in a letter to Gustaf Adolf, the crown prince of Sweden. In 1921, Andersson urged Gustaf Adolf, himself an amateur archaeologist always "ready to personally work and study in the field," to visit China and participate in an archaeological dig as a publicity stunt. "The fact is that decadent mandarinism has created a bias here against the participation of members of the upper class in any work that taxes the strength of the body," Andersson wrote. "We have encountered this difficulty, but we have been able to train a team of young government geologists, who see it as a natural thing to make use of their legs and arms in field work."[25] Shorn of the denigrating gloss on "decadent mandarinism," Andersson's statement captures well the difference between those Chinese elites who came of age in the second half of the nineteenth century versus those who came of age in the first two decades of the twentieth century. The unwillingness of the former to get their hands dirty in the field meant that they were confined to suburban excavations carried out through multiple intermediaries, such as we saw in chapter 2 with the Chinese officials and their Muslim begs in Xinjiang.

In addition to fieldwork, there was another crucial intellectual gap between these two generations of Chinese intellectuals. Both were receptive to Western ideas and eager to adapt them to the conditions of China, but only those who came of age during the twentieth century had actually digested these ideas through the unmediated tutelage of Western scientists themselves. This meant that they were true believers in new Western methodologies, unable to fall back on or take refuge in an alternative tradition of Confucian scholarship. Having come of age entirely under the banner of reform and revolution, most of these Westernized Chinese scholars evinced just as much hostility toward the old Confucian elite as their Western mentors did, if not more so. In 1928, Xu Xusheng, the co-leader of Sven Hedin's Sino-Swedish expedition who had studied abroad in France during his youth, passed just such a negative judgment on the views of a Confucian schoolmaster he met in Urumchi. "His thinking is that of the old way of twenty years ago," Xu wrote in his diary. "A bunch of nonsense about how 'there is no learning worthy of the name after the Zhou and Qin' and 'electricity and technology are not mentioned in the ancient books.' I could only refute him politely, and laugh at it all."[26]

Once trained to think and work like a Western scientist, this new crop of Chinese scholars found that it had less and less need of a Western mentor. Though Andersson is often credited by both Western and Chinese scholars with having played a pivotal role in the establishment and development of paleontology and paleoanthropology in China, such credit was slow to develop. After Andersson left China in 1925, some of his Chinese assistants later joined Hedin and Xu's Sino-Swedish expedition. In 1927, Hedin passed around a newspaper article in which Roy Chapman Andrews, the American paleontologist, defended himself against recent Chinese protests. Once they read the article, the Chinese members of the expedition grew furious. According to Huang Wenbi, the article quoted Andrews as saying "that China didn't know anything about stone artifacts originally until Andersson first discovered them. This made me really mad." The reason Huang was mad was because he believed that Andersson's Chinese colleagues deserved most of the credit. As proof, he recorded the results of his own interview with one of Andersson's former assistants. "In the evening, Zhuang Yongcheng returned from the mountains with numerous stone artifacts," Huang later wrote. "I asked him about the discovery of stone artifacts during his time with Andersson, and he informed me at length about how Andersson purchased his specimens of pottery. I thought about writing up everything he told me as a little history book about the Chinese discovery of stone artifacts, and mentioned this in a letter to Beijing. Then Andersson's story would fall apart of its own accord." Xu Xusheng seconded Huang's opinion. "As for his [Andrews's] claim that the Chinese only recognized the value of prehistoric artifacts after Andersson, this is completely wrong," Xu wrote. "The reason he went out and started to excavate was simply because there were many ancient artifacts in China, and at first he did many ridiculous things. We Chinese did not go out to search [for artifacts] because we did not have the financial resources to do so."[27]

Did the new crop of Chinese scientists lag behind their Western counterparts simply because the Westerners had more money? These disputes are difficult to untangle. When two scholars cut from the same intellectual and ideological cloth go into the field together, both men will feel entitled to claim credit for the results of their work. The truth of the matter is that neither Andersson, Ding, Zhuang, nor any other member of this revolutionary cohort of scholars in China ever acted entirely independent of one another. And yet it was Andersson and other Western scientists who were invited to serve in an advisory capacity in China, not vice versa. Furthermore, the Chinese scholars had no choice but to trace their intellectual pedigree back to a Western scholar in some capacity, be it in Europe, America, Japan, or China. Thus the Western "mentors" could not help but feel that they deserved the lion's share of the credit, either directly or indirectly, for the development of new Western scientific disciplines in China—even if many actual discoveries in the field were made by their Chinese "mentees." Conversely, these same Chinese understudies were more than ready to acknowledge their initial debt to Western scholarly institutions and advisors. At the same time, they also recognized the inherently transitory nature of any such course of tutelage. Once this course was complete, the new generation of Chinese scholars expected to be welcomed as fully legitimate members of the modern scientific club.

The Andersson model of cooperation with Chinese scholars in the postrevolutionary heartland was different from the model of cooperation that previous generations of Western archaeologists had experienced with the old Qing scholars and officials of northwestern China. In Xinjiang and Gansu, such cooperation was based more on a common class background and shared political ethos, with a clear and unbridgeable hierarchy between transimperial elites and their culturally "inferior" subjects. In the new China of the interior, however, such cooperation was based on a shared ideological commitment to the institutionalization of Western scientific practices on Chinese soil. Previously, there had been no pretense of intellectual equality between the Western scientist and Chinese scholar. Stein and Pelliot were doing things no Chinese had ever done before, and the Chinese admired them for having undertaken such pioneering work. But now the Chinese were fully capable of doing the same work themselves, and could boast of a Western educational pedigree equal to or better than that of any scholar from the West. Though men like Andersson had helped to bring about the new scientific order in China, once institutionalized, the continued presence of Western advisors was not merely superfluous. It was resented.

With respect to archaeology rather than paleontology or paleoanthropology, the situation was a bit different. The artifacts that Andersson collected and shipped away to Sweden all hailed from the prehistoric age. They shed light on an era of history that few scholars in China had ever thought existed. The archaeologists, however, dealt in historical artifacts. Whether inscribed with Chinese characters or not, everything collected during the course of an archaeological expedition could be contextualized to some degree by reference to the long venerated Confucian canon. From the perspective of the new generation of fully Westernized Chinese scholars, the export of historical artifacts such as these was a far more sensitive issue. By virtue of their very actions on the expedition trail, Westerners such as Stein had encouraged the Chinese to view such objects as priceless emblems of the empire or nation whose agents succeeded in discovering, preserving, and exhibiting them. It is entirely possible that the old generation of Confucian elites continued to regard such things as merely "precious" until the day they died. But they were absolutely priceless to the new generation of Western- or Japanese-educated scholars who came of age in the revolutionary heartland and now labored on behalf of new national universities, libraries, and museums modeled explicitly on their Western counterparts.

What this new generation of scholars still lacked, however, was a means of organizing their own archaeological expeditions. As alluded to by Xu Xusheng in the quote above, part of the problem was indeed simply financial. Expeditions were expensive undertakings, with most archaeologists being forced to rely on the generous patronage of a private patron or the closely monitored disbursements of a government stipend. The great misfortune of the first generation of Westernized Chinese scholars was to have come of age during a time when the finances of the central government in Beijing were utterly crippled. There was not even enough money to pay for basic administrative expenses of the state much less an ambitious scholarly expedition thousands of miles from the capital. In fact, Andersson himself once went three years without receiving a single penny of his official salary from the Chinese government.

The second misfortune of the new generation of fully Westernized Chinese scholars was to have come of age during the warlord era. After the death of President Yuan in 1916, few governors were willing to admit Chinese outsiders into their provinces. The not unfounded assumption was that anyone carrying papers from another jurisdiction could very well be a spy or assassin, regardless of their cover story. And archaeologists, long known to produce detailed maps of their travels and to collect valuable intelligence on local populations, were even more suspicious than most travelers. One of the reasons Andersson was able to gain access to warlord jurisdictions so often after 1916 was because he helped to identify exploitable mineral resources for his hosts. In 1920, in a letter to William Matthew, a curator at the American Museum of Natural History in New York, Andersson underscored this point. "Geological research as a State enterprise is quite new here in China, and consequently it is easier to raise the necessary funds for practical prospecting work especially concerning metalliferous deposits," he wrote. "It is only natural that the authorities are not inclined to spend large sums of money for such an entirely scientific undertaking as the study of the mammal remains."[28]

The other, and probably chief, reason was because he was a foreigner. Though the young Westernized Chinese scholars in Beijing were largely immune to the compensations of plunder, Republican warlords were not. Ever hopeful of securing the slightest edge over their rivals, most warlords still had much to gain and little to lose by cooperating with foreign scholars. The scant effort required to affix one's seal to a passport and issue orders for logistical support were easily repaid by the diplomatic, social, and economic capital still proffered by the foreign archaeologist and his consular backers. And if the foreigner's presence later proved damaging to the warlord's private interests in any way—such as Stein's presence in Turfan did to Governor Yang in 1915—he could always invoke the letter of new nationalist laws regarding the protection of cultural heritage to kick him out.

Unfortunately, most of the warlords had little expectation of receiving useful compensations from an unknown Chinese scholar bearing papers from a politically and financially impotent domestic patron. Accompanied by a prestigious Western archaeologist hailing from a powerful and wealthy foreign patron, however, these same Chinese scholars might be welcomed with open arms. In order to understand where, when, and how the first Westernized Chinese began to get attached to Western expeditions in China—and thus where, when, and how Chinese opposition to Western archaeological enterprise first materialized—we must turn our attention to Harvard art historian Langdon Warner and the ill-fated expeditions he undertook for the Fogg Museum.

THE FIRST FOGG EXPEDITION

The first American expedition to northwestern China appears to have been inspired by the French sinologist Paul Pelliot. In 1913, five years after Pelliot's famous visit to Dunhuang, the American art historian Langdon Warner (figure 21) tracked him down in Paris and told him of plans for the development of an American School of Archaeology in Beijing. Warner, then working as a curator of Asian art at the Boston Museum of Fine Arts, was traveling the world in search of Chinese and Japanese sculpture for his museum. Pelliot advised Warner to visit the French Archaeological School at Hanoi and to begin the task of amassing a great American collection of Asian art with a corpus of early Chinese inscriptions. After the outbreak of World War I, Warner once again crossed paths with Pelliot, this time in Beijing and Siberia. Both men were in the Far East on behalf of their respective governments, carrying out wartime intelligence operations under the guise of archaeology. When Warner told Pelliot of several failed proposals to establish an American archaeological presence in China, Pelliot proposed that he and Warner undertake a new expedition to Xinjiang after the war was over. "That would be an immense feather in our caps," Warner wrote to Frederick A. Whiting, the director of the Cleveland Museum of Art, "as he is the one who collected all the Tun-huang mss. and brought back the great T'ang paintings. Also he has several new sites for excavation up his sleeve, but will have no money to work them."[29]

Although the proposed joint expedition to Xinjiang never materialized, the proposal itself was an indication of how things had changed since the war. Europeans like Pelliot, Stein, and Le Coq had all the antiquities, experience, and fame, but they no longer had any money. By contrast, the Americans lacked antiquities, experience, and fame, but they had plenty of money. Edward Forbes and Paul Sachs, the director and associate director, respectively, of the Fogg Art Museum at Harvard, were eager to redress this imbalance. "I have, for years, been most anxious to send an expedition out from Harvard into Eastern Asia and I hope that it will be possible for us to do so in the near future," Forbes wrote to Pelliot in 1921. "I am just starting to raise money in the hopes that we can send an expedition out to follow your advice and bring to this part of the world the wonderful treasures about which you spoke in your public lectures." After securing Pelliot's blessing

Figure 21. Harvard Art Historian Langdon Warner. In two separate expeditions for the Fogg Museum in the early 1920s, Langdon Warner, desperate to build an Asian art collection in the United States that would not attract the pity of his European colleagues, pushed the boundaries of Western archaeological expeditions in China into uncharted waters. This undated photograph was likely taken at some point in the early 1930s, about a decade after his controversial expeditions to Dunhuang. Photographs of the Harvard Art Museums (HC 22), folder 3.291. Image number: VRS245177. Accession number: ARCH.0000.596. Harvard Art Museums Archives, Harvard University, Cambridge, MA.

for such an enterprise, Forbes and Sachs then recruited Langdon Warner from his post as director of the Pennsylvania Museum of Art. Warner was lured to Harvard by the promise of flexible teaching duties, ample time and money for travel, and a clear mandate to build up the Asian collections of the Fogg Museum. In 1922, as part of an application for funding submitted to John D. Rockefeller Jr., Warner highlighted the glaring disparity between American and European museums in the display of Gandharan art. "The British, the French, the Germans and the Russians, have, in the last twelve years, so added to our knowledge of the history of the human race, and incidentally enriched their museums with artistic monuments brought from Turkestan," Warner wrote, "that it has become almost a matter of reproach that America has contributed nothing in that direction."[30]

More than twenty years had passed, however, since the first European expeditions returned from Xinjiang. As a result, neither Forbes nor Warner was certain of what they might find. In 1921, Forbes wrote to Pelliot for more details regarding the Chinese removal of manuscripts from Dunhuang to Beijing in 1910. "May I ask you whether that means that since you were there the Government has taken most of the books and that the pictures and statues remain, or did the Chinese Government only take part of the books that still remain?" Unsure of what still lay unclaimed, the directors of the Fogg Museum tried to temper their expectations. "Director Forbes realizes that a mere report may be the sole result of the first expedition," Warner informed Rockefeller in his application for funding. Nonetheless, "it should certainly contain enough fresh material amply to repay the effort." Despite such modest declarations, it was clear that Forbes and Sachs still harbored great ambitions for their collections. In his letter to Rockefeller, Warner held out hope that "tangible results will be brought back in the form of archaeological collections," including "collections of sculptures or paintings or manuscripts or all of these things." Rockefeller, too, clearly expected just such a return on his investment. "It is not clear from your letter what disposition is to be made of such treasures and material," wrote Rockefeller's secretary, "but Mr. Rockefeller assumes Harvard University is to have whatever is found."[31]

In July 1923, Warner, accompanied by Horace Jayne, a longtime colleague from the Pennsylvania Museum of Art, arrived in Beijing. Their goal was to reach Kara-khoto, an ancient Tangut (and later Mongol) city located on the northwestern fringes of the Gobi Desert. En route, they would pass through most of Gansu province, including areas where the previous generation of European archaeologists had reaped their spoils. One major difference between Warner's expedition and theirs, however, was that Warner was obliged to start his journey in Beijing and pass through inner China. By contrast, the Europeans had all approached Xinjiang and Gansu from the west, either by climbing over the Himalayas from India or taking the Trans-Siberian railway through Russia. The Russian civil war now precluded the Trans-Siberian railway, while growing American ties in Beijing and the rise of the isolationist Governor Yang in Urumchi discouraged the Himalayan route. As we shall see, this put Warner in close proximity to the first generation of fully Westernized Chinese scholars, who now populated the increasingly prestigious universities and scholarly institutions of the capital. As a result, anything Warner did in China would quickly become known to the Westernized scholars of Beijing, men who felt just as qualified as Warner but lacked the financial and diplomatic ties to do as he did.

In 1923–24, during the first Fogg Museum expedition in China, Warner was treated in much the same way that Stein had been treated on his third expedition a decade earlier. Despite the ongoing political instability, Warner had no trouble securing safe passage through the domains of the warlords through whose realms he had to pass in order to reach Kara-khoto. In Henan, General Wu Peifu agreed to clear the road ahead for a couple of "modest scholars," and provided Warner and Jayne with an armed escort as far as Xi'an. After asking Warner to display an American flag on his vehicle, Wu proceeded to squeeze as much diplomatic capital out of this American delegation as he could, inviting thirty members of his staff to a lively dinner at which military songs were performed throughout the night. Once in Gansu, Warner found that General Wu's letters of introduction were capable of resolving any and all logistical difficulties, including a minor spat with the magistrate of Lanzhou.[32]

In November 1923, Warner and Jayne finally reached Kara-khoto, only to discover that the previous wave of European archaeologists had already cleared the site. Still hoping for tangible proceeds, Warner changed his plans and headed toward Dunhuang, this time without Jayne, who had fallen ill. Two months later, he reached the caves where both Stein and Pelliot had made their names. The beauty of the painted Buddhist wall murals in the grottoes left a deep impression on Warner, as did evidence of widespread vandalism and destruction since Stein's last visit. The worst infliction was that of several hundred White Russian soldiers, whom Governor Yang managed to disarm and intern in Dunhuang after they fled Bolshevik armies in Central Asia and attempted to plot their return to the battlefield from Xinjiang. "But across some of these lovely faces are scribbled the numbers of a Russian regiment," he informed his wife, "and from the mouth of the Buddha where he sits to deliver the Lotus Law flows some Slav obscenity."

Forbes had previously expressed to Warner his view that the separation of
"sculptures from living rock would be a vandalism which he does not approve." But now Warner had resolved to take drastic measures. "My job is
to break my neck to rescue and preserve anything and everything I can from
this quick ruin," he told his wife. "It has been stable enough for centuries,
but the end is in sight now."[33]

Five months later, the fateful result was delivered to the Fogg Museum
in Cambridge: twelve badly damaged paintings from Dunhuang, all stripped
from the walls of the caves through a complex process involving various
glues and chemicals. Warner also brought away a handful of Buddhist sculptures offered for sale by Wang Yuanlu, who had finally exhausted his seemingly endless supply of manuscripts and was now peddling other creative
forms of economic capital. What did the Chinese think about what Warner
had done? Reactions were diverse. According to Warner himself, the local
Chinese elites of Dunhuang, including the magistrate, knew full well what
he had done—and were fine with it. "When I left the caves and the town
I believe that I was in particular good odour," Warner later wrote to Stein.
"The magistrate dined and wined me and prominent citizens saw me on my
road with ceremony. Incidentally I made a point of telling the magistrate
what I [had] done and also telling him that I had seen no scrolls—the remaining few apparently were taken by the Russians."[34]

There is no reason to doubt Warner's claims here regarding the benign
disposition of the local magistrate. After all, this revelation was tendered
within the confines of a private letter to Stein and was not intended for
public consumption. Warner thus had little incentive to twist the truth.
Not only that, but the picture Warner paints of a cooperative northwestern
elite, steeped in the cosmopolitan ethos of yesteryear and eager to please
a prestigious foreign scholar, has a familiar ring to it. This was a classic
case of transimperial bonding between two educated elites. Though some of
these old Confucian elites would occasionally invoke the new discourse of
cultural sovereignty, such instances were rare and nearly always motivated
by personal agendas rather than altruistic principle. The case of Governor
Yang obstructing Stein at Turfan in 1915 is a case in point. Warner, too, fell
afoul of similarly motivated obstruction as he made his way back to Beijing from Dunhuang. Upon his arrival in Suzhou, Warner was confronted
by five Chinese soldiers sent by the local magistrate to demand the return
of a Six Dynasties bronze statue that the brother of the magistrate of Jinta
had given him as a gift several months earlier. In Warner's mind, the order
for its return appeared to originate in an ugly spat he had had with the

magistrate of Lanzhou, who, on learning that Warner had procured an antiquity, decided to enact his revenge by invoking the new antiquities law against him. Warner, indignant at being treated "like a thief" and cognizant of the petty origins of the affair, held onto the statue until he could procure a meeting with the military governor of Suzhou, "an old dear" with whom he got along well.

Warner's description of his meeting with the military governor (zhentai) of Suzhou perfectly illustrates the looming conflict between those who continued to subscribe to old transimperial mores and those who chose to invoke the newly enshrined nationalist principle of cultural sovereignty—sincerely or not. "I've just been to the Chent'ai with the bronze in my pocket," Warner wrote to his wife. "He knew all about the matter and when they demanded that he send a man to stop me he told them flatly that he would do no such thing but he would let them know when I struck town and they could send the man who gave me the bronze to ask it back as a favor!" Much as the magistrate of Dunhuang had done just a few weeks prior, the military governor of Suzhou also proceeded to wine and dine Warner, plying him with "3-Star Brandy and tinned corned beef for my foreign taste." While they ate, however, "word came that the Magistrate had warned the inn master not to let us leave town. You should have seen the Chent'ai explode! He was the old cavalry man again in a flash and he barked an order that the Magistrate was to be reprimanded and the inn man told to treat us like honored guests." The luncheon then continued, with "more 3-Star, and ham and eggs and more 3-Star, then the present of a Tibetan painting."[35]

The days of Aurel Stein and Pan Zhen, it seems, were not yet over. As for the art and antiquities removed by Warner from Dunhuang, it should not surprise us to find his Confucian hosts concerned only about ancient steles and manuscripts—hence Warner's special mention to the magistrate that he "had seen no scrolls," along with the same man's seeming indifference toward the twelve wall paintings Warner openly admitted to taking. After all, as we saw in previous chapters, the old Confucian elites tended to regard such things as vulgar religious "dreck" that was hardly worth their attention. But it was one thing to remove such things from the lands of the culturally disconnected Muslim peasants of Xinjiang, who were quick to dispose, destroy, or sell them. It was quite another to remove objects of religious worship among a population that still actively venerated them, as the Chinese peasants of Dunhuang did. As Stein would later tell Warner, he had "felt all along that the people of Tun-huang were a *gens religiosissima* and easily swayed by any agitator working upon their superstitions, etc." In

other words, the Confucian elites may not have cared much about the cave
murals removed by Warner, but the impoverished peasants who worshipped
them regarded them as absolutely priceless.[36]

Of course, Stein and Pelliot had also removed small portions of wall
murals from the Thousand-Buddha Caves. But these were tiny and insig-
nificant compared to what Warner had done. In addition, neither Stein nor
Pelliot had undertaken their handiwork against a backdrop of local drought
and famine. Warner did. As a result, his actions would be interpreted by
the peasants as a direct attack on the spiritual guardians of Dunhuang, who
enacted their revenge by ravaging the land. Soon after Warner's departure,
the locals discovered the gaping holes in their religious murals, most likely
during the annual pilgrimage undertaken in the spring. The reaction of the
villagers to Warner's activities is recorded in the diary of Chen Wanli (figure 22), a Chinese scholar destined to play a key role in the second Fogg
expedition to Dunhuang. In May 1925, during a conversation with Yang
Yiwen, the new magistrate of Dunhuang, Chen learned that after Warner's
departure the previous year, "the local people went en masse to the magistrate to question him about this matter." He further learned that some
of the locals had "accused" Wang Yuanlu of angering their gods. When the
magistrate who had wined and dined Warner the previous year was transferred to a new post, Chen learned that "he got as far as Xindianzi (a place
no more than a few miles east of Dunhuang township) when the people detained him, demanding that he return the wall paintings removed by Warner. At that point Warden Lu raced back to Dunhuang and brought back
several prominent citizens. Only then did the situation ameliorate."[37]

Thus far we have encountered four distinct Chinese reactions to the activities of Langdon Warner during the first Fogg expedition: the purely transactional assistance of a Republican warlord in search of diplomatic capital,
the eager cooperation of the old Confucian elite in exchange for social and
political capital, the cynical invocation of the new discourse of cultural
sovereignty by an opportunistic local official, and the principled indignation of impoverished peasants who perceived a priceless spiritual connection in the artifacts removed. The first three reactions evinced a pedigree
that went back to the earliest Western expeditions. The fourth and final
reaction, however, was very new indeed, for no previous Western scholar
had been so bold as to remove objects of active religious worship without
first reaching mutually agreed terms of compensation with the worshippers
themselves. The fact that Warner represented the belated collecting interests of a fledgling American museum, eager to catch up with its European
peers, is likely responsible for spurring him to such desperate measures. By

Figure 22. The Enigma of Chen Wanli. In 1925, Chen Wanli, an instructor in the Peking University School of Medicine, was selected to accompany the Second Fogg Expedition to Dunhuang. This marked the first time that a Westernized Chinese scholar was included as a member of a foreign archaeological expedition in China. Chen's precise role in the American expedition has long proved elusive, obscured by the deliberate misinformation Warner later circulated about the failed joint venture. Chen's Chinese-language diary, however, reveals him to be a far more complex—and sympathetic—character than that portrayed by Warner. Chen Wanli, *Xixing riji* [A diary of westward travels] (Beijing: Pushe, 1926), 3.

1924, the famous manuscripts of Dunhuang had all finally been dispersed. All that remained were public works of actively worshipped art, a taboo from which previous explorers had wisely kept their distance.

At the time Warner left Dunhuang, he knew nothing of the peasant wrath he had stirred up in his wake. This would come back to haunt him. Warner was also completely in the dark with respect to a fifth Chinese reaction, one that did not materialize until his return to Beijing. This was the reaction of Westernized Chinese scholars at national institutions of higher learning, and it would prove most fatal to the prospects of future work in China. The chain of events begins with two men: William Hung and Yuan Fuli. Hung, the dean of Yenching University, a prestigious Christian college in Beijing with close ties to Harvard, is notable for having adopted an English version of his Chinese name (Hong Ye). This shows just how Westernized he was, for none of the Chinese who interacted with Stein and Pelliot in the late Qing or early Republican eras ever adopted an English name. Like Ding Wenjiang, Andersson's colleague, Hung received all of his degrees at Western—in this case, American—universities. Hung's claim to fame stems from an interview he gave in 1978 to Susan Chan Egan, his Chinese American biographer. In early 1925, Hung said, Wang Jinren, the Chinese interpreter from Warner's first Fogg expedition, approached Hung with tears in his eyes to inform him that Warner was returning for a second expedition. Wang allegedly then told Hung what Warner had done at Dunhuang the previous year. Hung's response was to arrange a meeting with Qin Fen, the vice minister of education, and ask him to send an order to local officials throughout Gansu ordering them not to let Warner remove any more artifacts. He then told Wang "to go ahead with the trip and act as if nothing was happening."[38]

There are reasons to doubt parts of Hung's story. The most suspicious part of his account, told to a sympathetic biographer fifty years after the events in question, concerns the role of Wang Jinren, Warner's Chinese interpreter. In 1925, during a postmortem of the second expedition, Warner told Forbes that when he left Dunhuang the previous year, "the scene seemed quite set for another years work and everyone pleased with the foreigner's visit. Wang, the interpreter, told me at the time that it would be easier on the next trip!" In another letter to Paul Sachs, Warner claimed that "both Wang and I, when we left Tun Huang last year, thoroughly believed that the next year's work was made certain and that next time we should come as old friends." Warner also later told Stein that Wang Yuanlu, through whom all negotiations for the purchase of Buddhist statues and permission to remove wall paintings must have passed, "had been most friendly [to Interpreter] Wang on our former visit." All this suggests that Interpreter Wang was a most enthusiastic participant in Warner's removal of cave murals from Dunhuang in early 1924, of a type not unlike Stein's loyal Chinese secretary Jiang Xiaowan fifteen years earlier. It is thus difficult to imagine him turning heel virtually overnight and attempting to sabotage an undertaking he himself had done so much to bring about.[39]

But there is another reason to doubt Hung's claim as the first Western-ized Chinese scholar to obstruct foreign expeditions in China. In April 1925, just two months after the second Fogg expedition departed Beijing, Horace Jayne, who had taken over the party in Warner's absence, wrote a letter to Forbes recounting the exact moment he discovered just how much the Westernized Chinese scholars of Beijing knew about the activities of the first expedition. "You must realize that at this time I had no knowledge of one vital fact: that the people at [Peking] University and many others in Peking knew definitely that Warner last year had brought back frescoes from Tun Huang," Jayne wrote. He then singled out the role of Wang Jinren, the interpreter, in securing such knowledge. "We had not been on the road a fortnight before our Interpreter Mr. Wang discovered this in talking with Dr. Chen [Wanli]." Not only does Wang again come off as a loyal member of the American camp, someone who seems just as surprised as Jayne to learn that anyone in Beijing knew of the missing murals, but this passage also makes it clear that many more people in Beijing other than William Hung knew what had transpired in Dunhuang. More specifically, Jayne singles out Peking University—not Hung's Yenching University—as the primary source of information about the activities of the first Fogg expedition among Chinese scholars in Beijing.[40]

How did the Westernized Chinese scholars of Peking University learn about Warner's deeds? According to Jayne, there were three paths of trans-mission, none of which appear to lead directly to Wang Jinren or William Hung. "We have discovered the ways in which this information of Warner's activities last year reached Peking," Jayne continued in his letter to Forbes. The first two involved unnamed Chinese civil servants of the Gansu pro-vincial government: "an employee of the Lanchow post office who brought back the news" and "one or more members of the Kansu Provincial Gov-ernment who on being transferred related the story to friends in Peking." It is by no means clear whether these informants related the story of War-ner's actions at Dunhuang in the spirit of casual and benign gossip, or as an indignant commentary on foreign imperialism. Either way, it is certainly possible that William Hung's mysterious informant was in fact one of these men rather than Interpreter Wang. If so, then Hung can still claim a vaunted perch in the annals of modern Chinese nationalism as one of the first West-ernized Chinese scholars to take the lead in obstructing Western archaeolo-gists, regardless of whether his informants had intended to push him into such a role or not.[41]

Whatever Hung may or may not have done, the actions of a third man, Yuan Fuli, were likely far more damning to Warner's interests. "And also,"

Jayne informed Forbes, "there was one Mr. Yuan, [a] member of the Geological Survey of China who was in Lanchow as Dr. Andersson's assistant when Warner passed through last year." There are two reasons why Yuan Fuli's knowledge of Warner's activities at Dunhuang would prove so damaging to the work of foreign archaeologists in China. First, Yuan, a graduate of Columbia University, would have bristled at Jayne's characterization of him as Andersson's "assistant." In Yuan's eyes, he was a fully competent colleague of Andersson, in no way inferior in education, training, or experience. In other words, Yuan was the quintessential representative of the first generation of fully Westernized Chinese scholars, someone who was willing to get his hands dirty and saw no reason why any foreigner should take the lead in the field. The second reason Yuan's influence would reach further than Hung's was because of his institutional affiliation. As Jayne ruefully observed, "Mr. Yuan, in addition to his Survey job, is a professor in the Peking National University." Put these two considerations together, and the stage was set for conflict. In his letter to Forbes, Jayne drew equal attention to the importance of Yuan's affiliation with a national institution of Westernized higher learning and his willingness to confront his Western "mentors":

> When it came to dividing the spoils of Dr. Andersson's work, the Chinese, and Mr. Yuan in particular, were dissatisfied with what Dr. Andersson regarded an equal division. It is impossible to believe that Dr. Andersson was in any way unjust, yet it is true he may have regarded things in a slightly different light from when the agreement was made: he had received no pay for two years. Either way Mr. Yuan is without doubt critical of plans involving cooperation with foreigners, and Mr. Yuan is a member of the P.[eking] N.[ational] U.[niversity] faculty.[42]

In short, nearly everyone in China seemed to know what Warner had done. But it was only through the initiative of fully Westernized Chinese scholars like Yuan Fuli and William Hung in Beijing that such knowledge was finally translated into concrete action on the ground. This action took the form of numerous government telegrams sent back and forth between the central government in Beijing and the Chinese officials of Gansu, many of whom, as we saw during Warner's first trip in 1924, were more than happy to let him remove antiquities from their jurisdictions. Most likely Yuan and Hung both played a decisive role in getting various organs of the Chinese government to issue orders warning local officials in Gansu about Warner's return and publicizing what he had done the previous year. With regard to Hung, we can probably accept at face value his claim that he approached Qin Fen, the vice minister of education, and asked him to send out such orders. And we know for a fact that Yuan Fuli was instrumental in getting the Gansu provincial government to issue similar orders in the wake of disagreements concerning the division of artifacts with Andersson. As Jayne himself noted in 1925, "last year such a telegram was sent instructing the provincial governments to guard carefully all antiquities within their borders." As further evidence of this flurry of communications regarding the preservation of antiquities, we have the Chinese-language diary of Chen Wanli, who accompanied Jayne to Dunhuang on the second expedition. In May 1925, during a conversation with the local police warden of Dunhuang, Chen learned that "the offices of the Defense Commissioner and Circuit Intendant both have multiple secret orders [dieyou miling] that compel them" to prevent the party from removing any more murals.[43]

Although we may quibble over the details, the accounts of both Jayne and Hung presented above are in complete accord on three facts: the timing, location, and agents of the first sustained and principled obstruction efforts of Western archaeological enterprise in China. The year was 1925, the place was Beijing, and the men were Westernized Chinese scholars working outside of high political office: William Hung at Yenching University and Yuan Fuli at Peking University. Both men goaded their political leaders to act in a way that they probably would not have otherwise done, susceptible as they were to the allure of diplomatic capital. And whether or not Wang the interpreter did in fact play the unlikely role ascribed to him by Hung—if he did, then his acting skills were first rate—the end result was the same. That is, the obstruction of foreign archaeologists in China began as a direct response to Warner's attempt to revive the pre-Andersson model of solo Western expeditions, those that excluded fully equal and scientifically qualified Chinese colleagues. During the early days of Stein and Pelliot, such exclusion was perhaps unavoidable, if for no other reason than that there were so few (if any) fully Westernized Chinese scholars in China who were willing to venture out into the subzero desert for weeks at a time. Two decades later, however, the Andersson model of full and equal collaboration with Westernized Chinese colleagues was the only acceptable template for foreign archaeological enterprise in China—and even that was now coming under assault. The spark lit by William Hung and Yuan Fuli in 1925 would then be further inflamed by the unfortunate peasants of Dunhuang, who cared little for the abstract concerns of Yuan or Hung but were sorely upset at the despoilation of their gods.

The grievances of both these parties were something the previous generation of Western archaeologists had never before encountered. In hindsight, it seems that Warner was exceedingly fortunate to have ever made it to Dunhuang in the first place, much less removed anything from the country.

He would not be so lucky the second time around.

CHAPTER FIVE

Rise of the Apprentices

Preparations for a second Fogg Museum expedition to Dunhuang got underway almost immediately on Warner's return to Cambridge. Warner's dire warnings about the deteriorating conditions of the Thousand-Buddha Caves elicited much support from Forbes and Sachs for a more protracted stay at Dunhuang. "Information obtained on the first Fogg Museum expedition to China," Forbes wrote in July 1924, "makes it obvious that the work must, in the future, be amplified to include not only the study of the Tun Huang wall paintings but their preservation and their exhibition in America." This time a much larger team of seven scholars and technicians would be assembled, with the ultimate goal of removing entire wall frescos from multiple caves for reassembly at the Fogg Museum. It was also expected that an equal number of cave murals would be given to the Chinese for installation at a suitable institution in Beijing, as an unavoidable concession for their support. In preparation for the expedition, James Barney, a wealthy art collector from New York originally tapped to lead the expedition in place of Warner (whose wife was ill), found inspiration in none other than Pelliot's work. "I have been going over Pelliot's photographs of the frescoes this morning," Barney wrote to Forbes in June 1924. "I find that I want about 3/5ths of them. I should like to take caves 70 and 120 N. complete one for Peking one for the Fogg. (120 N for the Fogg, I hope)."[1]

In proposing to remove the artwork of entire caves from Dunhuang, Forbes knew that he was traversing uncharted territory. Aware that the Thousand-Buddha Caves was an active site of worship by the local peasants—though not aware that these same peasants had already discovered Warner's handiwork from the previous year—Forbes toyed with the remarkable idea of hiring an artist to accompany the second expedition. The job of this artist would be twofold. First, he could act on the suggestion of Pelliot, who "begged us to secure accurate copies of the frescoes, saying that he considered that to be as important a work as we could do in the Far East." Second, he could repaint any fresco that the expedition chose to remove from Dunhuang, an act "which may be undertaken for reasons of political expediency." It would also be undertaken for reasons of religious expediency. Such an artist, Forbes continued, "could undoubtedly make a copy in the place of the original which would doubtless fully satisfy the priests and the worshippers there." He then floated the name of Alexander Jacovleff, a Russian émigré artist based in Paris who was "very eager to go," having "begged me to send him with Langdon's first expedition."[2]

Although nothing came of this idea, the idea itself reveals the extent to which the backers of the second Fogg expedition knew that they were playing with fire in divesting Dunhuang of religious artwork that was still actively worshipped by the local population. Another indication that both Forbes and Warner knew just how morally dubious the goals of this second expedition were lay in the fact that both men evinced a high degree of anxiety regarding Pelliot's reaction to their proposed activities. They tried to allay their fears by courting Pelliot's blessing beforehand, but disagreed over how much to tell him. "I enclose copy, which I laboriously pounded out on the machine, of a letter which goes today to Pelliot," Warner informed Sachs in August 1924. "In it you will see that I have spoken of fresco removal as remote possibility. I do this because I fear his reaction if it is sprung on him at once. Edward [Forbes] is of the opposite opinion and characteristically wishes to lay all his cards on the table at once."[3]

For an American like Warner, the blessing of Pelliot, one of the giants of the first wave of European expeditions to northwestern China, was absolutely essential, "especially as Pelliot told me some years ago that he would never speak to me again if I tried to rob the chapels of Tun Huang." In his carefully composed letter to Pelliot, Warner took both the high and low roads, mixing lofty words about preservation in a museum with subtle and not-so-subtle appeals to the Frenchman's vanity. "I regard you as the tutelary deity of Tun Huang and should not want to suggest any work there which you do not sanction," Warner wrote in August 1924. "Please think the matter over seriously with the possibility of their being safe in the museum at Peking. In case such work were done by us no doubt a specimen could be presented by the Chinese government, or by the Fogg, to the Louvre or the Guimet in your name." In the end, Pelliot's vaunted approval was secured, though it came too late to soothe Warner's tormented conscience. "I saw Pelliot in Paris and told him that you had brought one statue back and showed him the photograph," Forbes informed Warner in July 1925, a month after the second expedition had already disbanded. "I also told him you had removed a few scraps experimentally and said that the present expedition, was armed with cameras and also that you were prepared with the consent of the Chinese authorities to remove some other pieces; and that you had a Chinese scholar with you. He said that if they were being destroyed he had changed his mind and approved of your saving them."[4]

In his description of the terms under which the second expedition set out from Beijing, Forbes gives the impression that Warner was working in harmony with Chinese scholars and government authorities. The truth of what actually transpired is far more complex, and it is made all the more so by the many deliberate half-truths Warner later told in an attempt to salvage his good name. What follows is the first systematic attempt in any language to reconstruct the actual course of events during the second Fogg expedition from Beijing to Dunhuang. In so doing, we must approach the available source material with extreme caution, since so much of it was produced in trying and acrimonious circumstances, with huge financial and political investments at stake. Our primary sources are of four types, listed in descending order of reliability: the unpublished English-language letters written by the other American members of expedition while in the field; the published Chinese-language diary of Chen Wanli, the Chinese scholar from Peking University who accompanied the expedition to Dunhuang; the unpublished letters of Warner, who initially stayed behind in Beijing and never reached Dunhuang; and finally, the published accounts of Warner intended for public consumption many years after he left China.

In a sense, it seems a bit odd that Warner's name should be so closely associated with the second Fogg expedition. After all, in the first three and half months after the vanguard party set out from Beijing, Warner was not with his American colleagues as they made their way toward Dunhuang (figure 23). Instead, he chose to remain behind in Beijing for several weeks in an attempt to negotiate an agreement with the scholars of Peking University for some sort of joint Sino-American school of advanced studies in Chinese history and culture. "My job," he told Sachs in August 1924, "will be to sound out the Pres.[ident] of Peking University in the hope that it will agree to some sort of liaison with H.[arvard] U.[niversity]." Warner's negotiating skills came to naught. Hu Shi, one of the most influential young intellectuals of the day with degrees from Cornell and Columbia, told Warner that the university could not possibly afford to be regarded as beholden to foreigners in either a scholarly or financial sense. With that, Warner decided to rejoin the expedition, setting out from Beijing at the end of March 1925.[5]

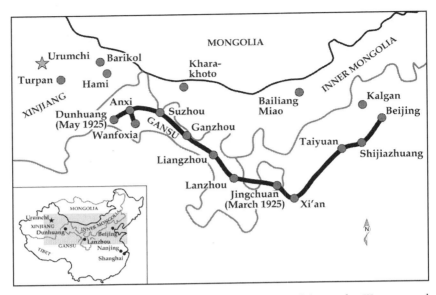

Figure 23. The Second Fogg Expedition to Dunhuang, 1925. While Langdon Warner stayed behind in Beijing to attend to other matters, Horace Jayne, a curator of Asian art at the Pennsylvania Museum of Art, led Chen Wanli and his American colleagues to Dunhuang, with plans to peel away several complete sets of cave murals. A scuffle with the peasants of Jingchuan over the disturbance of murals in the nearby Arhat Caves in March demonstrated the folly of this plan long before the expedition ever reached Dunhuang. Humiliated by his failure to deliver on any of his promises, Warner proceeded to blame Chen Wanli and the May 30 incident for the expedition's troubles at Dunhuang. Cartography by Debbie Newell.

It took Warner two and a half months to catch up with the other Americans. In the meantime, they were led by Horace Jayne, the twenty-seven-year-old curator of Asian art at the Pennsylvania Museum of Art. Jayne had already set out from Beijing a month and a half earlier with the six other members of the expedition. Minus Warner, however, there should only have been five. The unexpected sixth member of this party was Chen Wanli. Understanding Chen's role in the second Fogg expedition is critical, for he was the first fully Westernized Chinese scholar of the new generation—or any Chinese scholar of any generation, for that matter—to accompany an archaeological expedition into northwest China for the purpose of doing actual fieldwork. Unfortunately, the circumstances that led to his participation in the expedition, including his activities in the field, are still far from clear. Even more than Wang Jinren, Warner's interpreter, Chen Wanli is a frustrating enigma.

Like so much of what Warner would later say regarding the course of the second expedition, his comments regarding Chen are contradictory and colored by the inflamed passions in which he indulged on the failure of the expedition. On June 23, 1925, after reuniting with the vanguard party, Warner referred to Chen in a letter as "the representative of Peking Gov't. University—who went with us at our invitation. My hope was that by taking him I should persuade them of our intention and ability to cooperate." Just one year later, however, Warner denied extending any such invitation, informing Stein that the professors at Peking University "begged to have him go along and, though I wasn't very anxious to take him, I felt that if they wanted a spy on my actions I could best show my good faith by taking him with me. If they did not, he could do no harm." Warner then cited Jayne as telling him that Chen "never really believed that we would keep our word about not removing the treasures and that almost till the end he was aloof and suspicious." Finally, Warner adds, Chen repaid his debt to his American colleagues by writing "a series of articles about his amazing adventures with the foreigners, attributing to my young assistants the vilest motives." This series of alleged articles does not exist. What does exist is a Chinese-language diary, *A Diary of Westward Travels* (*Xixing riji*), published by Chen in 1926, one year after he returned to Beijing. As we shall see below, nowhere in Chen's diary does he attribute vile motives to any of his American companions or slander them in any way.[6]

As for Warner's claim that Jayne distrusted Chen from the outset and that Chen remained aloof and suspicious throughout the expedition, we have Jayne's own testimony to the contrary. On April 9, 1925, Jayne wrote a long and detailed letter to Forbes from Lanzhou. The timing of this letter is important: it was written before the debacle at Dunhuang, but after the revelation of widespread Chinese knowledge of what Warner had done on the first expedition, along with the subsequent awareness that such activities would not be permitted again. In his letter to Forbes, Jayne recounts how Warner's negotiations for a Sino-American scholarly partnership with the Chinese professors at Peking University prompted Warner himself to suggest that future expeditions be organized as joint Sino-American ventures. "This group was much pleased with the tentative suggestion that future expeditions should be composed of both Chinese and European scholars working for mutual benefit," Jayne recalled. Indeed, so much impressed were they that "they scurried around in the few days left before our departure from Peking and produced one Dr. Chen, a member of the University faculty, much interested in antiquities and skilled in photography; him they wished us to take along with us on the present expedition. In view of the Big Scheme and the value such a connection at the University offered, I accepted Dr. Chen as a member of the expedition." Jayne attributed two motives to the Chinese side, neither of them sinister: "first, and undoubtedly chiefest, they wanted to show their readiness to cooperate; and second, they very wisely desired to discover whether future expeditions representing Chinese and foreign institutions were feasible or not."[7]

From the beginning, some of the other American members of the expedition entertained the notion that Chen may have been sent to spy on them. Warner, despite spending no more than one week in Chen's presence toward the end of the expedition, clearly subscribed to this view. Alan Priest, a tutor in fine arts at Harvard, toyed with the idea soon after the party left Beijing. "We have brought with us at the request of Yenching University a Chinese scholar who may or may not have been sent to see what we are up to," Priest wrote to Forbes, mistaking one Beijing university for another. "In either case it is pure gain for us because he is already no end of use in dealing with the Chinese and on the strength of his coming the University has wired ahead to the governors of Shansi, of Shensi, and of Kansu and given us special passports." One month later, Priest heaped more praise on Chen, telling Sachs that "the doctor gives us a nice comfortable feeling of physical security and ingratiates us with the Chinese who appear from every direction whenever they get wind of him." About this same time, writing from Beijing well behind the rest of the party, Warner also seemed pleased with the addition of Chen, "who has gone ahead with the others [and] will contribute a chapter on the inscriptions and the literary evidence concerning the dating of the pictures." And Jayne himself, who interacted the most with Chen, concluded in his letter to Forbes that he was "sure that Dr. Chen himself was not instructed to spy on us or impede our work, and that as far as he knew he was merely the guest of the expedition, sent to help us and from us learn methods and whatever else of value to him and his associates." In the final analysis, Jayne regarded Chen as being "of much value and a distinct addition to the expedition in many ways."[8]

The charge that Chen was sent by Peking University to spy on the Americans appears to have originated in Warner's own contradictory and self-serving statements put forth after the conclusion of the expedition. No other member of the expedition—that is, the men who, unlike Warner, actually interacted with Chen on a daily basis—seriously entertained this notion. Unfortunately, it was Warner who went on to enshrine his version of the expedition into various publications for a Western audience, and it was his retroactive views of Chen that were destined to be accepted by future chroniclers of the second Fogg expedition.[9] Even some Chinese scholars, eager to embrace the idea of a humble college professor bringing down the foreign imperialists, have accepted Warner's claims at face value, in spite of the fact that Chen's own Chinese-language diary does not yield any support for this view. In 1930, Zhang Ji, a one-time revolutionary activist then holding high political office in Chiang Kai-shek's Nationalist Party, went so far as to claim that during both Fogg expeditions, Peking University "sent someone to maintain surveillance over them, but he was unable to fulfill his goal. This is something that the University still regrets to this day."[10]

The reason Zhang failed to supply a name for this alleged spy was because there was no such person on either expedition. In addition to the testimony of the American members of the expedition (including the early letters of Warner), along with the lack of evidence in Chen's own published diary, this conclusion is also supported by a simple deduction from the facts at hand. As we saw earlier, before any of the Americans ever left the capital, Yuan Fuli and William Hung had already managed to alert both the central government in Beijing and the provincial government in Gansu to the activities of Warner at Dunhuang. By the time the Americans—minus Warner—reached Dunhuang for the second time, Chen's diary reveals that local officials already had "multiple secret orders" (*dieyou miling*) to prevent their removal of any artifact or painting. In other words, there was no need of a spy. From Beijing to Dunhuang, the Chinese authorities, be they true believers in the discourse of cultural sovereignty like Yuan and Hung or simply determined to avoid further unrest among the peasantry of Dunhuang (a category into which most Gansu officials probably fell), were already under strict orders to monitor the expedition at every turn. Recall, too, the role of Wang Jinren, the Chinese interpreter. Jayne claimed that he first learned about the extent of Chinese knowledge of Warner's activities through Wang, who in turn heard it from Chen. If Chen was a spy sent to sabotage the Americans, then why didn't Wang, who was clearly willing to divulge other sensitive information regarding Chen, confide this fact to Jayne?

In light of all these revelations, we must still answer the most important question of all. If the Westernized Chinese scholars of Beijing knew all about Warner's vandalism at Dunhuang in 1924, and had already taken adequate measures to prevent a recurrence of such vandalism in 1925, then why did they let the expedition go into the field? After all, they knew the Americans would be thwarted in their primary objectives. The only reasonable answer is also the simplest one. Chen Wanli was exactly who his university said he was: a young Westernized Chinese scholar eager to obtain rare archaeological experience in a part of China that would otherwise be financially and politically inaccessible to him. As Shen Jianshi, the director of the School of

Sinology at Peking University, observed in one of three prefaces appended to Chen Wanli's published diary, "over the past twenty years foreigners have visited Dunhuang numerous times; among those of our countrymen who have visited for the purposes of archaeology, however, this trip signals the beginning of a new enterprise." In other words, the Westernized Chinese scholars of Beijing, aching to get out into the field and do as their Western "mentors" had long done, could best overcome the financial and political hardships of their day by attaching themselves to a well-funded and diplomatically secure American venture. The Chinese knew that the Americans were "dead men walking," so to speak, unable to fulfill any of their goals. Before the extent of that failure truly sunk in with the Americans, however, the Chinese saw no harm in going along for the ride, with the chance of procuring valuable experience in the field. In his endless search for a scapegoat, Warner seemed finally to grasp this simple calculus. "It now looks as if both Peking and the Provincial Officials (and possibly Dr. Chen) knew all along that we were going to be blocked," he wrote toward the end of the expedition, "and that they let us spend all this time and these thousands of dollars with their tongues in their cheeks."[11]

The Chinese master plan, if such there was, was not to humiliate Warner or his colleagues in any way. After all, there was still much to be gained by maintaining positive relationships with those influential Americans who controlled access to the wealth and prestige of Harvard. In recalling his meeting with Vice-Minister of Education Qin Fen fifty years later, William Hung described the order sent out under the Ministry of Education's cover as having instructed "the local authorities to provide these friends with ample protection and courteous treatment, but on no account allow them to touch any historical relics." No one was supposed to threaten or intimidate the Americans. The hope was that the Americans would gradually come to appreciate the value of a photographic record of the antiquities in lieu of the actual antiquities themselves. Chen Wanli, too, seems to have done all he could to maintain cordial relations with his American colleagues in spite of their unfounded suspicions of him. Far from the "vile motives" Chen was alleged by Warner to have ascribed to the Americans, Chen instead uses the first page of his diary to pay tribute to "the generous assistance of Warner and Jayne," who gave him "the opportunity to accompany the members of an American archaeological expedition to Dunhuang in order to conduct the first-ever on-site survey for my university's Graduate School of Sinology and its Committee on Archaeology." Despite spending less than three days at Dunhuang, "the joy and happiness I experienced are simply indescribable."[12]

What neither Warner nor Chen seem to have anticipated, however, was the extent to which the best laid plans of both the Americans *and the Chinese* would be thwarted by an oft-maligned force: the illiterate and impoverished peasants of China. These plans would be thwarted at two remote villages in Gansu: Jingchuan and Dunhuang. On March 23, 1925, Jayne, Priest, Chen, and the rest of the party arrived at Jingchuan, the county seat of six nearby villages, all located a little less than halfway on the road from Xi'an to Lanzhou. At a nearby temple, Jayne, still wholly ignorant of the impossibility of his removing even a single bodhisattva's head from any site on their journey, suggested to Chen that they take one of the "loose stones" strewn about the temple (Priest said it was an "incense pot") with an eye toward giving it to "the Museum in Peking" on their return. Jayne wanted to test Chen's response to such a course of action, in hope that this might set a precedent for the Americans to take additional artifacts for the Fogg later on. "He did not respond at all joyously to the suggestion," Jayne later wrote to Forbes. "I then suggested asking the local magistrate whether he would give us permission to take it for the Peking Museum. This Dr. Chen thought a good idea, and Priest and he interviewed the magistrate, who said he could not let us remove it, but he would take it himself to the Yamen for preservation, and perhaps later the Kansu government would let it go to Peking."[13]

The next day, the party hiked across the river to visit the Arhat Caves (*luohan dong*). It was in one of the eastern grottos that Jayne spotted "a very attractive small stone tablet, which, as soon as we saw it we planned to take to the Magistrate for preservation, with the hope that the magistrate might say that in this case we could have it for the Fogg." According to Jayne, Chen "evidently did not believe we intended to ask the Magistrate for it, for he bundled it up himself and put it in his own cart." Chen's diary narrates this episode somewhat differently. Claiming that he, not Jayne, was the first to spot "a long square-shaped rock lying tipped over horizontally at the foot of a pedestal," Chen quickly determined that it was the top portion of a stele once installed at a temple in the southern grotto. Chen mulled his options. Letting the Americans take it—even if ostensibly only to present it to the magistrate—was out of the question. Not only did Chen apparently not trust the Americans to do as they said they would, but he had also begun to doubt the ability of the magistrate to act in the interests of scientific preservation. Alluding to the fate of the incense pot from the day before, Chen concluded that any mention of the stele to the magistrate would result in "nothing more than an order to his security forces to move the stele to the county seat. After that, how would we be able to know anything regarding the fate of the stele?" In addition, Chen learned that the only reason this stele fragment had ended up in such a deplorable state of neglect in the first place was because the rest of the stele had been moved to another temple "due to a dispute concerning the temple's foundations." This meant that the last time the magistrate got involved in the handling of local artifacts, he had "not acted with the purpose of the preservation of ancient relics in mind." Instead, he had acted as a politician, with the concerns of his peasant subjects foremost in mind. As a result, Chen resolved to take the stele to Beijing. "When I told Jayne of my plan to take the stele remnant back to my university," Chen continued, in a sharp departure from Jayne's narrative of events, "he wholeheartedly endorsed the idea."[14]

In spite of these divergent accounts, it is instructive to note the ideological sympathy that Chen displays here for Western modes of scientific preservation and analysis. In less than twenty-four hours, Chen had managed to lose complete faith in the ability of his own government to treat artifacts the way he had been trained to treat them. His solution to the problem was to do as the Westerners did: take without asking. After all, to ask any non-Westernized Chinese official for permission to remove an artifact to a distant museum was to risk condemning the artifact in question to a turbulent existence within that official's own private networks, as a form of social or political capital. In this sense, Chen was much closer in spirit to his American colleagues than he was to his own government officials. The problem with the Americans was not, as it was with the Chinese officials, their commitment to science, preservation, or education. The problem with the Americans was that their commitment to science, preservation, and education would ultimately be fulfilled in America. In the end, Chen did not say a word to the magistrate about his stele, a fact that did not go unnoticed by Jayne, who had hoped to acquire it for the Fogg. Before the party left Jingchuan, Jayne "urged Dr. Chen to take the stone to the Yamen that the Magistrate might deal with it as he had with the one from the other cave. This he was reluctant to do, so I renounced any further interest and told him that if it went on in his cart it was his property and the expedition could not be responsible for it." In another letter to Forbes, Alan Priest took note of how "a small but lovely Wei tablet was borne off in triumph by Dr. Ch'en."[15]

The only source of tension between Chen and his American colleagues concerned the ultimate destination of the artifact. In nearly every other regard, they were mirror images of each other. This was evident not only in their interactions with the magistrate but also in their interactions with the peasantry. On the same day that the contested stele came to light, Chen and the Americans left the eastern grotto and began to work in the southern grotto. According to Jayne, "in the course of our work at this cave, we did considerable scraping of new mud restorations from the original stone figures in order to photograph, feeling free to do so since there was no indication that the temple was anything but completely abandoned." Toward the end of the day, however, "some of the local people gathered, considerably annoyed that their gods were being scratched up." As it turned out, once a year the headmen of the neighboring six villages would gather at the cave to worship. Unwittingly, Jayne found himself in a situation similar to that which Warner had brought about at Dunhuang the previous year—only this time, the perpetrator was caught red-handed.[16]

Because Jayne did not speak Chinese, the ensuing scuffle is best narrated by Chen, who added his own revealing gloss on what transpired. According to Chen, some twenty villagers showed up and prevented the party from returning to town. They grabbed the reins of the horses firmly and ordered Jayne to be searched for weapons while more villagers join the fray. One villager then "grabbed onto Jayne's sleeve," Chen wrote, "and told him that they would go to the temple together, and if they did not make arrangements for the compensation of the Buddhist statues they would not release him." Chen, who "began to fear the worst," implored an elderly man to act as mediator. "The mob had grown even larger by then, with many voices shouting out fiercely. They decided to convene a meeting right there in the field, and would not let us listen in." After Chen threatened to involve the magistrate, the villagers agreed to send several representatives into one of the caves with Jayne and Chen, where they settled on a price for the damage done to the statues: sixty-six American dollars. (Jayne later told Forbes that "the photographs of the caves are fully worth it.") Of greater interest than the scuffle itself, however, is Chen's reaction. "Though the peeling away of mud from the Buddhist statues on the walls of the southern grotto was Alan Priest's idea," Chen wrote, "I wholeheartedly believe that it was the correct method for the purpose of research, and I assisted in the process." Chen blamed himself for not anticipating the possibility of just such a debacle. "For burdening my friends with several hours of terror," he confessed, "I am deeply remorseful."[17]

The eventful stay at Jingchuan seems to have convinced Chen of several truths. First, though the Americans could not be trusted to leave artifacts within China, they could still be trusted to act in accordance with the ideals of scientific preservation, even if Warner had gone a little too far the previous year at Dunhuang. In that sense, the Americans and all other Western scholars were still regarded by their Westernized Chinese counterparts as respected and admired colleagues, ones who simply needed to learn to share a bigger piece of the archaeological pie. Second, no matter what sort of government regulations or orders were passed concerning the preservation of antiquities within China, Chinese officials still could not be trusted to implement them to the degree that Chen and other Westernized Chinese scholars in Beijing would have liked. And third, the peasants of China were an ignorant, superstitious lot who cared nothing for antiquities beyond what they could yield by prayer or necromancy. "The villagers here do not understand that they are supposed to cherish things like this," Chen observed with regard to his stele. Unless he removed the stele fragment to his university in Beijing, "how could its fate be anything other than eventual destruction?" As a result, Chen not only hid knowledge of his stele from the local magistrate but also from the village mob. "At that time I quickly ordered the driver to place it in my carriage, and those ten villagers who had supervised me in the grotto never got involved in the debate. How fortunate was I!" Jayne also witnessed this. "Unknown to them the stone came back to town with us in Dr. Chen's cart."[18]

As Chen's anxiety regarding the prospect of the villagers uncovering his stele clearly shows, the peasants of Jingchuan made no distinction between an archaeologist from Harvard or Beijing. As far as the illiterate villagers were concerned, both were "foreign imperialists," so to speak. This realization did not sit well with Gu Jiegang, one of the most influential historians of the day, who wrote one of the prefaces to Chen's published diary. "On the issue of ancient relics, it seems as if the viewpoint of my generation exists in an entirely different world from that of others," he wrote. "In our minds, things like statues and paintings are just old relics that reflect art and history, and we only want to study them. But in the eyes of other people, these things are regarded as religious objects and should only be preserved for the purposes of devotion and prayer." Referring to Chen's travails at the Arhat Caves as "a slight setback," Gu lamented the ways in which the peasants of Jingchuan construed Chen's actions "not as preservation, but rather destruction, or even as theft for our own monetary gain." Like Chen, Gu did not single out any of the Americans for blame. As far as he was concerned, the only people worthy of blame were men like Wang Yuanlu, "who has unlawfully profited from the sale of Dunhuang's ancient relics for over a decade."[19]

After their departure from Jingchuan, it took Chen and the Americans another seven weeks to reach Dunhuang. By this time, Jayne had already given up any hope of removing any more cave murals from Dunhuang without the complete knowledge and assistance of Chen and the local Chinese authorities. The experience at Jingchuan had allowed him to witness firsthand the perils of which Warner was still blissfully unaware. "First, it was plain that Dr. Chen would probably look with distinct disfavour on any removal of frescoes from there for the sole benefit of the Fogg," Jayne admitted to Forbes. Second, he now knew, as Warner did not, "that any extensive, unauthorized work could not be carried on without arousing a certain amount of local feeling which would make protracted work impossible and inevitably lead to complications with the provincial government." Jayne took pains to impress on Forbes "how closely the conditions under which the caves at Tun Huang are reverenced parallels the situation we met with at the Chinchow [Jingchuan] chapel." As a result, Jayne proposed a hastily formulated "Plan B" to Chen: apply to the governor of Gansu for permission to remove a complete cave from Dunhuang for display at Peking University, then "trust in the generosity of the University to reward us with a few pieces." According to Jayne, Chen was "very pleased with the idea."[20]

In a decision that must have aroused mixed feelings in Chen, "Plan B" was roundly rejected by the governor. With that, the contemporary record of events previously yielded by Jayne's and Priest's letters to Forbes ends, leaving us only with Chen's published diary and Warner's belated invective. Of the two, only Chen actually made it to Dunhuang. On May 18, 1925, after a visit with two local officials from Dunhuang, Chen tells us that Jayne resolved to return to Suzhou so that he could send a telegram to Warner warning him not to proceed to Dunhuang, since his presence might stir up hostility from the peasants to a degree far worse than that experienced at Jingchuan. On May 19, they reached the town of Dunhuang and met with Yang Yiwen, the local magistrate, along with three other officials. After Jayne confessed his original plans to remove an entire cave and promised only to take pictures—a proposal confirmed by Jayne's earlier letter to Forbes—all four officials became quite animated, talking in quick succession to one another. It was then that Jayne learned for the first time just how serious the peasant reaction to Warner's vandalism of the previous year had been. The previous magistrate himself had been "interrogated" by their headman, while pointed accusations against Wang Yuanlu had caused him to feign insanity and flee the district. The situation was further exacerbated by the lengthy drought afflicting the land, signs of which Chen himself had noted all along the road on placards that exhorted the people to pray piously for rain and not to slaughter any livestock. In order to prevent a recurrence of such troubles, Magistrate Yang told the Americans that they could reside in Dunhuang for no more than two weeks, and that any trips to the caves for the purposes of photography would have to be made as day trips from the town itself—a three-hour trek each way.[21]

With that, Chen recorded his profound disappointment at the failure of the expedition. "Jayne and the others are all quite upset and annoyed," he wrote. "As for me, I have to cancel all the plans I had for my work at Dunhuang. What a shame." In the end, the second Fogg expedition spent less than three full days at the caves before returning to Anxi to rendezvous with Warner. As consolation for their expulsion from Dunhuang, Warner and the rest of the party were granted a one-week stay at Wanfoxia, another series of Buddhist caves located a safe three days' march away from the peasants of Dunhuang. Daniel Thompson, one of the Americans who worked as a tutor of art at Harvard, told Chen that based on the total financial expenditures for the expedition, the actual time spent at the Thousand-Buddha Caves amounted to a cost of about forty cents per second. Unable to perform the work for which he had been hired, Thompson felt conflicted about drawing any more of his salary. "I came, of course, to transfer frescoes," he wrote to Forbes, "and as there are no frescoes to be transferred, I have cast about for some other means to justify my presence on the Expeditions." Warner also felt keenly the loss of so much time and investment. "Lord! how I hate to write you of failure and ask for money," he wrote to Sachs soon after meeting up with Jayne.[22]

With so much at stake, Warner was unwilling to admit that the chief goal of his Harvard patrons—an extended reconnaissance at Dunhuang—had been thwarted by superstitious peasants in an ugly debacle of his own making. Fortunately for Warner, developments elsewhere in China soon provided him with an alternative alibi. In early June, he received an alarming telegram from J. Leighton Stuart, the president of Yenching University and a close confidant of William Hung. "Recent acute development of nationalist feeling accompanied by obvious and natural demands create real danger of misinterpretation of your objects and actions which might imperil future prospects of your work and embarrass your country and university," Stuart wrote. "We strongly urge studying only and returning empty handed. Please acknowledge receipt." On June 23, Warner confirmed that he was indeed returning empty-handed. "By your telegraph I judge that some sort of Hell has popped in Peking of which I am ignorant," Warner responded. "It may be that this is the true explanation of Dr. Chen's grandmother's critical illness which called him home."[23]

The hell that popped loose was the May 30 incident, and it was indeed the true explanation for Chen's decision to withdraw from the expedition and return to Beijing alone. On May 30, 1925, a little over three weeks earlier, British police in the International Settlement of Shanghai had given an order to fire on Chinese students who were threatening to break into the station to secure the release of some of their classmates, who themselves had been jailed for protesting the death of a Chinese protester in a Japanese factory two weeks prior. The ensuing furor led to widespread street protests in cities throughout China, including Beijing, and provided the nascent Nationalist and Communist Parties with invaluable fodder for antiforeign propaganda. For Warner, too, the May 30 incident offered invaluable fodder for his own brand of propaganda. Here at last was a way to explain the fiasco at Dunhuang without calling attention to his own culpability in the affair. In his conclusion to *The Long Old Road in China* (1927), a book chiefly concerned with the first expedition, Warner made his first attempt to explain what happened at Dunhuang before May 30 by vague reference to events that occurred on and after May 30:

> I could not guess that in a short seven months the whole Chinese nation was to stir in its sleep and yawn so portentously that all we foreigners would be scuttling back to our Legations. *But in those months of the first return from the border, the Shanghai shooting* and the marchings and counter-marchings of Feng and Chang and Wu were not guessed. We had no idea of *the serious troubles a few months were to bring forth.* (Emphasis added)

This is a gross misrepresentation of the course of events that preceded the second expedition. The first expedition returned to Beijing in the spring of 1924. For Warner to suggest that the Shanghai shootings occurred in those amorphous months of the first return from the border (or, as he puts it in the following sentence, in the space of a few months) is deliberately to mislead his readers into thinking that the May 30 incident happened at some point in the second half of 1924. In *Buddhist Wall-Paintings* (1938), a collection of photographs from his one-week stay at Wanfoxia, Warner strengthened this misperception by declaring that the expedition's time in the northwest coincided with the death of "Old China," and that "nowhere were we welcome and seldom were we tolerated by the people, and little of our mission could be accomplished.[24]

In his public accounts of what transpired at Dunhuang, Warner constructed a deliberately vague and convoluted timeline, hoping that none of his readers would question his narrative too closely. But Chen Wanli's diary can easily set the record straight: the Americans reached Dunhuang on May 18 and left six days later on May 24. As its name suggests, the May 30 incident took place on May 30—nearly a week *after* the Americans left Dunhuang. It was thus impossible for the May 30 incident to have exerted any influence whatsoever on the expedition's reception there. Nevertheless, Warner found it useful to conflate one with the other. After all, he had some serious explaining to do: not only was he responsible for a virtual peasant rebellion against the local magistrate at Dunhuang, but he was also to blame for the expedition being permitted to spend only three short days at the Thousand-Buddha Caves, when they had planned for four long months. In a letter to Sachs, Warner privately confessed to "wak[ing] each morning to a strange feeling of failure to which I am not accustomed. Always in the past I have had the undeserved and inevitable luck of the red-headed."[25]

He would combat this strange feeling of failure by portraying the well-justified and situational malice of aggrieved peasants in Dunhuang as the premeditated hostility of all Chinese, regardless of class, context, and location. Before long, Warner was describing Jayne's stay at Dunhuang in terms that diverge starkly from Chen's diary. "When they had reached the Tun Huang oasis they were met by an angry mob of over 100 people who stayed by the inn gates and raised cain," Warner wrote in a letter to Roger S. Greene, the American director of the China Medical Board. To Stein, Warner declared that Jayne and the others "had been mobbed at Tun Huang and forbidden the caves." To Sachs, he declared that even a single scuffle with one of these peasants would have greatly reduced "our chances of bringing out the whole party alive."[26] In Chen's diary, however, there is no mob of any sort, and their stay at Dunhuang is portrayed as tense but uneventful. Of course, it is certainly possible that there was a mob, and that Chen or his publisher later edited this detail out from his diary. But this seems unlikely. After all, other unflattering portraits of superstitious Chinese peasants threatening foreign scholars did make the final cut: Chen's entries for the two days the party spent at Jingchuan fully attest to that. Far more likely is that Warner felt compelled to build up his own Dunhuang mob so as to draw a direct parallel with the urban protesters who took to the streets in other major Chinese cities in the weeks and months after the May 30 incident.

Mob or no mob, the lessons of the second Fogg expedition to Dunhuang remain the same. By 1925, a new generation of Westernized Chinese scholars had finally come of age in Beijing, one that was scarcely distinguishable from its Western counterpart. Warner, in his conflation of Westernized scholars such as Chen Wanli with the May 30 incident and the illiterate peasants of Jingchuan and Dunhuang, refused to acknowledge the fast-shrinking gap between educated Chinese scholars and their former Western mentors. He would not be the last to do so. Warner's wife Lorraine also swallowed her husband's story wholesale. "Evidently they've had one grand fiasco," she wrote to Forbes after reading Warner's letters, "which could perhaps have been avoided had the Chinese at Peking behaved like white men instead of like swine." On the contrary, it was precisely because Warner, in desecrating the gods of poor peasants afflicted by drought, had acted "like swine" at Dunhuang that the expedition failed to achieve any of its original goals. Similarly, it was precisely because Chen Wanli and his colleagues at Beijing had "behaved like white men" that the Americans failed to bring back even a single artifact from China. As Chen's diary clearly demonstrates, the Westernized Chinese scholars of Beijing echoed every single scientific sentiment on Warner's agenda but one: the removal of priceless antiquities to museums abroad. Short of that, the obstruction of foreign archaeologists was just as much the obstruction of the Chinese scholars who accompanied and sympathized with them. "Due to the malice of the locals toward Westerners," Gu Jiegang wrote in his preface to Chen's diary, "he was only able to spend three and a half days at the grottoes. This is cause for enormous regret."[27]

The second Fogg expedition showed that there was still a basis, anchored in mutual class prejudices against superstitious peasants, for collaboration between the Chinese and foreigners—but only if the foreigner was willing to pay for everything and take nothing. In other words, the foreign archaeologist must accept his new role as the glorified escort of a mirror image of himself. In his condemnation of Chen and Peking University as having known "all along that we were going to be blocked" and "that they let us spend all this time and these thousands of dollars with their tongues in their cheeks," Warner seems to have come to a belated understanding of the thankless role the Chinese now expected all Western archaeologists to play. The Westernized Chinese scholars of Beijing, unable to get into the field themselves or trust China's own government officials and illiterate peasants to fulfill the lofty Western mission of scientific preservation to which they themselves fully subscribed, decided instead to piggyback on resourceful foreign expeditions as a pragmatic means of getting into the field. In what turned out to be an ironic twist of fate, then, it was actually fortunate for the Chinese scholars in Beijing that most Western archaeologists were too arrogant to believe that their newly Westernized Chinese "understudies" were actually capable of keeping them to the letter of the law. This meant that the Chinese would continue to find opportunities to accompany yet another "dead man walking" to the northwestern frontier.

The fiasco of 1925 did not faze Warner in the least bit. Over the next five years, the chronic political instability of China apparently convinced Warner and other explorers who followed in his wake that it would still be possible to take first and ask later. It would fall to men like Yuan Fuli, William Hung, and Chen Wanli to make sure that the foreigners instead asked first—and took nothing later.

THE SINO-SWEDISH EXPEDITION

In 1925, Hugo Junkers, the German airplane designer, contacted Sven Hedin (figure 24), the Swedish explorer, to enlist his help in mapping out an air route from Berlin to Beijing. Hedin was on good terms with the Germans, having served as a war correspondent on the western front a decade earlier, during which time he spared no effort in publicizing the justness of their cause. The Great War had opened a wide rift within the community of Silk Road explorers, pushing men like Stein and Pelliot into opposite political camps of men like Le Coq and Hedin. In 1929, Stein's good friend Carl Keller passed along the news that Pelliot, then resident at Harvard, had finally made amends with Le Coq. "Pelliot told me that he had seen him several times," Keller wrote to Stein, "and that he had recovered from the war madness that afflicted him when he wrote several ridiculous letters to me back in '14, '15 and '16." Though Le Coq may have mellowed with time, Hedin had not. After the war, Hedin longed to do his part in reviving the German state, and he viewed Junkers's proposal as a means to that end. He wasted little time in composing a lengthy proposal for a multistage air route across the Soviet Union and Mongolia, drawing on his extensive prior experience in the field to identify potential airstrips and refueling depots. In 1926, Deutsche Lufthansa, the German state-owned airline, took over sponsorship of the project from Junkers and sent Hedin to Beijing to open negotiations with the Chinese.[28]

Once in Beijing, Hedin met with Zhang Zuolin, the warlord from Manchuria then in control of the capital. Zhang issued all the necessary paperwork and permissions without any fuss. To Zhang, a well-funded German expedition to the northwestern provinces offered numerous compensations. Not only could Zhang ingratiate himself with German industrialists and associate his regime with scientific research, but he could also use the expedition as a means of impinging on rival warlord domains. Certainly, all the Chinese officials in Gansu and Xinjiang with whom the expedition later came into contact believed that its members were sent by Zhang as thinly veiled clandestine agents. "Originally those in Xinjiang thought that we were sent by General Feng [Yuxiang] to attack Xinjiang," observed Xu Xusheng, one of the Chinese members of the expedition, in his diary, "while those in Gansu, cognizant of our having set forth from Beijing, then held by

Figure 24. Swedish Explorer Sven Hedin. In 1927, nearly thirty years after his last
expedition to Xinjiang, Sven Hedin returned to China with the goal of scouting out a
trans-Eurasian air route for Lufthansa. When opposition to his proposal for an "aerial
archaeological expedition" coalesced among the Westernized Chinese scholars of Beijing,
Hedin agreed to reorganize his outfit into a joint venture with the Chinese: the Sino-
Swedish Northwest Scientific Survey. In doing so, Hedin set an important precedent
for future negotiations with Western archaeologists in China. Sven Hedin, *History of
the Expedition in Asia, 1927–1935*, vol. 1 (Stockholm: Elanders boktryckeri aktiebolag,
1943), frontispiece.

the Fengtian clique, thought that we had been sent by Mr. Zhang Zuolin to attack Gansu!" During their time in Gansu, the Chinese members of the expedition also recorded an encounter with a Mongol prince who refused to meet with them until they could prove their lack of a political agenda, a border guard near Jinta instructed by the local magistrate to report on their movements, and a full two thousand soldiers sent to greet and disarm them at the border with Xinjiang.[29]

Whatever his agenda, Zhang Zuolin viewed Hedin's proposal through the lens of a pragmatic politician, not a university scholar. In the aftermath of Warner's expedition the previous year, however, the Westernized Chinese scholars of Beijing were now determined to have their say in the matter. The goal was not to send Hedin back to Europe. Rather, as with Warner, their goal was to turn Hedin into a toothless escort of his scientific equals in China. In order to do that, they would first have to raise a ruckus loud enough to capture Zhang's attention. Eschewing the quiet, behind-the-scenes maneuvering of William Hung and Yuan Fuli, the Chinese professors of Beijing decided to organize themselves into a more formal lobbying group: the Association of Chinese Scholarly Organizations (Zhongguo xue-shu tuanti xiehui), which would eventually evolve into the more famous Commission for the Preservation of Antiquities (Guwu baoguan weiyuan-hui). By publishing opinion pieces in the Chinese newspapers and organizing student demonstrations in the streets, the association certainly managed to catch Zhang's attention. "We were afraid of being overthrown by this Government," Hedin later wrote, "which sought popularity with the nationalistic mob, with its hoarse yell, 'Crucify! Crucify!'"[30]

As a result, Zhang brought Hedin back to the negotiating table. In order to satisfy the association, Zhang and Hedin signed a new agreement consisting of nineteen additional clauses. These new stipulations formally enshrined the principles of cooperation that had once been informally imposed on the second Fogg expedition. Instead of a lone Chinese scholar like Chen Wanli attached to an expedition in which the foreign members outnumbered him six to one, this time there would be a roughly equivalent number of Chinese and foreign members (in this case, mostly Swedish and German). Most importantly, one of these members would be elevated to the status of "codirector" with Hedin and be given equal decision-making powers. In addition, Hedin would not be allowed to remove any antiquities from China, nor could the expedition produce any maps on a scale larger than 1:300,000. Though Hedin would draw a nominal salary from the Chinese government, all other expenses, including those of the Chinese members of the expedition, were to be borne by Hedin. In other words, Hedin, much like Warner before him, could undertake scientific work in China, but only if he paid for everything, took nothing, and brought Chinese colleagues along for the ride. The reason Hedin agreed to such groundbreaking concessions was likely due to the nature of his mission: his job was to scout out potential airfields, install weather monitoring stations, and acquire permission from various warlords to allow Lufthansa planes to fly over their lands. Had he come to China chiefly as an archaeologist, hoping to acquire artifacts, it is unlikely he would have conceded so much ground.[31]

In May 1927, the newly reorganized Sino-Swedish Northwest Scientific Survey (Zhong Rui xibei kexue kaocha tuan) set out from Beijing (figure 25). In accordance with Chinese demands, both the official Chinese and English versions of the survey's name—if not the unofficial English version—avoided any mention of an "expedition" (Ch. *yuanzhengdui*), a word now deemed unsuitable to describe field research in a scientifically "advanced" country such as China. At the head of the party was Xu Xusheng, dean and

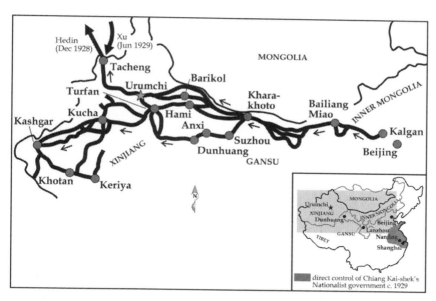

Figure 25. The Sino-Swedish Northwest Scientific Survey, 1927–30. In order to cover more ground, the Chinese and mostly Swedish and German members of the expedition often took divergent routes. Once reunited with his colleagues at Urumchi, Hedin was informed by Governor Yang Zengxin that he would not be permitted to carry out any of his proposed surveys for aerial routes through Xinjiang. After exiting the province empty-handed in December 1928, Hedin and his Chinese co-leader Xu Xusheng found that Chiang Kai-shek's new government in Nanjing was eager to sponsor another joint expedition to Xinjiang, for reasons of its own. Cartography by Debbie Newell.

professor of philosophy at Peking University, who was selected by the association to serve as Hedin's Chinese codirector. Also by his side, among many others, were Yuan Fuli and Huang Wenbi, both professors at the same university (in fact, Huang had personally seen Chen Wanli off at the train station two years earlier).[32] In a diary that remained unpublished during his lifetime, Huang noted the role he and his colleagues had played in bringing Hedin to heel. "Originally Hedin, a Swede, had planned to organize a large-scale expedition [*yuanzhengdui*] to northwestern China to excavate antiquities and study the geology, climate, etc.," he wrote in the very first entry. "Chinese scholars expressed their opposition. After negotiations, China sent five scholars and five students to accompany the Survey [*kaocha tuan*]. I was one of the scholars. As a result, our task was twofold. On the one hand, we were to supervise the foreigners, and on the other hand we were to carry out scientific investigations."[33]

In contrast to Huang, Xu Xusheng, Hedin's codirector, published his diary soon after the expedition returned to Beijing. Expressing his conviction that "knowledge and science are international, without national borders," Xu nonetheless drew attention to the fact that "those who gain the honor and distinction of conducting actual scientific research that furthers our knowledge of humanity are individual people who return to their individual countries." But now that "many of our students have returned from studying abroad in various countries" and "possess the ability to carry out such research," the Chinese themselves should earn the honor and distinction of carrying out field research within China. Unfortunately, however, "domestic troubles and foreign pressures have been unrelenting, inhibiting their ability to encourage or carry out these tasks." Therefore, foreign explorers such as Hedin, with "their superior finances," could still play a positive role in China, but only if they were "willing to cooperate with us." As for those "who adopt a policy of cultural invasion [*wenhua qinlüe*], hoping to pillage and carry off our precious resources, we will find a way to resist them and prevent their return to our land."[34]

In openly referring to the activities of foreign archaeologists who did not cooperate with their Westernized counterparts in China as "pillage" (*jueduo*), Xu was drawing a clear line in the sand. Gone was the culturalist mindset of the old Confucian elite. In its place was a nationalist claim to art and antiquities as the inviolable birthright of anyone who claimed membership in the new Chinese nation. Previously, no one in China had ever thought to characterize foreign archaeologists as "thieves" because they did not believe in the existence of a Chinese nation from which art and antiquities could be "stolen." Outside of active religious communities, art and antiquities were owned by private individuals or they were owned by nobody at all. In affixing his signature to the proposal for a joint scientific survey and promising not to remove anything from China, Hedin was injecting unprecedented legitimacy into the new nationalist definition of archaeological "theft" as put forth by the Westernized Chinese scholars of Beijing. From this point forward, it was their particular definition of "theft," long a minority position in China, that would increasingly come to monopolize the public discourse surrounding archaeological expeditions throughout the country.

In exchange for his blessing of the new nationalist order, Hedin was held up as a model for other foreign explorers to emulate. So long as the removal of artifacts was off the table, there was endless potential for constructive cooperation between a resourceful foreigner and the Chinese colleagues on his payroll. After all, despite the many ideological similarities between them, foreign explorers such as Hedin still had something the Westernized Chinese scholars of Beijing sorely lacked: decades of field experience. Just a few months into the expedition, Xu found it impossible to hide his admiration for Hedin's ingenuity and persistence in the field. After watching Hedin and Henning Haslund-Christensen, a Danish member of the expedition, wade repeatedly into a river in Inner Mongolia in order to measure the speed of its current, Xu took note of the "many things to admire" in his foreign colleagues. "No matter where they are, or how impossible the situation may seem, they always persist in finding a way to reach their goals," Xu wrote. "If at first they fail, they then try again, and then again a second time, until they finally succeed on their fifth or sixth attempt. There is no one who can help them, they must go in and do it themselves!" In an eerie echo of Wan Rong's preface to the first Chinese translation of Stein's *Preliminary Report* nearly thirty years earlier, Xu went on to criticize those Chinese who saw little benefit in cooperating with Hedin. "We Chinese may laugh at them now, but it is only later that we will come to realize that the levels of judgment and tolerance exhibited by foreigners are very difficult to reach."[35]

Huang Wenbi was far less enamored of Hedin and the rest of his Teuton colleagues. In contrast to Xu, who always refers to Hedin as "Mr. Hedin" (*Heding xiansheng*) in his published diary, Huang omits such honorifics in his unpublished account of the expedition, referring only to Xu as such. Not only that, but Huang also draws repeated attention to heated disagreements with the foreign members, episodes that Xu either omits entirely or quickly glosses over. The first instance occurred on June 26, 1927, just a few months after the expedition set out from Beijing. In his diary, Huang described the performance of a traveling "Flower and Drum Opera Troupe" near their camp. "Their performance and lyrics were very crass and depraved," Huang wrote. "To see this play performed here, way out in the desert, is quite an insult." Even though Chiang Kai-shek's newly resurgent Nationalist government had already banned the play in the southern regions of China, the foreign members of the expedition "decided to take a motion picture of it, with the intent of showing it to audiences overseas and exposing the backwardness of the Chinese race. How very humiliating!" In an attempt to stop them, Huang implored Xu to use his authority as codirector of the expedition to intervene. "But Mr. Xu did not approve [of my proposal]," Huang wrote. "What a shame."[36]

A similar incident occurred several months later, when one of the Chinese servants hired to attend to the expedition's camels attempted to abscond during the night, taking two of the camels in tow. His tracks were soon picked up by one of the Mongol guides, who returned the thief to camp. "I was greatly ashamed of this Chinese man, who has no self-respect and whose actions have led to a loss of face for all of us," Huang wrote in his diary. After talking to Xu, Huang and the other Chinese members of the expedition decided that the best course of action would be to deliver the camel thief to the local authorities. Not only would this "prevent the foreigners from applying their own private form of punishment," Huang concluded, but it would also "show that the Chinese follow the law and respect the integrity of its authority." They were too late. Unfortunately for Huang, "the foreigners have already tied him up in chains, verbally abused him, and even taken pictures of him. How many more such insults can our country bear?"[37]

Two weeks later, it was clear to Huang that the foreigners would continue to do as they pleased. "Today the foreigners tied up the camel thief and filmed him on camera," Huang noted with indignation. After Liu Yanhuai informed Huang, they went together "to tell Mr. Xu, and then all three of us went over to see what was going on. But they had already completed the filming by the time we got there. Foreigners all adopt an insulting attitude toward China, imposing a deep affront to our honor." Huang further noted that all of the motion pictures taken by the expedition were supposed to be subject to the review of a Chinese council in Beijing. Hedin, however, had admitted that the film would be sent to Germany for development and likely be premiered abroad, thus violating the text of the agreement. Not only that, Huang continued, but "movies can make profits, and the issue of how to divide these profits must be discussed." Huang, however, had already begun to lose faith in Xu's willingness to confront Hedin. "Mr. Xu's excessive weakness and pliability [guoyu ruanruo] are also a cause for concern."[38]

In his published diary, Xu narrated these incidents somewhat differently. The opera troupe, for instance, does not appear at all. As for the camel thief, despite being "filled with pity" on seeing him in chains, Xu nonetheless went out of his way to express his approval of Hedin's handling of the affair. "Mr. Hedin told me that when they set out the previous morning, he had already ordered [the rest of the foreigners] not to beat or otherwise abuse [the camel thief] after he had been tied up," Xu wrote. "For the safety of the group, however, neither could he allow the man to go free. I expressed my complete agreement with what Hedin said." When Liu and Huang informed Xu that the foreigners were in fact abusing the thief two weeks later, Xu rushed over to take a look. Unlike Huang, however, Xu concluded that they were merely adjusting the shackles to alleviate the prisoner's discomfort, "without any intent to abuse him." Accusing the prisoner of putting on "a trustworthy face" to conceal the fact that he was a "seasoned criminal" (jizei), Xu remain unmoved by his fate. Huang, however, came to express considerable sympathy with the thief. "This man is already more than fifty years old and he has great difficulty walking," Huang noted in his diary. "Thus he stole two camels, one to carry his possessions and the other for himself to ride. Other than his clothes and some other sundry possessions such as a few pieces of bread, he didn't touch any other important items. So to label him a thief rests upon a single moment of muddleheaded action; he is certainly not a seasoned criminal."[39]

Huang exhibited his dissatisfaction with Hedin on other occasions as well. In early July, Huang announced his plans to set off in search of the remains of an ancient wall near Bailingmiao that he suspected to be of Qin provenance (221–206 BC). "I decided to head out and investigate it," Huang noted in his diary, "but was prevented from doing so by the foreigners. This made me extremely angry and sad." Unwilling to back down, the next day Huang urged Xu to take up the topic once more with Hedin. "They talked endlessly," Huang wrote. "[Hedin] said that this part of the wall had already been noted on European maps." Huang, however, did not believe him. "I suspect that Hedin is simply trying to frustrate us," he continued. "Originally when we broached this matter with Hedin, he didn't know anything about it. Now that we've told him it might be the Qin wall, he says that it has already been discovered. Could it be that he doesn't want the Chinese to be the first to discover it?" In Huang's eyes, the foreigners had already taken enough credit for new scientific discoveries. It was time to let someone else bask in the spotlight. Just two days later, when Xu and Huang learned that Folke Bergman, the Swedish archaeologist, had already discovered more than a thousand stone artifacts, Huang comforted Xu "by saying that we should wait until the end to compare results, and then see who has pulled ahead. The moment of victory or defeat had not yet arrived." Four months later, Huang was still intent on outperforming his foreign colleagues. When Hedin announced that the first person to discover "another Loulan"—the lost desert oasis whose discovery in the 1890s had first catapulted Hedin to fame—would get five hundred dollars, Huang responded with undiluted bluster. "I laughed," Huang wrote later that same day, "and said that the discovery of one ancient city is nothing, for when I get to Xinjiang I expect to discover an entire kingdom."[40]

In addition to matters of cultural import, Huang also took careful note of Hedin's political agenda. Aware that the German members of the expedition evinced "a very deep national consciousness and all hold militaristic ideas," Huang worried about their ultimate designs on China. When Liu told Huang that "their goal for this expedition is entirely related to airplanes" and Xu later mentioned that "they are very desirous of being able to implement aerial archaeology," Huang immediately suspected the worst. "I am of the opinion that such a project as this absolutely cannot be countenanced," he confessed to his diary, "as the rights for aerial routes concern national security. If we permit airline routes, then Germany can simply fly straight into the heartland of China via Central Asia and the Pamir plateau, without having to travel around the ocean." Huang also observed that Hedin, though a Swede, "is fairly close to the old party German members. During the European war, he gave speeches on behalf of the old party, and was renounced by the British as a result." In the end, Huang concluded that both the Swedes and the Germans "should be restricted from any and all strategic military regions." Later, when the expedition reached the borders of Xinjiang and was escorted by government soldiers through a strategic mountain pass, Huang again voiced his disapproval. "To bring foreigners to this place seems inappropriate." Huang's constant surveillance of Hedin did not go unnoticed. When the Swedish geologist Erik Norin proposed mapping the sensitive Juyanhai district, both Xu and Huang expressed their disapproval. Hedin, however, "suspects that I am the true cause of obstruction." He was probably right. When Norin set out to gather data for his map anyway, Huang shadowed him for days. "What their intentions are I do not know," Huang wrote, "but whenever they see me they stop their secret discussions."[41]

Huang saw the expedition for what it was: a strategic political venture undertaken by duplicitous foreigners under the deceptive guise of aerial archaeology. Xu saw the expedition for what he and the other Westernized Chinese scholars of Beijing desperately wanted it to be: a fully cooperative scientific enterprise between modern Chinese scientists and a repentant imperialist eager to right the wrongs of the past by nurturing deserving young colleagues in China. Though Xu does reveal the occasional disagreement with Hedin, usually over benign logistical matters, such tensions never reach the level that they do with Huang. In his diary, Xu ascribes various "unreasonable" and "insulting" words and actions to many other Swedish and German members of the expedition, but never to Hedin, who is instead portrayed as bringing his haughty colleagues to heel. Despite a wealth of evidence that Hedin was not adhering to either the spirit or the letter of the nineteen-point agreement signed in Beijing, Xu was determined to preserve an image of Hedin that could be used as future leverage in negotiations with other foreign explorers. In other words, there is a reason why Xu's diary was published almost immediately on his return to Beijing, while Huang's diary never saw the light of day during his lifetime. Xu's portrayal of a penitent imperialist willing to treat his Chinese colleagues as equals was far more useful to the Westernized Chinese scholars of Beijing than Huang's indignant portrait of an unreformed foreigner who had conceded to Chinese demands only because he was convinced of their inability to enforce them.

Fortunately for Huang, the governor of Xinjiang, Yang Zengxin, was not nearly as weak and pliable as Xu. Thirteen years after he first drove Stein out of Turfan, Governor Yang still reigned supreme in Urumchi. And unlike the warlords and scholars of Beijing, Yang was not about to take Hedin's words at face value. Upon his arrival in Urumchi, Hedin found that no one in Yang's circle believed his cover story. On April 4, 1928, Hedin wrote a letter to Lufthansa executives in Berlin informing them of his failure to achieve any of their goals:

> The educated Chinese here, and those in power, say to me: You pretend that the Germans provide planes for you only to give you a chance to carry out aerial surveys of unexplored desert. You want us to believe that? That poor Germany is spending these sums to allow you to look at the desert! No, the Germans have other aims, political ones. These cannot be achieved now. But in ten or twenty years, when Germany is a great power once again.[42]

In his diary, Huang took great delight in narrating the course of the negotiations between Hedin and Governor Yang. On March 20, Huang learned that Xu had accompanied Hedin to discuss the matter of airplanes with Fan Yaonan, Yang's commissioner of foreign affairs. "Hedin then mentioned that [Fengtian warlord] Yang Yuting had already issued his approval, hoping to use this as an intimidation tactic against [Yang]," Huang recorded. "This is truly laughable." He then copied Fan's reply to Hedin verbatim:

> Fan said, "The situation in Xinjiang is different from that in the inner provinces. In all matters of finance and foreign affairs, we simply do as we see fit and report our actions to the ministries. Sometimes we do not even acknowledge the orders of the President himself. In other words, even if the President were to give his approval, it still would not mean anything." His words were roundabout and polite but the meaning was clear and unyielding. Truly, a professional diplomat of foreign affairs would have nothing on Fan.

Three weeks later, Yang informed Hedin of his final decision. "They were refused," Huang noted with glee. "I am thrilled. For many days now the air has been filled with the shrill voices of the Germans saying they will return home, but this is not enough to intimidate my countrymen."[43]

The Germans did return home. So did Hedin, who set out to find a new financial backer to replace Lufthansa. In the meantime, most of the Swedish and Chinese members of the expedition remained in Urumchi, where Governor Yang kept a careful watch over their activities. Though Huang may have rejoiced at the fate of the Germans, he knew that the governor also regarded the Chinese members of the expedition with equal parts suspicion. Back in Beijing, Wang Shu'nan, the retired commissioner of finance who had collected so many antiquities during his tenure in Xinjiang, warned Huang that Governor Yang, an ardent defender of the old Confucian order, was likely to be suspicious of a young Westernized scholar from Beijing. In preparation for his trip to Urumchi, Wang gave Huang a copy of the governor's own commentary on Laozi and urged Huang to mimic the same style of Confucian commentary of which Yang was a master. "He told me to annotate it with my notations of erroneous characters, so as to allay any misunderstandings Yang may harbor toward me." But Yang's suspicions were difficult to allay. When Xu met the governor for the first time, he concluded that "the way he talked at first seemed to suggest that he still suspected us of belonging to the radical camp." Just as Yang, a scion of the old Confucian imperial order, initially looked down on the young Westernized Chinese scholars of Beijing, they too, found it difficult to relate to Yang. In his diary, Huang described Yang as having "something about him that seems shallow and pedantic." Though the governor had "a pleasant voice, with a vocabulary to match, his mind is too old." In his diary, Huang noted with chagrin banners extolling Confucius and a public shrine dedicated to "virtuous women." In fact, Yang seemed so opposed to anything smacking of reform and revolution that Xu was astonished to find a book by Hu Shi, the Peking University professor who played a role in the frustration of Warner's plans in 1925, on the shelf of one of his officials. "To find such new culture books way out here in a closed-off frontier cannot but be a pleasant surprise!"[44]

As the weeks wore on, however, Yang, Fan, Xu, and Huang, the representatives of two radically divergent generations of Chinese intellectuals and statesmen, began to discover their shared interests. These were of two types: the Chinese antiquities of Xinjiang and the revival of the modern Chinese state. During the spring of 1928, Xu and Huang gradually managed to earn the trust of Chinese officials in Urumchi, dispelling any suspicions that they had come to sow revolutionary disorder in the province. In their diaries, Xu and Huang made repeated note of scheduled appointments to examine the antiquities in the offices of various officials, including those of Governor Yang. They got to know Pan Zuhuan, the son of the deceased Pan Zhen, with whom Stein had maintained continuous correspondence since his last expedition to Xinjiang. "In the morning I went to take rubbings," Huang wrote regarding one of his visits to examine the private collection of an official. "Chen introduced me to someone surnamed Pan, who is the [sic] nephew of the late Provincial Commissioner Pan. He once served as magistrate of Ruoqiang County. He is also fond of antiquities, and knows a great deal about archaeological sites."[45]

This shared respect and veneration for the Chinese antiquities of Xinjiang morphed seamlessly into a shared respect and veneration for the modern Chinese state. At the very moment the expedition was in Urumchi, Chiang Kai-shek's Nationalist forces were consolidating their power in the Yangzi delta, where they announced the relocation of the national capital from Beijing to Nanjing. Though their authority was limited to the environs of Nanjing and Shanghai, the Nationalists were able to secure formal recognition from most warlords throughout the country of the legitimacy of their rule. Yang Zengxin was no different. During a banquet organized in honor of the expedition, Yang rose to give a speech. According to Huang, Yang said that he did "not hold any bias against the southern government [i.e., the Nationalists]. If its armies were to take Beijing today, then I would raise the blue sky and white sun flag tomorrow. My approach is to worship the temple, not the gods within." In his diary, Huang applauded Yang's speech, characterizing his words as "very smart and efficient." In response, Huang also stood up and praised the governor. "I then gave a speech about Xinjiang being located on the distant frontier, with a complex array of peoples," Huang recounted. "At this time, when the central plains are beset by tur-

bulence and the power of the central government is insufficient to look
after this territory, it is no small accomplishment for the general to have
maintained this land for the Republic of China." According to Xu, Governor
Yang then took the Chinese members of the expedition to his office, where
he showed them two Sui and Tang steles from Turfan.[46]

Beyond the conflation of Chinese antiquities with the modern Chinese
state, the governor and Huang also bonded over concrete proposals to modernize Chinese infrastructure. Much as Stein and Pelliot had once given en-
gineering advice to local officials in Xinjiang, Huang did the same for Governor Yang. "When General Yang invited us to dine on the 11th," Huang
wrote on March 15, 1928, "we had talked about the water canals in the
streets of Dihua [Urumchi]. Whenever the snow melts in summer, the roads
become rivers. General Yang asked if there was any solution to this problem." Huang, using his expertise in geography, informed Yang that Urumchi "is located in the bottom of a basin, which is why the streets turn into
streams when water flows down from the mountains. But the land outside
the eastern gate is at a lower elevation than the city itself." The solution,
Huang said, would be to "dig a canal that would allow the water to flow
out the eastern gate. General Yang expressed his enthusiastic approval, and
issued orders to dredge a canal." Though Yang and Huang came from opposite ends of the political spectrum, both men found that they venerated the
political temple of China, regardless of the ideological gods within. Before
long, the Swedish and Chinese members of the expedition were granted
permission to leave Urumchi to conduct their research in the field. By now,
Yang trusted Huang so much that he even asked him to help keep tabs on
his local officials throughout the province. On April 16, as Huang took leave
of the provincial capital, the governor "entreated me to send him reports at
any time regarding local conditions, the performance of his officials, and
political conditions, so as to facilitate their improvement. I promised that
I would do so."[47]

Two months later, Yang Zengxin was dead, gunned down by agents of
another warlord as he rose for a toast during a banquet. In the ensuing chaos,
Jin Shuren (figure 26), a member of Yang's inner circle, seized power and
took immediate steps to purge the province of any and all threats, both
real and imagined. After pinning the assassination on Fan Yaonan and ordering his immediate execution, Jin took aim at the Sino-Swedish expedition. With political intrigue in the air, Jin no longer trusted any outsiders,
especially those bearing papers from another warlord in the interior. When
a shipment of crates from Europe filled with 1,200 bullets made it past border guards and found its way to Urumchi, Jin suspected that the Russians

Figure 26. Governor Jin Shuren. Having risen to power in the chaos surrounding the assassination of Yang Zengxin in 1928, Jin immediately adopted a hostile stance toward the members of the Sino-Swedish expedition, whom he associated with the warlord government in Beijing. But when Chiang Kai-shek's new government in Nanjing decided to throw its weight behind the expedition as a means of imposing its authority in distant Xinjiang, Jin struggled to explain why he was refusing to cooperate with a "purely scientific" enterprise that included numerous Chinese scholars among its ranks. This photograph includes a dedication from the governor to Colonel Reginald Schomberg, a British intelligence agent who helped deliver an arms shipment purchased by Jin from India to Urumchi in 1930–31. Courtesy of the Royal Society for Asian Affairs, RSAA/SC/SCH/2/15.

may be planning a coup through the foreigners or perhaps even the Chinese members of the expedition. With Hedin in Europe and most of the Swedes already in the field, Xu was left to explain the purpose of these bullets on his own. He was forced to confess, however, that he didn't really know much about such things. "As for whether or not they truly are designed only for hunting, I admitted to not knowing one way or another, and asked that he investigate thoroughly." Apparently, even Xu had begun to suspect that Hedin and the Germans might be up to no good.[48]

As Governor Jin continued to pry into the expedition's affairs, however, Xu became increasingly exasperated. "In the morning a Mr. Li from the Foreign Affairs Commission came with Zhao Cipeng," Xu wrote on August 29. "They said that the Foreign Affairs Commission had sent them to inspect our collections for anything that might impoverish Chinese culture. For the life of them, these officials simply cannot understand the nature of our expedition. All I can do is laugh." The generational divide only recently bridged under the late Governor Yang came back to the fore once more. "For people who have no understanding of what constitutes 'cultural significance' to be tasked with interrogating those who have specialized authority on cultural affairs—how can this not be considered a strange thing?" Xu wondered. Two days later, Governor Jin learned that one of the expedition members had sent a crate from Fuyuan to Urumchi containing human skulls. "It is the custom of our country to keep such things buried in the ground," Jin wrote on the report. "It is unbearable to see them exposed. Send a letter to the Survey informing its members that they are not allowed to dig up any more human skulls, as a gesture of respect."[49]

It was clear to Xu that the new governor was looking for a pretext to get rid of him. "But since they had no hard evidence of anything," Xu later wrote, "they did not dare to simply drive us out of the province, instead preferring to throw all sorts of obstacles in front of our work." By the time Hedin finally returned to Xinjiang in October, the situation had already become desperate. "Accompanied Mr. Hedin into the city to pay a visit to Chairman [Jin] De'an [Shuren]," Xu noted on October 4. "He really does not approve of our plans to excavate in the desert this winter. His reason is that Gansu has stationed troops [to the west of Dunhuang], and as a defensive measure, he has already sent soldiers to be stationed at Ruoqiang and Lop Nor. The entire Ruoqiang area is a military district, and it is not convenient to permit us to proceed there, etc." When Jin then asked Hedin to order Erik Norin and Folke Bergman back from Kara-shahr and Kucha, located far away from the troubled border with Gansu, Hedin finally snapped. "Perhaps there is some legitimate concern about provincial security near Charchan,"

Hedin conceded, referring to Xinjiang's most southeasterly oasis. "But Karashahr and Kucha are far away from the area in question, and surely the same concerns do not pertain there." Hedin, struggling to keep his temper under control, now went out of his way to antagonize Jin. "Furthermore," he concluded in his letter to Jin, "the proper name of our organization is either the Northwest Scientific Survey or the Chinese Northwest Scientific Survey. There is no other name. In a recent letter [from you] I noted an error on this account, and would appreciate it in the future if you could pay more attention to this matter."[50]

One month later, Huang Wenbi, now in the field, learned that Xu had been accused by Jin of "maintaining indirect communication with the inner provinces," with the result that all letters written by any member of the expedition now had to be vetted first in Urumchi before being sent out of the province. With that, Huang too decided to vent his anger. In consultation with Yuan Fuli, Huang drafted a strongly worded letter to the governor. "In the past scholars from both East and West have come numerous times to conduct excavations, and they have collected untold numbers of crates full of antiquities," Huang wrote. "In particular, the officials who hosted them were solicitous to the extreme in seeing to their needs. Today, however, when Chinese come, they are not even allowed to obtain a single glance. What will people say about this?" After one of the local officials told Huang that Jin would not respond well to such language, he removed the phrases "the officials who hosted them were solicitous to the extreme" and "What will people say about this?" before sending it out. But the brief détente experienced under Governor Yang was definitely over. When Huang informed Zhu Ruichi, another former Qing official left over from Stein's days, that he intended to abandon his work and leave the province for good, Zhu's response infuriated him. "I told him that there was no point in my staying here any longer, and that I intended to head back to Kucha," Huang wrote. "Zhu, a seasoned official, expressed his enthusiastic approval, and said that if any telegrams or letters came for me he would send them onward. But this is just what you say when you want to deceive a child. As he deploys only pleasing words, however, I had no choice but to respond in kind."[51]

In December 1928, both Hedin and Xu left Xinjiang. Instead of returning to Stockholm and Beijing, however, they made for Nanjing, the new capital of the Nationalist government. Chiang Kai-shek had apparently taken a personal interest in the fate of the expedition. Before he left Xinjiang, Xu wrote to Huang to let him know that Nanjing "is not asking the foreigners whether or not they wish to continue, but has determined to continue the expedition on its own." This was a stunning development. Apparently, the new central government had decided to throw its weight behind the first joint scholarly expedition between foreign and Chinese scientists. In other words, much as the Westernized Chinese scholars of Beijing had once concluded, the Nationalist government in Nanjing had also concluded that the symbolic value of a penitent and generous imperialist like Hedin was worth fighting for. It didn't matter that Hedin had already violated several of the provisions he had been forced to sign in Beijing the previous year. It also didn't matter that Hedin had returned to China with a radically new agenda for the expedition, one that should have caused an instant rift with his Chinese sponsors. This new agenda took root soon after he left Xinjiang in the wake of Governor Yang's refusal to grant aerial survey permissions. While passing through North America for medical attention, Hedin had managed to enlist the financial backing of a wealthy Swede in Chicago, Victor Bendix, as a replacement for Lufthansa. Bendix's money, however, came with strings attached: Hedin must bring back an entire Tibetan Lama temple, complete with hundreds of artifacts, for display at the 1933–34 World's Fair in Chicago.[52]

It is unclear at what point the Chinese learned of Hedin's new collecting agenda. What is clear, however, is that all interested parties—the Nationalist officials in Nanjing, the Westernized Chinese scholars in Beijing (now renamed Beiping), and the Chinese members of the expedition still in Xinjiang—did eventually learn of the plan. Though word of Hedin's taboo intent quickly caused a rift, it was not the rift we might expect. Instead, Hedin was rewarded for his symbolic yet duplicitous cooperation with Chinese scholars by being sent back into Xinjiang, this time with the full support of the Nationalist government in Nanjing. The motivation of the new government appears to have been exactly the same as that of the Beijing warlord Zhang Zuolin two years earlier: diplomatic and political capital. The Nationalists acquired political capital by associating themselves with a scientific venture capable of proving their "modern" credentials to other imperialist powers, thus laying the groundwork for the abolition of imperialist privileges such as extraterritoriality. They acquired diplomatic capital by forcing Jin Shuren, the newly ascendant warlord governor of Xinjiang entirely outside of Nationalist patronage networks, to acknowledge the authority of the central government by accepting scientific envoys bearing paperwork signed in Nanjing. The viability of both forms of capital depended entirely on Hedin's public renunciation of the imperialist privileges of yesteryear, along with his demonstrated commitment to taking Chinese peers with him into the field.

In February 1929, two months after his ignominious departure from the northwest, Hedin arrived in Nanjing, where he met up with Xu. Both men were received by Cai Yuanpei, one of the new breed of influential Nationalist officials occupying dual posts in government and academia. Cai, sensing a golden opportunity to test the waters in Xinjiang, promised to renew Xu and Hedin's visas, assuring them that "the government has the means to enforce its will" on Governor Jin. Two weeks later they were granted an audience with Chiang Kai-shek himself, then preoccupied with a warlord rebellion in north-central China. Chiang promptly signed off on a telegram to Jin, later recalled by Hedin as having instructed the distant governor to "facilitate their endeavours and in nowise to throw obstacles in their way." Chiang reminded Jin that "it is your duty to act in accordance" with these orders. Hedin, cognizant of Jin's likely response, preferred to delay costly preparations for a second expedition until some form of agreement had been hammered out. Nationalist officials, however, urged him to depart without delay, for "an order from the Central Government required no answer since in practice it must be obeyed." The Nationalists, eager to enhance the political and cultural legitimacy of the expedition, even allowed Hedin to print official commemorative Chinese stamps for sale to the general public (figure 27).[53]

For those members of Xu and Hedin's team still in Xinjiang—effectively under house arrest—these developments were most welcome news. Swedish geologist Erik Norin rushed to flaunt the new decree. "I have received a telegram from Dr. Hedin," he wrote to Jin on March 19, 1929. "It says that the Scientific Association of China has decided to extend our joint venture for an additional two years, and that the central government has also lent its approval. I trust Your Excellency has already been informed of this decision?" Jin played dumb. "My office has received no such notice," he told Norin. "Seeing as it will be difficult to extend the deadline, you are hereby to adhere to the original schedule. I trust you will obey." Hoping to get rid of Norin and the others before Hedin and Xu returned, Jin ordered the provincial Bureau of Education to discredit the expedition beyond repair. "They have been here for more than a year now, under the guise of academic inquiry, yet they have no accomplishments to speak of," bureau officials wrote to Nanjing. "Instead they send their men to dig things up, disturb corpses, and handle human skulls. These are grievous moral transgressions, and they have elicited the indignation of the Muslims." As for the celebrated inclusion of Chinese understudies, they "are nothing more than the tools of the Swedish scientists, assisting in the secret mapping of our land

Figure 27. Commemorating Equality. The political symbolism of a joint scientific expedition between Western and Chinese scholars was deemed so valuable by the Nationalist government in Nanjing that they allowed Hedin to print and sell official expedition stamps within China as a fund-raising measure. Stamps courtesy of Paul G. Pickowicz.

and surveying of important strategic sites." The bureau's correspondence ended by accusing the expedition of "destroying several thousand years' worth of antiquities."[54]

Nanjing was unmoved. "The members of this expedition are engaged in scientific survey," officers of the Ministry of Foreign Affairs replied two weeks later. "This is quite different from that of an ordinary traveler, and you are to admit them into the province." In order to defuse Jin's accusations of cultural theft, the ministry submitted for the governor's perusal a set of regulations Hedin had agreed to in Nanjing regarding the eventual deposit of all relics within a Chinese museum. To counter the governor's concerns regarding provincial security, the ministry described the expedition's weapons as nothing more than a "handgun, hunting rifles, and ammunition," all perfectly legal and necessary. The only thing Nanjing had not addressed was the supposed "indignation" of the Muslims. Jin took note. "Only through my unflagging efforts and timely intervention were we able to prevent their work on the outskirts and escort Hedin safely out of the province," Jin wrote on May 14, making it sound as if Hedin had barely escaped the clutches of a Muslim lynch mob. "If Hedin returns to Xinjiang again," the governor warned solemnly, "a misunderstanding is bound to occur, and the people will rise up." Sensing the need to grant himself a somewhat more impressive cultural résumé, Jin then went ahead and invented the nonexistent "Society for the Preservation of Antiquities" in Xinjiang. It, too, proceeded to denounce the expedition. With regard to Hedin and Xu's colleagues, eagerly awaiting the return of their codirectors in Urumchi, the governor insisted he had yet to see a "clear statement" of Nanjing's extension, and ordered them to leave the province at once.[55]

Events came to a head in June 1929. Five Swedish and two Chinese members of the expedition, having set off from Europe along the Trans-Siberian Railway, showed up at the border crossing in Tacheng with Nanjing-issued passports in hand. On orders from the governor, they were turned away. This snubbing at the border, Jin's first tangible repudiation of Nanjing's authority, necessitated the most spectacular justification to date. Unbeknownst to the Nationalist government, Jin now wrote, Hedin had once tried to transport "numerous firearms and a case of ammunition to the Torghut Mongols" in Kara-shahr. And it was certainly not a coincidence, Jin continued, that the Kara-shahr Mongols now evinced a hostile posture toward provincial authorities. "I had originally hoped to avoid publicizing this incident," the governor wrote, "but since matters have now come to this, I must marshal my courage and expose the details in a direct and honest manner." If the Sino-Swedish expedition did not leave the province immediately, Jin suggested, open rebellion against Han rule would ensue. He concluded with a final plea to consider the "the masses," who harbored "great antipathy" toward the expedition.[56] With that, Jin had thrown everything he had at the central government. In the face of such wily intransigence, were these archaeological proxies still worth fighting for?

The answer came one week later, as a reprimand from the Ministry of

Education to its administrative counterpart in Xinjiang. "This expedition is purely a scholarly venture, completely bereft of ulterior motives," officials at the ministry wrote. "If there are misunderstandings, then we will look to you to dispel the suspicions of the masses by means of logical explanation. You cannot simply echo popular sentiment and join in the attack." Liu Bannong, professor of literature at Peking University and a close colleague of Xu, urged the Nationalist government to do whatever was necessary to ensure the success of the expedition. After all, far more than science was at stake. "It seems that orders from the central government must be approved by Governor Jin first," Liu wrote from Beijing. "For a Chinese citizen equipped with a passport issued from his own central government to be unable to travel within the borders of our country—this is a frightening prospect." According to Liu, the governor's repeated invocation of Muslim indignation and popular antipathy was nothing more than a pretext to "openly despise the telegrams and passports of the central government." While damage to the expedition was inconsequential, "damage to the prestige of the central government [was] immense."[57]

Having thrice witnessed the determination of the new government to back its diplomatic proxies in Xinjiang, Governor Jin finally gave way. Quite miraculously, he claimed, owing to "strenuous efforts at clarification," the anger of the masses had suddenly dissipated. Likewise, the border guards at Tacheng came to the sudden realization that the expedition's marching orders "actually do benefit academic research." Jin, most begrudgingly, had once again admitted Xu and Hedin into his province, but he kept his eyes peeled for anything capable of discrediting them. He ordered the confiscation of the expedition's wireless telegraph box, authorized intimate inspections of every piece of luggage, and intercepted all postal communications. "If you see any boxes with an inspection seal that has been tampered with," the governor instructed his border guards in Hami, "open it up immediately, check its owner and his attendants for prohibited items on their persons, and submit a detailed description regarding any letter or report that is harmful to the security of Xinjiang." When the governor's agents discovered a letter from a Russian official in Novosibirsk addressed to a Russian consul in Tacheng, Jin postponed its delivery for two months while he mulled its significance. A translator was finally procured, and the mystery solved: "Move the equipment to [Urumchi] when the road is dry."[58]

The governor never found his smoking gun, and the Sino-Swedish Northwest Scientific Survey continued its work in the field for several more years. All the while, Sven Hedin managed to procure a full replica of a Tibetan Lama temple, along with 8,000 pieces of Mongolian art and handicrafts to accompany the temple on display. How did he manage to get these items out of the country? According to Hedin, Zhang Ji, the chairman of the Commission for the Preservation of Antiquities who also held a high position in the Nationalist government, told Hedin that no obstacles would be thrown in his way if he wanted to buy a couple of temples. It might even be possible, Zhang further suggested, that Nanjing could present Hedin with two temples as a gift. In searching for a large statue of the Buddha for the main hall of the temple, Hedin turned to Liu Bannong, the professor of literature at Peking University who had put so much pressure on Nanjing to support the expedition in its fight with Governor Jin. Eager to thank Hedin for all he had done for China, Liu found a suitable wooden statue from the Song dynasty, along with a fifteen-foot-tall bronze Buddha and a giant Avalokitesvara. Liu and his university then "quietly and without anyone's notice" helped Hedin "get the treasures out of the country."[59]

The roles of Zhang and Liu in helping Hedin to break the laws of their country and transgress the stipulations of the agreements he had signed with their own cultural and governmental bodies are nothing less than astounding. Apparently, the moment the Westernized Chinese scholars of Beijing chose to become enmeshed in the larger political concerns of their country, they too began to feel the patent allure of the compensations of plunder, in this case diplomatic capital. Huang Wenbi, however, seems to have kept his distance from such high-level political intrigue. As a result, though the evidence is sketchy on this point, it appears as if he was one of the only Chinese scholars to insist on calling out Hedin's duplicity. We already saw the many tensions between Huang and Hedin on display in Huang's diary, which may very well account for the inability to publish it during his lifetime. In addition, we also have Hedin's own words regarding the role of Huang on the second leg of the Sino-Swedish expedition, after Nanjing had already sent them back into the field. In an unprecedented display of public acrimony, Hedin used the official published account of the expedition to smear Huang's name. Claiming that Huang had turned various "dark forces" at Nanjing against him by daring to accuse the beloved Swede of illegally removing artifacts from China, Hedin characterized Huang's actions as "scoundrelism" and accused him of pursuing a "miserable plan of persecution against us."[60]

In hindsight, it appears that the opposite was true. In the fifteen years since the outbreak of World War I, the Chinese had come a long way toward reversing the archaeological imbalance in their country. The scientific achievements of Chinese scholars such as Ding Wenjiang and Yuan Fuli, who worked side by side with Johan Gunnar Andersson for more than a decade, are ample testament to this. But still the new generation of West-ernized Chinese scholars could not get over the intractable humps of finan-cial impoverishment and political instability. These handicaps forced them to continue working closely with resourceful foreigners long after they had surpassed their former mentors in scientific training. In a bold yet tenta-tive attempt to revise the terms of cooperation with such foreigners, the Westernized Chinese scholars of Beijing decided to use Langdon Warner as an unsuspecting escort into the field for Chen Wanli. For his part, Warner evinced a duplicitous agenda all his own, one he was convinced the Chinese would never uncover. When the Chinese ruse proved more successful than the American one, Warner responded by tarring all Chinese as nationalist fanatics incapable of understanding reason, initiating an ugly spat between Harvard and Peking University.

When Hedin showed up the very next year, the same professors decided to impose a similar model for cooperation on the Swedish explorer, this time without the subtle deception they had employed previously with Warner. Much to their surprise, Hedin agreed to the new terms. Though this was likely due to the specific nature of Hedin's Lufthansa mission, which was focused more on airfields and weather stations than antiquities, Hedin's un-expected concession was nonetheless powerfully symbolic of the new order conjured up by the Westernized Chinese scholars of Beijing. In fact, Hedin's voluntary cooperation with, and avowed respect for, the new generation of Chinese scientists proved so rewarding on so many fronts that both the Nationalist government in Nanjing and some of the Westernized Chinese scholars themselves decided not to hold Hedin to either the letter or spirit of the original agreement. Hedin, as both a political proxy for a weak but ambitious government and a financial wet nurse for Chinese scholars other-wise unable to get into the field, was too valuable to hold fully accountable. So long as he renounced imperialist privileges in theory and subordinated himself to domestic Chinese authority in practice, the Chinese were still willing to let him do as the imperialists of yore had done.

In the decade after the conclusion of World War I, it had become much harder for foreign archaeologists to undertake an expedition in China. In order to secure the support of the Beijing intellectuals, now indispensable for any enterprise, foreigners had to meet an ever-higher bar. And yet, as the complex evolution of the Sino-Swedish expedition clearly shows, once met, that bar was still embarrassingly flexible. In spite of this realization, Hedin was the only foreigner of his generation who proved even remotely willing to meet this bar, even in its heavily diluted state. For everyone else, the rise of Western ideological avatars in China was not an event to be celebrated. It was something to be confronted—and the most spectacular confrontation had yet to come. On May 29, 1930, Huang Wenbi, during an audience with the governor in Urumchi, learned of a new conflict on the horizon. "At 10 o'clock in the morning I went to call on Provincial Chairman Jin Shuren, and we talked for a long time," Huang wrote in his diary.[61]

"I learned that Stein is coming."

CHAPTER SIX

Foreign Devils Begone

On December 11, 1922, a little past three o'clock in the afternoon, three Americans attempted to drive two cars through a checkpoint in Kalgan, the last major city in China on the road from Beijing to Mongolia. In their trunks was ten thousand dollars' worth of silver. When they reached the sentry post, a group of soldiers stopped the convoy and discovered the silver. In accordance with a new ban on the export of silver promulgated by the military commander of Kalgan, the soldiers refused to let the Americans pass. Upon hearing of this, the local American consul declared such obstruction to be in violation of the treaties and ordered the cars to proceed at once. As the vehicles lurched forward, the soldiers fired a volley of warning shots. At that, two of the Americans, the consul and a man by the name of Charles Coltman, got out of the car and approached the soldiers. According to a report later filed with the US secretary of state by Roy Chapman Andrews, the famous American paleontologist, the soldiers "then rushed up and deliberately shot Coltman," who died from his injuries the next day. Afterward, according to Andrews, the soldiers "all laughed and acted much pleased that they had shot a foreigner."[1]

Whether or not the events in Kalgan unfolded exactly as Andrews alleged—American diplomats later determined that Coltman had indeed been attempting to smuggle unauthorized silver out of Kalgan—it is Andrews's response to the tragedy that most concerns us here. In his characterization of the soldiers as "unbearably insolent" and the orders of the local military commander as having "not the slightest legal right" to impinge on "the treaty rights of foreigners," Andrews gives us our first glimpse into his chronic contempt for the Chinese. In his report on the incident in Kalgan, Andrews, despite not having personally witnessed what transpired at the checkpoint, called for the immediate public execution of both the local military commander and the officer who gave the order to fire. He then admitted that he himself had repeatedly bowled through military checkpoints in China whenever he encountered resistance from local authorities, and that he was now concerned for his safety in the event he decided to do so again in the future. In the conclusion to his report, Andrews joked that "it is very fortunate that the Expeditions' work lies in 'uncivilized' Mongolia!" And yet it is clear that Andrews regarded both China and Mongolia as wholly uncivilized. In one of his best-selling books, Andrews bragged about how he and Coltman had once engaged in a harrowing shoot-out with unidentified "bandits" in Mongolia. "Bang, bang went our rifles," he later wrote. "Charlie's client sat down suddenly and rolled over. Mine did a magnificent swan dive right off the cliff."[2]

Henry Osborn, the president of the American Museum of Natural History in New York and Andrews's boss, was convinced that everything Andrews did in the field was motivated by altruistic concerns. "The United States has done everything in our power for China," Osborn told Charles Evans Hughes, the US secretary of state, in a short appendix to the report on the "murder" of Coltman. "Our own scientific workers are risking their lives daily for the future benefit of China." Since 1919, Andrews had been leading successive "Central Asiatic Expeditions" to Inner and Outer Mongolia (figure 28), both of which were intermittently controlled by Chinese, Mongol, and Russian armies. Supported by Osborn, Andrews set out to find fossil evidence of the "missing link" between man and ape. If found, it would provide fodder for a racist yet highly fashionable theory peddled by Osborn: that *Homo sapiens* were descended from the more palatable Mongoloid stock of "yellow Asia" rather than the undesirable Negroid stock of "black Africa."[3]

In nearly a decade of paleontological exploration, Andrews found nothing of the sort. He did, however, stumble on some dinosaur eggs, which he used to drum up popular and philanthropic support for his expeditions in influential New York circles. Much like Hedin, Andrews (figure 29) was a talented self-publicist who felt no shame in asking for money from friends in high places. He was also the first explorer to make extensive use of motor cars on an expedition and a pioneer in the business of accepting endorsements from commercial sponsors. With heightened drama on every page of his many best-selling books, Andrews imported the Hedin model of self-promotion into America, this time through the lens of paleontology. It is thus little wonder that he is often identified, quite erroneously, as the inspiration for the iconic Hollywood figure of Indiana Jones.[4] In cultivating such a profitable public image, Andrews drew the ire of his more reserved

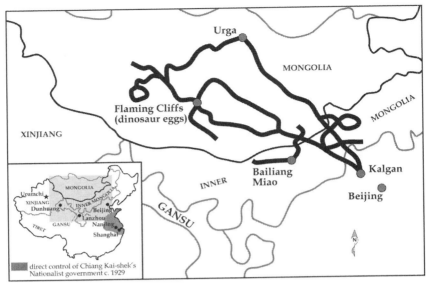

Figure 28. The Central Asiatic Expeditions. From 1919 to 1928, American paleontologist Roy Chapman Andrews led successive expeditions to Inner and Outer Mongolia on behalf of his home institution in New York, the American Museum of Natural History. Supported by Henry Osborn, the museum's president, Andrews hoped to find fossil evidence of the "missing link" between man and ape in "yellow Asia" rather than in "black Africa." Instead, Andrews found a collection of fossilized dinosaur eggs, which he used to garner commercial endorsements and promote his expeditions among the mainstream media. Cartography by Debbie Newell.

colleagues. In a letter to Stein, Langdon Warner criticized Andrews for his "contention that no support can be counted on and no money raised without a brass band and an atmosphere of commercial 'efficiency.'" In 1925, Carl Keller, a Harvard graduate on friendly terms with Warner, drew an implicit contrast between Andrews and the supposedly more dignified Stein. "I saw that Roy Chapman Andrews, our greatest advertising archeologist," Keller wrote to Stein, "is back in the United States and the papers are full again of addled and unaddled dinosaur eggs, hypothetical missing links and other things that keep the popular and vulgar mind interested."[5]

Key to keeping the popular and vulgar minds interested in Andrews's expeditions was the public display of tangible artifacts in the American Museum of Natural History in New York. This is where Andrews enters our story. For the first eight years of the Central Asiatic Expeditions, Andrews never encountered any opposition to the removal of fossils and skeletons from Chinese territory. On the contrary, in 1923, Ding Wenjiang, the

Figure 29. American Paleontologist Roy Chapman Andrews. Beginning in the fall of 1928, Andrews engaged in a series of acrimonious negotiations with the newly created Commission for the Preservation of Antiquities in Beijing, which wanted Andrews to reorganize his expeditions along the lines adopted by Hedin the previous year. Andrews, unwilling to submit to Chinese oversight or share his finds, responded by attacking the commission in the global press and terminating the Central Asiatic Expeditions. He later referred to the members of the commission as "returned students" who had "absorbed a superficial layer of Western culture" and "suffer from an inferiority complex." Roy Chapman Andrews, 12/22/23, LC-F8–28072, Library of Congress.

director of the Geological Survey then working closely with Andersson, assured Andrews that the American expedition "has every right to leave its collections—even the geological and palaeontological collections—in any museum or institution it may consider best suitable." With the force of many years' precedent behind him, a heroic public persona, marked disdain for the Chinese, professional dependence on the acquisition of artifacts, and a proven willingness to shoot his way through any dispute in China or Mongolia, Andrews was destined for an ugly confrontation with the Westernized Chinese scholars of Beijing.[6]

In the spring of 1928, Andrews was ready to head out from Kalgan for another season of work in Inner Mongolia. In his hands were papers issued by Zhang Zuolin, the warlord of Beijing. Zhang had issued similar papers to Sven Hedin a little over a year before, only to be pulled back to the negotiating table by Westernized Chinese scholars working under the institutional umbrella of the Association of Chinese Scholarly Organizations. Now reconstituted into a Commission for the Preservation of Antiquities, these same scholars began to set their sights on Andrews. Fully aware of Hedin's concessions and determined not to share his fate, Andrews took the extraordinary step of summoning all the Beijing correspondents for the major English-language newspapers of northern China. He then implored them not to publicize his latest expedition until after its departure, reasoning that this would be enough to defeat the commission. The journalists complied, and the expedition made it into the field without a hitch. Four months later, as the expedition made its way back to Beijing, a soldier at a military outpost near Kalgan attempted to detain Andrews over inconsistencies in his paperwork. True to form, Andrews resolved the situation by threatening to kill the soldier. "You will step aside and let my cars and my personnel into Kalgan according to our authorization and the order you have received from Peking," Andrews was reputed to have said, "or we will shoot our way through."[7]

Such bullying tactics would not work against the commission, which learned of Andrews's latest escapades soon after his departure from Kalgan. In August 1928, on his return to Beijing, Andrews learned that the crates containing the expedition's new fossil material had been detained at Kalgan on orders of the local Chinese garrison commander. It did not take long for Andrews to discover that the garrison commander in Kalgan had in turn been prodded into action by a telegram sent from the commission in Beijing. "I feel very much hurt at the telegram which your association is reported to have sent to the Kalgan authorities," Andrews wrote to Yuan Tongli, associate director of the Peking National Library. "For twelve years I have been carrying on scientific work in China and my relations with Chinese scientists always have been most friendly." Andrews bristled at any suggestion that he was, as Yuan alleged, "searching for oil and mineral wealth," "violating China's sovereign rights," or "robbing China of priceless treasures."[8] Unable to threaten Yuan with the same sort of brute force that had worked so well on the Mongolian frontier, Andrews was forced to submit a list of the paleontological specimens inside the crates for review by the commission. Then, on September 27, Andrews submitted to the indignity of having his laboratory inspected by members of the commission. Once the commission completed its review of the contents of the crates and laboratory with the master list provided by Andrews, however, they discovered a glaring discrepancy. The list contained mention of a humanoid skeleton, but no member of the commission had ever seen this skeleton during the actual inspection. Zhang Ji, acting director of the commission, was suspicious. "This case did not actually appear during the examination on that day," Zhang informed Andrews. "It is not known whether it is stored in your residence."[9]

One month later, Andrews finally handed over the skeleton. Now faced with the prospect of having all of his collections from the 1928 expedition confiscated by the Chinese, Andrews went on the offensive. Over the course of the following winter and spring, Andrews, with the full support of Osborn and the American diplomatic corps in Beijing and Washington, developed a new rhetorical strategy to combat the commission. It consisted of several major points. The first and important point was that Andrews was not an archaeologist in search of antiquities. He was a paleontologist in search of fossils. In other words, he did not collect the "works of man," but rather a mere "portion of the work of God," as he once so eloquently put it. According to Andrews, the last thing he wanted to do was to turn a profit off such objects. "Probably the entire collection could not be sold for $100," Andrews declared, in a condescending bluff. "Its only value is scientific." As such, the nationalist agenda of Westernized Chinese scholars, which "can well be understood and sympathized with," did not apply to "fossil remains of early prehistoric animal life, which are of interest to the entire civilized world." Building on this point, Andrews and his supporters then submitted a list of nineteen other "civilized" countries that supported similar work by the museum. "The governments of countries visited have not only approved but in many cases have assisted in these Museum expeditions," observed George Sherwood, the director of the museum, in a letter to Wu Chaoshu, the Chinese minister in Washington. Sherwood then added the dubious assertion that "the United States also welcomes explorations for fossils by any accredited expedition of a foreign country."[10]

This last statement was almost certain to raise the hackles of the members of the commission. In 1925, during the immediate aftermath of Warner's failed expedition to Dunhuang, Liu Bannong, one of the Peking University professors who was most instrumental in organizing the commission's institutional predecessors, pondered just such a hypothetical situation. "Let me ask you something," Liu wrote to Zhou Zuoren, a well-known writer and the younger brother of Lu Xun. "Xinjiang is Chinese territory. So how can Americans be allowed to go there and excavate freely? Just imagine if the situation was reversed and some antiquities were found on American soil. Would any Chinese be allowed to go there and excavate them freely?"[11]

There were other elements in Andrews's self-defense, including claims

that his expedition represented an economic stimulus for China and that
numerous Chinese assistants had been trained under his watch. The commission was unmoved. Either Andrews would submit to the same demands
as Hedin had done two years prior—a Chinese co-leader and retention of
the best fossils in China—or the commission would block the work of the
Central Asiatic Expeditions at every turn. Liu Bannong has left us a vivid
account of Andrews's reaction to any suggestion that he follow Hedin's lead.
"Although on the surface he said a whole bunch of different things," Liu
recalled later that year, "in reality, one thing stood out from the rest. He
never said it clearly, but we all detected it. Namely, that Sweden was a
small country, while America was a big country. And big countries, being
more powerful, do not have to do as small countries do."[12]

From start to finish, Andrews refused to consider handing his collection
over to the Chinese. But he was apparently willing to entertain the idea of
a Chinese co-leader, at least at first. In early April 1929, despite later claims
to the contrary, Andrews, according to a memo from the Department of
State, "reluctantly agreed to accept a so-called Chinese codirector but insisted that the expedition should not proceed unless the Museum should
have full direction of it and definite control of the disposal of any fossils discovered." Though the language in the second half of this memo effectively
negated the concession in the first half, Andrews still thought he had done
enough to appease the commission. He then gave the order for twenty-five
crates of paleontological specimens to be delivered to the customhouse in
Tianjin and thence onward to New York.[13]

They were detained yet again. Walter Granger, one of Andrews's clos-
est colleagues in the field, demanded an explanation from Ma Heng, the
director of the commission. "According to your letter and the statement
of Mr. Sun we expected to have the cases passed at once," Granger wrote.
"The Customs refused to do so, however, saying that they must have a
huchao [*huzhao*, 'passport'] from your Commission and that no telegram
had come from Nanking giving authority to ship the boxes." With that, Andrews called in the American diplomatic corps to help prosecute the battle
on his behalf. Nelson T. Johnson, the newly appointed minister to the Nationalist government, made the unhelpful suggestion that the commission
might be swayed by the argument that no one in China was qualified to assess the value of fossils recovered by the expedition. "The point is that the
authorities in the Museum in New York are the only ones who can classify
this material," he observed, apparently oblivious to the fact that Westernized Chinese scholars like Pei Wenzhong had been classifying such materials for years. "It cannot be done in Peking." For his part, Wu Chaoshu,

the Chinese minister in Washington, informed Osborn that the Nationalist government apparently had not accepted his claims about the interactions of museum expeditions with nineteen other "civilized" countries at face value, and were instead "investigating the practice in other countries and would conform to that."[14]

It was only when Andrews and Johnson managed to procure a meeting with top Nationalist diplomats, however, that they began to grasp the true power and autonomy of the commission. Jiang Menglin, the Nationalist minister of education, admitted to Andrews "quite candidly" that he himself "had never realized the distinction" between archaeological and paleontological objects, and that "now that he understood the matter better, he would interest himself in trying to bring about an arrangement which would enable the fossils to be taken in the first instance to the American Museum for the necessary study and comparison with its collections." Wang Zhengting, the minister of foreign affairs, also did his best to reassure Johnson, even going so far as to give his "personal assurance that arrangements satisfactory to you would be made," Johnson wrote. "He reiterated that we might completely rely upon his assumption of personal responsibility in the matter." Together, this was an extraordinary display of confidence by top Nationalist officials in the ability of the new government to enforce its will on the commission. Wu Chaoshu, the Nationalist minister in Washington, further echoed the sentiment of his colleagues in China, emphasizing the fact that the "demand for a Chinese expert to go as a co-director with Andrews had been made by the Chinese society, but not by the Chinese Government." As such, Wu "did not anticipate that there would be any trouble on that score."[15]

The Nationalists, whose effective political writ did not extend beyond the Yangzi River delta region, appeared to be pursuing a two-pronged agenda. On the one hand, much like the warlord Zhang Zuolin before them, they desperately wanted to curry favor with powerful and resourceful foreign governments. Issuing a passport for a scientific expedition sponsored by the avowedly anti-imperialist Americans was a cheap and easy way to do this. On the other hand, they also wanted to establish political footholds throughout the rest of the country, including Beijing. Attempting to take control of the commission's agenda and dictate the terms of engagement with foreign expeditions seemed like a promising way to set down roots in Beijing. Yet the members of the commission, rightly proud of their freelance victories over Langdon Warner and Sven Hedin in the years before the Nationalists seized power in Nanjing, were not about to relinquish control of their agenda to any outside party. The reason the commission and the

Nationalist government had been able to cooperate so effectively during the Sino-Swedish expedition was because Hedin proved willing to submit to nominal Chinese oversight. As a result, both the commission and the Nationalists found they could work together in pursuit of complementary goals. For the commission, this meant the procurement of invaluable field experience for its members and the enforcement of internalized Western ideals of cultural sovereignty for the new Chinese nation. For the Nationalists, this meant the imposition of its will and authority on Governor Jin Shuren in Xinjiang under the guise of a cooperative scientific venture between Chinese and foreigners.

Andrews, in refusing to do as Hedin had done, ensured that the political agenda of the Nationalists would come into conflict with the cultural agenda of the commission. Once again, Liu Bannong has left us the most complete account of how these tensions unfolded behind the scenes. During a hasty visit to Beijing, Wang Zhengting, the minister of foreign affairs, told the members of the commission that he "very much hoped that in the future the American secretary of state would help us to abolish consular jurisdiction" in China. Therefore, "it would be best if we could just yield [*rangbu*] on small matters [*xiaoshi*] like this." Liu and his colleagues were stunned. "So it turns out that everything we've been doing," he wrote later that same year, still seething from his encounter with Minister Wang, "is in fact detrimental to the abolition of consular jurisdiction and will make it difficult for the Republic of China, with its 'foreign relations revolution,' to win a big victory [*zhan bu dao da pianyi*]." According to Liu, after the assembled members of the commission offered a lukewarm assent to Wang's request, Wang "became very satisfied, let out a sigh, and drove away."[16]

Their assent, tendered in a state of shock, was soon retracted. On June 18, 1929, Johnson concluded that "the Cultural Society was not willing to accept the Government's word in the matter" and that "they were dictating themselves the terms under which the expedition should proceed." One week later, Secretary of State Henry Stimson wrote to Osborn to inform him that "we presented your conditions to the Cultural Society asking if they would abide by Nanking decision. Their answer was evasive. We were convinced that they will use all means to block expedition." Osborn, now in a panic, wrote to Minister Wu in Washington to warn him of a planned Soviet expedition to Mongolia. "I hope therefore in view of the proposed Russian entry into the same fossil fields," he informed the minister, "you will be able to convince the Cultural Society that it is for the very best educational and scientific interests of China to immediately withdraw their impractical demands and accept the most generous offer of the American Museum upon which they can absolutely rely."[17]

By July, it had become clear to all that the commission would not allow the Nationalist government to please the Americans at its expense. This was certainly the conclusion of the American legation in China. "If Ministers Wang and C. C. Wu [Wu Chaoshu] are actually seeking to control opposition to Cultural Society, their efforts thus far appear utterly fruitless, and the Society is manifesting an increasingly unfriendly attitude." Faced with such an intractable foe, Andrews began to impugn the motives of the commission itself. "Their idea of 'cooperation' is to let you do all the financing and all the work and they will take the results," he told Secretary Stimson. "Apparently they have not the slightest desire to advance world scientific knowledge. Their wish is merely to get something for nothing." Walter Granger seconded Andrews's sentiment, later declaring that submission to the commission's demands would effectively reduce the Central Asiatic Expedition into "Roy's Charity Organization." Osborn, deploring "the great wrong done Science and Education by this continued interference with our expedition since August last," made one last attempt to dangle the prospect of diplomatic compensations for the Nationalist government. "When China needs friends, confidence and trust on every side," he asked Minister Wu in Washington, "why continue to offend, delay, disappoint and obstruct scientific and educational cooperation of American Museum?"[18]

By now, however, Andrews knew full well that any such overtures to a Nationalist diplomat could only result in aspirational assent. "The Cultural Society has complete power here," he told Osborn in mid-July. "It is difficult for anyone who does not know intimately the present political situation in China, to realize that just because the Chinese Government in Nanking agrees to a proposal, does not mean that it will be acted upon. The Nanking authority in the north is precarious to say the least, and if a body like the Cultural Society takes a strong attitude against foreigners, Nanking does not dare oppose them." Nevertheless, Andrews continued to be irked at the extent to which an "unofficial" body like the commission could so easily deflect the combined might of the American diplomatic corps and the American Museum of Natural History. During one of his meetings with Wang Zhengting, the Nationalist minister of foreign affairs, Andrews brought along Harold Timperley, a journalist for the *Manchester Guardian*, to bear witness. "What is the status of the Cultural Society?" Timperley asked Wang. "Is it an official body?" Wang admitted it was not. But, he said, "it has great influence. Its members have made a close study of such matters." With Timperley by his side, Andrews resolved to play his final card. "There is just one way in which something might be done," he wrote to Osborn. "That is by unfavorable world publicity. The Chinese are very sensitive to criticism and ridicule."[19]

That publicity came the very next day. On July 19, 1929, the English-language newspapers of northern China were filled with shrill accusations and belittling insults, all directed toward the commission. "Peking Society Wins 'Face' at Expense of China and World," announced the front page of the *Peking Leader*. An article in the *North China Standard* attempted to discredit the "so-called" commission by reproducing an incendiary quote from Andrews, who referred to it as "a bigoted body unable to do the work itself." The motives of Andrews were portrayed as unimpeachably altruistic, while those of the commission were described in downright sacrilegious terms. "Nothing of the handiwork of man do we wish to keep," Mr. Andrews was quoted as saying. "Only a portion of the work of God." Apparently, Andrews was no longer content to equate obstruction of his expedition with the obstruction of science. Now, to defy Andrews was to defy God Himself. Unfortunately for Andrews, however, even God could not defeat the commission. Soon after the publication of these inflammatory articles, the American legation in Nanjing reported that the editor of the *Peking Leader* "was notified by local authorities that Ministry of Interior had ordered censorship of his paper."[20]

The commission won. Later that year, Liu Bannong reaffirmed the nobility of his cause. "Whenever I think of the work of the Commission for the Preservation of Antiquities," Liu wrote, "I cannot help but think of that scoundrel Andrews!" As far as Liu was concerned, Andrews, "a man of ordinary learning [*xuewen pingchang*] who merely dug up a few dinosaur eggs," had been treated far more generously than he deserved. Now that the "gangster" (*liumang*) Andrews had revealed his true nature by "going out of his way to insult and impugn" (*dama tema*) the commission in the foreign press, Liu urged his colleagues to pay no more heed to Andrews or his allies. "By nature, these crooked newspapers cannot help insulting the Chinese people," Liu concluded, "just as a dog, by its very nature, cannot help eating shit. So let us simply pay no attention to them anymore."[21]

For his part, Andrews, unable to contain his anger, told Osborn he intended to sell all the equipment in Beijing and leave China forever. Once Osborn informed Andrews that there might be a possibility of working together with the Russians, however, Andrews decided to stay put, thinking perhaps that the specter of cooperation with the Russians could be used as leverage with the commission. After two more years of fruitless negotiations, Andrews decided to send out feelers to the new Japanese-controlled puppet government of Manchukuo in China's far northeast. Though the Japanese initially expressed an interest in allowing Andrews to undertake an expedition in Manchukuo, it soon became clear that they, too, shared the same concerns of the commission in Beijing. "Should Manchukuo be content to receive only duplicates?" asked one Japanese official in the Manchurian government. Another letter from the Manchurian "Foreign Ministry" warned Andrews that "any Chinese or foreigner who harbor sinister designs upon this new state can not be welcomed and that some Manchurians or Japanese who are well versed in the line of your investigations may be attached to the party." In the end, nothing came of the proposal, with the Japanese citing political "unrest" as cause for postponement. Nonetheless, Andrews was gratified to learn of the alarm with which members of the commission responded to reports of his dealings with the Japanese. In a final attempt to denigrate the scientific credentials of the Westernized Chinese scholars of Beijing, Osborn and Andrews responded to the commission's protest by informing it that the members of the museum had "unanimously agreed" to "enter into negotiations with the new government of Manchukuo. It was hoped that a more liberal attitude toward international scientific work would be found among the authorities of the new state."[22]

Despite this apparently satisfying riposte, Andrews never got over the "humiliation" of his defeat at the hands of the commission. In 1932, after burning his final bridge with the commission, Andrews vented his frustrations to Frederick McCormick, the founder of the China Monuments Society. Referring to the members of the commission as "returned students" who had "absorbed a superficial layer of Western culture," Andrews concluded that they must all "suffer from an inferiority complex." They know "perfectly well that they cannot do the work themselves, but they feel that allowing foreigners to do it is a tacit admission that they are unable to do it and this makes them 'lose face.'" What Andrews never seemed to realize was just how little the commission had actually asked of him. If he had known anything about the clandestine dealings of the Sino-Swedish expedition, he would have learned that submission to the commission's demands was little more than window dressing. Once the scientific equality and credentials of both Chinese and foreign scholars were formally enshrined on paper, the Chinese were willing to treat the foreign explorer as one of their own. In the case of Sven Hedin, both the commission and the Nationalist government even proved willing to go so far as to suppress any and all dissent from domestic quarters, be it the principled idealism of Chinese archaeologist Huang Wenbi or the cynical opportunism of Xinjiang governor Jin Shuren.[23]

To men long accustomed to getting their way throughout the non-Western world, however, even nominal submission to "Oriental authority" was a difficult pill to swallow. Far from regarding the proven resolve of the commission as an insurmountable hurdle, most Western explorers chose to view the fates of Hedin and Andrews as cautionary tales about what not to do. After all, Hedin lacked a powerful patron, which crippled his ability to negotiate. Andrews was too impatient, too enamored of celebrity, and too quick to burn bridges. Perhaps most importantly, neither man had ever had much interest in cultivating close relations with his Chinese counterparts, scholars or otherwise. The same could not be said of the British archaeologist Aurel Stein. Famously cautious, meticulous, and patient, Stein had always shied away from the public limelight. Not only that, but he had excellent ties to the Chinese officials of Xinjiang, in some cases spanning many decades. His only weakness was his patron: interwar Britain was no longer the aggressive global powerhouse it had been just a few decades before. If he could only find a new patron, one willing to back him as Andrews had been backed, then the commission would face a foe unlike any other.

On July 15, 1929, just as Andrews was preparing to torch the commission in the press, Stein received a telegram:

Can you lead Asiatic expedition if Harvard will finance. Answer collect. Post details. Address Lyromo, Boston. Keller.[24]

THE RETURN OF SIR AUREL

This cryptic telegram was followed by a far less cryptic letter. In it, Carl Tilden Keller, a Harvard alumnus who split his time between a lucrative accounting business and the collection of obscure translations of *Don Quijote*, explained the origin of the telegram to his good friend Aurel Stein. "The story of it is that I was lunching with Langdon Warner, Curator of Asiatic Art in the Fogg Art Museum," Keller wrote to Stein, "and told him that sometime ago you had written that you were very anxious to make another expedition to Asia and intimated that you would be willing to do so under American auspices." According to Keller, Warner, "a very attractive and impulsive chap," suddenly jumped "on my neck and wanted me to cable you immediately, saying that he was convinced he could raise the funds, that you were the unique man on the universe and why hadn't I told him sooner." As Keller breathlessly explained, Harvard was willing to give Stein everything the British Raj could no longer guarantee. "By the way," he continued, "I neglected in my excitement to say that if you make the expedition for Harvard you can go when you will, where you will, how you will and make your own terms about everything." Keller begged Stein to reply at once. "You can imagine that Langdon Warner and I feverishly await an answer to yesterday's cable. God send that it come."[25]

In 1929, Stein was sixty-seven years old. No one who knew him, however, doubted his ability to lead an expedition into the desert at that age. In 1931, George Macartney, the former British consul at Kashgar, confessed to Stein that he was "beginning to realize that I am an old man, remaining not like you ever younger than your years." Nevertheless, in order to reassure his Harvard backers, Stein agreed to take along a young American assistant, Milton Bramlette. Bramlette, one of Ellsworth Huntington's graduate students in the geology program at Yale, had just returned from a three-year hiatus with Gulf Oil in Venezuela, Mexico, and Ecuador. His acclimation to a desk job in the tropics worried Stein's friend Fred Andrews, who found Bramlette unequal to the rigors of a shopping trip in England. "Entre nous, I think you will find it expedient to break him in gradually to physical strain," Andrews told Stein. "He seemed to tire with the walking about and shopping—probably due to his having had a sedentary period while studying." Later, when the elevations and subzero temperatures of the Himalayas proved far more taxing than the streets of London, Bramlette withdrew from the expedition and returned home. In a letter to Sachs, he confessed that it was not "easy to admit that a young man cannot stand up to conditions that one does of Sir Aurel's age."[26]

For his part, Stein much preferred to lead an expedition on his own, claiming that the logistics of camp and travel arrangements were "simplified when the needs of only one Sahib will have to be cared for." From Stein's perspective, too many sahibs spoiled the caravan. "You know that I do not feel lonely when doing my work without a white companion," Stein told his friend Percy Allen, "and since Br.[amlette]'s society was, I confess, at no time exactly stimulating and during the last two months or so owing to his physical discomfort somewhat depressing it will be easier for me to be once more by myself." Stein, however, eschewed not only the company of a white sahib but also that of a Chinese sahib. In December 1929, as he prepared to spend several weeks in Washington and Boston getting acquainted with his American patrons, Stein informed Sir Frederick Whyte, a British advisor to the Nationalist government in Nanjing, that he "could not contemplate hampering my work in the field by sharing control with a 'Chinese leader' or taking along a large party of Chinese students apart from the couple of competent Chinese literati, true scholars whom I am very anxious to secure as assistant." In expressing a wish to take along "competent Chinese literati," Stein was referring to someone like Jiang Xiaowan, the Kashgar secretary from his second expedition. For nearly two years, Jiang handled Stein's Chinese-language correspondence in the field, facilitated bilingual conversation with local officials, and helped to decipher Chinese inscriptions on ancient artifacts. Stein and Jiang got along extremely well and developed a genuine friendship, but it was a friendship that was nonetheless marked by clearly defined social, economic, and political boundaries. In other words, Jiang would not and could not give orders to Stein. He was Stein's "assistant," and Stein refused to travel with anyone—Bramlette excluded—who did not accept that hierarchical designation.[27]

On March 17, 1930, Stein arrived in Boston, where he met Langdon Warner amid the frenzied backdrop of the annual Saint Patrick's Day parade. Though Stein left no record of what he discussed with Warner during a "hasty lunch," it is almost certain that Warner reinforced Stein's determination not to accept the imposition of a Chinese co-leader or Westernized Chinese students. After all, just four years earlier, Warner had written a lengthy letter to Stein in which he asserted his belief that "some of the trouble" encountered on the second Fogg expedition to Dunhuang "may have been due to a Dr. Ch'ien [i.e., Chen Wanli] whom I brought with me from the Nat. University in Peking." Upon his arrival in Cambridge, however, Stein met with representatives from Yenching University, who had just cemented a formal partnership with Harvard in the guise of the Harvard-Yenching Institute in Beijing. Yenching University, which had agreed to sponsor Stein's expedition, was the institutional home of William Hung, who had played an instrumental role in undermining the second Fogg expedition under Warner. It was also home to many other Western scholars who were highly sympathetic to the demands of Westernized Chinese scholars to be treated as the scientific equals of men like Stein. One of these scholars was none other than John Leighton Stuart, the principal of the university who had hired Hung as dean and chairman of the history department. In June 1925, it was Stuart who cabled Warner in the field to advise him to return empty-handed, else he would "imperil future prospects of your work and embarrass your country and university." Another Western scholar affiliated with Yenching was George H. Chase, a professor of classical archaeology at Harvard. In 1924, Chase had warned Forbes that the second Fogg expedition "ought not to start unless there is a very clear understanding with the Chinese authorities (if such are discoverable) that we expect to be allowed to take some things out. We don't want to get into a position where anyone can accuse the University of countenancing the looting of China."[28]

After his meeting with the cautious Stuart and Chase, Stein noted his "surprise of insistence on arr[angement]s with Nat.[ional] Council of Cultural Soc[ietie]s. Andrew[s] & Hedin quoted as cases of satisfactory arrang[emen]ts!" In response, Stein opted to stall for time, promising to contact the commission only "if Sir F.[rederick] Whyte agreed." Three days later, William Hung, who had not been able to attend the first meeting with Stuart and Chase, joined the next conference with Stein. Hung was not as easily deflected as his Western colleagues had been. According to notes scribbled in Stein's pocketbook diary, Hung responded to Stein's second deferment to Whyte by offering "to write letter to Whyte which I promised to deliver." Stein, who would later deliver Hung's letter as promised, drafted a formal note on his conference with Stuart and Hung and insisted "on both treating matter as confidential." Knowledge that Yenching's share of the funds for his expedition had been approved by its trustees "on the definite understanding of our agreeing . . . about this reference to the National Council as an essential condition" was alarming, to say the least. Unsure if Stuart and Hung were bluffing—Stein says Stuart became evasive when he asked him whether or not "the Trustee's decision on this point had been communicated to Prof. Sachs or was otherwise on record"—Stein offered to wash their hands of the entire enterprise "by pointing out that my tour could be started without Y.[enching] funds. Visitors leave with their faces saved." Half a century later, Hung would tell his Chinese American biographer a very different version of his lone encounter with Stein. During a meeting arranged by Stuart with Stein at a Cambridge hotel, Hung supposedly attempted to persuade Stein to abandon the expedition entirely. According to Hung, instead of taking his advice, the "wizened old man" then arrogantly lectured him: "Mr. Hung, you are young; you do not know. I have been in China long before and many times. The Chinese officials—they do not care. I know how to manage them."[29]

As with Hung's alleged role in the Warner debacle of 1925, there is reason to believe that Hung and his biographer were indulging in a little bit of retroactive hagiography here. After their meeting at Cambridge, Hung wrote to Stein to express his "pleasure to have the honour of meeting you" and wished him "a most successful trip." Similarly, Stein told Hung that it had "been a great pleasure to make your acquaintance and I appreciate the value of the information you were good enough to give" as well as the "friendly interest you expressed in my planned labours." In spite of the dramatic caricatures Hung later imparted to his biographer, there is no denying his importance in leading the charge against Western expeditions in China. One month later, Stein arrived in Nanjing to apply for a passport with the

Nationalist government. Waiting to greet him and Whyte was an express letter from Roger Greene, the director of the China Medical Board and a close confidant of the Westernized Chinese scholars at Yenching. In his letter, Greene urged Stein to proceed "through Peking Council in interest of Yen-ching Univ.'s position, etc.," a suggestion Stein regarded as "obviously originat[ing] from line taken up at Harvard by Dr. Stuart & Hung." Whyte, however, did his best to downplay the letter, telling Stein that he "personally feels that he might well suppress it." Whyte then reassured Stein that everything was still proceeding as planned. "We need not be so easily alarmed," Stein recorded him as saying.[30]

Stein's brief visit to Shanghai and Nanjing marked the first time he had ever visited the eastern seaboard of China, having always entered and exited through the Himalayan passes southwest of Xinjiang. On April 22, 1930, he waxed poetic over his first glimpse of the eastern terminus of the Yangzi River, heretofore encountered only in the form of mountain glaciers. "By noon the colour of sea had changed to yellow," he wrote in his pocketbook, "thus bringing me within sight of the waters I had first touched in 1907 on the Su-lo-ho & Ta-tung watershed." Unimpressed with the "queerly mixed Western community" and "ostentatious 'business' display" and "gaiety" of Shanghai, Stein hurried onward to Nanjing for negotiations with the Nationalist government.[31]

Much like Sven Hedin and Roy Chapman Andrews before him, Stein found the new powerbrokers of China eager to please his diplomatic sponsors. From the perspective of the beleaguered Nationalist government in Nanjing, allowing Stein to undertake an expedition to Xinjiang killed three birds with one stone. Not only did it allow the Nationalists to once again impose their symbolic authority over Governor Jin Shuren, but it also enabled them to cultivate diplomatic capital with two resourceful Western powers: the British, who handled the formalities of Stein's passport and those of his Indian assistants, and the Americans, who tended both to Bramlette's passport and to the coffers and prestige of Harvard. Neither the British nor the Americans deemed it advisable to make any contact with either the Commission in Beijing or Governor Jin in Urumchi. "Sir Miles [Lampson] & [Eric] T.[eichman] agree with Wh.[yte] that submission to National Council of Cult[ura]l Assoc[iation]s undesirable," Stein noted in his diary, and "that telegraphic reference to Urumchi must be avoided (break of wire at this season would imply indefinite delay)." Nelson Johnson, the American minister in Nanjing, echoed the opinion of his British colleagues, informing Stein that he did "not think it advisable in my case" to court the attention of the commission.[32]

The Nationalists agreed. On May 1, Stein met with Wang Zhengting, the minister of foreign affairs.[33] Just one year earlier, Wang had given his personal assurance to Johnson that the Nationalist government would resolve matters between Andrews and the commission to everyone's satisfaction. Having failed to fulfill that promise, Wang decided to go it alone this time around. During his interview with Stein, Wang did not broach any topic likely to stir the passions of all those involved. "No question about arch.[aeological] proceeds raised," Stein wrote in his diary soon after the meeting. "At conclusion Dr. W.[ang] promises all facilities for work as asked." Much to Stein's relief, Wang did not make any mention of the commission. "No reference had been made to that 'National Council' at Peking and the conditions it might wish to impose," he later wrote. "So obviously my desire to keep clear altogether of the old capital and its nationalist wise men was justified and approved." Instead, Wang preferred to focus on how the expedition might breach Governor Jin's defenses. "Opinion of Provincial Adm[inistratio]n is not to be telegraphed for in view of delay foreseen through seasonal breakdown of wires," Stein noted. "But Gov[ernmen]t permission to be communicated to Tihwa [i.e., Urumchi] after issue of passport."[34]

Later that same day, Johnson learned that Stein's expedition had already received approval. "Dr. Wang told me that he had seen Sir Aurel Stein with the British Minister today," he wrote in a memo back to Washington, "and that, so far as he was concerned, the matter was being quickly arranged." Eric Teichman, the only British diplomat in Nanjing who had foreseen difficulties in securing a passport, was surprised at the lack of obstacles thrown in Stein's way. "Yesterday had passed without feared disturbance," Stein wrote in his diary the next day. "Called away to see Teichman by 11.40. Reported yesterday's interviews. T.[eichman] pleasantly surprised of easily secured result. W.[ang] had not mentioned 'proceeds' nor insisted on previous reference to Provincial Gov[ernmen]t." As the days passed with no further signs of disturbance, Stein began to wonder whether Wang had been too eager to oblige him. In his final meeting with Sir Miles Lampson, the British minister, Stein "hinted at risk of similar methods being used as in L.[angdon] Warner's case." That is, the Chinese may let him go forth on the expedition trail, but once there, all manner of passive obstruction would be thrown in his way. Lampson, however, "does not believe recourse to them likely." Nor should he. The sparse Chinese archival record of Stein's visit to Nanjing is notable only for its complete lack of diplomatic drama. Stein came to Nanjing and asked for a passport. Wang Zhengting duly issued said passport (figure 30), then sent out an order to Governor Jin to admit Stein

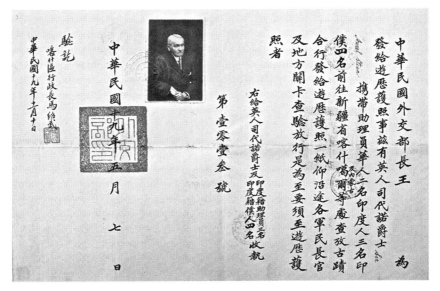

Figure 30. Passport for Stein's Fourth Expedition to Xinjiang. In May 1930, the Nationalist government in Nanjing issued Stein a passport to undertake a new archaeological
expedition to Xinjiang. Stein, who was surprised by the "easily secured result" of his
application, nonetheless expressed reservations about the wording of the passport. Once
he reached Xinjiang, much debate would ensue as to the precise meaning of the intention-
ally ambiguous phrase *chakao guji* ("to survey and investigate ancient relics"; *fourth line
from right*). Stein Papers, Bodleian Library, MS 283. Reprinted with the kind permission
of the British Academy.

into his province. As far as top Nationalist officials were concerned, it was
as if the commission in Beijing didn't even exist.[35]

All this seems to constitute a stunning display of naivete on the part
of the Chinese, British, and American officials in Nanjing, each of which
had repeatedly witnessed the awesome power of the commission in Beijing
to bend foreign and domestic diplomats to its will. One way to account for
such perplexing complaisance on the part of Stein's many sponsors, however, is to highlight the unique resources that Stein brought to the table.
Unlike every one of his archaeological peers, Stein had cultivated and maintained substantive relationships with important Chinese officials stationed
in the area of his proposed expedition. In one of his first letters after accepting Warner's offer of an expedition sponsored by Harvard, Stein told Keller
that he "could probably to a considerable extent rely there upon the personal good will of the Mandarins of the old scholarly type who understood
my scientific aims, who still hold an influential position in the provincial

administration and among whom I still count old friends." In January 1930, Stein received a letter from Reginald Charles Francis Schomberg, a British colonel who had just spent several years in Xinjiang. "He found quite a number of my old Mandarin friends still in office and all of them remembering me very kindly," Stein informed Keller.[36]

Stein's trump card, however, was Pan Zuhuan. The son of the late Pan Zhen, Stein's beloved mandarin friend, Pan Zuhuan had easy access to all the top Chinese officials in Xinjiang, including the governor. In 1928, after several years of work in the provincial government in Urumchi, Pan was transferred to Kashgar to take up the position of magistrate of Shule County. The very next year, Stein wrote to Pan to ask him if he could help smooth the way for a fourth expedition to Xinjiang. Pan replied immediately. "Your plan of visiting Sinkiang again for having more scholarly research will be heartily welcome from my part," Pan wrote to Stein in English, "but before starting it would be very necessary to have some agreements with our Nanking Government and Sinkiang authorities respectively. During the recent years the foreign expedition working in this Provinces is not so free as you were here formerly." Pan then told Stein all about the trials and tribulations of the Sino-Swedish expedition. In his reply, Stein assured Pan that he completely agreed "that it would be essential to have the proper recommendation from the Nan-king government in order that no difficulties or obstacles should be locally raised. For this very purpose endeavours are being made at Nan-king on the part of the British and American diplomatic representatives."[37]

Pan's telegraphic reply to Stein's latest missive—"TRYING BEST HELP YOU WISH TO KNOW RESULT YOU GOT"—could not have come at a better time. It arrived in Nanjing on May 1, the same day Stein met with Wang Zhengting and other top Nationalist officials in order to make his case for a passport. One of these officials was Hu Hanmin, the head of the Legislative Yuan and "after Chang Kai-shek most important person in Gov[ernmen]t." During the meeting with Hu, Stein talked "about ancient routes in Turk.[estan], my friends there and hoped for work along T'ien-shan." After telling Hu about "those scholarly Mandarins who had been such helpful friends on my former expeditions," Stein was delighted to learn that Hu "had heard of P'an Taj-en [Pan Zhen], the best of them, and was evidently pleased by what I could tell of my attachment to his memory and the respect P'an had commanded throughout the province." It was at this point that Stein produced Pan Zuhuan's telegram for Hu and his secretaries to see. "Such close touch with my old Chinese patron's son," Stein later wrote, "did not fail to make due impression." Indeed, it did not. After this meeting,

Zhang Fengjiu and Wang Ruyi, the Nanjing representatives of Governor Jin who had sat in on Stein's audience with Hu, chose to cast Stein's expedition in a decidedly sympathetic light. "Mr. Stein has been to Xinjiang three times," they wrote to the governor in Urumchi, "and maintained a close friendship with Department Head Pan. He imparted many favorable impressions of Xinjiang to us." Convinced that Stein's agenda was "scholarly in nature and did not include any illegal activity," Zhang and Wang asked Governor Jin to instruct his officials in Kashgar to lend all necessary support, so that "Mr. Stein can complete his work with piece of mind."[38]

The diplomatic corps of Nanjing, be they British, American, or Chinese, were all convinced that Stein was special. And because he was so special, the new rules regarding foreign expeditions in China, reformulated and refined by the commission during endless negotiations with Hedin and Andrews over the previous three years, simply did not apply. As a result, if the members of the commission in Beijing wanted to prevent the Nationalist government from getting its pound of diplomatic capital at the expense of "the Chinese nation," then they would have to do it all by themselves—again. Just like Andrews, however, Stein had chosen to eschew any and all publicity in hopes of sneaking into Nanjing and Xinjiang undetected by the commission. "I am thoroughly convinced that your judgment is as usual correct," Keller told Stein a few months before his arrival in Nanjing in a scarcely veiled jab at Andrews and Hedin, "in slipping into Chinese Turkestan with an inconspicuous expedition rather than chasing in with automobiles, airplanes, submarines and what-not, especially the what-not." It is not entirely clear when the members of the commission first learned of Stein's presence in Nanjing. Stein's diary, however, does provide some tantalizing clues. On May 3, just two days after his meetings with Wang and Hu, Stein recorded the visit of Zhang Xinhai ("H. H. Chang"), a young official in the Ministry of Foreign Affairs. The two men shared a cordial lunch, with Zhang inviting Stein over to his house for tea the next day. There Stein met "two other Harvard students" and shared printed transcripts of some of his previous lectures. Stein also asked Zhang if he could help him find a Chinese literatus in the mold of Jiang Xiaowan. Three days later, Zhang wrote to Stein to assure him that he was "still looking for the man whom you want to accompany you in your next trip to Central Asia" and reiterated his "admiration for your work," the results of which "will be most deeply treasured by me."[39]

Zhang then made a curious request. "Dr. Li Chi, the author of that work on 'The Formation of the Chinese People' whom I had occasion to mention to you," Zhang wrote to Stein, "is arriving in Nanking today and I was told that his present trip is for excavating in the vicinity of those lions and that pagoda of which you have seen the pictures." Li Ji ("Li Chi"), who received his PhD from Harvard, was one of the most prominent archaeologists in China and an influential member of Westernized scholarly circles in Beijing. Most importantly, he was also a member of the commission. Innocently or not, Zhang suggested that Stein and Li meet. "I am anxious that Dr. Li sees you before you leave Nanking. May I arrange a meeting as soon as I see him?" Whether or not he was aware of the danger of meeting Li, Stein must have agreed, for the two men met the very next day. After returning from a brief excursion to a nearby temple with Johnson and Jiang Menglin, the Nationalist minister of education, Stein "reached station in time for 2.50 train. There met Dr. Li, of Chinese archaeol. Dept., who had returned from inspection of some similar tomb remains N. of railway." Though Zhang does not appear to have accompanied the party on this occasion, it is hard to believe that this meeting with Li Ji, which took place just one day after Zhang's proposal, could have been a coincidence.[40]

Either way, knowledge of Stein's presence in Nanjing had now spread beyond diplomatic quarters. Having met Stein in person, Li Ji would not fail to notify the commission in Beijing. Nor would he hide this information from his colleagues at the newly established Academia Sinica, a prestigious government-funded research institution then overseeing excavations at the Shang-era site of Anyang. In and of itself, however, Stein's mere presence in China was not evidence of a crime. For that, Stein would have to make it clear that he had no intention of sharing his expedition with the Chinese. And on this point, Stein received fatal advice from his British handlers. From the moment he arrived in Shanghai, Stein was constantly on the lookout for a learned Chinese assistant to accompany him into the desert. Having failed to identify a suitable person, Stein decided to enlist the help of Zhang Xinhai, who assured Stein that "there is prospect of my succeeding." On May 9, however, just two days after Zhang's optimistic note to Stein, Teichman informed Stein that the British government in India had reversed its assessment of the desirability of Stein taking a Chinese assistant from the inner provinces. "Am to be strongly advised not to take Chinese Ass[istan]ts with me as Chairman [Jin Shuren] may refuse them admission," Stein wrote in his diary, reflecting the British understanding of the complex relations between the Nationalist government and the autonomous warlords of the outer provinces.[41]

As Stein noted in his pocketbook diary, this was "timely advice," since he was scheduled to have dinner with Zhang Xinhai that very same evening. "Glad to meet once more Mr. & Mrs. Chang," Stein wrote later that night. Amid the interjections of a "somewhat grating" American mission-ary couple, Stein "had long talk with Chang about Hs.[uan]-tsang's [Xuan-zang's] desert crossing & how my tracing of his route illustrates need of sur-veys." He then let slip the fateful news. "Refer to diff[icult]y about taking Chinese ass[istan]ts for journey. Ch.[ang] wants to know from whom this advice. Obliged to keep reply indefinite. . . . Had better omitted this piece of news." Zhang, who was close to securing the much sought after Chinese companion, responded by asking Stein "to let cooperate Chinese in working up results," to which Stein "could well agree, once reproduction & publi-cation is assured." Though the night still ended with a "hearty farewell," the damage had been done. Li Ji knew Stein was in Nanjing; Zhang Xinhai knew Stein was not going to take a Chinese companion with him into the desert—and Zhang and Li knew each other.[42]

On May 12, 1930, Stein returned to Shanghai and boarded a Japanese steamer to Hong Kong, from whence he would proceed to India and then on to Kashmir and Xinjiang. Five days later, the commission began its at-tack. The opening salvo came in the form of a curt but incendiary telegram from Zhang Ji, chairman of the commission in Beijing, to the Administra-tive Yuan in Nanjing. "The British [traveler] Stein has applied for a pass-port from the Ministry of Foreign Affairs in order to permit him to work in Xinjiang and Gansu," Zhang wrote. "Previously, however, this person was sent by the Indian government to draw military maps of the routes from Xinjiang to Lanzhou. He also plundered the Dunhuang manuscripts and destroyed antiquities in the desert regions of Khotan. As his return on this occasion carries serious implications for our national defense and sover-eignty, we entreat you to order the Ministry of Foreign Affairs to reject [his application]."[43]

Over the next two weeks, Cai Yuanpei, the president of the Academia Sinica in Nanjing and former president of Peking University, further fanned the flames of protest. Once it became clear that Zhang Ji had failed to block the issuance of Stein's passport, Cai decided to paint Stein as a seasoned criminal. "Stein has been to Xinjiang three times in the past," Cai wrote to the Ministry of Foreign Affairs, "and each time he has stolen many different types of Chinese antiquities, never once obtaining the permission of our country beforehand. The amount of historical materials that China has lost in this manner is incalculable." After reminding the ministry of the strict conditions imposed on Hedin and Andrews, Cai concluded that Stein must be treated in the same way. Worst of all, according to Cai, was that Stein "did not get in touch with any domestic [scholarly] organizations during his visit to Nanjing." Cai ended his letter by insisting that the ministry submit a detailed copy of Stein's itinerary to the academy for review. To the Administrative Yuan, Cai portrayed Stein as someone who "plunders by habit and nature" (*daoqie xingcheng*) and questioned the ability of local officials in Xinjiang to monitor his activities. As a remedy, Cai asked the Administrative Yuan to send special instructions to all the officials along Stein's route demanding that they implement "strict surveillance" over his every movement.[44]

With that, it was time for Wang Zhengting, the minister of foreign affairs, to attend to damage control. He resorted to his usual tactic: strategic ambiguity. Noting that Stein had only been issued a "common traveler's passport" (*putong youli huzhao*), Wang assured Zhang and Cai that Stein "has no other motives on this trip and that everything is in accord with the various statutes." Of course, in the event that Stein went so far as to "excavate antiquities and transport them out of the country without our authorization," Wang continued, then he would indeed be acting "within the realm of prohibited activities." In claiming that he had only issued a "common traveler's passport" to Stein, Wang was telling the truth. But it was only half the truth. On May 7, the Ministry of Foreign Affairs had issued Stein a passport that permitted him to undertake "the investigation of historical traces including relics of art and writing." Stein, who found the English translation of the Chinese wording to be strange, asked for further clarification from Sir Miles Lampson. The next day, Lampson informed Stein that this was a translation of four carefully worded Chinese characters (see figure 30): *chakao guji* ("to survey and investigate ancient relics"). Lampson's own translation, "to trace ancient vestiges & ar[chaeological] remains," seemed to imply the collection of historical artifacts. There was a reasonable basis for this interpretation: the character *kao* ("investigate"), when combined with the character for "antiquity" (*gu*), produces the Chinese word for "archaeology" (*kaogu*). Similarly, Stein's passports for his previous expeditions had used almost identical language—*kaocha guji*, with the position of *kao* and *cha* reversed—to permit his earlier activities, which clearly involved both excavation of antiquities and their removal from Chinese territory. But what about maps? On this point, both Lampson and Stein took comfort in Wang's personal assurance, tendered over dinner, that "to 'trace vestiges' implies surveying." Accordingly, Stein was told that "no further represent[atio]n needed."[45]

Had the British diplomats of Nanjing witnessed Wang's negotiating tactics with the Americans during the Andrews affair, they might have experienced a sense of déjà vu. In seeking to cultivate diplomatic goodwill from Britain and the United States, Wang was eager to give the sort of verbal assurances that his Western counterparts wanted to hear. But he was careful not to put such promises into writing. This gave him room to maneuver between inflated Western expectations and the inevitable domestic Chinese backlash. This is perhaps also the reason why, in his meeting with Stein, Wang did not broach the subject of the ultimate destination of any antiquities that Stein was sure to uncover during the course of "tracing" ancient "vestiges and remains" in Xinjiang. (Wang did raise the topic in a preliminary meeting with Lampson before Stein's arrival, but he dropped the subject when met with assurances that any such proceeds would be "rubbish heap contents.") After all, Wang needed to preserve the prospect of plausible denial, and detailed minutes of the meeting with Stein had been recorded on both sides. Having placed himself in an awkward yet eminently defensible position, Wang now adopted the hat of neutral intermediary, providing an institutional conduit for the outraged scholars of China to direct their vitriol at the equally outraged foreign diplomats.

In early June 1930, Sir Miles Lampson received an urgent telegram from Minister Wang, which summarized the complaints and demands of Cai Yuanpei's earlier protest. Lampson then forwarded the telegram to the Indian Foreign Office in Simla, so as "to communicate with Stein and furnish a reply." In an appended comment, Lampson concluded that "it is evident that same type of people who made trouble for R.[oy] Andrews and other explorers having got wind of Stein's plans have written to Wai Chiao-pu [Ministry of Foreign Affairs], and that latter not daring to do otherwise have passed their communication on to me in above form." By the time Stein learned of these developments, he had already made it back to his summer haunt in Kashmir and was finalizing preparations to cross over the mountain passes into Xinjiang. Considering the stakes involved, Stein reacted with remarkable calm, declaring that he was "not altogether surprised of it." Notwithstanding the strict avoidance of publicity, Stein had apparently already resigned himself to the realization that official approval of his plans would not long "escape the attention of the Chinese who for reasons of their own are jealous of foreign scholarly enterprise and anxious either to prevent or to hamper it by conditions mainly intended to serve their own ends." Key to Stein's optimistic assessment of the situation was his unshakeable faith in "the good will of the local authorities" in Xinjiang, without which "the tracing and surveying of ancient routes and remains . . . would in any case be practically impossible."[46]

In other words, so long as the local officials in Xinjiang "know that the Central Government have taken formal cognizance of my plan," Stein believed that the remnants of "Old China" in Xinjiang would allow him to return to the good old days of Pan Zhen. He was very nearly right. Soon after furnishing his reply to the British Legation in Nanjing, Stein wrote to Pan Zuhuan in Kashgar for help. "A short while ago I was informed by the Legation that the Wai Chia-pu had been addressed by the Central Research Institution claiming that I ought to put myself into touch with national scientific organs about my plan," Stein wrote to Pan in early July. "I earnestly hope that you who know the true character of my aims will very kindly help to remove any misapprehensions if such were to arise at Urumchi. Of course on my return the collaboration of Chinese scholars on eventual results will be very desirable and welcome." Confident that his decades of friendship with Pan Zhen would now pay dividends through his son, Stein wrote to Keller to assure him that all would depend on the attitude of the Chinese administration in Xinjiang. "Fortunately its dependence on Nanking is more or less nominal," Stein observed, "and as the enclosed copy of a letter from old friend Pan Ta-jen's son shows, I may still count on friendly remembrance. All the same, it all causes cares which one might well be spared."[47]

In several of the letters Stein wrote to various friends and colleagues about this time to defend his position, he enclosed a copy of Pan Zuhuan's latest epistle as evidence of the support he could expect from within Chinese official circles in Xinjiang to combat the baneful influence of the commission. In it, Pan reminisced about having seen Stein engaged in "a very friendly talk" with his father in 1907, back when Pan was just fourteen years old. He then promised to do everything within his power to smooth Stein's way. "Now you cannot imag[in]e how I will be delighted and charmed if I could see you again personally to talk over all the memories," Pan wrote. "So it is my duty to try my best in smoothing the way for you." In recognition of this duty to his departed father, Pan informed Stein that he had "written already to our Governor at Urumchi confidentially about your past valuable works and the present aim." With a Nationalist passport in one hand and a letter like this in the other, it is little wonder that Stein remained nonplussed about the commission's assault on his reputation. "In closing wish you a great success in your coming plan and the best of health," Pan ended his letter, "and wait for the unspeakable pleasure of meeting you again."[48]

That unspeakable pleasure would have to wait. On August 20, as Stein passed a British garrison near the remote mountain kingdom of Hunza, he learned that "Young China" had succeeded in turning Governor Jin against him. The news was delivered in a "telephone message of Major Todd that Hunza Mir has received definite report of Sarikol Begs having been ordered to oppose my entry!" Three days later, Stein learned that Jin, "under tele-graphic orders from Administrative Yu[an]," had "directed Kashgar Tao-yin to stop my entering Sarikol." This was the first tangible fruit of the letters of protest sent to the Administrative Yuan by Cai Yuanpei and Zhang Ji. Apparently unwilling to place their trust in Minister Wang alone, Cai and Zhang had pursued the most direct path to the governor of Xinjiang him-self. Documents held in the Xinjiang archives give a sense of what spurred the governor to refuse Stein entry into Xinjiang. A letter from the commis-sion in Beijing informed Jin that Stein had previously "removed materials of considerable value, the manuscripts of Dunhuang standing as a prime example." The commission urged Jin not to be fooled by any promises Stein may have made to the Ministry of Foreign Affairs. "The passport that he has obtained for his present trip to the northwest does not allow for the col-lection of antiquities," it wrote. "However, as this man is extraordinarily greedy and cunning, it is certain that he intends to pursue precisely this goal. Because this matter pertains to our national polity, defense, and cul-ture, he should be driven out of the country."[49]

As if this wasn't enough, Jin was also given a Chinese translation of inflammatory remarks Stein was alleged to have made during one of his lectures at Harvard the previous year:

> I only know Old China and do not pay the least attention to the slogans and catch-words of Young China. The Kuomintang is most disreputable and should not be heeded by foreigners. . . . Moreover, Sinkiang is not Chinese territory, and there is no central government in China. Sinkiang is not fully civilized. I think I can do with Sinkiang officials today what I used to do with those of the old regime. If you can give me some addi-tional money with which to bribe them, I can have everything my own way in Sinkiang.

As one of Stein's previous biographers has pointed out, neither the tone nor content of these words conforms to Stein's cautious rhetorical habits. This was particularly the case during his time at Harvard, when Stein, wary of publicity, refrained from discussing his plans with anyone not already in the know.[50] All this points to an obvious candidate for the dissemination of such a devastating smear campaign: William Hung, the one Western-ized Chinese scholar in Cambridge to have met with Stein to discuss his plans. Likely suspecting that Stein never delivered his letter to Whyte as promised, Hung seems to have taken matters into his own hands by giving the opposition camps in Beijing and Nanjing a valuable incendiary to throw at Stein.

With any other explorer, the expedition likely would have ended here. But Stein's supporters were just getting started. As soon as the order to obstruct Stein arrived in Kashgar, the British diplomatic corps sprung into action by submitting formal protests on several fronts. Perhaps the most effective was that conveyed by the British consul of Kashgar, who informed Governor Jin that "the Indian Government would be immeasurably grateful" to him if he could allow Stein into Kashgar for additional discussions of his plans. There was an unspoken subtext to the consul's words, which was further elaborated over the coming weeks. That is, prior to Stein's expedition, Governor Jin had already inked an agreement for a shipment of arms from India into Xinjiang. As "only a small installment has so far reached the province," Stein later explained to his friend Percy Allen, "the further supply would obviously have to depend on the attitude now shown by the Chairman as regards myself." Jin was furious when he learned that the British had decided to use the arms shipment as leverage for Stein's expedition. "It defies logic for the British consul in Kashgar to use the purchase of armaments as an excuse to meddle in this affair," he wrote to Pan Zuhuan. "There is absolutely no connection between this case and the arms purchase, and they cannot be discussed together. If the British consulate in Kashgar does as he is suggesting and reneges on the agreement, then responsibility for any fallout will redound to him. I expect you to transmit these sentiments onward."[51]

With diplomatic unpleasantries on the rise, Minister Wang attempted to broker a compromise agreement. Unlike with Hedin and Andrews, the solution was not to impose a Chinese co-leader on Stein or to saddle him with Chinese students in the field. The wily Brit had recourse to too many allies and resources to feel pressured to make such concessions. Rather, it was to let him enter Xinjiang as planned, but make sure that all the officials on his route exercised the strictest surveillance of his activities. "According to statements made by the British consul," Wang wrote to both the Administrative Yuan and Governor Jin, "this British subject does not have as a goal on this trip the pursuit and collection of antiquities. We expect the provincial government to permit his entry into the province and issue an order to local officials informing them that they are to send personnel to maintain surveillance on him at all times and ensure that he does not excavate antiquities or take any out of the country." Jin Shuren, now afraid that enforcement of the commission's protest would endanger the shipment of

British arms from India, was quick to accept Wang's proposal. "Since a passport has already been issued," Jin wrote to his officials in Kashgar, "we are obliged to maintain the reputation of the central government. When Stein arrives in Xinjiang, he will be placed under the strictest surveillance, so as to prevent the excavation of antiquities."[52]

Stein was elated. Convinced that "the local Chinese authorities, disposed to be considerate for various reasons, would find a way to get over that obstructive Nanking order," he eagerly pushed on toward Kashgar. As he crossed the Chinese border at Tashkurgan (figure 31), Stein reveled in a "happy feeling at having regained the ground where 30 years ago I first reached my C.[entral]-A.[sian] goal." Once in Kashgar, he came face to face with the son of his late patron (see figure 16). "Warm welcome extended in his father's quiet genial way," Stein wrote in his diary. "Talk of plans & explain need of supplem.[entary] surveys. . . . Light lunch served as was custom in Pan Ta-jen's house." The last time these two men met, Pan had

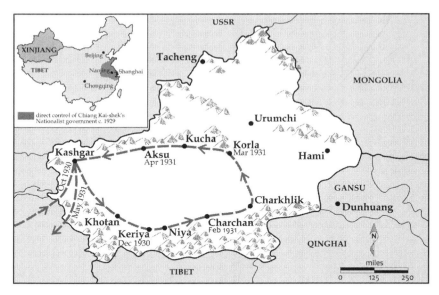

Figure 31. Stein's Fourth Expedition in Xinjiang. In October 1930, with the help of Pan Zuhuan, son of the late Pan Zhen, Stein managed to reach Kashgar. After subsequent negotiations, Stein received permission to proceed to Urumchi for an audience with Governor Jin Shuren via the southern circuit of the Taklamakan Desert. By his side was Zhang Hongsheng, sent to ensure that Stein did not remove any antiquities along the way. When Stein heard that his passport had been canceled in response to the protests of the commission in Beijing, he decided to return to Kashgar via the northern route. Cartography by Debbie Newell.

been a teenager. Now all grown up, Pan was determined to do for Stein as his father had done three decades earlier. In a letter to Allen, Stein noted that Pan, "who remarkably resembles his father in outlook and personal sympathies is doing his best to secure full freedom for my tasks." During the subsequent rounds of visits with the Chinese officials of Kashgar, Pan served as an effective advocate for Stein. On October 8, Stein met with Circuit Intendant Ma Shaowu, the most powerful official in Kashgar. By Stein's side was Pan, who "did his best to explain my aims." At an audience with Tao Mingyue, Ma's secretary of foreign affairs, Pan again "helped in explaining my objects." In a final call on Jin Lun, the governor's special agent in Kashgar, Pan "takes word on my behalf & fully explains scope of hoped for work." The next day, Stein was full of praise for Pan. "He has been indefatigable in his efforts to smooth my way ahead," Stein informed Allen, and "played the part of a devoted councilor & interpreter of my objects in the interviews" with the Chinese officials of Kashgar.[53]

Throughout the month of October, a flurry of communications passed back and forth among Beijing, Nanjing, Urumchi, and Kashgar, all urging Jin to treat Stein in one way or another. In response, Jin, aware that the commission could tarnish his own reputation just as quickly as it had done to warlords and Nationalist politicians before him, began to vacillate once more. Stein, itching to get out of Kashgar, began to wonder if the commission could ever truly be defeated. "Cares as to future moves oppress," he confessed to his diary on October 27. Then, in a remarkable show of solidarity with Stein, both Pan Zuhuan and Jin Lun made one last attempt to dispel the governor's anxieties. On October 30, Jin Lun, who had gravitated into Stein's camp under the influence of Pan, made the case for letting Stein go forth. "The present expedition undertaken by Stein is intended to culminate his life's work," Jin wrote with considerable sympathy. "And as he enjoys the support of both the British and American governments, it will be impossible to stop him." Jin then suggested that the governor "grant permission for Stein to travel from Keriya to Kara-shahr and thus on to the capital," accompanied all the while by someone specially selected to monitor his every move. "To act thus would not stand in violation of any of the proposals put forth by the scholarly community in the interior." The very same day, Pan forwarded to the governor a strongly worded telegram from the British consul in Kashgar, who renewed the threat of halting the arms shipment from India. Pan then appended his own comments. "In the interests of appeasing all sides," Pan wrote to Governor Jin, "I beg you to permit Stein to proceed as requested. We can send a suitable person ahead to accompany him to Khotan and monitor his movements."[54]

On November 3, Stein was summoned to Ma Shaowu's yamen. Once there, he found Jin and Pan also in attendance. "Chairman agreed to my going to Khotan-Keriya, etc., as proposed," Stein was informed, and "coming via Kara-shahr to U.[rumchi] & come to an agreement about further travel there." Against all odds, Stein had prevailed. It had been more than five years since Langdon Warner's debacle at Dunhuang, three years since Sven Hedin's capitulation at Beijing, two years since Roy Chapman Andrews had been stymied at Kalgan, and two months since Milton Bramlette had succumbed to the rigors of alpine travel. And yet here was the sixty-eight-year-old Stein, about to head out into the deserts of Xinjiang with the full permission of the Chinese central government and the governor of Xinjiang, with nary a Chinese co-leader or student in sight. Warner, who had recruited Stein to do what he himself could not, would have been proud. "I confess that my heart was in my mouth when I reached Sir Miles Lampson's telegram telling of the protest by the Society for the Preservation (sic) of Chinese Culture and the comments of the Wai-chiao-pu," Warner had written to Stein just two months earlier, while Stein was held up at Hunza. "You will have accomplished a miracle if you can do your work in Hsin-chiang—and I thoroughly believe that you can."[55]

Now there was the question of who would accompany Stein into the desert. Stein, long dismissive of the Confucian aversion to manual labor, warned Ma Shaowu that the person selected "must be of sound physique & prepared to walk on foot on desert ground." Heady with success, Stein deluded himself into thinking that Pan Zuhuan might be chosen. "No question raised as to remuneration but I mention how happy I should be to have a man like Pan with me," he recounted in his diary. Instead, Ma selected Zhang Hongsheng, an inspector in the Kashgar post office. Little is known about Zhang. On meeting him for the first time, Stein described him as a "pleasant lively person who anyhow will talk." (This was a backhanded jab at Li Yuansun [see figure 11], Stein's much-reviled secretary from his third expedition who largely ignored Stein's requests to practice conversational Chinese.) Hoping to purchase Zhang's loyalties, George Sherriff, the British consul in Kashgar, dropped in on the meeting and urged Stein to make a "reference to T.[aotai Ma Shaowu] about remuneration." Stein followed suit, offering to pay Zhang's salary for the journey. "Express my satisfaction with choice of Chang Hou Saing," Stein wrote. "Offer to pay his T.A. not accepted but his gratuity left to Chairman's approval." Instead, Ma, recognizing Sherriff and Stein's gambit for what it was, cabled to the governor in Urumchi to ask for permission to increase Zhang's salary himself, so as to diminish the allure of financial compensation from Stein. "To accompany a foreigner into the desert over vast distances during the wintertime," Ma wrote to Jin, "is an exceptionally difficult task." Jin agreed. Instead of receiving forty *liang* per month, Zhang would now receive eighty.[56]

On November 11, 1930, Stein finally set off from Kashgar. In addition to Zhang, his caravan also included two servants from his previous expeditions. "One of them is Hasan Akhun, the great camel factotum," Stein told Allen. "In spite of his white beard he is as keen as ever for work in the desert." But it wasn't just former employees who gravitated back toward Stein. Everyone, it seems, remembered him with great fondness. Even before he reached Kashgar, Stein encountered a village headman near Tashkurgan who "remembered my three preceding visits. Then on passing new Sarai greeted by Nadir Khan, my guide of 1900, & other notables." En route from Kashgar to Khotan, Stein "met with sturdy trader from Charchan who remembered my passage there seventeen years ago," followed by "my old host of 1900 still hale & eager to offer hospitality." At the Imam Jafar Sadik mazar near Niya, Stein found that "some of the Shaikhs still remember my first visit among them." At Charchan, Stein's "passage of 1913 remembered by some of the older people. Ismail Pawan my guide of that year and 1906 turned up, too." Not to be outdone, a "police magistrate who remembers my visit to Ju Tao-tai at Aksu in 1915" also sought out Stein in Charchan. Then there was the venerable Zhu Ruichi ("Ju Tao-tai") himself, who twenty years earlier had sent an effusive letter of praise to Stein (see figure 2). "Passed on way carriage with Chiu Tao-tai, of Aksu, an old acquaintance of 1908 and 1915," Stein noted near Korla, "who to Chang expresses remembrance of our meetings."[57]

Here we get our first glimpse of a fascinating development. Zhang Hong-sheng's job was to impose strict surveillance over Stein's movements and prevent him from doing anything that would draw the wrath of the commission in Beijing toward Governor Jin in Urumchi. In exchange for his efforts, Zhang received both a generous salary and a chance to impress the Chinese governor in Urumchi, whom he expected to meet in person. Previously, the Muslim and Chinese peasants of northwestern China had eagerly served foreign sahibs on their expeditions in hopes of improving their lot in life. On this score, we might recall Huntington's guide Da'ud, who began his spectacular rise to local fame and fortune after Huntington brought him along for an audience with Governor Liankui in 1906. Much like Da'ud and so many others before him, Zhang, a lowly postal inspector from Kashgar, must have viewed his role in Stein's expedition as the opportunity of a lifetime. By 1930, however, Zhang's road to promotion was fraught with far more pitfalls than those of his predecessors. These pitfalls are evident in Stein's description of the meeting with Zhu Ruichi quoted above. Instead of joining the chorus of hostility toward Stein and thanking Zhang for keeping a close eye on him, Zhu, one of the most powerful and influential officials in Xinjiang, expressed "remembrance of our meetings" to Zhang.

As a result, Zhang had to balance a complex set of priorities that were in constant tension with one another. On the whole, it is clear that nearly everyone in Xinjiang remembered Stein with fondness and was eager to facilitate his endeavors as before. Even before he left Kashgar, Pan Zuhuan had called Zhang into his yamen, where Pan "talked to [Zhang] evid.[ently] about my work & shown Plates of I.[nnermost] A.[sia] with objects of 'no value' found on surface." At Khotan, Zhang stood by as the local circuit intendant showered Stein with gifts, including "a big & tasteless carpet with animal figures which shows what Khotan designing has come to." If Zhang wanted to impress Chinese men in high places, he could not profess allegiance to the hostile agenda of the Westernized Chinese scholars of Beijing and Nanjing. And yet his marching orders demanded that he defend the interests of the commission, which Governor Jin needed to appease. What was a humble postal clerk to do? Stein's diary provides the answer. One week after leaving Kashgar, the local officials of Yarkand paid Stein a visit. Following Stein's lead in the discussion of the light his past labors had shed on the history of the Tang dynasty, Zhang attempted to display "sympathetic interest in those subjects but obviously lacks literary familiarity with them." When Stein met with a rare display of obstruction by the magistrate of Keriya, Zhang "attribute[d] all trouble to obstruction from Nanking & hopes for change once matters are explained to Chairman." Much like Huntington's servant Da'ud nearly three decades earlier, Zhang wanted more than anything to meet Governor Jin, and Stein was key to realizing that dream. In February 1931, when Stein began to question whether or not a visit to Urumchi was truly worth the trouble, Zhang urged him to stay the course. "Evid.[ently] he has been reassured by the Hsien-kuan's friendly feeling for me and is prompted also by his own personal interest in reaching Urumchi."[58]

The clearest evidence of Zhang's delicate balancing act came toward the end of the expedition, when Stein passed through Luntai. Deng Jingwen, the local magistrate, displayed his "unmistakable knowledge of ancient geography & interest in Turkestan antiquities" and told Stein all about sites he had visited near Domoko. Zhang, sensing Deng's sympathetic posture toward Stein, began to relate "at length obstructive action of Keriya Amban & his Ssu-yeh which he now ridicules & condemns—after having before fallen in with it." Peeved, Stein now branded Zhang "a clever opportunist who knows how to turn his coat." Later that night, Deng returned for another visit with Stein. As the two men reminisced about Pan Zhen and discussed various archaeological sites in Xinjiang, Zhang suddenly began to talk of Stein's supposedly "harmless survey of Niya Site & is evidently bent to display his superior comprehension of such work & his sympathy with my aims." When Deng, "evidently no admirer of Nanking," later told Stein that the obstruction efforts of Nanjing and Beijing "can be due only [to] ignorance of my aims & labours," Zhang chimed in "sympathetically to suit our guest, forgetting apparently his conduct at Malakalagan, Niya Site, Koyumal & ill-disguised threat at Temenpo." One week later, Zhang acted similarly for the next magistrate down the road. "Amban returns visit by 3 P.M. when I show him Chavannes' *Documents*," Stein wrote in his diary. "Lively interest shown in contents & script. Chang as usual adopts attitude corresponding to that of visitor & displays hearty sympathy with my aims. How different from his conduct in Keriya area!"[59]

In stark contrast to his dodgy performance in the field, in his reports to Urumchi, Zhang took great pains to portray a staunch adherence to Governor Jin's agenda. On January 28, 1931, Zhang submitted a detailed account of Stein's tumultuous stay at Keriya, where the local magistrate, Chen Shi, was one of the few Chinese officials to take the obstruction orders against Stein seriously.[60] "Several times Stein asked if he could take pictures of the area, and then proceeded to order his men to clear the sand from a stupa," Zhang wrote. "When I prevented him from doing so, he said that he was only removing the lowest layer of sand in order to determine its true height and appearance, and that he was not damaging or removing traces of any antiquities. He said that 'examination' [*cha*] and 'excavation' [*caijue*] were different things, which seems to permit its allowance." Things got far more contentious when Stein came across some fragments of Buddhist relics on the ground. "Stein insisted on going over to collect them," Zhang reported to Governor Jin, "and it was only through the repeated efforts of myself and Zhang Zhouquan, a man sent by Keriya magistrate Chen Shi to assist in my surveillance, that we managed to take them back. They are now in my custody, and I plan to hand them over for perusal upon reaching the capital. I only permitted Stein to take two photographs." Two weeks later, Zhang again reassured the governor that Stein had done nothing that would get Jin in trouble with Chinese scholars on the eastern seaboard. "Other than the daily entries he makes in his diary, which I cannot prevent," Zhang noted, "your deputy has managed both to maintain complete surveillance over him and to prevent him from excavating and collecting antiquities or drawing maps. As a result, Mr. Stein has been able to obey the laws of our country and has not engaged in any transgressive behavior."[61]

The governor was pleased with Zhang's performance. But it was not enough to insulate him from the growing outcry in Beijing and Nanjing. In the months since Stein left Kashgar and embarked on his route in the desert, reports of his movements began to appear in various English-language newspapers, much to Stein's chagrin. "I do not think it desirable in any way for news of my doings getting 'publicity' in view of the 'Young China' opposition at Peking, etc.," Stein wrote his friend Fred Andrews in August 1930. "I was sorry for some Simla friend's communication about my plans which got into the Statesman & thus into home papers also. However, it may be forgotten by now." It was not. Nor were the secret reports of the Chinese members of the Sino-Swedish expedition, who by now were scattered all throughout the southern oases. Cai Yuanpei, the president of the Academia Sinica, later said that he was informed of Stein's arrival in Kashgar and his negotiations with Governor Jin from an unnamed member of the Sino-Swedish expedition. These reports were most likely written by Yuan Fuli, who had done so much to block Warner and Hedin in preceding years. On March 2, 1931, Yuan, who was in regular contact with Governor Jin in Urumchi and the commission in Beijing, urged Jin to kick Stein out of the province at once. "It seems that in matters of foreign affairs," Yuan wrote, "the central government can use the present situation as an opportunity to hold Stein accountable for all of his past deceptions in earlier years."[62]

Just as damaging as these reports of Stein's comings and goings in Xinjiang was new information about the extent of the financial support he had been given at Harvard. According to Cai Yuanpei, during the summer of 1930, articles in the American press claimed that Stein had already overcome all Chinese opposition and was en route to Xinjiang with the equivalent of one million Chinese yuan. And indeed, Stein's backers at Harvard had managed to raise $100,000 for his use, with a small percentage contributed by the British Museum and the government of India. Thus, by the time Stein set out from Kashgar in early November, the Westernized scholars of Beijing and Nanjing were in possession of several pieces of damaging intelligence. First, Stein's expedition was generously endowed. This meant that his Harvard sponsors did not expect him to come home empty-handed, as Stein and the Anglo-American diplomats of Nanjing had repeatedly claimed. Second, unlike Hedin and Andrews, Stein had successfully managed to overcome the first wave of resistance put forth by Cai and Zhang Ji during the summer of 1930. Not only that, but he had followed up this unlikely victory by commencing negotiations directly with Governor Jin in Urumchi regarding an itinerary for the field, using a British arms shipment from India as leverage. And third, he had managed to get into the field without a Chinese co-leader or student in tow.[63]

If there was one thing the members of the commission knew better than anything else, it was that Chinese politicians, be they warlords or members of the Nationalist Party, could not be trusted to enforce new ideas about the cultural sovereignty of the Chinese nation. Lofty rhetoric notwithstanding, it was painfully clear that neither Jin Shuren in Urumchi nor Wang Zhengting in Nanjing could be counted on to do the "right" thing. As a result, the commission decided to take a page out of Andrews's playbook and initiate a global smear campaign against Stein, hoping that negative publicity could accomplish what principled words had not. On November 20, 1930, just nine days after Stein set off from Kashgar, the commission issued a devastating press release. In a "Statement regarding Sir Aurel Stein's Archaeological Expedition in Chinese Turkestan," nineteen of the most eminent scholars in China accused the Harvard-Yenching Institute, Archaeological Survey of India, and Trustees of the British Museum of sponsoring a duplicitous scientific enterprise designed to deprive China of its cultural heritage.[64]

The four-page statement, signed by Zhang Ji, Cai Yuanpei, Yuan Fuli, Xu Xusheng, Ma Heng, Li Ji, and Huang Wenbi, among others, went into great detail regarding Stein's activities on his first three expeditions. From the outset, the statement made a mockery of Stein's well-known invocation of the Buddhist pilgrim Xuanzang, portraying this as "his favourite excuse" to engage in "commercial vandalism." Using lengthy quotations from Stein's own books in order to expose his many "dishonourable acts" on prior expeditions, the statement portrayed Stein—and his institutional sponsors by extension—as operating under a "false pretence." It then made note of the "satisfactory" terms to which Hedin had consented and drew attention to recent antiquities laws passed by the Nationalist government. "While we welcome foreign participation in Chinese archaeological studies," the statement continued, "we will use every means to resist any attempt on the part of foreigners like Sir Aurel Stein to carry out excavations under false pretence and to smuggle secretly historical and archaeological objects out of the country." The final sentence, which invoked the politically disinterested ideals of science, was directed squarely at Stein's institutional backers. "We believe that in doing so we have on our side the sympathy of all true students of scientific archaeology all over the world, and that when the scientific institutions that have promised Sir Aurel Stein their financial support have been informed of the questionable methods used by him and the disastrous results expected, will withdraw their support in the interest of true science and good international relations."[65]

This letter was accompanied by a hostile propaganda campaign conducted on multiple fronts. Unlike the commission's formal statement, which relied on Stein's own published words to frame the case against him, publicity was also directed toward the derogatory comments he was supposed to have uttered at Harvard the previous year. The headline of one Chinese newspaper in Tianjin was representative: "Antiquities Preservation Committee Requests Immediate Expulsion of Stein; Under Pretense of Travel, Stein Plunders Xinjiang Antiquities; Outrageous Speeches in America Insult Chinese Nation." As Stein later noted in a letter to Allen, these "outrageous speeches" were a total fabrication. "I never had an occasion there to appeal for funds or to deliver an 'address' on my plan," he wrote. "As you know, all this was spared to me by the quiet effort of my friends from the Fogg Art Museum. But evidently there are people in Peking sufficiently inflamed by nationalist jealously of foreign scholarly enterprise to think it necessary to supplement the misstatements of that Council by still more absurd inventions about my personal attitude towards modern China, etc." According to Stein, the commission's letter was marred by "misstatements." But the tales concerning his time at Harvard were "absurd inventions."[66]

Fortunately for Stein, he was spared knowledge of a sarcastic—and apparently untranslated—polemic published less than a month later by Wu Jinding, a Chinese archaeologist at the Academia Sinica. Wu's essay, which stretched to nearly seven thousand characters, expanded the attack on Stein well beyond his interactions with art and antiquities, characterizing all his previous expeditions as the result of imperialist coercion, personal deceit, and domestic corruption. Wu even took issue with the titles of Stein's books, observing that none of them used the official Chinese name of "Xinjiang" to describe the geographic backdrop of his expeditions. The essay concluded with a spirited rhetorical flourish:

> According to reliable reports, Stein is now back in China and has already been to Shanghai and Nanjing, claiming that all he wants to do is "follow the traces of Xuanzang." Come on, Mr. Stein! Are you really going to use an old lie that once worked to deceive the Chinese of twenty years ago to try and deceive the Chinese of today? Then let me tell you something plainly. The instability of our country will soon be resolved, our government has already killed off Pan *daren*, and not all of our people are like Daoist priest Wang [Yuanlu]. So stop dreaming about pulling out *Journey to the West* to conduct foreign relations with us! Even if you build a thousand temples to that Tang monk in Nanjing and erect ten thousand shrines to Xuanzang in Beiping, we will still resist to the

end Stein-style archaeology: walk ten thousand miles, steal ten thousand manuscripts, and write ten thousand boring articles.[67]

Such gleeful vitriol was wholly without precedent in the history of Western expeditions in China. In sizing up their most formidable adversary to date, the commission and its allies had deemed it necessary to resort to extraordinary measures. The reaction within China was swift. Just four days after Wu's polemic began to circulate within Nationalist diplomatic circles, the Administrative Yuan, citing Stein's "substantial funds and personnel" and continued freedom of movement in Xinjiang, ordered Governor Jin to "bring his work to a halt and secure his exit from the province without delay." Not only that, but the Ministry of Foreign Affairs was also "hereby directed to cancel his traveler's passport." In formulating his reply, Governor Jin tried to reassure Nanjing that Stein "has not traveled to any local sites," nor had he been "permitted to carry out any archaeological work" or undertake "any surveys of military matters." These claims were only partially true: as Jin knew full well from Zhang's reports, Stein had visited multiple sites and attempted to engage in substantive work at all of them, with varying degrees of success. That Jin knew of Zhang's incomplete efforts in the field is evident in a telegram he later sent to several of his magistrates in the southern oases, in which he chastised Zhang for allowing Stein to "survey" the land. But Jin also knew that only he had access to Zhang's reports from the field. As such, he could adhere to whatever version of the truth proved most useful in dealing with the commission. "With him en route is a special deputy by the name of Zhang Hongsheng, who is monitoring him," Jin informed Nanjing. "Thus it has been extremely difficult for him to enact his crafty plots."[68]

It took a bit longer for news of these developments to reach Stein. On January 31, 1931, Sherriff wrote to Stein to tell him that the end was near. "I am very sorry to have to tell you that I fear your expedition in this country must almost certainly be regarded as finished," Sherriff wrote. Receipt of this news in Stein's camp seemed to disturb Zhang, who had hoped to meet the governor in Urumchi, more than it did Stein. "Chang upset by fresh orders of Urumchi reporting Nanking's demand for my return," Stein noted in his diary. Stein, who had always anticipated the possibility of failure, took some solace in the fact that the governor had permitted him to return to Kashgar via the northern route of the Taklamakan, thus allowing him to complete his farewell tour among old haunts. "My circumambulation of the great basin affords me welcome chances of paying farewell visits to familiar scenes full of happy memories," Stein wrote to Allen, "from bits of 'true desert' to hospitable Turki homesteads such as the one from which I write this. It is very cheering to find myself so well remembered by old friends like Roze Beg, my host."[69]

The reason that Stein reacted to news of his defeat with such calm resignation was because he had not yet seen the rhetorical barbs that preceded it. Edward Forbes, one of Stein's chief allies at the Fogg Museum, reacted with indignation when he first saw the commission's letter. "Some members of the young China party who call themselves the National Commission for the Preservation of Antiquities have written a very savage letter to me, to Paul Sachs, Langdon Warner, George Chase and others attacking Sir Aurel Stein and saying that he is a most immoral and unscrupulous person and that he has behaved very badly towards China," Forbes wrote to his brother William, the American ambassador in Japan. "I am writing a letter in reply to this telling them of our complete belief in Sir Aurel Stein's honor and integrity." On April 10, 1931, a full five months after the publication of the commission's letter and Stein's alleged comments at Harvard, Stein finally learned what had precipitated the fatal order for his expulsion from the province. "But it is from your enclosures that I learned for the first time that resort had been had also to such ridiculous allegations about remarks I am supposed to have made at Harvard," he wrote to Allen. Stein then turned his attention to a detailed refutation of each of the allegations against him. "Afternoon has to be sacrificed to dealing with allegations in Waichiaopu's Memo.," he wrote in his diary, "a sad waste of time caused by Young China & by Harvard-Yenching representative whom it holds under its thumb." For Stein, who had long extolled the moral rectitude of Pan Zhen and so many other Chinese officials in Xinjiang, allegations of moral misconduct cut deep. "It is an unpleasant task to deal with such misrepresentations of one's past labours and objects."[70]

Amid all the outcry, considerable confusion remained as to whether or not Stein's passport had actually been canceled. In May 1931, after receiving conflicting reports in the field regarding the status of his passport, Stein made it back to Kashgar. There he found Ma Shaowu, the circuit intendant, still professing "to be without information about withdrawal of cancellation order! The game obviously continues to be played from Nanking." Indeed, it was. The Chinese archives reveal that Wang Zhengting, the minister of foreign affairs, had responded to the Administrative Yuan's orders to cancel Stein's passport by challenging the legal basis for those orders. On February 9, 1931, Wang reminded his colleagues in the Administrative Yuan that the British diplomats handling Stein's application had promised that he would not remove any antiquities from the country. As noted earlier, this was a disingenuous claim at best. According to all available evidence concerning Stein's stay in Nanjing, Wang had raised the question of archaeological proceeds but once and had quickly dropped the subject when Sir Miles Lampson assured him that Stein would only collect the contents of ancient "rubbish heaps." Other than this one exchange, it is clear that Wang carefully avoided the topic, opting instead for deliberate ambiguity and undocumented "verbal assurances" off the record.[71]

Wang's careful maneuvering of the year before now provided him with an opportunity to please all sides. "It is the opinion of the Ministry," Wang wrote, "that the decision to cancel [Stein's] passport must hinge upon whether or not any antiquities have been collected [on this expedition]." Though Wang admitted there was "cause for suspicion" regarding Stein's first three expeditions to Xinjiang, he disputed the relevance of Stein's past actions as cause for obstruction on the present expedition. "We cannot use his activities from previous trips as evidence to support the cancellation of his traveler's passport on this occasion." Yet again, here we see the internal divisions of various political factions within China coming to the fore. As minister of foreign affairs, Wang was determined to preserve what little shred of diplomatic capital he could still hope to salvage from the British and Americans. As such, he would not cancel Stein's passport unless irrefutable evidence emerged to prove that he had attempted to remove antiquities from China on his latest expedition—evidence that Wang knew could not be procured until Stein was ready to leave Xinjiang.[72]

When Stein returned to Kashgar, such evidence finally came to light. With the commission breathing down the neck of Governor Jin, Ma Shaowu was directed to order Stein to unpack every single box in his possession. On May 4, Stein "arranged 'antiques,' a poor show, for Tao-tai's inspection. . . . He inspected stuccoes & documents on wood, showing mild interest in Chinese slips & coins." In addition, Consul Sherriff was forced to provide a master list of everything Stein had managed to collect in secret during his circumambulation around the Taklamakan. Hoping to salvage something on Stein's behalf, Sherriff pleaded with Ma to ask Jin for permission to allow the objects to be sent to London for further study before being returned to China. "If we are to adhere to the interests of scholarship," Sherriff argued, "then all of the items on the list must be sent out of Xinjiang so that their value can be properly assessed by experts. This is particularly the case with regard to the short wooden slips bearing writing; it is absolutely imperative that they be sent to Europe for research."[73]

From the perspective of Governor Jin, the very presence of so many antiquities in Kashgar was all the proof the commission needed to accuse Jin of failing to safeguard the cultural heritage of the Chinese nation. Furious at all the trouble Stein had brought him, Jin informed Sherriff that the Chinese were more than capable of studying their own history. "As only a common traveler, Stein exceeded his authority by collecting more than a hundred antiquities," Jin wrote. "Not only that, many of these antiquities consist of inscribed wooden tablets and Indian manuscripts, which bear a strong relationship to the local history of this province. To allow us only to take photographs of them, and then let them leave the country on the pretext that we cannot study them adequately is absolutely not something we can permit." When Sherriff persisted in touting Stein's unique qualifications to study the Indian materials, Jin lost his temper. "Under no condition can the Chinese side approve of this," he fired back. "Furthermore, the Chinese people know very well the importance of research and scholarship as a means of advancing the development of culture throughout the world, and have made substantial contributions to this endeavor. On what basis does your letter refer to the lack of anyone here qualified to conduct such research?"[74]

At long last, Stein's humiliation was complete. Carl Keller, who had played such a key role in organizing the expedition, attempted to console Stein with the revelation that he had "cursed most vigorously and profoundly the ignorant Nationalism of china which is endeavoring to preserve the National Antiquities, even such ridiculous things as fossil[s]." He most fervently hoped, he said, "that this present bunch of idiots will be thoroughly and completely overthrown." Keller then indulged in a racist tirade. "Somehow the Chinese people make me think of masses of objectionable insects, like aphids, or corn borers, or army worms," he continued. "What earthly use there is of having any country as full of people as China is beyond my comprehension." In his reply to Keller, Stein ignored his friend's racist invective but fully echoed the desire for revenge. "What you wrote about the pranks of Young China and the need of having it brought to its senses is only too true," he wrote. "I quite agree with you that the lesson China is likely to receive from the Japanese will be well deserved and perhaps beneficial in the end." Not all of Stein's friends were as sympathetic to his travails as was Keller, though. "The Chinese officials were not very helpful to you," wrote Lionel Barnett, a British scholar of Sanskrit, "but I think that it is wonderful that they were not even more obstructive: you never seem to realize your own risks! There seems to me to have been no real reason, beyond the quotation of Hsuan Tsang, why they should not have had you quietly knocked on the head, and finally closed the whole discussion by your deeply regretted death of some fatal disease."[75]

On May 16, 1931, as Stein prepared to leave China for the last time, Sherriff attempted to pay tribute to Stein's past labors by hiring a Chinese opera troupe to perform the tale of Xuanzang on the rooftop of the British consulate in Kashgar. Stein was unimpressed. "A shouting farce with acrobatics supposed to tell Hsuan-tsang's story." The following evening, Sherriff arranged a farewell party at the Kashgar consulate for Stein. Among the guests were Ma Shaowu, Zhang Hongsheng, and Pan Zuhuan. Before dinner, Zhang informed Stein that he had been ordered to accompany him up to the border at Tashkurgan. "Sh.[erriff] overheard this cleverly & during dinner tells Tao-Tai plainly that he would [consider] this escorting an unfriendly act. Spy's face reflects his discomfiture. A relief to me." This emphatic protest, Stein later wrote to Allen, "rid us of the sneaky Mr. Chang who all through the journey around the Tarim basin had accompanied us by order from Urumchi as spy and guard against surveys." A dinner of twelve courses followed, with Pan seated on Stein's right. During the meal, Sherriff rose for a toast, referring to Stein as the "best friend of China." Stein then joined the ritual, offering good wishes "to those administr[ator]s who guard Hsinchiang's peace & order."[76]

During his final days in Xinjiang, Stein might have been forgiven for thinking that the "good old days" of Pan Zhen had never really passed. Pan Zuhuan gave Stein a present as an "everlasting souvenir for your unvariable friendship and kindness to my father and me." After expressing a wish for a future reunion with Stein on his summer camp in Kashmir, Pan asked Stein if he would undertake a survey of Karakul Lake on his way out of the province, with an eye toward increasing the supply of water for new agricultural settlements under his jurisdiction. Stein promised to do so, later submitting a lengthy report filled with mathematical calculations. Of course, before leaving China, Stein was forced to submit once more to an inspection of his cases at Tashkurgan. Though the inspection itself was a novelty, its denouement was not. "Finished with request for medicines," he noted in his diary. Three days later, at the loneliest border crossing in all of China, Stein met with a "hearty welcome by a poor decrepit Chinese official who inspects my passport." The border clerk, a "living relic of a kindlier past," impressed Stein with his Confucian regard for learning. "His care for the education of his little son touching."[77]

And then he was gone.

CONCLUSION

On November 20, 1937, readers of the *Saturday Evening Post* were treated to a short story about hard-hitting cops and the bad guys they busted. Four pages into the action, "The Last Wayne" wraps its text around a one-panel cartoon by David Huffine (figure 32). The cartoon depicts a dock somewhere on a river in New York City, with the Statue of Liberty in the background. On the dock stand three men: a casually attired African American janitor, a white porter in suit and tie, and a scantily clad black man with an oar in his hand. Beneath them, still floating on the water, are three more men sitting in a canoe, each drawn to resemble the third man on the dock. They, too, have black skin, few clothes, and tribal adornments, all of which suggest a journey from the jungles of Africa. Below them is the punch line, delivered by the African American janitor to the smartly dressed white porter: "He say dey is a expedition, come heah to get stuff fo' dey museum."[1]

To our eyes today, everything about this cartoon is cringe-worthy, from its pejorative representation of African American speech patterns to its stereotypical depiction of dark-skinned tribal peoples from the jungle. At the time of its publication, however, the humor of the cartoon would have been readily apparent to anyone with even a passing familiarity with the history of Western archaeological expeditions over the previous century. Langdon Warner certainly seems to have thought it was funny. On December 17, 1937, Warner cut this cartoon out of the *Saturday Evening Post* and included it in a letter to his good friend Roy Chapman Andrews in New York.[2] Just a decade earlier, both men had succumbed to nationalist obstruction of their scholarly expeditions in China. To Warner and Andrews, the Huffine cartoon offered a rare chance to laugh at their misfortune. In its depiction of an unlikely role reversal in the world of archaeological expeditions, the cartoon poked fun at the idea that dark-skinned natives from an uncivilized

"*He say dey is a expedition, come heah to get stuff fo' dey museum.*"

Figure 32. Role Reversal in the *Saturday Evening Post*. In December 1937, Harvard art historian Langdon Warner cut this cartoon out of the latest issue of the *Saturday Evening Post* and included it in a letter to his good friend Roy Chapman Andrews at the American Museum of Natural History in New York. A decade earlier, both men had been forced to abandon their plans for additional archaeological work in China. Cartoon by David Huffine, the *Saturday Evening Post*, November 20, 1937, 50; letter from Warner to Andrews, December 17, 1937, Andrews Papers, Administrative Papers 1920–1940, box XV, folder 41.

land might be interested in, or even capable of, removing art and antiquities from civilized white people in developed Western cities.

By 1937, however, the laughter was bittersweet. Although the "natives" were not paddling their way to New York in a canoe in order to "get stuff fo' dey museum," Western-educated elites both in China and throughout the independent countries of the Middle East and Latin America had long slammed the door on unrestricted Western archaeological enterprise within their lands. And in some cases, they dreamed of doing far more. "When will our countrymen measure up to the Stein and Pelliot spirit," asked one Chinese pundit in 1936, "and venture out into the world, unearth and gather up exquisite cultural treasures, and bring them back to our country, all for the greater glory of our nation?"[3] The publication of the *Saturday Evening Post* cartoon thus coincided with the end of an era. With the demise of unilateral Western expeditions and excavations, the men who had once led those ventures passed into legend. In 1940, Carl Keller sent to Stein a transcript of a high school skit performed by the seventeen-year-old daughter of his niece as part of a report on the history of printing. The niece, apparently unaware that Stein was one of her great-uncle's best friends, had reenacted for her class Stein's acquisition of a copy of the *Diamond Sutra*, the earliest printed book in the world, from the cave library at Dunhuang:

The Discovery of the Diamond Sutra

Time: April 22, 1908
Place: The British Museum
Characters: Sir Aurel Stein and Sir Henry Drayton

HENRY: Well, Aurel, I understand that you are turning over your findings to the British Museum. Which of all your expeditions did you find the most interesting?
AUREL: Oh, by all means my latest one in northwestern China. There, in a certain cave called "The Thousand Buddhas," I made some interesting discoveries.
HENRY: I hear you found some very valuable manuscripts.
AUREL: Yes, but I made an even more exciting discovery. Let me tell you about how I found it.

The scene changes to "The Caves of the Thousand Buddhas" in China. Characters are Sir Aurel and his servant.

AUREL: Come over here, Ming, and tell me about these beautiful frescoes.

MING: These were being restored by a mendicant priest about seven years ago when he discovered that some were on brick rather than stone. He then discovered a secret chamber behind the bricks filled with some old manuscripts.

AUREL: How interesting. I wonder if they are still here. That's funny. Shouldn't the wall curve here instead of jutting out? Maybe there is an old cell in back of these bricks. Help me take them out.

MING: Look, Sir Aurel. It does open and there is some sort of a room here.

AUREL: Let's go in. Shine your light over here and be careful that you don't fall because it's very dark and dangerous here. Look!!! Piles of manuscripts! I wonder how old they are. They are very yellow and musty so I imagine they must be centuries old. The dry climate must have preserved them. I hope I will be able to take them back to England with me.

The scene switches back to England.

AUREL: I never realized, Henry, what a nerve-racking time I would have trying to bring some of the valuable ones back to England.

HENRY: What was the reason?

AUREL: Well, it seems that the natives had some superstition that nothing could be taken out of the sacred cave but I finally persuaded them to let me have the "Diamond Sutra" and some old woodblock prints.

HENRY: Aurel, what exactly is this "Diamond Sutra"?

AUREL: Well, Henry, it's the earliest printed book in existence. It was made by a Chinese merchant, Wangchieh, in 868 on May 11th. He made it for free distribution to perpetuate the memory of his parents. He printed it on mulberry paper and pasted it into a continuous roll. Of course this book would not have been printed if the Chinese had not invented a rag paper in 105 A.D. I also found the oldest known woodblock in existence.

HENRY: Aurel, you certainly have had some interesting experiences. What are you going to do with all your discoveries? Keep them in your collection?

AUREL: No, Henry. I am giving some of them, as you know, to this museum so all the world can benefit by their interesting material.

HENRY: That's wonderful of you, Aurel. I am sure the museum will always treasure them as one of their most valued possessions.

Finis.

This short high school script, infused with the self-serving Enlightenment discourse of science, preservation, and education, thoroughly amused Stein. "I was greatly pleased to find myself made an interlocutor in the amusing little dialogue composed by the young daughter of Mrs. Keller's niece," he wrote back. "I should never have thought that any young American lady would know something of that early blockprint I brought away from the 'Thousand Buddhas'—or of my 'unworthy person.'"[4]

In China, too, Stein quickly entered the realm of myth. In 1936, just five years after Stein had been driven out of Xinjiang, the British traveler Peter Fleming heard tales from the local Muslims about Ishtin Sahib, "a superhuman figure whom, after initial perplexity, we identified as Sir Aurel Stein."[5] Among educated Chinese elites, the name of Stein gradually became etched into the mythic landscape of northwestern China as well. We can see this clearly in the proliferation of fake Chinese colophons attached to manuscripts purported to have come from the caves of Dunhuang. In one such colophon appended to the end of a *Lotus Sutra*, the following comments are attributed to Mu Shouqi, a lifelong Gansu official:

In the twenty-ninth year of Guangxu [1903–4], the Hungarian Stein, who was a specialist in Central Asian geography, set out to investigate the geography of Central Asia and its ancient cultures. Traveling as a representative of the British Indian government, he brought with him a translator named Jiang and traveled to the Mogao Grottoes in order to view the cave murals, which are all from the Six Dynasties era. Then he saw an ancient manuscript on the desk of Daoist priest Wang, and proceeded to enter into secret negotiations with him in order to gain entrance into the treasure cave. Once inside, he saw manuscripts, banners, papers, silks, paintings, and other miscellaneous articles piled high from the ground to the ceiling. It measured about ten English feet high, with a total volume of about five hundred English cubic feet. After giving the Daoist priest Wang three hundred silver taels, [Stein] stole twenty-four boxes of manuscripts, along with five additional boxes of various items such as paintings. This all occurred on May 22, 1907 of the Western calendar.[6]

The colophon is signed and dated to the second month of spring in the first year of the Xuantong emperor—February 1909. And therein lies proof of the forgery: at this early date, no one in China possessed such precise knowledge of the circumstances surrounding Stein's acquisitions of the Dunhuang manuscripts. In every other Chinese colophon from these early years, Stein is consistently identified as either German or British; precious few, if any, seemed to know that he was born in Hungary. Other details—such as the cubic dimensions and total volume of the cave library (given in "English feet" no less!), the number of cases of manuscripts and paintings removed, and the exact date of Stein's transaction at the caves—were not made public until the publication of *Ruins of Desert Cathay* in 1912. Even a preliminary report published by Stein in the *Geographic Journal* did not appear until September 1909, seven months after this colophon was supposedly written. When this report was hastily translated into Chinese and included in Luo Zhenyu's *Visiting the Ancients among the Shifting Sands* (*Liusha fang gu ji*, 1909), the name of Stein's Chinese secretary, Jiang Xiaowan, was rendered not as "Jiang" (as in the colophon) but rather as "Zhang Shuyi"—a strictly phonetic translation of Stein's original "Chiang-ssu-yieh" (*Jiang shiye*, or "Secretary Jiang").[7]

In other words, in order to lend an air of authenticity to a forged manuscript in hopes of securing a higher price for its sale, some shady Chinese entrepreneur decided to include an implausibly precise summary of Stein's second expedition, a summary that could only have been assembled in China after the publication of *Ruins of Desert Cathay* in 1912—provided the person in question could read English, which Mu Shouqi most certainly could not. With all evidence pointing in the direction of a scam, the jarring description of Stein having "stolen" manuscripts from Dunhuang can be readily explained: the colophon was written not in 1909, when Stein was more likely to be regarded by the Chinese as hero than thief, but rather at some point after the adoption of such criminalizing discourse by Westernized Chinese on the eastern seaboard in the 1920s and '30s. In another colophon attributed to Yang Zengxin and dated to September/October 1908, four years before Yang became the governor of Xinjiang, the name of French sinologist Paul Pelliot was similarly invoked. At the end of a *Commentary on the Great Perfection of Wisdom* manuscript, an enterprising crook writing in Yang's name gives a complete account not only of Pelliot's time at Dunhuang—which had occurred just a few months prior to the date of the colophon and was known only to Wang Yuanlu and the French members of Pelliot's party—but also the subsequent shipment of ten cases of manuscripts back to Paris; his trip to Shanghai to share news of his discovery with Chinese scholars; and the Ministry of Education's order the following year for officials in Gansu to ship the remaining manuscripts to Beijing. But unless Yang had somehow managed to build a time machine and had visited the future, he could not possibly have been privy to events that had not yet occurred at the time he was purported to have written this colophon.[8]

That both of these colophons managed to fool not only their original purchasers but also the modern Chinese scholars who reproduced them as authentic texts shows just how little is known regarding the actual circumstances under which Western archaeologists acquired art and antiquities from China. But the Chinese are not alone in their anachronistic adherence to cherished nationalist myths regarding the age of Western archaeological expeditions. In 2015, during an academic conference on Stein held in New Delhi, I was ushered into a room where a solemn ceremony was being held by my Indian hosts to inaugurate the proceedings. Much to my astonishment, I was greeted with an elaborately constructed shrine to Stein, complete with his portrait, burning candles, wreaths of flowers, incense, and group prayer. As the conference unfolded over the next several days, it gradually dawned on me that Stein had become a nationalist Indian icon of sorts, one whose pursuit of Gandharan art and Indic scripts throughout Central Asia was imagined to have played a seminal role in linking the cultural pasts of Kashmir and Xinjiang to that of India. This nationalist apotheosis of Stein in India made for some awkward moments during the conference proceedings, none more so than when I gave voice to Stein's many derogatory statements about that country's "absence of history," the incapacity of its people for self-government, and the similarities of Xinjiang and India in requiring the agents of a more civilized race to bring about peace and prosperity.[9]

None of this ignorance appears to be willful. Instead, it is rooted in our passive acceptance of whichever version of Western archaeological expeditions proves most useful for current political agendas. In other words, most politicians and scholars have had little incentive to dig beneath the surface narratives of these expeditions. As a result, we have made only half-hearted attempts to penetrate the fog of nationalist disinformation that arose in the years after Western archaeologists packed up their bags and went home. Our collective ignorance is empowering. It allows the Chinese to portray themselves as sympathetic victims who would have resisted Stein from the outset had he not been such a cunning imperialist bully and the Qing officials of the old imperial order so corrupt and dim. It makes it possible for the Indians to claim a carefully manicured image of Stein as a nationalist

icon, despite his abhorrence at the idea of an independent India. The curators of major Western museums can justify the retention of their collections
by reference to Stein's books, which never fail to couch the removal of art
and antiquities from China as an altruistic service performed in devotion
to science, preservation, and education. Conversely, those Western scholars
who are inclined to be critical of Stein, Hedin, or Pelliot can point to their
deeply insensitive comments on race and class as evidence of the moral
bankruptcy not only of their work along the expedition trail but also of
Western imperialism writ large.

Although the above examples of ignorance may not be willful, they are
unique to the present age. For, as we have seen throughout the preceding
chapters, almost everyone who crossed paths with Western archaeologists
in northwestern China knew exactly what he was doing and how he was
doing it. The ignorance is ours, not theirs. From the Qing official isolated
in his *yamen* clear on down to the Muslim or Han peasant toiling in the
fields, it was common knowledge that the Westerner was a haughty and
arrogant man who found it difficult to hide his scorn and disdain for the
lower classes and occasionally even the local elites. If someone or something displeased him enough, he could call on the diplomatic support of
one of the most powerful empires on the planet to get his way. But that
was rarely necessary: most daily conflicts and irritants could be resolved
through a public whipping or the threat of detention in a local prison. Even
for those who managed to escape the Westerner's ire, the conditions of employment could often be brutal. Though Stein once quipped that "the trip
over the Karakorum has become a tour for ladies," it is clear that all manner of physical hardship and privation afflicted those who joined his caravans. Even Stein himself once lost a toe to frostbite and narrowly averted
death when his horse reared back and fell on top of him. Milton Bramlette,
the young American geologist selected to accompany Stein on his fourth
expedition, found the rigors of the expedition trail too much to bear, in
spite of all the material "comforts" someone in his position could expect
to enjoy. (Le Coq once referred to Stein's "Champagne-lubricated style" of
expeditions!)[10]

All these facts were known. And yet the people of northwestern China
were no less aware of them in 1900, the year of Stein's first expedition, than
they were in 1931, when Stein was forced to abandon his fourth expedition.
In neither case did the ultimate fate of Stein's expeditions hinge on the application of Western force or deception on the supposedly corrupt and ignorant Chinese and Muslims. In 1900, the Qing court felt confident enough
to declare war on all the Western and Japanese powers and lay siege to their

legations in Beijing. And yet they still admitted Stein into Xinjiang even as war raged on the other side of the country. "I have already told you that the country is perfectly quiet," Stein wrote to Allen from the oasis of Karghalik in September 1900, as the embers of war in Beijing continued to smolder. "The Chinese officials have so far been all most attentive and I hope will give no trouble to me thereafter."[11]

Three decades later, China had descended into a patchwork quilt of competing warlord domains, with a central government whose authority did not even extend beyond the Yangzi River basin. And yet this was the backdrop against which Stein would be kicked out of the country. In other words, he was welcomed into Xinjiang while China was at war with the Western powers, but he was expelled from Xinjiang during a time when China was at war with itself. Like the emir of Afghanistan, the Chinese could have refused to issue a passport to Stein for any one of his four expeditions without fear of anything other than a rhetorical backlash, if that. All they had to do was say "no." Though wars can lead to the looting of art and antiquities, the prospect of such looting is generally not a motivating factor in the declaration of war. Museums may benefit from the tangential spoils of imperialist wars, but museums themselves do not have armies. All this is to say that Western archaeologists did not shoot their way into China, nor did they get shot out. Quite simply, they came to China when the Chinese said "yes," and they left China when the Chinese said "no."

But why did the Chinese say "yes" and why did they say "no"? This book has attempted to answer these questions by developing a new explanatory framework, one that looks beyond the anachronistic nationalist valuation of artifacts as priceless and attempts to understand how such objects could be treated when they were merely viewed as profitable or precious. In so doing, we have drawn attention to the material and immaterial incentive structure that governed interactions between Western archaeologists and those people with whom they were obliged to interact in order to secure support for their activities in the field. The gross disparity between the Western imperial powers and the rest of the world certainly established the context for these interactions. But this context merely provided the *incentive* to give the Western scholar what he wanted. It did not impose an obligation. The geopolitical conditions of the day imposed but two obligations on the Chinese who hosted Stein: to ensure his safety and to throw no obstacles in his way. Both of these obligations could be met with far less enthusiasm and assistance than is evident in the historical record.

Their enthusiasm was rooted in the pragmatic incentive structure referred to in the preceding chapters as "the compensations of plunder." In

CONCLUSION 279

exchange for offering their services to a Western expedition and for tolerating the hazards, hardships, or liabilities associated with such service, the people of China received a host of compensations in return. Most importantly, these compensations were nearly always perceived to be of greater—sometimes much greater—value than that which the foreigner took away. The majority of the people with whom the Western archaeologist interacted did not think of themselves as victims of imperialism. Instead, they tended to regard themselves as the beneficiaries of a resourceful and cultured agent of modernization from one of the most powerful and advanced empires in the world. To the mostly lower-class Muslims, he was a "sahib in the desert," one who was expected to dispense liberal doses of economic capital to anyone who rendered him a service—even if the sahib did not want that service. And if they were lucky, the powerful sahib with his scientific arts just might prove capable of overcoming the desert *jinns* and discovering a new cache of hidden gold—or perhaps he would even introduce them to the governor. To the highly educated Chinese upper classes, the Western archaeologist was a "gentleman of empire," with whom they could bond over matters of perceived social, cultural, and political import. And if he was lucky, the Chinese official just might find himself featured in a best-selling book about the trailblazing scientific adventures of a cultured celebrity that would provide conversational fodder for generations to come.

In both cases, the people of northwestern China had a vested interest in exaggerating the importance of "their" sahib or gentleman. The reason is simple: the greater the personage, the greater the compensations he could dole out to those in his favor. As a result, as we saw in chapters 1 and 3, the Western archaeologist was often forced to "perform" certain social, economic, and political roles with which he himself was deeply uncomfortable. But perform them he did. Much like the Qing official who weighed the liabilities of a treaty-protected foreigner against the prospect of obtaining rare social and political capital or the Muslim peasant who considered the risks of a week's labor in the hostile winter desert against the allure of attractive wages and perhaps a promotion to a begship, the Western archaeologist, too, had to weigh the inconveniences and irritations of performing the onerous roles expected of a "great man" against the prospect of securing greater support for his expedition. Though this obligation clashed most memorably with the professed egalitarian ethos of American climatologist Ellsworth Huntington and his traveling companion Daniel Barrett, even the European explorers, who were generally much more comfortable with rigid distinctions of class and title, privately vented against such nuisances in their diary.

In formulating the compensations of plunder framework, this study has displaced the retroactive nationalist fetishization of the inanimate artifact with an empirical analysis of the contemporary valuation of a professional relationship with the living Western archaeologist. The reason we are unable to understand why the Chinese were so eager to aid and abet the Western archaeologist is because we have projected our own priceless valuation of art and antiquities back to a time and place where they were not yet viewed as priceless by those who lived within their midst. To such people, the only thing that was priceless was a personal relationship with a Western sahib or gentleman. By contrast, the objects the Westerner targeted were generally viewed as either profitable or precious, but not priceless.

We saw this clearly in the collecting habits of the same Muslim and Chinese who later lent their assistance to the Western archaeologist. Whenever the Muslims and Chinese collected these artifacts on their own, without the assistance or involvement of Westerners, they proceeded to exchange them among themselves for the exact same sort of economic, political, and social capital that they would later procure from the Westerners. In each and every case, these forms of capital were perceived to be of greater value than the object exchanged for that capital, even when Westerners were not involved in the transaction in any way. At the end of the day, of course, the Chinese certainly thought it was "unfortunate" that Westerners had gotten the lion's share of art and antiquities. But they did not regard their misfortune as the result of a morally dubious act. In their eyes, men like Stein were simply engaging the same pragmatic barter arrangement in which they themselves had long participated. The only difference was that Stein had greater resources with which to barter—and that the results of his bartering would end up in a museum or library halfway around the world, permanently encased in a glass cabinet without the possibility of further transfer.

As the value of the object within China increased, the value of what the Westerner could offer in exchange for its removal decreased. The devaluation of Western compensations began with the 1911 revolution. More specifically, it began with the valorization of an ostensibly classless "Chinese nation" (*Zhonghua minzu*) as the basis of political legitimacy for the new Republic of China. In the realm of art and antiquities, nationalism was written into the cultural identity of the new state through constitutional provisions for the establishment of a national museum and laws regulating the protection of artifacts within China. Even though neither provision would be adequately enforced for another four decades, together they brought about a dramatic shift in how art and antiquities would be perceived in China. Instead of profitable or precious commodities reflective of one's individual virtue, artifacts were now viewed as the collective property of the abstract Chinese nation. To acquiesce in their removal was now a criminal act—a betrayal of the Chinese nation itself. As Xiaowei Zheng, Judd Kinzley, and Timothy Brook have shown, a similar shift was also evident in other realms of political and economic concern, such as the nationalization of privately funded railroads in Sichuan, the reconceptualization of natural resources as national patrimony, and the transition from exclusive expressions of individual loyalty to a monarch to collective demonstrations of loyalty to an abstract nation and its symbols.[12]

The idea that art and antiquities could be priceless rather than precious was an idea that Westerners brought to China. For it was Westerners who first viewed cultural artifacts as representative of the political legitimacy of an empire composed of many nations; to exert dominion over the material remains of these idealized nations was to claim the right to exert dominion over the descendants of those same nations today. Within the analytical framework adopted in this book, art and antiquities became priceless once they were tethered to the political legitimacy of a state that claimed to protect the newly reimagined cultural heritage of its collective nation or nations rather than the exclusive cultural property of individual elites. Though national (or more often imperial) museums and antiquities preservation laws were essential ingredients in the rising domestic valuations of artifacts, they alone were not enough to produce a "priceless" valuation. After all, the Imperial Ottoman Museum in Istanbul opened its doors in 1846 and the Bulaq Museum in Cairo followed suit in 1863. The unregulated export of Ottoman art and antiquities to Western museums, however, continued for more than half a century after the establishment of both institutions.

More specifically, it continued until the Ottoman Empire itself was partitioned into a host of successor states in the aftermath of World War I. In those successor states that attained full independence, such as Turkey and Egypt, Western archaeological digs, such as that of Howard Carter at the tomb of Tutankhamun, were stopped almost immediately. In states that were subjected to the semicolonial imposition of a British or French "mandate," however, such as Palestine, Syria, or Iraq, no such opposition materialized until the mandate was lifted. Once that mandate was lifted, however, opposition surfaced almost instantly. In Iraq, for example, the dissolution of the British mandate in 1932 was followed soon thereafter by the obstruction of American Egyptologist James Henry Breasted. In China, we saw how Governor Yang Zengxin undertook the first attempt to obstruct Stein in 1914, just two years after the establishment of the new state. Even though Yang's obstruction was highly cynical and motivated by personal profit, more principled obstruction efforts occurred almost immediately on the resumption of Western expeditions in the 1920s—even if those efforts were, as we saw in chapters 5 and 6, still compromised by the political and economic crises then afflicting China.

In each case, museums and antiquities laws were prerequisites to a domestic priceless valuation and the obstruction that such valuation instigated. But they alone were not enough. What was needed was a rhetorical repudiation of the old imperial order and its crippling dependence on the Western powers. In the Middle East, it was World War I and the subsequent dismemberment of the Ottoman Empire that prompted this repudiation in the successor states of Turkey and Egypt and eventually in Iraq. In China, it was the 1911 revolution that gave rise to a repudiation of the old Qing order. The situation in China was perhaps more similar to that of Iran, which began to obstruct French and American archaeologists only after the overthrow of the imperial Qajar dynasty in 1925. Whether by war or revolution, however, the Westernized elites of these young states were united in their need for a new political identity, one that was distinct from the old imperial ideology and rooted in the identities of the new Westernizing nations they now claimed to represent.

To the Westernized scholars of the post-1911 era in China, the artifacts removed by Stein and other Western archaeologists were no longer viewed as the private possessions of the gentleman who had acquired them by dint of his own labor and resources. Instead, they were now regarded exactly as Stein himself regarded them: as the priceless abstract patrimony of a nation on whose behalf both collectors claimed to speak. As such, the Westernized Chinese scholars who accompanied Langdon Warner and Sven Hedin into Gansu and Xinjiang, such as Chen Wanli, Xu Xusheng, and Huang Wenbi, were no longer willing to countenance the removal of the material basis of this new political identity. Conflict was thus unavoidable. In 1915, as the domestic valuation of antiquities in Xinjiang began to soar, Stein indulged in a bit of nostalgia for the marketplace of the nineteenth century. "Statues, MSS. and the like were fortunately of no saleable value in those happy days," Stein wrote in his diary. For Stein and other Western archaeologists, that was the golden age: when they alone regarded the art and antiquities of northwestern China as priceless. So long as all possible domestic competitors regarded them as merely worthless, profitable, or precious, the Westerner could take advantage of a highly favorable "exchange rate," so to speak, one that, as Stein put it after acquiring his first batch of Dunhuang manuscripts, "will make our friends at the Br.[itish] Mus.[eum] chuckle."[13]

Those early years were what we might refer to as the "Age of Content": when every party emerged from the archaeological transaction convinced he had gotten something of great value in exchange for something of little value. When a new generation of Westernized Chinese scholars in Beijing began to project an equally priceless valuation on the exact same art and antiquities, however, the Age of Content gave way to the "Age of Discontent." Most Western archaeologists and their supporters, having grown up amid a very different ideological and geopolitical backdrop, found it difficult to accept young Westernized Chinese as their intellectual and political equals. "It seems to me that nothing so ruins an Oriental as to veneer him with Western education," Keller informed Stein after the conclusion of his fourth expedition, "which apparently is so disharmonic with their past that it destroys in them what was good in their own tradition without giving them what is admirable in ours." In 1932, Frederick McCormick, the founder of the China Monuments Society, assured his good friend Roy Chapman Andrews that he had been right to spurn Chinese demands for "cooperation." "I wish my China Monuments Society had turned out better for the archaeologists, paleontologists, and geographers," McCormick wrote to Andrews. "The Chinese whom I interested in cultural objects and their protection took just that one word for their activities in succession to my enterprise, and, according to press reports have made life miserable for the explorers and students, educational institutions and museums abroad." Keller and McCormick, unable to appreciate the irony of Westernized Chinese scholars defending their newly reimagined cultural heritage exactly as Western scholars had long done, refused to recognize the legitimacy of the Commission for the Preservation of Antiquities, with McCormick referring to it as an "autocratic institution" with "no legal basis for its actions."[14]

Fortunately for men like Stein—or perhaps unfortunately, in light of the much delayed and tortuous result—the one thing Chinese politicians still desired, even as late as 1930, was diplomatic capital from Western countries. For political elites throughout the world, diplomatic capital was—and perhaps still is—the only form of capital capable of matching the priceless nationalist valuation of antiquities. (To the impoverished lower classes, economic capital continues to serve as sufficient recompense to target the contents of ancient tombs and other archaeological sites, both in China and elsewhere.) When the pragmatic pursuit of diplomatic capital by Nationalist Minister of Foreign Affairs Wang Zhengting drew the highly publicized ire of principled nationalist scholars in Beijing, Stein's defeat—and subsequent criminalization of all previous expeditions—was assured. In March 1931, as Stein prepared to leave Xinjiang for the last time, Chen Yuan, a prominent historian based in Beijing, put the finishing touches on his mon-umental *Dunhuang jieyu lu*. Though discreetly translated into English as *An Analytical List of the Tun-huang Manuscripts in the National Library of Peiping*, anyone proficient in Chinese could have provided a more accurate translation: *An Index of the Dunhuang Manuscripts Remaining after the Plunder*. With the once priceless compensations of Western archaeological expeditions now grossly devalued or simply undetected, all that remained was the "plunder." No longer content merely to express their discontent, this new generation of Westernized Chinese scholars ushered in the "Age of Obstruction."[15]

When the discourse of criminalization unique to the era after World War I was projected backward onto the era before the war, those people who knowingly and willingly facilitated the success of Western archaeological expeditions became little more than caricatures of their actual historical selves. There were few other options: if Wang Yuanlu was not a greedy simpleton, if Pan Zhen was not a corrupt bureaucrat, and if Aurel Stein was not a dishonest and deceptive imperialist, then what else could account for each man's unforgivable and inexplicable betrayal of the now valorized "Chinese nation"? If we truly want to restore agency to long neglected his-torical figures from the non-Western world, however, we cannot assume that they shared the priorities of their nationalist descendants. To speak on behalf of those whose voices we have made no attempt to recover is, in fact, the very embodiment of imperialist arrogance. In order to restore historical agency to Wang Yuanlu and Pan Zhen, we must accept the possibility that they were rational human beings who knew exactly what they were doing, and that what they were doing made sense within the ideological, social, economic, and geopolitical contexts of their day.

Most Chinese historians have been unwilling to accept this possibility. Wang Yuanlu, in particular, has consistently borne the brunt of condemna-tion within China. Whereas Confucian collectors of the late Qing and early Republican eras once vilified Wang for depriving "people like us" (*wubei* or *wuren*) of the opportunity to accumulate individual social and political capital—that is, in class terms—later Chinese historians have vilified him for depriving "the Chinese nation" of its collective cultural heritage. Rong Xinjiang, one of the foremost scholars in the field of Dunhuang studies, has even gone so far as to describe Wang as "the one who will be remembered in history as the person who stole the Dunhuang treasures and sold them to foreigners. His tombstone and stūpa should not be a tourist destination but rather be kept standing in front of the Mogao caves as a shame pole." Historian Wang Jiqing has taken Rong's vindictive nationalist assessment of Wang and applied it to all of the principle actors involved in Stein's four expeditions to northwestern China. Pelliot has fared somewhat better than Stein, likely because his contributions to the field of Sinology and productive scholarly relationships with leading Chinese historians of his day can be interpreted in redemptive nationalist terms. Nevertheless, even Pelliot is occasionally lumped together with the criminal behavior of Western imperialists like Stein.[16]

To the late Qing and early Republican elites who interacted with the archaeologist along the expedition trail or heard about his activities through contemporary Chinese commentaries and translations of his works, however, "plunder" was an alien concept. But it did not take long for a new generation of Westernized Chinese elites to warm up to the idea. To this generation, the same words and actions that had once made Stein a widely admired "hero"—both to Chinese and foreigners alike—now made him a "thief." In casting doubt on Stein's character and reputation, the commission had not turned up any new evidence of Stein's alleged misdeeds. Instead, it simply turned his own published words back against him. Stein had not changed—the world around him had. "Perhaps," Stein wrote in response to the commission's statement against him, anticipating yet another ideological shift in the future, "the time may not be too distant when competent Chinese scholars will be prepared to recognize that researches bearing on the cultural past of their country have suffered by the obstacles which unjustified agitation has raised against the continued work of a confrere who had done as much as any one to throw light on the great and beneficial part played by ancient China in the history of Central Asia."[17]

Such agitation on the part of the Westernized Chinese scholars of Beijing may not have been unjustified. But it was certainly rooted in a gross misunderstanding of what had once transpired during the course of a Western expedition or excavation in China. As we have seen, the expedition trail could be the site of many tensions and sometimes even hostilities. None of these conflicts, however, had anything to do with the "agitation," justified or not, of the members of the commission in Beijing decades hence—or of the moral barometer that they have bequeathed to our own day and age. When tensions flared up, as they often did, they were rooted in mundane logistical concerns wholly unrelated to the nationalist discourse of cultural sovereignty: cold desert winds, a snoring tent mate, disrespectful seating arrangements, fear of *jinns*, unpaid bills, a jilted lover, the inconvenience of billeting, garnished wages, or an elderly mother left behind. In fact, it was the decidedly banal nature of such tensions that virtually ensured the resourceful Western archaeologist would get his way, so long as he was willing to dispense with his resources. In other words, we might say that the reason why China lost its treasures was because few people in China at the time of their removal actually regarded them as "China's treasures." Instead, they were profitable or precious objects that just happened to be found within the borders of the Qing Empire. The moment the Chinese themselves regarded them as the priceless patrimony of their newly conceived nation or nations, the compensations of plunder plummeted in value and the age of unregulated Western archaeological enterprise came to an end.

ACKNOWLEDGMENTS

The first time I ever heard of Aurel Stein, Xinjiang, and the Silk Road was in Daniel Waugh's undergraduate seminar on the Silk Road at the University of Washington. Over the years, as I strayed off into other pursuits, I always retained a vivid memory of the endless slideshows of Central Asian art and antiquities that had first entranced me as a freshman. That seed, long dormant, eventually bore fruit in graduate school. Ever since then, Stein, Xinjiang, and the Silk Road have dominated my intellectual agenda. Through it all, Dan has proven my most steadfast supporter, frankest critic, and most prized colleague. Twenty years after he first broadened my horizons to a world beyond China, it gives me great pleasure to acknowledge my considerable debt to one of the most indefatigable and exacting scholars ever to have studied the Silk Road.

My interest in these topics could not have blossomed, however, without the tangible and intangible support of my graduate advisors at the University of California, San Diego. It was Joe Esherick who first suggested that the Chinese officials in Xinjiang may have welcomed Stein into their jurisdictions in part simply because they were lonely. At the time, I thought he was joking. Turns out he was right. Paul Pickowicz oversaw my first attempt at understanding how the Chinese "confronted Indiana Jones" and later donated his own collection of Sino-Swedish commemorative stamps to the cause. Both Joe and Paul provided generous financial support for my early research efforts, making it possible for me to complete a full encirclement of the Taklamakan Desert (by bus, not camel!) and later to attend a Stein conference in Budapest. Not too many second-year graduate students can expect such support from their advisors.

I could not have carried out the research for this project without the patient and able assistance of many archival caretakers throughout the world.

In this regard, I am pleased to acknowledge the generous assistance of Colin Harris, who let me examine all the original Stein papers at the Bodleian Library in Oxford without having to squint at endless reels of microfilm; Susan Whitfield, who has provided timely insight into numerous queries over the years; Håkan Wahlquist, who hosted me at the Museum of Ethnography in Stockholm and helped to uncover a spectacular photograph of Yang Zengxin; Cristina Cramerotti, who guided me through the Pelliot papers at the Musée Guimet in Paris; Megan Schwenke, who facilitated generous access to the Harvard Art Museums Archives in Cambridge, Massachusetts; Rosie Llewellyn-Jones, who kindly granted access to the Schomberg papers at the Royal Society for Asian Affairs in London; and many other helpful curators at Harvard's Houghton Library, Yale University Library, Philadelphia Museum of Art, American Museum of Natural History, and Getty Museum. I am grateful to the British Academy for permitting the publication of numerous images from the Stein papers held at the Bodleian Library.

The ideas presented in this book have benefited from fruitful discussions over the years with numerous colleagues in the field, including Maggie Greene, James Wicks, Eric Schluessel, David Brophy, Lilla Russell-Smith, Joshua Freeman, Sanchita Balachandran, Ágnes Kelecsényi, Helen Wang, Clayton Brown, Wendy Doyon, Fletcher Coleman, Patricia Graham, Caren Dreyer, and Imre Galambos. Judd Kinzley was generous enough to read through several chapters of an early draft of this manuscript and provide a brutal but necessary critique. I look forward to returning the favor one day. I am also grateful to the organizers and participants of several conferences for providing me with a venue to present some of my preliminary findings. Imre Hamar has twice welcomed me to Budapest, Radha Sarkar hosted me in New Delhi, and Xuan Li facilitated a fruitful series of talks in Chengdu. I am particularly indebted to Karl Gerth for making it possible to stay at Merton College during an extended research trip to Oxford. I have also benefited greatly from comments received during numerous public talks I have given at Live and Learn Bethesda, Profs. and Pints, Oasis, and the Smithsonian Associates Program.

The subject matter of this project has forced me to move beyond my intellectual comfort zone and tackle source material in unfamiliar forms and languages. Ye Wa's patient assistance was indispensable in helping me to decipher the flowing calligraphy of Chinese colophons on the Dunhuang and Turfan manuscripts. Jenny Huangfu Day also lent her keen eye for a crucial translation of mine from one of the modern Dunhuang colophons, while He Jiajie provided a flawless transcription in record time of a nigh impenetrable handwritten letter in Chinese. Shilah Marks harnessed her masterful command of French to open up the fascinating world of Pelliot's field diary and letters, and provided much needed insights into Pelliot's puzzling references to "a summer of Saint Martin" and the lecherous Duke of Richelieu. As in all my work, the wonderful cartographic work of Debbie Newell is on display in each of the maps included in the chapters herein.

At American University, I am fortunate to be able to interact on a regular basis with supportive and brilliant colleagues. In particular, I would like to thank Max Paul Friedman, who read through a complete draft of the manuscript, along with Lisa Leff and Eric Lohr, both of whom have long supported my undignified interest in studying "Indiana Jones in history." I also acknowledge with pleasure the generous and recurring support of AU Faculty Mellon Grants, which have taken much of the financial pinch out of my visits to archives and conferences around the world. Parts of chapter 5 first appeared in "Nationalist China's Great Game: Leveraging Foreign Explorers in Xinjiang, 1927–1935," *Journal of Asian Studies* 73, no. 1 (February 2014): 43–64.

Priya Nelson first reached out to me about this project in 2014 and maintained her editorial support for many years and through several painful revisions. I am very grateful for her patience and understanding and only wish that I had been an easier author to work with. Two anonymous reviewers for the University of Chicago Press offered critical insights and suggestions during the final round of revisions. James Millward has supported my career and research in so many ways for so long now that words feel inadequate to express my debt. Neither I nor my book would have made it this far without him, and it is an honor to have my work included within his Silk Roads series.

What would life be like without kids? I cannot imagine, nor do I want to. May Sasha and Lance always pull me back into the twenty-first century and its familial delights. Central to those delights is the eternal drive, energy, and bounce—especially the bounce—of my wife Cindy. In our marriage lies the fountain of youth.

bao 刨

baocun difang gu wu 保存地方古物

bilin 鄙吝

bing 兵

boxue haogu 博學好古

boya junzi 博雅君子

bu yun 不允

Cai Yuanpei 蔡元培

caijue 採掘

Cen Dongshi 岑董士

cha 查

Chai Hongshan 柴洪山

chakao guji 查考古蹟

chanbao 鏟刨

chantou 纏頭

Chang Tingjiang 長汀江

Chang Yongqing 常永慶

Che Yuheng 車玉衡

Chen Jikan 陳季侃

Chen Shi 陳湜

Chen Wanli 陳萬里

Chen Wengan 陳問淦

Chen Zhigao 陳芷皋

Cheng Zongyi 程宗伊

Da ban niepan jing 大般涅槃經

dalu 大路

dama tema 大罵特罵

daren 大人

Da Yingguo zongli Yindu jiaoyu dachen 大英國總理印度教育大臣

da zhidu lun 大智度論

dai 帶

Dai Chengmo 戴承謨

daihui Yingguo 帶回英國

Dan Qi 單騎

dao 盜

daoqie xingcheng 盜竊性成

daotai 道台

de 得

Deng Jingwen 鄧竟文

di bu ai bao 地不愛寶

dieyou miling 疊有密令

Ding Wenjiang 丁文江

Dong Kang 董康

Duanfang 端方

Duan Yongen 段永恩

Enguang 恩光

Fan Yaonan 樊耀南

Feng Sizhi 馮司直

Feng Yuxiang 馮玉祥

Foshuo foming jing 佛說佛名經

futai 撫臺

gaoliang 高粱

gouhui yi bufen 購回一部分

Gu Jiegang 顧頡剛

guan 官

guanlan kaocha 觀覽考查

guoyu ruanruo 過於軟弱

Guwu baoguan weiyuanhui 古物保管委員會

guwu shi er da xiang 古物十二大相

Haiwangcun　海王村

Han Yaoguang　韓瑤光

hao dongxi　好東西

haogu duowen　好古多文

haogu shenxin　好古深心

He Jiadong　賀家棟

Heding xiansheng　赫定先生

hen　恨

Hong Ye　洪業

Hu Dianhua　胡莫華

Hu Hanmin　胡漢民

Hu Shi　胡適

Hu Wenbing　虎文炳

Huang Wenbi　黃文弼

huawen　華文

huo　獲

huzhao　護照

ji　寄

Jia Lu　賈魯

jiang ge jian nazhu bowuyuan　將各件納諸博物院

Jiang Menglin　蔣夢麟

Jiang shiye　蔣師爺

Jiang Xiaowan　蔣孝琬

Jin Chengyin　金承蔭

Jin Lun　金掄

Jin Shuren　金樹仁

jin yu ci duanjian　僅餘此斷簡

jingming lianda　精明練達

jizei　積賊

jue　掘

jue de guwu shen huo　掘得古物甚夥

jue qi jingying　擇其菁英

jueduo　攫奪

Kang Youwei　康有為

kaocha tuan　考查團

kaogu 考古

ke bei 可悲

ke hen 可恨

ke xi 可喜

kexi 可惜

kuikai 愧慨

lao pengyou 老朋友

laoye 老爺

Li Ji 李濟

Li Chenglin 李成林

Li Shengduo 李盛鐸

Li shiye 李師爺

Li Shurong 李樹榮

Li Yingshou 李應壽

Li Yougeng 李又庚

Liang Suwen 梁素文

Liankui 聯魁

lingren qinyang wuji 令人欽仰無極

Liu Bannong 劉半農

Liu Mo 劉謨

liunan zuzhi 留難阻滯

Liu Pingguo 劉平國

Liu Yanhuai 劉衍淮

liumang 流氓

Liusha fanggu ji 流沙訪古記

lunyi yi jin 渝夷以盡

Luo Zhenyu 羅振玉

luohan dong 羅漢洞

Ma Fuxing 馬福興

Ma Heng 馬衡

Ma Shaowu 馬紹武

Ma Xulun 馬叙倫

minzhu guo 民主國

Mu Shouqi 慕壽祺

Pan Zhen 潘震

Pan Zuhuan 潘祖煥

Pei Jingfu 裴景福

Pei Wenzhong 裴文中

Peng Xuzhan 彭緒瞻

putong youli huzhao 普通遊歷護照

qi ming ze wei E lingshi 其名則為俄領事

Qianfodong 千佛洞

qishi ji wei longduan zhi suo 其實即為壟斷之所

Qigong 啟功

Qin Fen 秦汾

Qinyu 秦浴

qu 取

rangbu 讓步

Rao Yingqi 饒應祺

shangyi yuan 上議院

Shen Jianshi 沈兼士

shiye 師爺

shi jue shi xian 時掘時現

Shoulengyan sanmei jing 首楞嚴三昧經

Song Xiaolian 宋小濂

suiyi wajue 隨意挖掘

Tang Yongshan 湯詠山

Tao Mingyue 陶明樾

ti 體

titai 提台

wa 挖

Waiwubu 外務部

Wan Rong 萬榮

Wang Guowei 王國維

Wang Jiayan 王家彥

Wang Jinren 王近仁

Wang Kangnian 汪康年

Wang Min 王憨

Wang Ruyi 王汝翼

Wang Shu'nan 王樹楠

Wang Yingqi   王迎琦

Wang Yuanlu   王圓籙

Wang Zhengting   王正廷

wei ren wenwen jinya, yi shi jiezhe   為人溫文謹雅, 亦是杰者

wei shijie ge guo suo bu xu   為世界各國所不許

Wen Lishan   文立山

wenhua qinlüe   文化侵略

Wu Aichen   吳藹宸

Wu Chaoshu   伍朝樞

Wu Jinding   吳金鼎

Wu Jingshan   吳靜山

Wu Peifu   吳佩孚

wubei   吾輩

wuren zhi dachi   吾人之大恥

xi   惜

xi ru xing feng   希如星鳳

Xixing riji   西行日記

Xi you ji   西遊記

xiayi yuan   下議院

xiaoshi   小事

xie   攜

Xie Bin   謝彬

xiequ   攜去

Xie Weixing   謝維興

Xinjiang fanggu lu   新疆訪古錄

Xinjiang tuzhi   新疆圖志

Xu Chengyao   許承堯

Xu Xusheng   徐旭生

Xu Yili   許以栗

Xuanzang   玄奘

xuewen pingchang   學問平常

xunfang guji   尋訪古蹟

yamen   衙門

Yang Jinbang   楊金榜

Yang Yiwen   楊繹闻

Yang Zengxin 楊增新

Yao Wenlin 姚文林

Ye Changchi 葉昌熾

yide baoyuan 以德報怨

yong 用

you Hua fanggu ji 游華訪古記

you lingren qinyang 尤令人欽仰

Yuan Dahua 袁大化

Yuan Fuli 袁復禮

Yuan Hongyou 袁鴻祐

Yuan Shikai 袁世凱

Yuan Tongli 袁同禮

Yuan Wenbai 袁文百

Yuan Yanxun 袁彥熏

yuanjing zhengshi 援經證史

yuanzhengdui 遠征隊

yun 運

Yun Yuding 惲毓鼎

Zailan 載瀾

Zeng Binghuang 曾炳爌

Zeng Liangsheng 曾良升

zhan bu dao da pianyi 佔不到大便宜

Zhang Fengjiu 張風九

Zhang Hongsheng 張鴻升

Zhang Huaiji 張懷寂

Zhang Ji 張繼

Zhang Jian 張騫

Zhang Shaobo 張紹伯

Zhang Shuyi 張叔伊

Zhang Xinhai 張歆海

Zhang Zaoguang 張璪光

Zhang Zuolin 張作霖

Zhao Weixi 趙惟熙

zhaoyue tuowei baohu 照約妥為保護

zhengui zhi pin 珍貴之品

zhentai   鎮台

zhengxiang gelie   爭相割裂

zhi zhi jian, xin zhi rui   志之堅, 心之銳

zhigan chajiu   致干查究

Zhongguo xueshu tuanti xiehui   中國學術團體協會

Zhonghua minzu   中華民族

Zhong Rui xibei kexue kaocha tuan   中瑞西北科學考查團

Zhu Ruichi   朱瑞墀

Zhuang Yongcheng   庄永成

INTRODUCTION

1. Diary entry, April 1, 1901, Stein Papers, ms. 193; and Stein, *Sand-Buried Ruins of Khotan*, 421.

2. Zhongguo Xinjiang Weiwuer zizhiqu dang'an guan and Riben fojiao daxue Niya yizhi xueshu yanjiu jigou, *Jindai waiguo tanxianjia Xinjiang kaogu dang'an shiliao*, 108–9.

3. Galambos, "Forgotten Chinese Translation," 56.

4. Letters (in Chinese) sent to Stein from Zhu Ruichi (October 30, 1908), Xie Weixing (August 2, 1908), Pan Zhen (one dated 1908 and three more undated), Dai Chengmo (December 6, 1913), and Li Shurong (October 1914), Stein Papers, mss. 341–42. My thanks to Ely Finch for his generous assistance in helping me produce a more accurate translation of Dai Chengmo's letter.

5. Zhongguo di er lishi dang'an guan, *Zhonghua minguo shi dang'an ziliao huibian*, vol. 5, no. 1 (wenhua), 688, 700–701.

6. For a scholarly overview of these expeditions, see Trümpler, *Das grosse Spiel*, 147–225. A somewhat less scholarly but far more accessible overview is Hopkirk, *Foreign Devils on the Silk Road*.

7. McClellan, *Inventing the Louvre*; and St. Clair, *Lord Elgin and the Marbles*. On the subtle measures adopted by the British Museum in the late eighteenth and early nineteenth centuries to ensure that only the well connected or well educated could gain admittance to the museum, see Colla, *Conflicted Antiquities*, 57–58; and Moser, *Wondrous Curiosities*, 53–54.

8. Hume, *Belzoni*; Evans, *Romancing the Maya*; Allen, *Finding the Walls of Troy*; Reid, *Whose Pharaohs?*; Shaw, *Possessors and Possessed*; and Goode, *Negotiating for the Past*.

9. Hume, *Belzoni*, 63; and Allen, *Discovering the Walls of Troy*.

10. Ray, *The Rosetta Stone and the Rebirth of Ancient Egypt*; Colla, *Conflicted Antiquities*, 53; Shaw, *Possessors and Possessed*; and Goode, *Negotiating for the Past*, 208.

11. Metcalf, *Ideologies of the Raj*, 148–50; and Evans, *Romancing the Maya*.

12. Le Coq, *Buried Treasures of Chinese Turkestan*, 79.

13. Stein, *Ruins of Desert Cathay*, 1:149; and diary entry, November 29, 1907, Stein Papers, ms. 200.

14. Letter to Allen, September 7, 1930, Stein Papers, ms. 21; and Skrine letter, October 21, 1924, quoted in Waugh, *Skrine at Kashgar*.

15. Pringle, *Master Plan*, 145–76; Colla, *Conflicted Antiquities*; Reid, *Whose Pharaohs?*; and Evans, *Romancing the Maya*.

16. Diary entry, August 12, 1908, Stein Papers, ms. 202; letter from Huntington to his sister Beth, December 22, 1905, Huntington Papers, box 1, folder 2; Pelliot, *Carnets de route*, 124; letter to Allen, June 9, 1907, Stein Papers, ms. 4; letter from Lorraine Warner to Edward Waldo Forbes, August 13, 1925, Forbes Papers (HC 2), folder 363; and letter from Keller to Stein, June 16, 1931, Stein Papers, ms. 22.

17. Huntington, *Civilization and Climate*, 16; and letter from Stein to Schomberg, September 14, 1940, Schomberg Papers, 2/53.

18. Letter from Paul H. Alling to Paul Sachs, November 2, 1943, Keller Papers, folder 53.

19. Letter to Andrews, October 1, 1907, Stein Papers, ms. 37; Mannerheim, *Across Asia from West to East*, 70–71; and Skrine letter, April 27, 1924, included in Waugh, *Skrine at Kashgar*. On the covert intelligence activities of Western archaeologists during the First and Second World Wars, see Harris and Sadler, *Archaeologist Was A Spy*; and Allen, *Classical Spies*.

20. Diary entry, November 2, 1907, Stein Papers, ms. 200.

21. Xie, *Xinjiang youji*, 99.

22. Stein, *Ancient Khotan*, 1:vii; and letter to Colonel G. D. Ogilvie, June 24, 1930, Stein Papers, ms. 21.

23. Skrine letter, September 22, 1923, included in Waugh, *Skrine at Kashgar*; and diary entry, April 23, 1901, Stein Papers, ms. 194.

24. Zhongguo Xinjiang Weiwuer zizhiqu dang'an guan et al., *Xinjiang yu E Su shangye maoyi dang'an shiliao*, 231.

25. Letter from Huntington to unidentified recipient, October 9, 1905, Huntington Papers, Series I, box 6, folder 63.

26. Stein, *Ruins of Desert Cathay*, 1:104.

27. Pelliot, "Trois ans dans le Haute Asie," 10. The Chinese-language passport issued by the Qing state for Stein's second expedition can be found in Stein Papers, ms. 283. It is dated to the eighth month of the thirty-first year of the reign of the Guangxu emperor [i.e., September 1905]. Pelliot's passport is reproduced in Giès, "Die Mission Pelliot (1906–1909)," 214; and Boxihe, *Boxihe Xiyu tanxian riji 1906–1908*, plate 2. For a more extended analysis of the diplomatic complications that foreign archaeologists presented to Qing officials in Xinjiang, see Jacobs, "Cultural Thieves or Political Liabilities?"

28. Wang, "Sitanyin di er ci Zhong Ya kaocha qijian suo chi Zhongguo huzhao jianxi," 76; Liu and Meng, *Dunhuang bai nian*, 1:72; and Wang, "Jiang Xiaowan wannian shiji kaoshi," 163.

29. Mirsky, *Sir Aurel Stein*, 204–5.

30. Goode, *Negotiating for the Past*.

31. Diary entry, January 12, 1901, Stein Papers, ms. 193; diary entry, April 23, 1901,

Stein Papers, ms. 194; diary entry for October 9, 1906, Stein Papers, ms. 197; diary entries, December 3, 5, 13, 1906, and January 17, 19, 1907, Stein Papers, ms. 198.

32. Diary entry, March 13, 1907, Stein Papers, ms. 198; letter to Allen, April 26, 1907, Stein Papers, ms. 4; diary entry, July 22, 1907, Stein Papers, ms. 199; diary entries, August 29, October 3, and October 20, 1907, Stein Papers, ms. 200; letter to Allen, May 12, 1908, Stein Papers, ms. 5; and letters (in Chinese) from Pan Zhen to Stein (undated), and Li Shurong to Stein, October 1914, Stein Papers, ms. 341–42.

33. Zhongguo Xinjiang Weiwuer zizhiqu dang'an guan and Riben fojiao daxue Niya yizhi xueshu yanjiu jigou, *Jindai waiguo tanxianjia Xinjiang kaogu dang'an shiliao*, 107–8.

34. Zhongguo Xinjiang Weiwuer zizhiqu dang'an guan and Riben fojiao daxue Niya yizhi xueshu yanjiu jigou, *Jindai waiguo tanxianjia Xinjiang kaogu dang'an shiliao*, 108.

35. For a full English translation of Wan Rong's preface, see Galambos, "A Forgotten Chinese Translation of the Preliminary Report of Aurel Stein's First Expedition," 56. For a complete facsimile reproduction of the entire Chinese translation, see Liu and Zhou, *Guojia tushuguan cang guji zhenben youji congkan*, 5:2423–524.

36. Liu and Zhou, *Guojia tushuguan cang guji zhenben youji congkan*, 5:2429.

37. Stein, *Preliminary Report*, 47.

38. Liu and Zhou, *Guojia tushuguan cang guji zhenben youji congkan*, 5:2487.

39. Stein, *Preliminary Report*, 69, 63, 69; and Liu and Zhou, *Guojia tushuguan cang guji zhenben youji congkan*, 5:2519, 2509, 2520.

40. Diary entry, November 11, 1907, Stein Papers, ms. 200; Pelliot, *Carnets de route*, 211; and diary entry, December 4, 1913, Stein Papers, ms. 215.

41. Chinese letters to Stein from Pan Zhen (1908 and one undated), Dai Chengmo (December 6, 1913), and Wang Min (1925), Stein Papers, ms. 341–42.

42. Letter (in Chinese) from Wang Min to Stein, 1925, Stein Papers, ms. 341–42; and Beijing daxue tushuguan and Shanghai guji chubanshe, *Beijing daxue tushuguan cang Dunhuang wenxian*, 1:124.

43. Wang Shu'nan, *Xinjiang fang gu lu*, 13, 36, 16, 20.

44. Mannerheim, *Across Asia from West to East*, 91–92; and Jacobs, "Cultural Thieves or Political Liabilities?"

45. See, for example, Mirsky, *Sir Aurel Stein: Archaeological Explorer*; Hopkirk, *Foreign Devils on the Silk Road*; Walker, *Aurel Stein: Pioneer of the Silk Road*; Kish, *To the Heart of Asia: The Life of Sven Hedin*; Whitfield, *Aurel Stein on the Silk Road*; Gallenkamp, *Dragon Hunter*; and Dreyer, *Abenteuer Seidenstrasse*. Many of these explorers and archaeologists also make cameo appearances in Meyer and Brysac, *Tournament of Shadows*; Meyer and Brysac, *China Collectors*; and Torma, *Turkestan-Expeditionen*.

46. Johansson, *Saluting the Yellow Emperor*; and Danielsson, *Explorer's Roadmap to National-Socialism*.

47. Balachandran, "Object Lessons."

48. Johansson, *Saluting the Yellow Emperor*, 56.

49. See, for example, Drège and Zink, *Paul Pelliot: De l'histoire à la légende*; Gumbrecht, "Chinese Passports for the German Turfan Expeditions"; Galambos, "Another Hungarian Looting China's Treasures?"; Galambos, "An English Boy in Chinese Turkestan"; Galambos, "Japanese Exploration of Central Asia"; Galambos, "A Forgotten

Chinese Translation of the Preliminary Report of Aurel Stein's First Expedition"; Jacobs, "Cultural Thieves or Political Liabilities?"; Jacobs, "Langdon Warner at Dunhuang: What Really Happened?"; Jacobs, "Huang Wenbi: Pioneer of Chinese Archaeology in Xinjiang"; and Jacobs, "Nationalist China's 'Great Game.'"

50. Reid, *Whose Pharaohs?*; Reid, *Contesting Antiquity in Egypt*; Colla, *Conflicted Antiquities*; Shaw, *Possessors and Possessed*; and Goode, *Negotiating for the Past.*

51. Cannadine, *Ornamentalism*; and Pringle, *The Master Plan*, 145–46.

52. Banner, *How the Indians Lost Their Land.*

53. St. Clair, *Lord Elgin and the Marbles*, 88; Shaw, *Possessors and Possessed*, 133; and Jasanoff, *Edge of Empire*, 305.

54. Brown, *Pastimes*; and Ebrey, *Accumulating Culture.*

55. Wu, *Story of Ruins*, 13–91.

56. Wu, *Story of Ruins*, 13–91.

57. Wang, "Qing Imperial Collection, circa 1905–25," 322.

58. See Pelliot, *Carnets de route.* Pelliot's diary has also been translated into Chinese as Boxihe, *Boxihe Xiyu tanxian riji 1906–1908.*

59. Sommer, *Sex, Law, and Society in Late Imperial China*; Sommer, *Polyandry and Wife-Selling in Qing Dynasty China*; and Hegel, *True Crimes in Eighteenth-Century China.*

60. Diary entries, December 14–15, 1906, Stein Papers, ms. 198; and diary entry, April 13, 1907, Stein Papers, ms. 199.

61. Pelliot, *Carnets de route*, 34–35, 119, 130.

62. Letter to Allen, December 2, 1907, Stein Papers, ms. 4; letter to Allen, January 15, 1915, Stein Papers, ms. 13; and Popova, "S. F. Oldenburg's First Russian Turkestan Expedition," 153.

63. Pelliot, *Carnets de route*, 254–55.

64. Letter from Huntington to unidentified recipient, October 30, 1905, Huntington Papers, Series I, box 6, folder 63.

65. Diary entry, July 14, 1907, Stein Papers, ms. 199.

66. Le Coq, *Buried Treasures of Chinese Turkestan*, 75–76; and letter from Huntington to unidentified recipient, March 14, 1906, Huntington Papers, Series I, box 6, folder 65.

67. The Uyghur-language materials can be found in Stein Papers, ms. 341–42. I am grateful to David Brophy and Jun Sugawara for their generous assistance in helping me to understand the content of these documents.

CHAPTER ONE

1. Pelliot, *Carnets de route*, 89, 92, 365.

2. Popova, "Russian Expeditions to Central Asia," 45, 20; diary entry, January 15, 1908, Stein Papers, ms. 201; and Xie, *Xinjiang youji*, 266.

3. Diary entries, October 29, 1914; January 20, 1915; January 19, 1915; November 2, 1914; and February 1, 1915, Stein Papers, ms. 216.

4. Diary entry, October 4, 1906, Stein Papers, ms. 197; diary entry, January 22, 1901, Stein Papers, ms. 193; and Pelliot, *Carnets de route*, 376.

5. Le Coq, *Buried Treasures of Chinese Turkestan*, 58–59; diary entry, December 13, 1907, Stein Papers, ms. 200; diary entry, January 19, 1908, Stein Papers, ms. 201; diary entry, November 16, 1914, Stein Papers, ms. 216; Xu, *Xu Xusheng xiyou riji*, 182; and Beijing daxue tushuguan and Shanghai guji chubanshe, *Beijing daxue tushuguan cang Dunhuang wenxian*, 1:126.

6. Tugusheva, "Expeditions to Central Asia and the Discovery of Early Medieval Turkic Manuscripts," 42; Popova, "Russian Expeditions to Central Asia," 29; letter from Edward Waldo Forbes to Langdon Warner, September 2, 1924, Forbes Papers (HC 2), folder 2053; diary entry, April 5, 1915, Stein Papers, ms. 217; Xu, *Xu Xusheng xiyou riji*, 182; and Huang, *Huang Wenbi Meng Xin kaocha riji*, 514–15.

7. Thum, *Sacred Routes of Uyghur History*, 38.

8. Huang, *Huang Wenbi Meng Xin kaocha riji*, 279; and Le Coq, *Buried Treasures of Chinese Turkestan*, 152.

9. Pelliot, *Carnets de route*, 364, 122–23; and letter to Allen, November 12, 1914, Stein Papers, ms. 11.

10. Pelliot, *Carnets de route*, 364.

11. Skrine letter, November 26, 1922, quoted in Waugh, *Skrine at Kashgar*; and diary entry, April 25, 1901, Stein Papers, ms. 194.

12. Le Coq, *Buried Treasures of Chinese Turkestan*, 84–85.

13. Letter to Allen, October 10, 1906, Stein Papers, ms. 3; and diary entry, November 3, 1914, Stein Papers, ms. 216.

14. Pelliot, *Carnets de route*, 186, 90; and diary entry, December 22, 1907, Stein Papers, ms. 200.

15. Diary entry, January 28, 1901, Stein Papers, ms. 193; and Pelliot, *Carnets de route*, 123, 364, 89.

16. Stein, "Explorations in Central Asia, 1906–8," 16. On the phrase "subsistence diggers," see Matsude, "Subsistence Diggers."

17. Letter from Huntington to his sister Beth, February 19, 1905, Huntington Papers, box 1, folder 1.

18. Letter from Huntington to unidentified recipient, June 22, 1905, Huntington Papers, Series I, box 6, folder 62; and letter from Huntington to unidentified recipient, July 10, 1905, Huntington Papers, box 1, folder 1.

19. Diary entry, September 24, 1930, Stein Papers, ms. 224; letter from Huntington to unidentified recipient, July 9, 1905, Huntington Papers, Series I, box 6, folder 62; letters from Huntington to unidentified recipients, October 9, 1905 and February 2, 1906, Huntington Papers, Series I, box 6, folder 63; diary entry, September 14, 1907, Stein Papers, ms. 200; letter from Huntington to unidentified recipient, July 10, 1905, Huntington Papers, box 1, folder 1; and diary entry, April 4, 1907, Stein Papers, ms. 199.

20. Letters from Huntington to unidentified recipients, July 2, 1905, and July 22, 1905, Huntington Papers, Series I, box 6, folder 62.

21. Skrine, *Chinese Central Asia*, 94; letter from Huntington to unidentified recipient, June 27, 1905, Huntington Papers, box 1, folder 1; letter from Huntington to unidentified recipient, March 14, 1906, Huntington Papers, Series I, box 6, folder 65; letter from Huntington to unidentified recipient, October 12, 1905, Huntington Papers, Series I, box 6, folder 63; and Hedin, *History of the Expedition in Asia*, 1:250–1.

22. Letter from Huntington to unidentified recipient, June 27, 1905, Huntington Papers, box 1, folder 1; letter from Huntington to unidentified recipient, December 22, 1905, Huntington Papers, Series I, box 6, folder 63; and letter from Huntington to unidentified recipient, July 2, 1905, Huntington Papers, Series I, box 6, folder 62.

23. Pelliot, *Carnets de route*, 186, 171; and letter (in Chinese) from Zhu Ruichi to Stein, October 30, 1908, Stein Papers, ms. 341–42.

24. Letter from Huntington to unidentified recipient, March 14, 1906, Huntington Papers, Series I, box 6, folder 65.

25. Letter to Allen, September 14, 1906, Stein Papers, ms. 3; diary entry, April 5, 1908, Stein Papers, ms. 201; diary entry, December 6, 1913, Stein Papers, ms. 215; diary entry, December 23, 1914, Stein Papers, ms. 216; diary entry, May 5, 1915, Stein Papers, ms. 217; and diary entry, September 27, 1930, Stein Papers, ms. 224.

26. Diary entry, July 17, 1908, Stein Papers, ms. 202; diary entry, April 2, 1901, Stein Papers, ms. 193; Mannerheim, *Across Asia from West to East*, 102–3; letter from Huntington to unidentified recipient, July 10, 1905, Huntington Papers, box 1, folder 1; and Pelliot, *Carnets de route*, 234–35. The letter from Sir Kander Khan is included in the Stein papers at the Bodleian Library at Oxford; regrettably, I can not identify from which file it emerged.

27. Letter from Huntington to unidentified recipient, October 12, 1905, Huntington Papers, Series I, box 6, folder 63.

28. Pelliot, *Carnets de route*, 35, 83, 130; and diary entry, December 26, 1907, Stein Papers, ms. 200.

29. Letter to Allen, April 28, 1907, Stein Papers, ms. 4; and Quirke, *Hidden Hands*, 59, 101.

30. Diary entries, December 5, 10, 1906 and February 4, 1907, Stein Papers, ms. 198; and diary entry, January 27, 1908, Stein Papers, ms. 201.

31. Mannerheim, *Across Asia from West to East*, 184, 227; diary entry, June 9, 1908, Stein Papers, ms. 202; diary entry, October 14, 1914, Stein Papers, ms. 216; and diary entry, March 12, 1907, Stein Papers, ms. 198. My thanks to Imre Galambos for providing a transcription and translation of the Hungarian word "kvártélyozás."

32. Mannerheim, *Across Asia from West to East*, 184, 426–27; diary entry, October 15, 1914, Stein Papers, ms. 216; diary entry, March 23, 1907, Stein Papers, ms. 198; and Pelliot, *Carnets de route*, 44. For Stein's detailed account books, see Stein Papers, mss. 364, 366.

33. Pelliot, *Carnets de route*, 30, 95.

34. Le Coq, *Buried Treasures of Chinese Turkestan*, 147, 65; Xie, *Xinjiang youji*, 224; and Pelliot, *Carnets de route*, 18.

35. Pelliot, *Carnets de route*, 67; Wang, "Boxihe yu Pei Jingfu de jiaowang," 430; diary entry, December 26, 1907, Stein Papers, ms. 200; letter to Mrs. Allen, July 27, 1908, Stein Papers, ms. 5; and diary entries, June 28, July 4, June 16, 1914, Stein Papers, ms. 216.

36. Letter from Andrews to J. P. Morgan, November 9, 1921, Andrews Papers, C446, 1921–1930, box 1, folder 8; diary entries, February 14, 1931, and March 17–19, 1931, Stein Papers, ms. 224; and Hedin, *History of the Expedition in Asia*, 1:250.

37. Pelliot, *Carnets de route*, 62; and diary entry, April 1, 1901, Stein Papers, ms. 193.

38. Diary entry, September 26, 1914, Stein Papers, ms. 216; letter from Huntington to unidentified recipient, December 22, 1905, Huntington Papers, box 1, folder 2; letter to Allen, December 17, 1906, Stein Papers, ms. 3; and letter to Allen, August 21, 1907, Stein Papers, ms. 4.

39. Pelliot, *Carnets de route*, 83, 29; Walker, *Aurel Stein: Pioneer of the Silk Road*, 59; and diary entry, September 12, 1913, Stein Papers, ms. 215.

40. Diary entry, January 8, 1908, Stein Papers, ms. 201; letter to Allen, January 11, 1908, Stein Papers, ms. 5; and diary entry, November 9, 1914, Stein Papers, ms. 216.

41. Le Coq, *Buried Treasures of Chinese Turkestan*, 129; Hedin's fatal trek is retold in Kish, *To the Heart of Asia*, 45–47. Stein's conversation with Kasim is documented in a November 15, 1913, diary entry, Stein Papers, ms. 215.

42. Diary entries, March 5 and January 31, 1908, Stein Papers, ms. 201; diary entry, July 29, 1907, Stein Papers, ms. 199; and diary entry, July 13, 1914, Stein Papers, ms. 216.

43. Diary entry, November 18, 1930, Stein Papers, ms. 224; Pelliot, *Carnets de route*, 20; and diary entry, February 18, 1907, Stein Papers, ms. 198. The interview with the elderly man who recalled guiding Stein to the Niya ruins in 1906 is included in "Across the Taklmakan Desert," episode 6 of the jointly produced CCTV-NHK *Silk Road* documentary series.

44. Diary entry, December 6, 1906, Stein Papers, ms. 198; diary entry, September 10, 1907, Stein Papers, ms. 200; and diary entry, October 17, 1913, Stein Papers, ms. 215.

45. Regarding the name of "Li Yuansun," I have only been able to find one mention of his given name in all of Stein's diaries, letters, and other papers. In his diary entry for September 24, 1913 (Stein Papers, ms. 215), Stein wrote that during the morning he had settled arrangements "with Chiang's substitute Li Yuan Sun, a quiet little man in quaint Europe clothes." Thereafter, Stein always refers to Li by some orthographic variant of "Li ssu-yeh" (*Li shiye*, or "Secretary Li"). Stein does not provide the Chinese characters for Li's name, nor does any Chinese-language documentation regarding his association with Stein survive. It is impossible to know, of course, whether Stein, whose grasp of Chinese was shaky, accurately transcribed Li's name or not. Even if he did, "Yuansun" could have been Li's courtesy name rather than his given name. The Chinese historian Wang Jiqing claims to have found mention in Stein's papers of one "Li Zhuohua," which he believes may be the true identity of Secretary Li. Since Wang himself admits there is no way to confirm or deny his theory (nor does he reveal the source of this name in Stein's papers), I have opted to use the form of Li's name as recorded in Stein's diary entry in 1913. On Wang Jiqing's theory, see Wang, *Sitanyin di si ci Zhongguo kaogu riji kaoshi*, 275–76.

46. Diary entry, December 27, 1913, Stein Papers, ms. 215; diary entry, March 27, 1914, Stein Papers, ms. 216; letter to Allen, April 13, 1914, Stein Papers, ms. 11; diary entries, November 19, 1914 and April 7, 1914, Stein Papers, ms. 216; and diary entry, June 17, 1915, Stein Papers, ms. 217.

47. Diary entries, June 20–21, 1907, Stein Papers, ms. 199.

48. Diary entry, April 29, 1907, Stein Papers, ms. 199; diary entry, January 1, 1914, Stein Papers, ms. 215; and diary entry, February 12, 1908, Stein Papers, ms. 201.

49. Diary entry, May 16, 1915, Stein Papers, ms. 217; diary entry, December 14, 1906, Stein Papers, ms. 198; Stein, *Sand-Buried Ruins of Khotan*, 383; and Pelliot, *Carnets de route*, 20, 293.

50. Pelliot, *Carnets de route*, 64, 89, 364; and diary entry, October 17, 1913, Stein Papers, ms. 215.

51. Letter to Allen, August 27, 1906, Stein Papers, ms. 3; and letter to Allen, April 28, 1907, Stein Papers, ms. 4.

52. Pelliot, *Carnets de route*, 139.

53. Letter to Allen, June 9, 1907, Stein Papers, ms. 4; Wang, "Jiang Xiaowan wannian shiji kaoshi," 162; letter from Skrine to Stein, September 17, 1922, Stein Papers, ms. 107; and diary entry, August 11, 1930, Stein Papers, ms. 224.

CHAPTER TWO

1. Letter (in Chinese) from Prince Zailan to Pelliot, September 7, 1908, Pelliot Papers, box 79; and Pelliot, "Trois ans dans la Haute Asie," 12.

2. Pelliot, *Carnets de route*, 254–55.

3. Ebrey, *Accumulating Culture*; Brown, *Pastimes*; Jang, "Culture of Art Collecting in Imperial China"; and Lawton, *Time of Transition*.

4. Donnelly, *Journey through Chinese Hell*, 12; letter from Edward Waldo Forbes to Langdon Warner, September 2, 1924, Forbes Papers (HC 2), folder 2053; and Huang, *Huang Wenbi Meng Xin kaocha riji*, 279.

5. Pelliot, *Carnets de route*, 66–67, 139.

6. Letters to Allen, August 16, 1907, and October 14, 1907, Stein Papers, ms. 4; and unpublished and undated personal narrative for Stein's visit to Shanghai and Nanjing to secure a passport for his fourth expedition, Stein Papers, ms. 264.

7. Diary entry, September 30, 1913, Stein Papers, ms. 215; and Mannerheim, *Across Asia from West to East*, 84.

8. Galambos, "A Forgotten Chinese Translation of the Preliminary Report of Aurel Stein's First Expedition," 56–57.

9. Xie, *Xinjiang youji*, 92; and diary entry, March 29, 1901, Stein Papers, ms. 193.

10. Diary entry, August 3, 1900, Stein Papers, ms. 192; diary entry, May 5, 1915, Stein Papers, ms. 217; diary entry, June 30, 1906, Stein Papers, ms. 196; diary entry, June 16, 1907, Stein Papers, ms. 199; and Huang, *Huang Wenbi Meng Xin kaocha riji*, 326, 478, 484.

11. Letter to Allen, December 2, 1907, Stein Papers, ms. 4; letter to Mrs. Allen, January 28, 1908, Stein Papers, ms. 5; and letter to Allen, January 16, 1908, Stein Papers, ms. 5.

12. Wang, *Xinjiang fang gu lu*, 9, 13; and Xie, Xinjiang youji, 89.

13. Mannerheim, *Across Asia from West to East*, 400; Gansu cang Dunhuang wenxian bianweihui et al., *Gansu cang Dunhuang wenxian*, 3:326; and Dan, "Xinjiang lüxing ji," 2724.

14. Shanghai guji chubanshe et al., *Shanghai bowuguan cang Dunhuang Tulufan wenxian*, 1:113; Galambos, "An English Boy in Chinese Turkestan," 95; and Zhongguo shudian cang Dunhuang wenxian bian weihui, *Zhongguo shudian cang Dunhuang wenxian*, 79.

15. Yang, "Yang Zengxin deng suo cang liang jian Tulufan Dunhuang xiejing," 43; and diary entries, November 16, 1914, January 19–20, 1915, and January 22, 1915, Stein Papers, ms. 216.

16. Diary entries, September 27, 1913 and December 2, 4, 1913, Stein Papers, ms. 215.

17. Ebrey, *Accumulating Culture*.

18. Pelliot, *Carnets de route*, 279. On the early dispersal of Dunhuang manuscripts among Qing officials of Xinjiang and Gansu, see Rong, *Eighteen Lectures on Dunhuang*, 79–108.

19. Rong, *Eighteen Lectures on Dunhuang*, 90. On Ye Changchi's involvement with the Dunhuang manuscripts, including revealing excerpts from his diary, see Li, "Lun Dunhuang shibao ji Ye Changchi 'Yuan Dulu riji chao,'" 36–39; Cai, "Ye Changchi yu Dunhuang wenwu bushuo," 95–103; and Rong, "Ye Changchi: Pioneer of Dunhuang Studies," 1–4.

20. Facsimiles of the modern Chinese colophons appended to ancient manuscripts from Dunhuang and Turfan can be found in five multivolume collections published in China over the past thirty years. These include manuscripts that ended up in the Shanghai Museum, Peking University Library, the Tianjin Municipal Museum of Art, various institutions in Gansu, and the China Bookstore conglomerate in Beijing. See Shanghai guji chubanshe and Shanghai bowuguan, *Shanghai bowuguan cang Dunhuang Tulufan wenxian*; Beijing daxue tushuguan and Shanghai guji chubanshe, *Beijing daxue tushuguan cang Dunhuang wenxian*; Shanghai guji chubanshe and Tianjin shi yishu bowugua, *Tianjin shi yishu bowuguan cang Dunhuang wenxian*; and Gansu cang Dunhuang wenxian bianweihui, Gansu renmin chubanshe, and Gansu sheng wenwu ju, *Gansu cang Dunhuang wenxian*.

21. For a more complete analysis of the content of these colophons, see Jacobs, "An Analysis of Modern Chinese Colophons on the Dunhuang Manuscripts."

22. Beijing daxue tushuguan and Shanghai guji chubanshe, *Beijing daxue tushuguan cang Dunhuang wenxian*, 1:124.

23. Beijing daxue tushuguan and Shanghai guji chubanshe, *Beijing daxue tushuguan cang Dunhuang wenxian*, 1:124–27; Shanghai guji chubanshe and Tianjin shi yishu bowuguan, *Tianjin shi yishu bowuguan cang Dunhuang wenxian*, 5:162; Beijing daxue tushuguan and Shanghai guji chubanshe, *Beijing daxue tushuguan cang Dunhuang wenxian*, 1:67; and Shanghai guji chubanshe and Shanghai bowuguan, *Shanghai bowuguan cang Dunhuang Tulufan wenxian*, 1:60–61.

24. Shanghai guji chubanshe and Shanghai bowuguan, *Shanghai bowuguan cang Dunhuang Tulufan wenxian*, 1:199, 61.

25. Shanghai guji chubanshe and Shanghai bowuguan, *Shanghai bowuguan cang Dunhuang Tulufan wenxian*, 1:92–93.

26. Gansu cang Dunhuang wenxian bianweihui, Gansu renmin chubanshe, and Gansu sheng wenwu ju, *Gansu cang Dunhuang wenxian*, 3:152; Gansu cang Dunhuang wenxian bianweihui, Gansu renmin chubanshe, and Gansu sheng wenwu ju, *Gansu cang Dunhuang wenxian*, 5:308; Gansu cang Dunhuang wenxian bianweihui, Gansu renmin chubanshe, and Gansu sheng wenwu ju, *Gansu cang Dunhuang wenxian*, 2:176; and Shanghai guji chubanshe and Shanghai bowuguan, *Shanghai bowuguan cang Dunhuang Tulufan wenxian*, 1:199–200.

27. Dewey, *Letters from China and Japan*, 195; and Beijing daxue tushuguan and Shanghai guji chubanshe, *Beijing daxue tushuguan cang Dunhuang wenxian*, 1:124–25.

28. Gansu cang Dunhuang wenxian bianweihui, Gansu renmin chubanshe, and Gansu sheng wenwu ju, *Gansu cang Dunhuang wenxian*, 3:326; Shanghai guji chubanshe and Shanghai bowuguan, *Shanghai bowuguan cang Dunhuang Tulufan wenxian*, 1:113; Gansu cang Dunhuang wenxian bianweihui, Gansu renmin chubanshe, and Gansu sheng wenwu ju, *Gansu cang Dunhuang wenxian*, 3:152; Beijing daxue tushuguan and Shanghai guji chubanshe, *Beijing daxue tushuguan cang Dunhuang wenxian*, 1:66–67; and Yang, "Yang Zengxin deng suo cang liang jian Tulufan Dunhuang xiejing," 43.

29. Shanghai guji chubanshe and Shanghai bowuguan, *Shanghai bowuguan cang Dunhuang Tulufan wenxian*, 2:246; and Beijing daxue tushuguan and Shanghai guji chubanshe, *Beijing daxue tushuguan cang Dunhuang wenxian*, 1:125.

30. Shanghai guji chubanshe and Shanghai bowuguan, *Shanghai bowuguan cang Dunhuang Tulufan wenxian*, 1:60, 113; and Bowie, *Langdon Warner through His Letters*, 118.

31. Gansu cang Dunhuang wenxian bianweihui, Gansu renmin chubanshe, and Gansu sheng wenwu ju, *Gansu cang Dunhuang wenxian*, 5:308.

32. Pocketbook entry, April 22, 1930, Stein Papers, ms. 250; Beijing daxue tushuguan and Shanghai guji chubanshe, *Beijing daxue tushuguan cang Dunhuang wenxian*, 1:126–27.

33. Elliot and Shambaugh, *Odyssey of China's Imperial Art Treasures*, 56–66.

34. Lawton, *Time of Transition*; and Netting, *Perpetual Fire*, 94–95.

35. Jing, "The Genesis of the Academic Library in China," 161–74.

36. Letter (in Chinese) from Pan Zhen to Stein, undated, Stein Papers, ms. 341–42.

37. Letters (in Chinese) from Pan Zhen (undated) and Wang Min to Stein (1925), Stein Papers, ms. 341–42; and letter (in Chinese) from Prince Zailan to Pelliot, September 7, 1908, Pelliot Papers, box 79.

38. Diary entry, March 5–6, 1901, Stein Papers, ms. 193; Pelliot, *Carnets de route*, 355; diary entry, September 9, 1907, Stein Papers, ms. 200; diary entry, May 19, 1907, Stein Papers, ms. 199; Pelliot, *Carnets de route*, 117, 183; letter to Allen, October 5, 1914, Stein Papers, ms. 11; and letter to Macartney, December 6, 1913, Stein Papers, ms. 96.

39. Diary entry, June 30, 1906, Stein Papers, ms. 196; and Pelliot, *Carnets de route*, 67.

40. Xie, *Xinjiang youji*, 253, 170.

41. Wang, *Xinjiang fang gu lu*, 20; and Wu and Pan, *Zhongguo jiaguxue shi*, 11–12.

42. Luo, "Dunhuang shishi shumu ji faxian zhi yuanshi," 46; Xie, *Xinjiang youji*, 231; and Wang, *Xinjiang fang gu lu*, 20.

43. Beijing daxue tushuguan and Shanghai guji chubanshe, *Beijing daxue tushuguan cang Dunhuang wenxian*, 1:124–26. Yun Yuding's diary entry is reproduced in Rong and Wang, "Paul Pelliot en Chine" (original Chinese text kindly provided by Wang).

44. Letter from Luo Zhenyu to Wang Kangnian is reproduced in Rong and Wang, "Paul Pelliot en Chine" (original Chinese text kindly provided by Wang).

45. On Pelliot's subsequent trip to the eastern seaboard on the conclusion of his expedition in Xinjiang and Gansu, see Wang, "Boxihe 1909 nian Beijing zhi xing xiangguan riqi bianzheng," 139–44; and Rong and Wang, "Paul Pelliot en Chine (1906–1909)."

On Pelliot's relationship with Chinese scholars, see Wang, "Boxihe yu Pei Jingfu de jiaowang," 427–50.

46. Pelliot, "Trois ans dans la Haute Asie," 15; Luo, *Liusha fang gu ji*, 37; and Shanghai guji chubanshe and Shanghai bowuguan, *Shanghai bowuguan cang Dunhuang Tulufan wenxian*, 1:60–61.

47. Rowe, *Saving the World*, 298.

CHAPTER THREE

1. Galambos, "A Forgotten Chinese Translation of the Preliminary Report of Aurel Stein's First Expedition," 56–57.

2. For a detailed study of the implementation of the "New Policies" in Xinjiang, see Qi, "Lun Qingmo Xinjiang 'xinzheng,'" 31–39.

3. Pelliot, *Carnets de route*, 214, 305; Mannerheim, *Across Asia from West to East*, 63–64, 83–84; and diary entry, March 31, 1908, Stein Papers, ms. 201.

4. Diary entry, June 5, 1908, Stein Papers, ms. 202; Pelliot, *Carnets de route*, 115; diary entry, April 11, 1931, Stein Papers, ms. 224; and Xu, *Xu Xusheng xiyou riji*, 169.

5. Letter from Huntington to unidentified recipient, March 14, 1906, Huntington Papers, Series I, box 6, folder 65; Pelliot, *Carnets de route*, 42; and Mannerheim, *Across Asia from West to East*, 491.

6. Mannerheim, *Across Asia from West to East*, 114; diary entries, October 19, 1907, November 18, 1907, Stein Papers, ms. 200; diary entries, May 6, 1908, June 4, 1908, May 4, 1908, Stein Papers, ms. 202; and letter to Allen, May 12, 1908, Stein Papers, ms. 5.

7. Galambos, "An English Boy in Chinese Turkestan," 94; diary entry, December 4, 1913, Stein Papers, ms. 215; and letters to Andrews, October 27, 1914 and January 13, 1915, Stein Papers, ms. 42.

8. Pelliot, *Carnets de route*, 148, 316.

9. Diary entries, March 25, 28, 1908, Stein Papers, ms. 201; letter to Allen, March 31, 1908, Stein Papers, ms. 5; and diary entry, May 16, 1908, Stein Papers, ms. 202.

10. Diary entry, December 19, 1913, Stein Papers, ms. 215; diary entries, May 15, 27, 1931, Stein Papers, ms. 225; and letter to Allen, June 5, 1931, Stein Papers, ms. 22.

11. Rowe, *Saving the World*, 297; and Schluessel, "Muslim Emperor of China," 89–90.

12. Letters to Allen, February 15, 1915, and January 15, 1915, Stein Papers, ms. 13; and letters to Andrews, February 6, 1915 and January 3, 1915, Stein Papers, ms. 42.

13. Letters to Allen, September 10, 1907, and August 16, 1907, Stein Papers, ms. 4; diary entry, August 12, 1908, Stein Papers, ms. 202; and Pelliot, *Carnets de route*, 121, 124.

14. Letter from Pan Zuhuan to Stein, December 19, 1929, Keller Papers, Series II, folder 114.

15. Letter from Stein to Pan Zuhuan, March 1, 1930, Keller Papers, Series II, folder 114; diary entry, September 19, 1907, Stein Papers, ms. 200; letter to Allen, July 15, 1908, Stein Papers, ms. 37; diary entry, October 19, 1907, Stein Papers, ms. 200; and letter from Stein to Carl Keller, June 21, 1930, Keller Papers, Series I, folder 3 of 6.

16. Le Coq, *Buried Treasures of Chinese Turkestan,* 150; and letters from Stein to Carl Keller, August 2, 1930, from Keller to Stein, May 6, 1930, and from Keller to Stein, June 12, 1930, Keller Papers, Series I, folder 29, subfolder 3 of 6; and letter from Sir Aurel Stein to Carl Keller, January 14, 1932, Sachs Papers (HC 3), folder 1052.

17. Letter to Allen, March 5, 1907, Stein Papers, ms. 4; diary entry, March 21, 1907, Stein Papers, ms. 198; diary entry, September 1, 1907, Stein Papers, ms. 200; diary entry, June 5, 1908, Stein Papers, ms. 202; letter to Allen, May 12, 1908, Stein Papers, ms. 5; and letter from Huntington to unidentified recipient, February 25, 1906, Huntington Papers, Series I, box 6, folder 63.

18. Wang, "1907 nian Sitanyin yu Wang Yuanlu ji Dunhuang guanyuan zhijian de jiaowang," 62; and Huangfu, "Internalizing the West," 21.

19. Letter from Huntington to unidentified recipient, July 10, 1905, Huntington Papers, box 1, folder 1; letter to Allen, April 9, 1907, Stein Papers, ms. 4; Pelliot, *Carnets de route,* 312; and Mannerheim, *Across Asia from West to East,* 81–82.

20. Mannerheim, *Across Asia from West to East,* 114; Pelliot, *Carnets de route,* 261, 101, 236; diary entry, October 19, 1907, Stein Papers, ms. 200; and China Expedition journal of Alan Priest, Feburary 20, 1925, Forbes Papers (HC 2), folder 1659.

21. Diary entry, May 5, 1908, Stein Papers, ms. 202; letters (in Chinese) from Xie Weixing and Zhu Ruichi to Stein, Stein Papers, ms. 341–42; and diary entry, December 30, 1914, Stein Papers, ms. 216.

22. Diary entry, July 27, 1907, Stein Papers, ms. 199; diary entry, September 16, 1907, Stein Papers, ms. 200; diary entry, May 5, 1908, Stein Papers, ms. 202; and Pelliot, *Carnets de route,* 208.

23. Pelliot, *Carnets de route,* 43, 116–17, 96, 208.

24. Diary entry, December 5, 1906, Stein Papers, ms. 198; diary entry, April 6, 1908, Stein Papers, ms. 201; diary entry, January 9, 1914, Stein Papers, ms. 215; diary entry, July 3, 1914, Stein Papers, ms. 216; diary entries, April 15, 1915 and March 27, 1915, Stein Papers, ms. 217; and diary entry, July 15, 1914, Stein Papers, ms. 216.

25. Diary entry, September 15, 1906, Stein Papers, ms. 197; diary entries, August 25, 1907, September 9–10, 1907, and October 8, 1907, Stein Papers, ms. 200; Mannerheim, *Across Asia from West to East,* 83, 492; letter from Huntington to unidentified recipient, July 16, 1905, Huntington Papers, box 1, folder 1; letter from Huntington to unidentified recipient, July 22, 1905, Huntington Papers, series I, box 6, folder 62; and Mannerheim, *Across Asia from West to East,* 114.

26. Diary entry, May 18, 1915, Stein Papers, ms. 217; diary entry, June 24, 1914, Stein Papers, ms. 216; letter from Huntington to unidentified recipient, July 16, 1905, Huntington Papers, box 1, folder 1; diary entry, April 6, 1908, Stein Papers, ms. 201; and diary entry, May 20, 1915, Stein Papers, ms. 217.

27. Skrine letters, September 23, 1923, and October 1, 1923, included in Waugh, *Skrine at Kashgar.*

28. Letter to Allen, October 12, 1900, Stein Papers, ms. 1; letter from Huntington to unidentified recipient, July 16, 1905, Huntington Papers, box 1, folder 1; letter to Andrews, September 14, 1906, Stein Papers, ms. 37; letter to Allen, June 19, 1906, Stein Papers, ms. 3; diary entry, June 30, 1906, Stein Papers, ms. 196; and diary entry, January 7, 1931, Stein Papers, ms. 224.

29. Mannerheim, *Across Asia from West to East*, 82–83, 63–64; diary entries for June 12, 1907 and July 23, 1907, Stein Papers, ms. 199; diary entry, December 30, 1913, Stein Papers, ms. 215; and diary entry, November 22, 1930, Stein Papers, ms. 224.

30. Schomberg, "A Second Turkestan Diary, 1930–1931," 30, Schomberg Papers, box 14, unpublished manuscript; diary entries, October 6, 1914, and December 26, 1914, Stein Papers, ms. 216; and diary entry, Mary 19, 1915, Stein Papers, ms. 217.

31. Diary entries, December 1, 1930, and November 18, 1930, Stein Papers, ms. 224; diary entries for May 2, 17, 1931, Stein Papers, ms. 225; and diary entry, May 4, 1908, Stein Papers, ms. 202.

32. Letter (in Chinese) from Wang Min to Stein, 1925, Stein Papers, ms. 341–42; and letter from Pan to Stein, 1930, Stein Papers, ms. 21.

33. Letters (in Chinese) to Stein from Wang Min (1925), Li Shurong (October 1914), and Zhu Ruichi (1908), Stein Papers, ms. 341–42. On the literary conventions deployed in earlier eras, see Zhang, *Transformative Journeys*.

34. Skrine, *Chinese Central Asia*, 115, 256; and letter from Ibrahim Beg to Skrine, February 2, 1924, Stein Papers, ms. 97.

35. Mannerheim, *Across Asia from West to East*, 444; and diary entry, October 30, 1907, Stein Papers, ms. 200.

36. Pelliot, *Carnets de route*, 88, 96; Mannerheim, *Across Asia from West to East*, 492; and letter (in Chinese) from Liankui to the French embassy, October 13, 1907, Pelliot Papers, box 55.

37. Diary entry, May 4, 1930, Stein Papers, ms. 224; and letters from Wu to Stein, September 14, 1939 and January 22, 1940, Stein Papers, ms. 112.

38. Diary entry, October 21, 1907, Stein Papers, ms. 200; Pelliot, *Carnets de route*, 237; diary entry, June 14, 1908, Stein Papers, ms. 202; and letters (in Chinese) to Stein from Pan Zhen (undated), Wang Min (1925), Xie Weixing (August 2, 1908), and Li Shurong (October 1914), Stein Papers, ms. 341–42.

39. Pelliot, *Carnets de route*, 103, 156, 321.

40. Diary entry, June 12, 1907, Stein Papers, ms. 199; diary entries, October 7, 1914, and December 27, 1914, Stein Papers, ms. 216; Skrine letter, August 14, 1922, included in Waugh, *Skrine at Kashgar*; diary entry, September 15, 1906, Stein Papers, ms. 197; and unsigned letter to Stein, January 15, 1915, Stein Papers, ms. 13.

41. Mannerheim, *Across Asia from West to East*, 189; letter from Pan Zuhuan to Stein, June 25, 1926, Stein Papers, ms. 101; and letter from Stein to Pan Zuhuan, March 1, 1930, Keller Papers, Series II, folder 114.

42. Pelliot, *Carnets de route*, 155, 170; diary entry, October 7, 1914, Stein Papers, ms. 216; and diary entry, September 27, 1930, Stein Papers, ms. 224. Regarding the name of Li Chenglin, Pelliot refers to him in his diary as Li Tanglin, without providing the Chinese characters for Li's name. On a list of Chinese officials compiled for Stein's second expedition by his Chinese secretary, however, the name of Li Chenglin is listed as the military commandant for Kucha during the same time frame.

43. Mannerheim, *Across Asia from West to East*, 200–201, 203–4.

44. Xu, *Xu Xusheng xiyou riji*, 169; and Hedin, *History of the Expedition in Asia*, 1:228.

45. Mannerheim, *Across Asia from West to East*, 350–51, 332.

46. Letter from Huntington to unidentified recipient, June 23, 1905, Huntington Papers, series I, box 6, folder 62; Mannerheim, *Across Asia from West to East*, 98, 124–25; and Skrine letter dated September 20, 1922, included in Waugh, *Skrine at Kashgar*.

47. Diary entry, January 9, 1907, Stein Papers, ms. 198; diary entry, November 12, 1907, Stein Papers, ms. 200; diary entries, July 14, 1908, and May 5, 1908, Stein Papers, ms. 202; letter to Allen, June 2, 1906, Stein Papers, ms. 3; and letter from Alan Priest to Edward Waldo Forbes, February 17, 1925, Forbes Papers (HC 2), folder 1659.

48. Diary entry, July 30, 1907, Stein Papers, ms. 199.

49. Letter (in Chinese) from Wang Min to Stein, 1925, Stein Papers, ms. 341–42; letter from Skrine to Stein, September 17, 1922, Stein Papers, ms. 107; and diary entry, May 18, 1915, Stein Papers, ms. 217.

50. Letter from Allen to Stein, January 18, 1908, Stein Papers, ms. 5; diary entry, May 5, 1908, Stein Papers, ms. 202; diary entries, December 23, 30, 1914, Stein Papers, ms. 216.

51. Letter from Pan Zuhuan to Stein, June 25, 1926, and letter from Stein to Pan, September 23, 1928, Stein Papers, ms. 101; letter from George Sherriff to Stein, November 20, 1942, Stein Papers, ms. 33; and letter from Pan Zuhuan to Stein, December 19, 1942 (received September 1, 1943), Stein Papers, ms. 34.

CHAPTER FOUR

1. Brown, "Luo Zhenyu and the Predicament of Republican Period Antiques Collecting," 66; Claypool, "Zhang Jian and China's First Museum"; and Shao, "Exhibiting the Modern," 691.

2. Letter (in Chinese) from Duanfang to Edmond Bapst, November 3, 1908, Pelliot Papers, box 79; and Shao, "Exhibiting the Modern," 695–96.

3. Hong, "A Newly Made Marketable 'Leftover,'" 144–50; and Yang, "Yang Zengxin deng suo cang liang jian Tulufan Dunhuang xiejing," 43.

4. Brown, "Preserving China's Past," 4–10; and letter from McCormick to Andrews, August 25, 1932, Andrews Papers, Administrative Papers 1920–1940, Central Asiatic Expedition 1932, box VII, folder 3.

5. Lu, *Museums in China*, 91, 96; Elliot and Shambaugh, *Odyssey of China's Imperial Art Treasures*, 58; and Wang, "The Qing Imperial Collection, circa 1905–25."

6. Wei, "Dunhuang shishi," 38–39; and Xie, *Xinjiang youji*, 231, 246.

7. The most comprehensive treatment of political developments in Xinjiang in the immediate aftermath of the 1911 revolution, including the rise of Yang Zengxin, can be found in Li, *Yang Zengxin zai Xinjiang*, 23–97. See also Jacobs, "Empire Besieged," 79–112; and Forbes, *Warlords and Muslims in Chinese Central Asia*, 11–13.

8. Diary entries, September 24, 1913; September 12, 1913; September 20, 1913; and October 1, 1913, Stein Papers, ms. 215.

9. Diary entries, January 6, 1914; January 12, 1914; and June 1, 1913, Stein Papers, ms. 215.

10. Letter to Andrews, June 1, 1913, Stein Papers, ms. 42; Guang, *Guang Lu huiyilu*, 54; and Yang, *Buguozhai wendu*, 1:70.

11. Reginald C. F. Schomberg, "A Turkestan Diary," 41, unpublished manuscript, Schomberg Papers, Box 14.

12. Diary entry, September 30, 1913, Stein Papers, ms. 215; and Zhongguo Xinjiang Weiwuer zizhiqu dang'an guan and Riben fojiao daxue Niya yizhi xueshu yanjiu jigou, *Jindai waiguo tanxianjia Xinjiang kaogu dang'an shiliao*, 118.

13. Letter from Ch'ang Yung-ch'ing (Chang Yongqing) to Macartney and the British Embassy in Beijing, December 25, 1913, Stein Papers, ms. 96; and diary entry, January 23, 1914, Stein Papers, ms. 215.

14. Letter from Jordan to Macartney, January 22, 1914, and letter from Macartney to Stein, June 14, 1914, Stein Papers, ms. 97. On Stein's makeshift passport and other logistical matters surrounding his third expedition, see Wang, "Sitanyin di san ci Zhong Ya kaocha suo chi Zhongguo huzhao fenxi," 21–30. Wang suggests that Stein and Macartney, taking advantage of the chaos of the 1911 revolution, engaged in deliberate deception and trickery in their dealings with Qing officials in Kashgar. As a result, he concludes that everything Stein removed from China during this expedition was taken out of the country "illegally."

15. Diary entry, December 29, 1914, Stein Papers, ms. 216; and letter to Allen, December 29, 1914, Stein Papers, ms. 11.

16. Diary entry, February 1, 1915, Stein Papers, ms. 216; and letter (in Chinese) from Hu Wenbing to Stein, February 11, 1915, Stein Papers, ms. 97.

17. Letter from Macartney to Stein, March 3, 1915, Stein Papers, ms. 97; letter to Allen, February 15, 1915, Stein Papers, ms. 13; and diary entry, February 13, 1915, Stein Papers, ms. 216.

18. Diary entries, April 4, 15, 1915; May 18–19, 1915; and June 5, 1915, Stein Papers, ms. 217.

19. Huang, *Huang Wenbi Meng Xin kaocha riji*, 174, 177; and Xu, *Xu Xusheng xiyou riji*, 194.

20. Diary entries, February 5, 12, 11, 1915, Stein Papers, ms. 216.

21. Letter from Williamson to Stein, October 11, 1928, Stein Papers, ms. 112.

22. Letter to Allen, August 14, 1914, Stein Papers, ms. 11; diary entry, August 22, 1914, Stein Papers, ms. 216; Walker, *Aurel Stein*, 226; and letter to Allen, January 15, 1915, Stein Papers, ms. 13.

23. Goode, *Negotiating for the Past*; Colla, *Conflicted Antiquities*; and Reid, *Contesting Antiquity in Egypt*.

24. Fiskesjö and Chen, *China before China*; and Shen, *Unearthing the Nation*. For an accessible account of Andersson's career in China, see Andersson, *Children of the Yellow Earth*.

25. Fiskesjö and Chen, *China before China*, 38.

26. Xu, *Xu Xusheng xiyou riji*, 246–47.

27. Huang, *Huang Wenbi Meng Xin kaocha riji*, 36–37; and Xu, *Xu Xusheng xiyou riji*, 32.

28. Letter from Andersson to W. D. Matthew, May 15, 1920, Andrews Papers, C446, 1921–1930, box 1, folder 3.

29. Bowie, *Langdon Warner through His Letters*, 41, 87.

30. Letter from Edward Waldo Forbes to Paul Pelliot, December 7, 1921, Forbes Papers (HC 2), folder 2196; and form letter outlining plan for the Fogg Museum's China Expedition, undated, Forbes Papers (HC 2), folder 2196.

31. Letter from Edward Waldo Forbes to Paul Pelliot, December 7, 1921, Forbes Papers (HC 2), folder 2196; form letter outlining plan for the Fogg Museum's China Expedition, undated, Forbes Papers (HC 2), folder 2196; and letter from Charles A. Heydt to Edward Waldo Forbes, August 16, 1922, Forbes Papers (HC 2), folder 2196.

32. Bowie, *Langdon Warner through His Letters*, 106–12.

33. Bowie, *Langdon Warner through His Letters*, 115–16; and form letter outlining plan for the Fogg Museum's China Expedition, undated, Forbes Papers (HC 2), folder 2196.

34. Balachandran, "Object Lesson," 14–15; and letter from Warner to Stein, December 26, 1926, Stein Papers, ms. 111.

35. Bowie, *Langdon Warner through His Letters*, 118–20.

36. Letter from Stein to Warner, February 21, 1927, Stein Papers, ms. 111.

37. Chen, *Xixing riji*, 80–82.

38. Egan, *Latterday Confucian*, 114.

39. Letter from Langdon Warner to Edward Waldo Forbes, May 28, 1925, Forbes Papers (HC 2), folder 362; letter from Langdon Warner to Paul J. Sachs, May 3, 1925 (clearly a mistake for June 3, 1925), Forbes Papers (HC 2), folder 363; and letter from Warner to Stein, December 26, 1926, Stein Papers, ms. 111.

40. Letter from Horace Jayne to Edward Waldo Forbes, April 9, 1925, Forbes Papers (HC 2), folder 362.

41. Letter from Horace Jayne to Edward Waldo Forbes, April 9, 1925, Forbes Papers (HC 2), folder 362.

42. Letter from Horace Jayne to Edward Waldo Forbes, April 9, 1925, Forbes Papers (HC 2), folder 362.

43. Chen, *Xixing riji*, 92.

CHAPTER FIVE

1. Draft letter and "Plan for the Second Expedition to Tun Huang," July 18, 1924, Forbes Papers (HC 2), folder 2205; and letter from James W. Barney to Edward Waldo Forbes, June 27, 1924, Forbes Papers (HC 2), folder 368.

2. Draft letter and "Plan for the Second Expedition to Tun Huang," July 18, 1924, Forbes Papers (HC 2), folder 2205; and letter from Edward Waldo Forbes to Paul J. Sachs, August 19, 1924, Forbes Papers (HC 2), folder 371.

3. Letter from Langdon Warner to Paul J. Sachs, August 20, 1924, Forbes Papers (HC 2), folder 371.

4. Letter from Langdon Warner to Paul J. Sachs, August 20, 1924, Forbes Papers (HC 2), folder 371; letter from Langdon Warner to Paul Pelliot, August 20, 1924, Forbes Papers (HC 2), folder 371; and letter from Edward Waldo Forbes to Langdon Warner, July 31, 1925, Forbes Papers (HC 2), folder 362.

5. Letter from Langdon Warner to Paul J. Sachs, August 20, 1924, Forbes Papers (HC 2), folder 371; and Bowie, *Langdon Warner through His Letters*, 126.

6. Extract of letter from Langdon Warner to Roger S. Greene, June 23, 1925, Forbes

Papers (HC 2), folder 363; and letter from Warner to Stein dated December 26, 1926, Stein Papers, ms. 111.

7. Letter from Horace Jayne to Edward Waldo Forbes, April 9, 1925, Forbes Papers (HC 2), folder 362.

8. Letter from Alan Priest to Edward Waldo Forbes, February 17, 1925, Forbes Papers (HC 2), folder 1659; letter from Alan Priest to Paul J. Sachs, March 15, 1925, Sachs Papers (HC 3), folder 540; and letter from Langdon Warner to Edward Waldo Forbes, March 27, 1925, Forbes Papers (HC 2), folder 364.

9. Warner's characterization of Chen as a spy was first tendered in numerous letters to Stein, Sachs, and Forbes, and later reproduced by Bowie, *Langdon Warner through His Letters*; Hopkirk, *Foreign Devils on the Silk Road*; and Balachandran, "Object Lessons."

10. Zhongguo di er lishi dang'an guan, *Zhonghua minguo shi dang'an ziliao huibian*, vol. 5, no. 1 (wenhua), 690.

11. Chen, *Xixing riji*, 3; and extract of letter from Langdon Warner to Roger S. Greene, June 23, 1925, Forbes Papers (HC 2), folder 363.

12. Egan, *Latterday Confucian*, 114; and Chen, *Xixing riji*, 1. The supportive role of Chen is also noted in Hu, "Chen Wanli jianshi, zuzhi Huaerna daoqie Dunhuang bihua yi shi de zhiyi," 89–94.

13. Letter from Horace Jayne to Edward Waldo Forbes, April 9, 1925, Forbes Papers (HC 2), folder 362; and letter from Alan Priest to Edward Waldo Forbes, March 23, 1925, Forbes Papers (HC 2), folder 1659.

14. Letter from Horace Jayne to Edward Waldo Forbes, April 9, 1925, Forbes Papers (HC 2), folder 362; and Chen, *Xixing riji*, 43.

15. Letter from Horace Jayne to Edward Waldo Forbes, April 9, 1925, Forbes Papers (HC 2), folder 362; and letter from Alan Priest to Edward Waldo Forbes, March 24, 1925, Forbes Papers (HC 2), folder 1659.

16. Letter from Horace Jayne to Edward Waldo Forbes, April 9, 1925, Forbes Papers (HC 2), folder 362.

17. Chen, *Xixing riji*, 42–45.

18. Chen, *Xixing riji*, 43, 45; and letter from Horace Jayne to Edward Waldo Forbes, April 9, 1925, Forbes Papers (HC 2), folder 362.

19. Chen, *Xixing riji*, 8.

20. Letter from Horace Jayne to Edward Waldo Forbes, April 9, 1925, Forbes Papers (HC 2), folder 362.

21. Chen, *Xixing riji*, 79–80.

22. Chen, *Xixing riji*, 80; letter from Daniel V. Thompson to Edward Waldo Forbes, April 11, 1925, Forbes Papers (HC 2), folder 362; and letter from Langdon Warner to Paul J. Sachs, May 3, 1925 (clearly a mistake for June 3, 1925), Forbes Papers (HC 2), folder 363.

23. Letter from Langdon Warner to Paul J. Sachs, June 29, 1925, Forbes Papers (HC 2), folder 363; and extract of letter from Langdon Warner to Roger S. Greene, June 23, 1925, Forbes Papers (HC 2), folder 363.

24. Warner, *Long Old Road in China*, 149–50; and Warner, *Buddhist Wall-Paintings*, xv.

25. Letter from Langdon Warner to Paul J. Sachs, June 29, 1925, Forbes Papers (HC 2), folder 363.

26. Extract of letter from Langdon Warner to Roger S. Greene, June 23, 1925, Forbes Papers (HC 2), folder 363; letter from Warner to Stein, December 26, 1926, Stein Papers, ms. 111; and letter from Langdon Warner to Paul J. Sachs, June 29, 1925, Forbes Papers (HC 2), folder 363.

27. Letter from Lorraine Warner to Edward Waldo Forbes, August 13, 1925, Forbes Papers (HC 2), folder 363; and Chen, *Xixing riji*, 8.

28. Letter from Keller to Stein dated January 11, 1929, Keller Papers, Series I, folder 29, subfolder 2 of 6. For background on Hedin's relationship with Junkers and Lufthansa, see Kish, *To the Heart of Asia*, 111–13; Johansson, *Saluting the Yellow Emperor*, 67–69; and Danielsson, *Explorer's Roadmap to National-Socialism*, 120–22. For a brief scholarly summary of the Sino-Swedish expedition, see Mehmel, "Sven Hedin in Peking," 437–47. Recent Chinese scholarship on the Sino-Swedish expedition includes Feng, "Zhong Rui xibei kexue kaocha tuan yu Zhongguo Xinjiang sheng zhengfu de guanxi chutan," 75–81; and Li, "Zhong Rui xibei kexue kaocha tuan zujian zhong de zhengyi," 5–15.

29. Xu, *Xu Xusheng xiyou riji*, 6, 96; and Huang, *Huang Wenbi Meng Xin kaocha riji*, 104.

30. Hedin, *History of the Expedition in Asia*, 1:20.

31. Zhongguo Xinjiang Weiwuer zizhiqu dang'an guan and Riben fojiao daxue Niya yizhi xueshu yanjiu jigou, *Zhong Rui xibei kexue kaocha dang'an shiliao*, 3–5.

32. For a brief introduction to the career of Huang Wenbi and his relationship with Hedin, see Jacobs, "Huang Wenbi: Pioneer of Chinese Archaeology in Xinjiang," 122–31. For a fuller treatment of Yuan Fuli, see Yuan et al., *Xibei kexue kaocha de xianxingzhe*.

33. Huang, *Huang Wenbi Meng Xin kaocha riji*, 1.

34. Xu, *Xu Xusheng xiyou riji*, 1–2.

35. Xu, *Xu Xusheng xiyou riji*, 94.

36. Huang, *Huang Wenbi Meng Xin kaocha riji*, 24.

37. Huang, *Huang Wenbi Meng Xin kaocha riji*, 68, 86.

38. Huang, *Huang Wenbi Meng Xin kaocha riji*, 68, 86, 34.

39. Xu, *Xu Xusheng xiyou riji*, 64; and Huang, *Huang Wenbi Meng Xin kaocha riji*, 68.

40. Huang, *Huang Wenbi Meng Xin kaocha riji*, 26–28, 112.

41. Huang, *Huang Wenbi Meng Xin kaocha riji*, 33–34, 147, 112.

42. Hedin's letter to Lufthansa executives is quoted in Kish, *To the Heart of Asia*, 115.

43. Huang, *Huang Wenbi Meng Xin kaocha riji*, 176, 178.

44. Huang, *Huang Wenbi Meng Xin kaocha riji*, 157, 174; and Xu, *Xu Xusheng xiyou riji*, 190–91. The book Xu referred to was Hu Shi's *A History of Chinese Philosophy* (1918), and it was in the possession of Burhan Shahidi, a Russian Tatar who had adopted Chinese citizenship and served Governor Yang in various official capacities.

45. Huang, *Huang Wenbi Meng Xin kaocha riji*, 177.

46. Huang, *Huang Wenbi Meng Xin kaocha riji*, 175; and Xu, *Xu Xusheng xiyou riji*, 194.

47. Huang, *Huang Wenbi Meng Xin kaocha riji*, 175, 179.

48. Xu, *Xu Xusheng xiyou riji*, 240. On the official inquiry into the bullets, see also Zhongguo Xinjiang Weiwuer zizhiqu dang'an guan and Riben fojiao daxue Niya yizhi xueshu yanjiu jigou, *Zhong Rui xibei kexue kaocha dang'an shiliao*, 17–19. This volume

also includes more than two hundred primary source documents on the Sino-Swedish expedition drawn from the Xinjiang Uyghur Autonomous Region archives. The most revealing and unique documents are those written to and from Governor Jin Shuren after the assassination of Yang Zengxin.

49. Xu, *Xu Xusheng xiyou riji*, 243; and Zhongguo Xinjiang Weiwuer zizhiqu dang'an guan and Riben fojiao daxue Niya yizhi xueshu yanjiu jigou, *Zhong Rui xibei kexue kaocha dang'an shiliao*, 21.

50. Xu, *Xu Xusheng xiyou riji*, 260, 253; and Zhongguo Xinjiang Weiwuer zizhiqu dang'an guan and Riben fojiao daxue Niya yizhi xueshu yanjiu jigou, *Zhong Rui xibei kexue kaocha dang'an shiliao*, 24–25, 31.

51. Huang, *Huang Wenbi Meng Xin kaocha riji*, 323, 373, 381–82.

52. Huang, *Huang Wenbi Meng Xin kaocha riji*, 362; and Johansson, *Saluting the Yellow Emperor*, 90.

53. Hedin, *History of the Expedition in Asia*, 2:50–52; and Zhongguo Xinjiang Weiwuer zizhiqu dang'an guan and Riben fojiao daxue Niya yizhi xueshu yanjiu jigou, *Zhong Rui xibei kexue kaocha dang'an shiliao*, 47.

54. Letters between various members of the Sino-Swedish expedition and Jin Shuren (March–April 1929), along with the Bureau of Education's telegram to Nanjing, can be found in Zhongguo Xinjiang Weiwuer zizhiqu dang'an guan and Riben fojiao daxue Niya yizhi xueshu yanjiu jigou, *Zhong Rui xibei kexue kaocha dang'an shiliao*, 48–50.

55. Letters between various Nationalist government organs in Nanjing and their administrative counterparts in Xinjiang (April–May 1929) can be found in Zhongguo Xinjiang Weiwuer zizhiqu dang'an guan and Riben fojiao daxue Niya yizhi xueshu yanjiu jigou, *Zhong Rui xibei kexue kaocha dang'an shiliao*, 51–53; and Hedin, *History of the Expedition in Asia*, 2:58–59.

56. Jin Shuren's accusations of inappropriate activities of the various members of the Sino-Swedish expedition (June 1929) can be found in Zhongguo Xinjiang Weiwuer zizhiqu dang'an guan and Riben fojiao daxue Niya yizhi xueshu yanjiu jigou, *Zhong Rui xibei kexue kaocha dang'an shiliao*, 58–59.

57. Zhongguo Xinjiang Weiwuer zizhiqu dang'an guan and Riben fojiao daxue Niya yizhi xueshu yanjiu jigou, *Zhong Rui xibei kexue kaocha dang'an shiliao*, 60–62.

58. Jin's continued attempts to monitor and discredit the members of the expeditions are documented in Zhongguo Xinjiang Weiwuer zizhiqu dang'an guan and Riben fojiao daxue Niya yizhi xueshu yanjiu jigou, *Zhong Rui xibei kexue kaocha dang'an shiliao*, 77, 63, 89–91, 93–94, 100.

59. Johansson, *Saluting the Yellow Emperor*, 92, 95.

60. Hedin, *History of the Expedition in Asia*, 3:302, 304.

61. Huang, *Huang Wenbi Meng Xin kaocha riji*, 555.

CHAPTER SIX

1. Letter from Andrews to Henry Osborn, December 15, 1922, National Archives, RG 59, decimal file 1910–29, box 4643.

2. Letter from Andrews to Osborn, December 15, 1922, National Archives, RG 59, decimal file 1910–29, box 4643; and Andrews, *Under a Lucky Star*, 150.

3. Letter from Osborn to Hughes, January 20, 1923, National Archives, RG 59, decimal file 1910–29, box 4643; and Gallenkamp, *Dragon Hunter*.

4. On the lack of historical inspiration for the Indiana Jones film franchise, see my analysis of the topic in Jacobs, *Indiana Jones in History*, 225–50. For an accessible though overly sympathetic biography of Andrews based entirely on English-language sources, see Gallenkamp, *Dragon Hunter*.

5. Letter from Warner to Stein, August 23, 1903 (but clearly a mistake for 1930), Stein Papers, ms. 22; and letter from Keller to Stein, November 12, 1925, Keller Papers, Series I, folder 29, subfolder 1 of 6.

6. Letter from Ding to Andrews, January 6, 1923, Andrews Papers, C446, 1921–1930, box 5, folder 18.

7. Gallenkamp, *Dragon Hunter*, 230–32, 250.

8. Letter from Andrews to Yuan, September 1, 1928, Andrews Papers, C446, 1921–1930, box 5, folder 30.

9. Letter from Yuan Tongli to Andrews, September 26, 1928, Andrews Papers, C446, 1921–1930, box 5, folder 30; and letters from Zhang Ji (on behalf of Ma Heng) to Andrews, October 25, 27, 1928, Andrews Papers, C446, 1921–1930, box 6, folder 9.

10. State Dept. "Memorandum," July 9, 1929, National Archives, RG 59, decimal file 1910–29, box 0292; letter from Andrews to Yuan Tongli, September 1, 1928, Andrews Papers, C446, 1921–1930, box 5, folder 30; and letter from Sherwood to Wu, May 11, 1929, Andrews Papers, C446, 1921–1930, box 5, folder 27.

11. Wang, "Liu Bannong yu Meiguo ziranshi bowuguan Zhong Ya kaocha tuan jiaoshe shimo," 324. In his thorough and detailed account of Andrews's negotiations with the Commission and the Nationalist government, Wang repeatedly highlights the perspective of Liu Bannong through his diary and letters.

12. Wang, "Liu Bannong yu Meiguo ziranshi bowuguan Zhong Ya kaocha tuan jiaoshe shimo," 340.

13. Memo, July 2, 1929, Andrews Papers, C446, 1921–1930, box 5, folder 27.

14. Letter from Granger to Ma, May 18, 1929, Andrews Papers, C446, 1921–1930, box 3, folder 19; telegram from Johnson to Secretary of State Henry Stimson, June 4, 1929, National Archives, RG 59, decimal file 1910–29, box 0292; and record of a discussion between Wu Chaoshu, Osborn, and the assistant secretary of state, June 7, 1929, National Archives, RG 59, decimal file 1910–29, box 0292.

15. Letter from Johnson to Andrews, June 8, 1929, Andrews Papers, C446, 1921–1930, box 7, folder 22; and State Dept. minutes of a meeting with Chao-Chu Wu (Wu Chaoshu), June 24, 1929, National Archives, RG 59, decimal file 1910–29, box 0292.

16. Wang, "Liu Bannong yu Meiguo ziranshi bowuguan Zhong Ya kaocha tuan jiaoshe shimo," 340–41.

17. Memo by Nelson Johnson, June 18, 1929, National Archives, RG 59, decimal file 1910–29, box 0292; letter from Stimson to Osborn, June 24, 1929, National Archives, RG 59, decimal file 1910–29, box 0292; and letter from Osborn to Wu, June 19, 1929, RG 59, decimal file 1910–29, box 0292.

18. Paraphrase of a telegram for Secretary Stimson in Washington, DC, July 2, 1929, Andrews Papers, C446, 1921–1930, box 5, folder 27; letter from Andrews to Stimson, June 27, 1929, National Archives, RG 59, decimal file 1910–29, box 0292; and telegram

from Osborn to Wu, July 12, 1929, National Archives, RG 59, decimal file 1910–29, box 0292.

19. Letter from Andrews to Osborn, July 18, 1929, National Archives, RG 59, decimal file 1910–29, box 0292.

20. Newspaper clippings from the *Peking Leader* and the *North China Standard*, July 19, 1929, National Archives, RG 59, decimal file 1910–29, box 0292; and report of J. V. A. MacMurray, July 31, 1929, National Archives, RG 59, decimal file 1910–29, box 0292.

21. Wang, "Liu Bannong yu Meiguo ziranshi bowuguan Zhong Ya kaocha tuan jiaoshe shimo," 332.

22. Letter from Osborn to Nelson T. Johnson, August 12, 1929, National Archives, RG 59, decimal file 1910–29, box 0292; and letters from K. Shinamura to Andrews, August 2, 1932, from Manchurian Department of Foreign Affairs to Andrews, June 1932, and unsigned letter from the Museum to an unidentified recipient of the Commission, 1932, Andrews Papers, Administrative Papers 1920–1940, box VII, folder 3.

23. Letter from Andrews to McCormick, October 4, 1932, Andrews Papers, Administrative Papers 1920–1940, box VII, folder 3.

24. Telegram from Carl Keller to Stein, July 15, 1929, Keller Papers, Series I, folder 29, subfolder 2 of 6.

25. Letter from Keller to Stein, July 16, 1929, Keller Papers, Series I, folder 29, subfolder 2 of 6. For Chinese scholarship on Stein's fourth expedition to Xinjiang, see Wang, "Zhong Ying guanyu Sitanyin di si ci Zhong Ya kaocha suo huo wenwu de jiaoshe neimu," 242–57; Wang, "Wang Zhengting yu Aolaier Sitanyin jueshi 1930 nian Nanjing huiwu neimu," 9–14; Sun, "Sitanyin di si ci lai Xin zhi jingguo ji suo huo guwu kao," 85–91; and Wang, *Sitanyin di si ci Zhongguo kaogu riji kaoshi*. A brief summary of the expedition from the perspective of Stein's papers is also included in Walker, *Aurel Stein*, 263–87.

26. Letter from Macartney to Stein, May 16, 1931, Stein Papers, ms. 22; letter from Andrews to Stein, July 9, 1930, Stein Papers, ms. 52; and Brysac, "Sir Aurel Stein's Fourth 'American' Expedition," 21.

27. Letter to Allen, November 5, 1930, Stein Papers, ms. 21; and letter from Stein to Whyte, December 13, 1929, Keller Papers, Series II, folder 137.

28. Letter from Warner to Stein, December 26, 1926, Stein Papers, ms. 111; telegram from Stuart to Warner dated to sometime in June 1925, Forbes Papers (HC 2), folder 363; and letter from George A. Chase to Edward Waldo Forbes, July 27, 1924, Forbes Papers (HC 2), folder 369.

29. Pocketbook entries for March 18, 21, 1930, Stein Papers, ms. 250; Stein's memo on meeting with Stuart and Hung, March 21, 1930, Keller Papers, Series II, folder 151; and Egan, *Latterday Confucian*, 122.

30. Letters to and from Hung and Stein, March 22, 1930, Keller Papers, Series II, folder 82; and diary entry, April 30, 1930, Stein Papers, ms. 224.

31. Pocketbook diary entry, April 22, 1930, Stein Papers, ms. 250.

32. Diary entries, April 28, 30, 1930, Stein Papers, ms. 224.

33. For a Chinese account of Stein's negotiations with Wang Zhengting, see Wang, "Wang Zhengting yu Aolaier Sitanyin jueshi 1930 nian Nanjing huiwu neimu," 9–14.

The Chinese archival source base for Stein's fourth expedition begins with his arrival in Nanjing in April 1930. Documents produced by Nationalist officials in Nanjing, including their correspondence with the Commission in Beijing, are included in Zhongguo di er lishi dang'an guan, *Zhonghua minguo shi dang'an ziliao huibian*, vol. 5, no. 1 [Culture], 679–719. For the perspective of Governor Jin Shuren and various officials in Xinjiang, including their correspondence with Nationalist officials in Nanjing and the Commission in Beijing, see Zhongguo Xinjiang Weiwuer zizhiqu dang'an guan and Riben fojiao daxue Niya yizhi xueshu yanjiu jigou, *Jindai waiguo tanxianjia Xinjiang kaogu dang'an shiliao*, 134–53; and Zhongguo Xinjiang Weiwuer zizhiqu dang'an guan and Riben fojiao daxue Niya yizhi xueshu yanjiu jigou, *Sitanyin di si ci Xinjiang tanxian dang'an shiliao*.

34. Diary entry, May 1, 1930, Stein Papers, ms. 224; and undated, unpublished, and unfinished personal narrative for Stein's fourth expedition, Stein Papers, ms. 264.

35. Johnson memo, May 1, 1930, Keller Papers, Series II, folder 141; diary entry, May 4, 1930, Stein Papers, ms. 224; and Zhongguo Xinjiang Weiwuer zizhiqu dang'an guan and Riben fojiao daxue Niya yizhi xueshu yanjiu jigou, *Sitanyin di si ci Xinjiang tanxian dang'an shiliao*, 1–2.

36. Letter from Stein to Keller, July 18, 1929, Keller Papers, Series I, folder 29, subfolder 2 of 6; and letter from Stein to Keller, January 31, 1930, Keller Papers, Series I, folder 29, subfolder 3 of 6.

37. Letters from Pan Zuhuan to Stein, December 19, 1929 and March 1, 1930, Keller Papers, Series II, folder 114.

38. Diary entry, May 1, 1930, Stein Papers, ms. 224; undated, unpublished, and unfinished personal narrative for Stein's fourth expedition, Stein Papers, ms. 264; and Zhongguo Xinjiang Weiwuer zizhiqu dang'an guan and Riben fojiao daxue Niya yizhi xueshu yanjiu jigou, *Sitanyin di si ci Xinjiang tanxian dang'an shiliao*, 7–8.

39. Letter from Keller to Stein, February 14, 1930, Keller Papers, Series II, folder 29, subfolder 3 of 6; and diary entries, May 3, 4, 7, 1930, Stein Papers, ms. 224. Stein's decision to avoid all contact with the commission in Beijing appears to represent a change of strategy on the part of the American and British diplomatic corps in Nanjing. In a draft proposal written three years earlier for a new expedition funded by Boxer Indemnity Funds, Stein echoed the recommendations of Eric Teichman, who "emphasized the necessity of a preliminary visit to Peking," where Stein could obtain the "good will" of the members of the commission by explaining "the exact object and scope of the planned explorations" so as "to assure their sympathetic attitude in respect of the desired grant." See draft proposal to Sir John Marshall, May 7, 1927, Stein Papers, ms. 20.

40. Letter from H. H. Chang to Stein, May 7, 1930, Keller Papers, Series II, folder 67; and diary entry, May 8, 1930, Stein Papers, ms. 224.

41. Diary entry, May 9, 1930, Stein Papers, ms. 224.

42. Pocketbook entry, May 9, 1930, Stein Papers, ms. 250; and diary entry, May 9, 1930, Stein Papers, ms. 224.

43. Zhongguo di er lishi dang'an guan, *Zhonghua minguo shi dang'an ziliao huibian*, vol. 5, no. 1 (wenhua), 679.

44. Zhongguo Xinjiang Weiwuer zizhiqu dang'an guan and Riben fojiao daxue Niya yizhi xueshu yanjiu jigou, *Sitanyin di si ci Xinjiang tanxian dang'an shiliao*, 2; and

Zhongguo di er lishi dang'an guan, *Zhonghua minguo shi dang'an ziliao huibian*, vol. 5, no. 1 (wenhua), 679–80.

45. Chinese-language passports for Stein's second expedition (issued in the eighth month of the thirty-first year of the reign of the Guangxu emperor [i.e., September 1905]) and fourth expedition (issued May 7, 1930), Stein Papers, ms. 283; diary entries, May 8, 9, 1930, Stein Papers, ms. 224; and pocketbook entry, May 8, 1930, Stein Papers, ms. 250.

46. Telegram from Lampson to Indian Foreign Office in Simla, June 12, 1930, Stein Papers, ms. 21; and letter from Stein to Colonel G. D. Ogilvie in Kashgar, June 24, 1930, Stein Papers, ms. 21.

47. Letter from Stein to Pan Zuhuan, July 10, 1930, Keller Papers, Series II, folder 114; and letter from Stein to Keller, July 12, 1930, Keller Papers, Series I, folder 29, subfolder 3 of 6.

48. Letter from Pan Tsi-lu (Pan Zuhuan) to Stein, April 20, 1930, Stein Papers, ms. 21.

49. Diary entries, August 20, 23, 1930, Stein Papers, ms. 224; and Sun, "Sitanyin di si ci lai Xin zhi jingguo," 85.

50. Stein's alleged remarks at Harvard appear in a couple of forms. For the Chinese translation seen by Jin Shuren in Urumchi, see Sun, "Sitanyin di si ci lai Xin zhi jingguo," 86. For the longer English-language version published by newspapers in China, see Walker, *Aurel Stein: Pioneer of the Silk Road*, 283–84.

51. Zhongguo Xinjiang Weiwuer zizhiqu dang'an guan and Riben fojiao daxue Niya yizhi xueshu yanjiu jigou, *Sitanyin di si ci Xinjiang tanxian dang'an shiliao*, 8; letter from Stein to Allen, October 23, 1930, Stein Papers, ms. 21; and Sun, "Sitanyin di si ci lai Xin zhi jingguo," 87.

52. Sun, "Sitanyin di si ci lai Xin zhi jingguo," 85–86; and Zhongguo di er lishi dang'an guan, *Zhonghua minguo shi dang'an ziliao huibian*, vol. 5, no. 1 (wenhua), 685.

53. Letters to Allen, September 12, October 9, and October 23, 1930, Stein Papers, ms. 21; and diary entries, September 21, 1930, and October 7–8, 1930, Stein Papers, ms. 224.

54. Sun, "Sitanyin di si ci lai Xin zhi jingguo," 86–87; and Zhongguo Xinjiang Weiwuer zizhiqu dang'an guan and Riben fojiao daxue Niya yizhi xueshu yanjiu jigou, *Jindai waiguo tanxianjia Xinjiang kaogu dang'an shiliao*, 140.

55. Diary entry, November 3, 1930, Stein Papers, ms. 224; and letter from Warner to Stein, August 23, 1903 (clearly a mistake for 1930), Stein Papers, ms. 22.

56. Diary entries, November 3, 7, 9, 1930, Stein Papers, ms. 224; and Zhongguo Xinjiang Weiwuer zizhiqu dang'an guan and Riben fojiao daxue Niya yizhi xueshu yanjiu jigou, *Jindai waiguo tanxianjia Xinjiang kaogu dang'an shiliao*, 141.

57. Letter to Allen, October 23, 1930, Stein Papers, ms. 21; and diary entries, September 26; November 20, 1930; January 15, February 13, 16, 1931; March 24, 1931, Stein Papers, ms. 224.

58. Diary entries, November 11, 18, 1930; December 6, 1930; January 12, 1931; February 13, 1931, Stein Papers, ms. 224.

59. Diary entries, March 26, April 4, 1931, Stein Papers, ms. 224.

60. In his diary, Stein does not describe the nature of the obstruction he met with at Keriya. But Colonel Reginald Charles Francis Schomberg, who passed through Keriya soon after Stein, has left an indignant account of what he heard. "Under instructions from

on high, he [Keriya magistrate Chen Shi] had insulted Sir Aurel Stein in every possible manner, in those disagreeable petty ways which are a perpetual disgrace to the Chinese who have always loved to practise them. He had tried, again under orders, to rummage in this distinguished scientist's boxes, he had guarded this friend of China as no malefactor would be, and he had conducted him out of the town as a close prisoner." Later at Niya, Schomberg, too, found his movements restricted by the local Muslim begs, who gave "as a reason all the trouble that Sir Aurel Stein had caused the local people by digging. This I knew to be a falsehood, and a clumsy one; as Sir Aurel paid well, and never lacked diggers." See Schomberg's unpublished manuscript, "A Second Turkestan Diary. 1930–1931," 35, 37–38, Schomberg Papers, box 14.

61. Zhongguo Xinjiang Weiwuer zizhiqu dang'an guan and Riben fojiao daxue Niya yizhi xueshu yanjiu jigou, *Jindai waiguo tanxianjia Xinjiang kaogu dang'an shiliao*, 148–50.

62. Letter to Andrews, August 10, 1930, Stein Papers, ms. 52; and Zhongguo Xinjiang Weiwuer zizhiqu dang'an guan and Riben fojiao daxue Niya yizhi xueshu yanjiu jigou, *Jindai waiguo tanxianjia Xinjiang kaogu dang'an shiliao*, 151. Reports of Stein's movements in China during his fourth expedition, along with Chinese demands for expulsion, were reported regularly in *The Times*. See Wang, *Sir Aurel Stein in the Times*, 101–9.

63. Zhongguo di er lishi dang'an guan, *Zhonghua minguo shi dang'an ziliao huibian*, vol. 5, no. 1 (wenhua), 687–88.

64. The complete English-language text of the Commission's statement is reproduced as a facsimile in Zhongguo Xinjiang Weiwuer zizhiqu dang'an guan and Riben fojiao daxue Niya yizhi xueshu yanjiu jigou, *Sitanyin di si ci Xinjiang tanxian dang'an shiliao*, 31–32. I have not been able to identify any other published source that reproduces the entirety of the Commission's statement. All previous scholars who have quoted from it have done so from copies held in various unpublished archival holdings.

65. Zhongguo Xinjiang Weiwuer zizhiqu dang'an guan and Riben fojiao daxue Niya yizhi xueshu yanjiu jigou, *Sitanyin di si ci Xinjiang tanxian dang'an shiliao*, 31–32.

66. *Tianjin dagongbao*, December 27–28, 1930; and letter to Allen, April 10, 1931, Stein Papers, ms. 22.

67. Zhongguo di er lishi dang'an guan, *Zhonghua minguo shi dang'an ziliao huibian*, vol. 5, no. 1 (wenhua), 692–701.

68. Zhongguo Xinjiang Weiwuer zizhiqu dang'an guan and Riben fojiao daxue Niya yizhi xueshu yanjiu jigou, *Jindai waiguo tanxianjia Xinjiang kaogu dang'an shiliao*, 143, 152; and Sun, "Sitanyin di si ci lai Xin zhi jingguo," 87.

69. Letter from Captain G. Sherriff to Sir Aurel Stein, January 31, 1931, Forbes Papers (HC 2), folder 1944; diary entry for February 11, 1931, Stein Papers, ms. 224; and letter to Allen, February 22, 1931, Stein Papers, ms. 22.

70. Letter from Edward Waldo Forbes to William Cameron Forbes, February 16, 1931, Forbes Papers (HC 2), folder 1945; letters to Allen, April 10, 1931, and May 5, 1931, Stein Papers, ms. 22; and diary entry, May 4, 1931, Stein Papers, ms. 225.

71. Diary entry, May 11, 1931, Stein Papers, ms. 225; and Zhongguo di er lishi dang'an guan, *Zhonghua minguo shi dang'an ziliao huibian*, vol. 5, no. 1 (wenhua), 701.

72. Zhongguo di er lishi dang'an guan, *Zhonghua minguo shi dang'an ziliao huibian*, vol. 5, no. 1 (wenhua), 701.

73. Diary entry, May 4, 1931, Stein Papers, ms. 225; and Sun, "Sitanyin di si ci lai Xin zhi jingguo," 89–90.

74. Sun, "Sitanyin di si ci lai Xin zhi jingguo," 89–90.

75. Letter from Keller to Stein, June 16, 1931, Stein Papers, ms. 22; letter from Sir Aurel Stein to Carl Keller, January 14, 1932, Sachs Papers (HC 3), folder 1052; and letter from Lionel Barnett to Stein, July 4, 1931, Stein Papers, ms. 22.

76. Diary entries, May 16–17, 1931, Stein Papers, ms. 225.

77. Letter from Pan to Stein, May 16, 1931, Stein Papers, ms. 22; and diary entries, May 29, June 1, 1931, Stein Papers, ms. 225.

CONCLUSION

1. *Saturday Evening Post*, November 20, 1937, 50.

2. Letter from Warner to Andrews, December 17, 1937, Andrews Papers, Administrative Papers 1920–1940, box XV, folder 41. The Huffine cartoon was found placed on top of Warner's December 17 letter to Andrews within a folder labeled "Warner, Langdon—Archaeologist." With the publication date of the cartoon (November 20) coming so close to the date of the letter on which it was placed in the archives, the evidence strongly suggests that it was Warner who cut the cartoon out of his copy of the *Saturday Evening Post* and mailed it to Andrews in New York.

3. Yi Tuo, "Du 'Dunhuang shishi fangshu ji' ji 'Sitanyin Qianfodong qujing shimo ji' hou," 50.

4. Letter from Keller to Stein, May 16, 1940, and letter from Stein to Keller, July 12, 1940, Keller Papers, Series I, folder 29, subfolder 5 of 6. The skit was written by Virginia Kingsley and Sally West.

5. Fleming, *News from Tartary*, 311.

6. Gansu cang Dunhuang wenxian bianweihui, Gansu renmin chubanshe, and Gansu sheng wenwu ju, *Gansu cang Dunhuang wenxian*, 3:155–56.

7. Stein, "Explorations in Central Asia, 1906–8," 241–64; and Luo, *Liusha fang gu ji*, 4.

8. Yang, "Yang Zengxin deng suo cang liang jian Tulufan Dunhuang xiejing," 43–44.

9. Jacobs, "The Relevance of 'India' for Aurel Stein's Expeditions in Xinjiang."

10. Mirsky, *Sir Aurel Stein*, 88; and letter from Edward Waldo Forbes to Langdon Warner, September 2, 1924, Forbes Papers (HC 2), folder 2053. In his letter to Warner, Forbes recounts a recent visit to Le Coq in Berlin, where Le Coq assured Forbes that his previous excavations in Turfan and Kucha were "run on meagre lines—living 'like and *with* the natives, not in Stein's Champagne-lubricated style.'"

11. Letter to Allen, September 20, 1900, Stein Papers, ms. 36.

12. Zheng, *Politics of Rights and the 1911 Revolution in China*; Kinzley, *Natural Resources and the New Frontier*; and Brook, Walt van Praag, and Boltjes, *Sacred Mandates*.

13. Diary entry, January 19, 1915, Stein Papers, ms. 216; and letter to Andrews, June 15, 1907 (but likely a typo for June 25), Stein Papers, ms. 37.

14. Letter from Keller to Stein, October 29, 1931, Keller Papers, folder 29, subfolder 3 of 6; and letter from McCormick to Andrews, August 25, 1932, Andrews Papers, Administrative Papers 1920–1940, Central Asiatic Expedition 1932, box VII, folder 3.

15. Chen, *Dunhuang jieyu lu*.

16. Rong, *Eighteen Lectures on Dunhuang*, 108. For a representative sampling of Wang Jiqing's voluminous scholarship on Stein, see Wang, "Sitanyin di er ci Zhong Ya kaocha qijian suo chi Zhongguo huzhao jianxi"; Wang, "Sitanyin di san ci Zhong Ya kaocha suo chi Zhongguo huzhao xiping"; Wang, "1907 nian Sitanyin yu Wang Yuanlu ji Dunhuang guanyuan zhijian de jiaowang"; and Wang "Jiang Xiaowan wannian shiji kaoshi." For the more redemptive Chinese views on Pelliot, see Jacobs, "Confronting Indiana Jones," 79–80; Wang, "Boxihe yu Pei Jingfu de jiaowang"; and Rong and Wang, "Paul Pelliot en Chine (1906–1909)."

17. Stein's public response to the Commission, May 25, 1931, Stein Papers, ms. 22.

BIBLIOGRAPHY

UNPUBLISHED ARCHIVAL SOURCES

Andrews Papers

Andrews, Roy Chapman. Papers, 1912–44. American Museum of Natural History. New York, NY.

Forbes Papers

Forbes, Edward Waldo. Papers. Harvard Art Museum Archives, Harvard University, Cambridge, MA.

Huntington Papers

Huntington, Ellsworth. Papers. Manuscripts and Archives, Yale University Library, New Haven, CT.

Keller Papers

Keller, Carl Tilden. Carl Tilden Keller Collection concerning Sir Aurel Stein. Houghton Library, Harvard University, Cambridge, MA.

National Archives

National Archives and Records Administration (NARA). College Park, MD.

Pelliot Papers

Notes et manuscrits de Paul Pelliot. Pel. Mi. Musée national des Arts asiatiques (Guimet). Paris, France.

Sachs Papers

Sachs, Paul J. Papers. Harvard Art Museum Archives, Harvard University, Cambridge, MA.

Schomberg Papers

Papers and correspondence of Colonel Reginald Charles Francis Schomberg. Royal Society for Asian Affairs. London, UK.

Stein Papers

Papers and correspondence of Sir Marc Aurel Stein. Bodleian Library, Oxford University. Oxford, UK.

Warner Papers

Warner, Langdon. Letters to Horace Howard Furness Jayne, 1923–1953. Houghton Library, Harvard University, Cambridge, MA.

PUBLISHED ARCHIVAL SOURCES

Beijing daxue tushuguan and Shanghai guji chubanshe, eds. *Beijing daxue tushuguan cang Dunhuang wenxian* [Dunhuang manuscripts stored in the Peking University Library]. 2 vols. Shanghai: Shanghai guji chubanshe, 1995.

Bowie, Theodore. *Langdon Warner through His Letters*. Bloomington: Indiana University Press, 1966.

Gansu cang Dunhuang wenxian bianweihui, Gansu renmin chubanshe, and Gansu sheng wenwu ju, eds. *Gansu cang Dunhuang wenxian* [Dunhuang manuscripts stored in Gansu]. 6 vols. Lanzhou: Gansu renmin chubanshe, 1999.

Huang Wenbi. *Huang Wenbi Meng Xin kaocha riji: 1927–1930* [The diary of Huang Wenbi during a survey of Mongolia and Xinjiang: 1927–1930]. Compiled by Huang Lie. Beijing: Wenwu chubanshe, 1990.

Liu Jiaping and Zhou Jiming, eds. *Guojia tushuguan cang guji zhenben youji congkan* [Old and rare travel accounts in the collection of the National Library of China]. 16 vols. Beijing: Xianzhuang shuju, 2003.

Mannerheim, C. G. *Across Asia from West to East in 1906–1908*. Helsinki: Otavia Publishing, 2008.

Pelliot, Paul. *Carnets de route, 1906–1908*. Paris: Les Indes savantes, 2008.

Shanghai guji chubanshe and Shanghai bowuguan, eds. *Shanghai bowuguan cang Dunhuang Tulufan wenxian* [Dunhuang and Turfan manuscripts stored in the Shanghai Museum]. 2 vols. Shanghai: Shanghai guji chubanshe, 1993.

Shanghai guji chubanshe and Tianjin shi yishu bowuguan, eds. *Tianjin shi yishu bowuguan cang Dunhuang wenxian* [Dunhuang manuscripts stored in the Tianjin Municipal Museum of Art]. 7 vols. Shanghai: Shanghai guji chubanshe, 1996.

Yang Zengxin. *Buguozhai wendu* [Records from the Studio of Rectification]. 6 vols. [1921] Taibei: Wenhai chubanshe, 1965.

Zhongguo di er lishi dang'an guan, ed. *Zhonghua minguo shi dang'an ziliao huibian—di wu ji, di yi bian: wenhua* [Collection of archival materials concerning the history of the Republic of China—vol. 5, no. 1: Culture]. Nanjing: Jiangsu guji chubanshe, 1994.

Zhongguo Shudian cang Dunhuang wenxian bianweihui, ed. *Zhongguo Shudian cang Dunhuang wenxian* [Dunhuang manuscripts stored in the China Bookstore]. Beijing: Zhongguo shudian, 2007.

Zhongguo Xinjiang Weiwuer zizhiqu dang'an guan, ed. *Xinjiang yu E Su shangye maoyi dang'an shiliao* [Historical documents on commerce and trade between Xinjiang and Russia/Soviet Union]. Wulumuqi: Xinjiang renmin chubanshe, 1994.

Zhongguo Xinjiang Weiwuer zizhiqu dang'an guan and Riben fojiao daxue Niya yizhi xueshu yanjiu jigou, eds. *Jindai waiguo tanxianjia Xinjiang kaogu dang'an shiliao* [Archival materials concerning the archaeological expeditions of foreign explorers in modern Xinjiang]. Wulumuqi: Xinjiang meishu sheying chubanshe, 2001.

———. *Sitanyin di si ci Xinjiang tanxian dang'an shiliao* [Archival materials concerning Stein's fourth expedition to Xinjiang]. Wulumuqi: Xinjiang meishu sheying chubanshe, 2007.

———. *Zhong Rui xibei kexue kaocha dang'an shiliao* [Archival materials concerning the Sino-Swedish Northwest Scientific Survey]. Wulumuqi: Xinjiang meishu sheying chubanshe, 2005.

Zu Yanfu and Daxiya Wei'aihe-Luosi, eds. *Shi yu wu: Zhongguo xuezhe yu Faguo hanxuejia lunxue shuzha jizhu* [An annotated collection of letters between Chinese scholars and French sinologists]. Beijing: Shangwu yinshuguan, 2015.

OTHER PRIMARY AND SECONDARY SOURCES

Abt, Jeffrey. *American Egyptologist: The Life of James Henry Breasted and the Creation of His Oriental Institute*. Chicago: University of Chicago Press, 2013.

Allen, Susan Heuck. *Classical Spies: American Archaeologists with the OSS in World War II Greece*. Ann Arbor: University of Michigan Press, 2011.

———. *Finding the Walls of Troy: Frank Calvert and Heinrich Schliemann at Hisarlik*. Berkeley: University of California Press, 1999.

Andersson, J. Gunnar. *Children of the Yellow Earth: Studies in Prehistoric China*. London: Kegan Paul, Trench, Trubner, 1934.

Andrews, Roy Chapman. *Under a Lucky Star: A Lifetime of Adventure*. New York: Viking, 1943.

Balachandran, Sanchita. "Object Lessons: The Politics of Preservation and Museum Building in Western China in the Early Twentieth Century." *International Journal of Cultural Property* 14 (2007): 1–32.

Banner, Stuart. *How the Indians Lost Their Land: Law and Power on the Frontier*. Cambridge, MA: Harvard University Press, 2005.

Boxihe [Paul Pelliot]. *Boxihe Xiyu tanxian riji, 1906–1908* [Pelliot's diary of his expedition to the Western Regions, 1906–1908]. Translated by Geng Sheng. Beijing: Zhong-guo zangxue chubanshe, 2014.

Brook, Timothy, Michael van Walt van Praag, and Miek Boltjes, eds. *Sacred Mandates: Asian International Relations since Chinggis Khan.* Chicago: University of Chicago Press, 2018.

Brown, Clayton D. "Preserving China's Past: Sino-American Collaboration in Archaeology and Cultural Heritage Management, 1912–1940." Paper presented at the Association for Asian Studies Annual Conference, Seattle, 2016.

Brown, Shana J. "Luo Zhenyu and the Predicament of Republican Period Antiques Collecting." In *Lost Generation: Luo Zhenyu, Qing Loyalists, and the Formation of Modern Chinese Culture,* edited by Yang Chia-Ling and Roderick Whitfield, 58–73. London: Saffron Books, 2012.

———. *Pastimes: From Art and Antiquarianism to Modern Chinese Historiography.* Honolulu: University of Hawai'i Press, 2011.

Brysac, Shareen. "Sir Aurel Stein's Fourth 'American' Expedition." In *Proceedings of the British Museum Study Day 23 March 2002,* edited by Helen Wang, 17–22. London: British Museum, 2004.

Cai Fuquan. "Ye Changchi yu Dunhuang wenwu bushuo" [Additional comments on Ye Changchi and Dunhuang cultural relics]. *Dunhuang yanjiu* 2 (2011): 95–103.

Cannadine, David. *Ornamentalism: How the British Saw Their Empire.* Oxford: Oxford University Press, 2002.

Çelik, Zeynep. *About Antiquities: Politics of Archaeology in the Ottoman Empire.* Austin: University of Texas Press, 2016.

Chen Wanli. *Xixing riji* [A diary of westward travels]. Edited by Yang Xiaobin. 1926; Lanzhou: Gansu renmin chubanshe, 2000.

Chen Yuan, ed. *Dunhuang jieyu lu* [Index of the Dunhuang manuscripts remaining after the plunder]. Beijing: Guoli zhongyang yanjiuyuan lishi yuyan yanjiusuo, 1931.

Claypool, Lisa. "Zhang Jian and China's First Museum." *Journal of Asian Studies* 64, no. 3 (August 2005): 567–604.

Colla, Elliott. *Conflicted Antiquities: Egyptology, Egyptomania, Egyptian Modernity.* Durham, NC: Duke University Press, 2007.

Danielsson, Sarah. *The Explorer's Roadmap to National-Socialism: Sven Hedin, Geography, and the Path to Genocide.* Burlington, VT: Ashgate, 2012.

Dewey, John. *Letters from China and Japan.* New York: E. P. Dutton, 1920.

Donnelly, Neal. *A Journey through Chinese Hell: "Hell Scrolls" of Taiwan.* Taipei: Artist Publishing, 1990.

Drège, Jean Pierre, and Michel Zink, eds. *Paul Pelliot, de l'histoire à la légende: colloque international organisé par Jean-Pierre Drège, Georges-Jean Pinault, Cristina Scherrer-Schaub et Pierre-Étienne Will au Collège de France et à l'Académie des inscriptions et belles-lettres (Palais de l'Institut), 2–3 octobre 2008.* Paris: Académie des inscriptions et belles-lettres, 2013.

Dreyer, Caren. *Abenteuer Seidenstrasse: Die Berliner Turfan-Expeditionen, 1902–1914.* Leipzig: E. A. Seemann, 2015.

Ebrey, Patricia Buckley. *Accumulating Culture: The Collections of Emperor Huizong.* Seattle: University of Washington Press, 2008.

Egan, Susan Chan. *A Latterday Confucian: Reminiscences of William Hung (1893–1980)*. Cambridge, MA: Harvard University Press, 1987.

Elliot, Jeannette Shambaugh, and David L. Shambaugh. *The Odyssey of China's Imperial Art Treasures*. Seattle: University of Washington Press, 2005.

Elliott, Mark C. *Emperor Qianlong: Son of Heaven, Man of the World*. New York: Pearson Longman, 2009.

Evans, R. Tripp. *Romancing the Maya: Mexican Antiquity in the American Imagination, 1820–1915*. Austin: University of Texas Press, 2004.

Feng Chengjie. "Zhong Rui xibei kexue kaocha tuan yu Zhongguo Xinjiang sheng zhengfu de guanxi chutan" [A preliminary investigation into the relations between the Sino-Swedish Northwest Scientific Survey and the Xinjiang provincial government]. *Xinjiang daxue xuebao*, no. 4 (2017): 75–81.

Fiskesjö, Magnus, and Chen Xingcan. *China before China: Johan Gunnar Andersson, Ding Wenjiang, and the Discovery of China's Prehistory; A Companion Volume for the New Exhibit at the Museum of Far Eastern Antiquities*. Stockholm: Museum of Far Eastern Antiquities, 2004.

Fleming, Peter. *News from Tartary*. London: Cape, 1936.

Forbes, Andrew D. W. *Warlords and Muslims in Chinese Central Asia: A Political History of Republican Sinkiang, 1911–1949*. Cambridge: Cambridge University Press, 1986.

Galambos, Imre. "Another Hungarian Looting China's Treasures? Sir Aurel Stein, Lajos Ligeti, and a Case of Mistaken Identity." *Tonkō shahon kenkyū nenpō* 4 (2010): 195–207.

———. "An English Boy in Chinese Turkestan: The Story of Orlando Hobbes." *Studia Orientalia Slovaca* 10, no. 1 (2011): 81–98.

———. "A Forgotten Chinese Translation of the Preliminary Report of Aurel Stein's First Expedition." In *Dunhuang Studies: Prospects and Problems for the Coming Second Century of Research*, edited by Irina Popova and Liu Yi, 55–58. Saint Petersburg: Russian Academy of Sciences Institute of Oriental Manuscripts, 2012.

———. "Japanese Exploration of Central Asia: The Ōtani Expeditions and Their British Connections." *Bulletin of the School of Oriental and African Studies* 75, no. 1 (2012): 113–34.

———. "The Third Ōtani Expedition at Dunhuang: Acquisition of the Japanese Collection of Dunhuang Manuscripts." *Journal of Inner Asian Art and Archaeology* 3 (2008): 29–35.

Gallenkamp, Charles. *Dragon Hunter: Roy Chapman Andrews and the Central Asiatic Expeditions*. New York: Viking, 2001.

Giès, Jacques. "Die Mission Pelliot (1906–1909)." In *Das grosse Spiel: Archäologie und Politik zur Zeit des Kolonialismus (1860–1940)*, edited by Charlotte Trümpler, 202–17. Cologne: Dumont, 2008.

Goode, James F. *Negotiating for the Past: Archaeology, Nationalism, and Diplomacy in the Middle East, 1919–1941*. Austin: University of Texas Press, 2007.

Guang Lu. *Guang Lu huiyilu* [Memoirs of Guang Lu]. Taibei: Zhuanji wenxue, 1969.

Gumbrecht, Cordula. "Acta Turfanica: Die deutschen Turfan-Expeditionen gesehen in den Archiven von Urumchi und Berlin." PhD diss., Freie Universität Berlin, 2002.

————. "Chinese Passports for the German Turfan Expeditions." In *Turfan Revisited—The First Century of Research into the Arts and Cultures of the Silk Road*, edited by Desmond Durkin-Meistererernst et al., 111–20. Berlin: Dietrich Reimer Verlag, 2004.

Harris, Charles H., and Louis R. Sadler. *The Archaeologist Was a Spy: Sylvanus G. Morley and the Office of Naval Intelligence*. Albuquerque: University of New Mexico Press, 2003.

Hedin, Sven Anders. *History of the Expedition in Asia, 1927–1935*. 4 vols. Stockholm: Elanders boktryckeri aktiebolag, 1943.

Hegel, Robert E. *True Crimes in Eighteenth-Century China: Twenty Case Histories*. Seattle: University of Washington Press, 2009.

Hevia, James L. "Looting and Its Discontents: Moral Discourse and the Plunder of Beijing," In *The Boxers, China, and the World*, edited by Robert Bickers and R. G. Tiedemann, 93–113. New York: Rowman and Littlefield, 2007.

Hong Zaixin. "A Newly Made Marketable 'Leftover': Luo Zhenyu's Scholarship and Art Business in Kyōto (1911–1919)," In *Lost Generation: Luo Zhenyu, Qing Loyalists, and the Formation of Modern Chinese Culture*, edited by Yang Chia-Ling and Roderick Whitfield, 142–71. London: Saffron Books, 2012.

Hopkirk, Peter. *Foreign Devils on the Silk Road: The Search for the Lost Cities and Treasures of Chinese Central Asia*. Amherst: University of Massachusetts Press, 1980.

Hu Tongqing. "Chen Wanli jianshi, zuzhi Huaerna daoqie Dunhuang bihua yi shi de zhiyi" [Questions concerning Chen Wanli's surveillance and obstruction of Warner during his theft of the Dunhuang murals]. *Dunhuang yanjiu*, no. 2 (2011): 89–94.

Huangfu, Zhengzheng. "Internalizing the West: Qing Envoys and Ministers in Europe, 1866–1893." PhD diss., University of California, San Diego, 2012.

Hume, Ivor Noël. *Belzoni: The Giant Archaeologists Love to Hate*. Charlottesville: University of Virginia Press, 2011.

Huntington, Ellsworth. *Civilization and Climate*. New Haven, CT: Yale University Press, 1915.

Jacobs, Justin M. "An Analysis of Modern Chinese Colophons on the Dunhuang Manuscripts." *The Silk Road* 17 (2019): forthcoming.

————. "The Compensations of Plunder: Why Chinese Officials Aided and Abetted Foreign Explorers in Xinjiang." Paper presented at the Association for Asian Studies Annual Conference, Seattle, 2016.

————. "Confronting Indiana Jones: Chinese Nationalism, Historical Imperialism, and the Criminalization of Aurel Stein and the Raiders of Dunhuang, 1899–1944." In *China on the Margins*, edited by Sherman Cochran and Paul G. Pickowicz, 65–90. Ithaca, NY: Cornell University Press, 2010.

————. "Cultural Thieves or Political Liabilities: How Chinese Officials Viewed Foreign Archaeologists in Xinjiang, 1893–1914." *The Silk Road* 10 (2012): 117–22.

————. "Empire Besieged: The Preservation of Chinese Rule in Xinjiang, 1884–1971." PhD diss., University of California, San Diego, 2011.

————. "Huang Wenbi: Pioneer of Chinese Archaeology in Xinjiang." *The Silk Road* 12 (2014): 122–31.

————. *Indiana Jones in History: From Pompeii to the Moon*. Pulp Hero Press, 2017.

———."Langdon Warner at Dunhuang: What Really Happened?" *The Silk Road* 11 (2013): 1–11.

———. "Nationalist China's 'Great Game': Leveraging Foreign Explorers in Xinjiang, 1927–1935." *Journal of Asian Studies* 73, no. 1 (February 2014): 43–64.

———. "The Relevance of 'India' for Aurel Stein's Expeditions in Xinjiang." Paper presented at the "Marc Aurel Stein with Special Reference to South and Central Asian Legacy: Recent Discoveries and Research" conference, New Delhi, 2015.

———. *Xinjiang and the Modern Chinese State.* Seattle: University of Washington Press, 2016.

James, T. G. H. *Howard Carter: The Path to Tutankhamun.* London: Tauris Parke, 2001.

Jang, Scarlett. "The Culture of Art Collecting in Imperial China." In *A Companion to Chinese Art,* edited by Martin J. Powers and Katherine R. Tsiang, 47–72. Malden, MA: John Wiley and Sons, 2016.

Jasanoff, Maya. *Edge of Empire: Lives, Culture, and Conquest in the East, 1750–1850.* New York: Knopf, 2006.

Johansson, Perry. *Saluting the Yellow Emperor: A Case of Swedish Sinography.* Boston: Brill, 2012.

Kinzley, Judd C. *Natural Resources and the New Frontier: Constructing China's Modern Borderlands.* Chicago: University of Chicago Press, 2018.

Kish, George. *To the Heart of Asia: The Life of Sven Hedin.* Ann Arbor: University of Michigan Press, 1985.

Kuhn, Philip A. *Soulstealers: The Chinese Sorcery Scare of 1768.* Cambridge, MA: Harvard University Press, 1992.

Lawton, Thomas. *A Time of Transition: Two Collectors of Chinese Art.* Lawrence: Spencer Museum of Art, University of Kansas, 1991.

Le Coq, Albert von. *Buried Treasures of Chinese Turkestan.* 1928; Oxford: Oxford University Press, 1985.

Li Jianhong. "Lun Dunhuang shibao ji Ye Changchi 'Yuandu Lu riji chao'" [On the loss of the Dunhuang treasures and Ye Changchi's "Draft of the diary of Yuandu Lu"]. *Dunhuang yanjiu* 64 (2000): 36–39.

Li Xincheng. *Yang Zengxin zai Xinjiang* [Yang Zengxin in Xinjiang]. Taipei: Guoshiguan, 1993.

Li Xuetong. "Zhong Rui xibei kexue kaocha tuan zujian zhong de zhengyi" [Controversy over the organization of the Sino-Swedish Northwest Scientific Survey]. *Zhongguo keji shiliao,* no. 2 (2004): 5–15.

Liao, Jing. "The Genesis of the Modern Academic Library in China: Western Influences and the Chinese Response." *Libriares and Culture* 39, no. 2 (Spring 2004): 161–74.

Liu Shiping, and Meng Xianshi. *Dunhuang bai nian* [Dunhuang centennial]. 2 vols. Taipei: Yuanliu chuban shiye gufen youxian gongsi, 2002.

Lu, Tracy L-D. *Museums in China: Power, Politics, and Identities.* London: Routledge, 2014.

Luo Zhenyu. "Dunhuang shishi shumu ji faxian zhi yuanshi" [Index of the Dunhuang stone cavern and an account of its discovery]. *Dongfang zazhi* 10 (September 1909): 42–46.

———. *Liusha fang gu ji* [Visiting the ancients among the shifting sands]. N.p., 1909.

Matsuda, David. 2005. "Subsistence Diggers." In *Who Owns the Past? Cultural Policy, Cultural Property, and the Law*, edited by Karen Fitz Gibbons, 255–64. New Brunswick, NJ: Rutgers University Press.

McClellan, Andrew. *Inventing the Louvre: Art, Politics, and the Origins of the Modern Museum in Eighteenth-Century Paris*. Berkeley: University of California Press, 1999.

Mehmel, Astrid. "Sven Hedin in Peking." In *Das grosse Spiel: Archäologie und Politik zur Zeit des Kolonialismus (1860–1940)*, edited by Charlotte Trümpler, 437–47. Cologne: Dumont, 2008.

Metcalf, Thomas R. *Ideologies of the Raj*. Cambridge: Cambridge University Press, 1998.

Meyer, Karl E., and Shareen Blair Brysac. *The China Collectors: America's Century-Long Hunt for Asian Art Treasures*. New York: Palgrave Macmillan, 2015.

———. *Tournament of Shadows: The Great Game and the Race for Empire in Central Asia*. New York: Basic Books, 1999.

Mirsky, Jeannette. *Sir Aurel Stein: Archaeological Explorer*. Chicago: University of Chicago Press, 1977.

Moser, Stephanie. *Wondrous Curiosities: Ancient Egypt at the British Museum*. Chicago: University of Chicago Press, 2006.

Netting, Lara Jaishree. *A Perpetual Fire: John C. Ferguson and His Quest for Chinese Art and Culture*. Hong Kong: Hong Kong University Press, 2013.

Pelliot, Paul. "Trois ans dans la Haute Asie." *Asie française* (January 1910): 3–16.

Popova, I. F. "Russian Expeditions to Central Asia at the Turn of the 20th Century." In *Russian Expeditions to Central Asia at the Turn of the 20th Century*, edited by I. F. Popova, 11–39. Saint Petersburg: Slavia, 2008.

———. "S. F. Oldenburg's First Russian Turkestan Expedition (1909–1910)." In *Russian Expeditions to Central Asia at the Turn of the 20th Century*, edited by I. F. Popova, 148–75. Saint Petersburg: Slavia, 2008.

Pringle, Heather. *The Master Plan: Himmler's Scholars and the Holocaust*. New York: Hyperion, 2006.

Qi Qingshun. "Lun Qingmo Xinjiang 'xinzheng': Xinjiang xiang jindaihua maijin de zhongyao kaiduan" [On the "New Policies" in Xinjiang: an important beginning for advancing the modernization of Xinjiang]. *Xiyu yanjiu*, no. 3 (2000): 31–39.

Quirke, Stephen. *Hidden Hands: Egyptian Workforces in Petrie Excavation Archives, 1880–1924*. London: Gerald Duckworth, 2010.

Ray, John. *The Rosetta Stone and the Rebirth of Ancient Egypt*. Cambridge, MA: Harvard University Press, 2007.

Reid, Donald Malcolm. *Contesting Antiquity in Egypt: Archaeologies, Museums, and the Struggle for Identities from World War I to Nasser*. Cairo: American University in Cairo Press, 2015.

———. *Whose Pharaohs? Archaeology, Museums, and Egyptian National Identity from Napoleon to World War I*. Berkeley: University of California Press, 2002.

Rong, Xinjiang. *Eighteen Lectures on Dunhuang*. Translated by Imre Galambos. Boston: Brill, 2013.

———. "Ye Changchi: Pioneer of Chinese Studies." *IDP News* 7 (1997): 1–4.

Rong, Xinjiang, and Wang Nan. "Paul Pelliot en Chine (1906–1909)." In *Paul Pelliot: De l'histoire à la légende*, edited by Jean-Pierre Drège and Michel Zink, 83–119. Paris: Académie des inscriptions et belles-lettres, 2013.

Rowe, William T. *Saving the World: Chen Hongmou and Elite Consciousness in Eighteenth-Century China*. Stanford, CA: Stanford University Press, 2001.

Schluessel, Eric T. "The Muslim Emperor of China: Everyday Politics in Colonial Xinjiang, 1877–1933." PhD diss., Harvard University, 2016.

Shao, Qin. "Exhibiting the Modern: The Creation of the First Chinese Museum, 1905–1930." *China Quarterly* 179 (September 2004): 684–702.

Shaw, Wendy M. K. *Possessors and Possessed: Museums, Archaeology, and the Visualization of History in the Late Ottoman Empire*. Berkeley: University of California Press, 2003.

Shen, Grace Yen. *Unearthing the Nation: Modern Geology and Nationalism in Republican China*. Chicago: Chicago University Press, 2014.

Skrine, C. P. *Chinese Central Asia: An Account of Travels in Northern Kashmir and Chinese Turkestan*. 1926; Oxford: Oxford University Press, 1986.

Snyder-Reinke, Jeff. "Afterlives of the Dead: Uncovering Graves and Mishandling Corpses in Nineteenth-Century China." *Frontiers of History in China* 11, no. 1 (2016): 1–20.

Sommer, Matthew H. *Polyandry and Wife-Selling in Qing Dynasty China: Survival Strategies and Judicial Interventions*. Berkeley: University of California Press, 2015.

———. *Sex, Law, and Society in Late Imperial China*. Stanford, CA: Stanford University Press, 2000.

St. Clair, William. *Lord Elgin and the Marbles: The Controversial History of the Parthenon Sculptures*. Oxford: Oxford University Press, 1998.

Stein, Marc Aurel. *Ancient Khotan: Detailed Report of Archaeological Explorations in Chinese Turkestan*. 3 vols. Oxford: Clarendon Press, 1907.

———. "Explorations in Central Asia, 1906–8." *Geographical Journal* 34, no. 1 (July 1909): 5–36.

———. "Explorations in Central Asia, 1906–8 (Continued)." *Geographical Journal* 34, no. 3 (September 1909): 241–64.

———. *Innermost Asia: Detailed Report of Explorations in Central Asia, Kan-su and Eastern Īrān*. 4 vols. Oxford: Clarendon Press, 1928.

———. *Preliminary Report on a Journey of Archaeological and Topographical Exploration in Chinese Turkestan*. London: Eyre and Spottiswoode, 1901.

———. *Ruins of Desert Cathay: Personal Narrative of Explorations in Central Asia and Westernmost China*. 2 vols. London: Macmillan, 1912.

———. *Sand-Buried Ruins of Khotan: Personal Narrative of a Journey of Archaeological and Geographical Exploration in Chinese Turkestan*. London: Hurst and Blachett, 1903.

———. *Serindia: Detailed Report of Explorations in Central Asia and Westernmost China*. 5 vols. Oxford: Clarendon Press, 1921.

Sun Boxin. "Sitanyin di si ci lai Xin zhi jingguo ji suo huo guwu kao" [An analysis of the course of Stein's fourth expedition to Xinjiang and the antiquities he obtained]. *Zhongguo bianjiang shidi yanjiu* 13, no. 1 (March 2003): 85–91.

Thum, Rian. *The Sacred Routes of Uyghur History*. Cambridge, MA: Harvard University Press, 2014.

Torma, Franziska. *Turkestan-Expeditionen: Zur Kulturgeschichte deutscher Forschungs-reisen nach Mittelasien (1890–1930)*. Bielefeld: Transcript Verlag, 2011.

Trombert, Éric. "La Mission Archéologique de Paul Pelliot en Asie Centrale (1906–1908)." In *Paul Pelliot: De l'histoire à la légende*, edited by Jean-Pierre Drège and Michel Zink, 45–82. Paris: Académie des inscriptions et belles-lettres, 2013.

Trümpler, Charlotte, ed. *Das grosse Spiel: Archäologie und Politik zur Zeit des Kolonial-ismus (1860–1940)*. Cologne: Dumont, 2008.

Tugusheva, L. Yu. "Expeditions to Central Asia and the Discovery of Early Medieval Turkic Manuscripts." In *Russian Expeditions to Central Asia at the Turn of the 20th Century*, edited by I. F. Popova, 40–49. Saint Petersburg: Slavia, 2008.

Walker, Annabel. *Aurel Stein: Pioneer of the Silk Road*. London: John Murray, 1995.

Walravens, Hartmut, comp. *Paul Pelliot (1878–1945): His Life and Works — A Bibliog-raphy*. Bloomington: Indiana University Research Institute for Inner Asian Studies, 2001.

Wang, Cheng-hua. "The Qing Imperial Collection, circa 1905–25: National Humiliation, Heritage Preservation, and Exhibition Culture." In *Reinventing the Past: Archaism and Antiquarianism in Chinese Art and Visual Culture*, edited by Wu Hung, 320–41. Chicago: Center for the Art of East Asia, 2010.

Wang Jiqing. "Boxihe 1909 nian Beijing zhi xing xiangguan riqi bianzheng" [Pelliot's trip to Beijing in 1909 and an analysis of the timeline of his travels]. *Dunhuang xue jikan*, no. 4 (2011): 139–44.

———. "Jiang Xiaowan wannian shiji kaoshi" [An analysis of events in the later years of Jiang Xiaowan]. *Dunhuangxue jikan* 3 (2013): 153–63.

———. "Liu Bannong yu Meiguo ziranshi bowuguan Zhong Ya kaocha tuan jiaoshe shimo" [An account of negotiations between Liu Bannong and the Central Asiatic Expeditions of the American Museum of Natural History]. *Xiyu wenshi* 12 (2018): 319–48.

———. "1907 nian Sitanyin yu Wang Yuanlu ji Dunhuang guanyuan zhijian de jiaowang" [The interactions among Stein, Wang Yuanlu, and Dunhuang officials in 1907]. *Dun-huangxue jikan* 3 (2007): 60–76.

———. "Sitanyin di er ci Zhong Ya kaocha qijian suo chi Zhongguo huzhao jianxi" [A brief analysis of the passport Stein held during his second expedition to Central Asia]. *Zhongguo bianjiang shidi yanjiu* 4 (1998): 69–76.

———. "Sitanyin di san ci Zhong Ya kaocha suo chi Zhongguo huzhao xiping" [An analysis of the passport Stein held during his third expedition to Central Asia]. *Xiyu yanjiu* 4 (1998): 21–30.

———. *Sitanyin di si ci Zhongguo kaogu riji kaoshi* [An analysis of Stein's diary from his fourth archaeological expedition to China]. Lanzhou: Gansu jiaoyu chubanshe, 2004.

———. *Sitanyin yu Riben Dunhuang xue: Yingguo Niujin daxue cang Sitanyin kaogu dang'an Riben Dunhuang xue shi wenxian yanjiu* [Stein and Dunhuang studies in Japan: research on historical documents concerning Dunhuang studies in Japan held in the Stein papers at Oxford University]. Lanzhou: Gansu jiaoyu chubanshe, 2004.

Wang Nan. "Boxihe yu Pei Jingfu de jiaowang: Yi Zhong Fa xuezhe youguan Dunhuang cangjingdong zuichu yanjiu wei zhongxin" [The relationship between Paul Pelliot and Pei Jingfu: A study centered on the earliest research among Chinese and French scholars concerning the hidden cave library]. *Dunhuang Tulufan yanjiu* 11 (2008): 427–50.

Wang Shu'nan. *Xinjiang fang gu lu* [Record of antiquities in Xinjiang]. N.p., 1911.

Warner, Langdon. *Buddhist Wall-Paintings: A Study of a Ninth-Century Grotto at Wan Fo Hsia*. Cambridge, MA: Harvard University Press, 1938.

———. *The Long Old Road in China*. London: Arrowsmith, 1927.

Waugh, Daniel. *Skrine at Kashgar*. Draft manuscript, 2016.

Wei Juxian. "Dunhuang shishi" [The stone cavern at Dunhuang]. *Shuowen yuekan* 3, no. 10 (1943): 21–45.

Whitfield, Susan. *Aurel Stein on the Silk Road*. London: British Museum Press, 2004.

Wu Haokun, and Pan You. *Zhongguo jiaguxue shi* [A history of the study of oracle bones in China]. Shanghai: Shanghai renmin chubanshe, 1991.

Wu, Hung. *A Story of Ruins: Presence and Absence in Chinese Art and Visual Culture*. Princeton, NJ: Princeton University Press, 2012.

Xie Xiaozhong [Xie Bin]. *Xinjiang youji* [A record of travels in Xinjiang]. 1923; Lanzhou: Gansu renmin chubanshe, 2002.

Xu Xusheng [Xu Bingchang]. *Xu Xusheng xiyou riji* [A diary of Xu Xusheng's western travels]. 1930; Yinchuan: Ningxia renmin chubanshe, 2000.

Yang Ming. "Yang Zengxin deng suo cang liang jian Tulufan Dunhuang xiejing" [Two manuscripts from Dunhuang and Turfan collected by Yang Zengxin and others]. *Xiyu yanjiu* 2 (1995): 42–44.

Yi Tuo. "Du 'Dunhuang shishi fangshu ji' ji 'Sitanyin Qianfodong qujing shimo ji' hou" [After reading "An account of a visit to the library of the stone caverns of Dunhuang" and "A complete account of Stein's acquisition of manuscripts at the Thousand-Buddha Caves"]. *Haichao yin* 17, no. 2 (December 1936): 48–53.

Yuan Jiang, Yuan Gang, Yuan Yang, Yuan Fang, and Yuan Ding, eds. *Xibei kexue kaocha de xianxingzhe: Dixuejia Yuan Fuli de zuji* [Pioneer of scientific survey in the northwest: The tracks of geologist Yuan Fuli]. Beijing: Xinhua chubanshe, 2007.

Zhang, Cong Ellen. *Transformative Journeys: Travel and Culture in Song China*. Honolulu: University of Hawai'i Press, 2011.

Zheng, Xiaowei. *The Politics of Rights and the 1911 Revolution in China*. Stanford, CA: Stanford University Press, 2018.

INDEX

Page numbers in italics refer to illustrations.

Printed in Great Britain
by Amazon